D1918632

Challenges at the Bank for International Settlements

Bottmingen, Jan / Feb 2016

Dear Douglas

with my best wishes
to you and M.-C.

Elmar

Elmar B. Koch

Challenges at the Bank for International Settlements

An Economist´s (Re)View

With 19 Figures and 56 Tables

Springer

Dr. Elmar B. Koch, LLD, MBA, PhD
Bank for International Settlements
4002 Basel
Switzerland
chrkoch@bluewin.ch

Library of Congress Control Number: 2007932729

ISBN 978-3-540-72789-7 Springer Berlin Heidelberg New York

Springer is a part of Springer Science+Business Media

springer.com

Production: LE-TEX Jelonek, Schmidt & Vöckler GbR, Leipzig
Cover-design: WMX Design GmbH, Heidelberg

SPIN 12069477 43/3180YL - 5 4 3 2 1 0 Printed on acid-free paper

Foreword

For a number of reasons I am pleased that Elmar has asked me to write a foreword to this volume, which assembles together a number of pieces that he wrote over the course of the decade between 1997 and 2007. The first reason is that it gives me the opportunity to thank him for the work he has carried out so conscientiously and ably in his role as an economist working for the BIS. I would, however, be remiss if I did not also thank him for his earlier efforts, contributing in particular to the statistical output of the MED, and also the broader contribution he made as president of the Sports Club from 2004 to 2007. A second reason for being pleased is that the research contained in this volume was drawn from the period when I was chief of the MED and very much involved in discussions of the important issues to which these papers are directed. Time goes fast when one is busy, and it is all too easy to forget what was yesterday's central question. This volume constitutes a kind of reintroduction to old friends, and that is always a pleasure.

The papers in this volume are grouped into four time periods, during each of which Elmar had been given different responsibilities. The interesting point is that, taken together, they imply an interest in essentially all the important topics of interest to the BIS. The earliest years, 1997 to 2000, when his attention was focused on the economic prospects of central and eastern Europe, as well as Africa and India, provided insights into matters pertaining to both monetary and financial stability. These are key issues for central bankers today. Subsequently, from 2002 to 2006, the focus was redirected towards matters having to do with the governance of the international financial system, as seen from the perspective of the G10 Deputies. Such issues continue to be hotly debated today. Most recently, Elmar's work has been directed to matters related to the governance and internal management of central banks. Such topics probably preoccupy Governors during 50 percent of their working day, and international comparisons of practices are thus extremely valuable at a practical level.

The discerning reader will note in the above a 2-year gap, between 2000 and 2002, when Elmar provided invaluable assistance to Hans Meyer, the previous president of the Swiss National Bank, in mediating a financial dispute between the successor states of the former Yugoslavia. While there was no successful outcome, the work done in preparing background material will prove invaluable when, as seems certain, this issue comes up again. One important reason for relying on Elmar in this case was his training as a lawyer, as well as an economist, and of course his language skills. Indeed, it is worth noting that in the governance area, both with respect to individual central banks and the international financial system, the insight of both lawyers and economists are crucial in formulating good policy. The BIS was lucky to have someone who could in fact bring both sets of skills to the table.

During the period when these articles were written, Elmar was involved in Secretariat support work rather than having a research function as such. Not many people in such positions, subject to many demands from clients and day-to-day responsibilities, succeed in finding time to write thoughtful articles. Elmar deserves a special thanks for having succeeded in this endeavor and for producing documents that generally provide the measured balance of views that the BIS has become well known for. Lastly, even in difficult times, he never lost his enthusiasm or his willingness to cooperate and contribute to the work of the BIS. The colleagues he leaves behind all wish him a happy and a fruitful retirement.

Bill White
Head of the Monetary and Economic Department
Bank for International Settlements

Contents

1 Introduction

This book contains a range of contributions written mainly while the author was working as an economist in the Monetary and Economic Department (MED) of the Bank for International Settlements (BIS)[1] over the last few years.[2]

During this time Bill White, who joined the BIS in 1995, was economic advisor at the MED, and I was fortunate enough to be asked to address the range of challenging issues discussed in this book, some of which remain to be resolved. These include, for example, cross-border issues in financial contracts, collective action clauses in sovereign bonds, the state bank deposit guarantee in the former Yugoslavia, the role of the private pension fund industry and governance at central banks. This monograph also reflects the wealth of mainstream monetary policy and financial stability issues, including topics such as monetary policy transmission mechanisms and monetary policy model building and analysis, and includes as well articles on financial crises, bank restructuring and external debt.

In the last decade I have been in the MED's Secretariat and have not been involved in research. The main function of the MED Secretariat is to prepare intellectual input for substantive discussions at BIS meetings rather than conduct pure research.

The contributions in this book are in chronological order starting with the most recent;[3] the following personally coloured comments observe this same time sequence as well.

The governance period (2004–2007)

In 2006, the BIS created a Secretariat called Central Banking Studies. This Secretariat assists central banks in finding governance structures appropriate

---

1 See annex for a short summary of the BIS.

2 See annex for author's CV.

3 The articles or contributions appear as they were written, unedited. Co-authors were Marco Sorge, Philip Wooldridge and Iikka Korhonen for Chapters 5, 8 and 9 respectively. Chapters 5, 7, 11 and 13 are published here for the first time.

for them. The recognition of the importance of governance for central banks implies, *inter alia*, solid research in a range of important areas like decision-making theory, optimal organisational design, efficiency and performance measurement, optimal flow of information and principles of governance. Central bank governors regularly exchange views on these areas. Over the past few years, this large and growing governance domain has become of major concern at central banks, as reflected in Chapter 2, *Challenges for governance at central banks*.

Activity, in the form of conferences and written works, in this area is growing rapidly. For example, in 2003 I participated in a workshop on central bank efficiency organised by the Sveriges Riksbank chaired by Lars Heikensten. I was struck by the different approaches to efficiency in monetary policy vs. payment systems vs. governance. Representatives of the People's Bank of China (SAFE) visited the BIS in late 2004, and I gave a presentation on communication and transparency by central banks in foreign exchange markets, a typical governance topic.

In a short period of time, the book by Alan S. Blinder[4] has become a 'classic' in terms of governance principles, and much more is in the pipeline. Central banks are now considerably more inclined to consider developments in the area of private-sector governance than ever before.

The G10[5] period (2002–2006)

The years 2005–2006 saw the winding down of the G10 as the key substantive G10 meetings and reports of the deputy finance ministers and central bank governors were discontinued – an event which almost went unnoticed outside the G10. Philipp Hildebrand of Switzerland, as last chairman of the G10 deputies, had been asked to terminate the G10 deputies process. The issue of terminating the G10 deputies had already been addressed in earlier years. A history of the G10 needs to be written.

I was fortunate to have been involved in the last few years in the work of the G10 and its final substantive studies on pension system reform (2005), insolvency and contract enforceability (2003) and contractual clauses in sovereign bonds (2002). In 2004 there was also an important unpublished report on the finances of the IMF called the *Financial position of the IMF*. This latter report must be seen in the light of the then existing concentration of IMF lending in only a few countries. In fulfilling this remit, this G10 report looks at the size and composition of the Fund's

---

[4] Blinder, Alan S. (2004) The Quiet Revolution, Central Banking Goes Modern. Yale University Press.

[5] See annex for a short summary of the G10.

financial portfolio, highlighting similarities and differences from past experience, and at the Fund's ability to cope with future demands on its resources. This report concludes a 40-year-long history of independent evaluation of IMF policies by the G10. How this gap in the international financial architecture is to be filled remains an open question. The *Note on the consequences of a potential default by Argentina to the IMF* (Chapter 5) falls within this time period and reflects the concern of the international financial community at that time.

The last report by the G10 deputies was in fact released in 2005. The *Report on ageing and pension system reform: implications for financial markets and economic policies* was produced under the chairmanship of Ignazio Visco from Italy. This authoritative report currently constitutes the latest cross-country study in this domain and will be a good benchmark in the near future for many governments. While the study reviews the data on 'dependency ratios' and summarises the prediction of the likely development of this ratio in future, it also deals in broad strokes with the role of the public and private sectors in the provision of pensions for the aged and the financial underpinnings of this large financial sector.

My paper on *Insolvency laws – a review of the international dimension* (Chapter 3) was inspired by the G10 study 'Insolvency arrangements and contract enforceability' (www.bis.org/publ/gten06.htm) and the subsequent symposium at the ECB in 2003, which was mainly organised by me on behalf of the BIS together with the Federal Reserve Bank of New York (under first Vice President Christine Cumming), the Bank of England and the Bank of Italy. The symposium revealed philosophically different starting points in tackling insolvency issues. For financial supervisors, deposit insurers, rating agencies and financial analysts the way in which cross-country claims were being settled was relevant. The inconsistency between the territoriality principle as predominantly applied in the USA and the consolidation/universality principle applied in civil-law countries is essential in understanding many cross-border discussions. How far and why certain financial contracts should be netted or carved out in a cross-border dispute remains an important issue. An understanding of the underlying domestic legal frameworks is absolutely essential as they tie the hands of any supervisor or deposit insurer. Domestic law will still prevail in spite of many arrangements by the international supervisory community. 'Comity' remains a weak concept in this domain. A key concern is fragility – the house-of-cards concept – when looking at a potential meltdown of large, complex internationally active financial institutions. The G10 would perhaps have reviewed progress in this domain in 2007 or 2008, but with its demise, it is hoped that others will step forward to perform this task.

Another important contribution of the G10 deputies was the September 2002 report on contractual clauses (www.bis.org/publ/gten08.htm). It is widely recognised that an important factor complicating the rapid and orderly resolution of sovereign-debt crises is the collective action problem, whereby the incentives for individual creditors diverge from those of creditors as a whole (hold-out creditors). This problem became more acute as bond finance had accounted for an increasing share of sovereign borrowing, leading to growing interest by the international financial community in mechanisms to facilitate faster and more orderly debt restructuring.

In that context, the G10 Ministers and Governors approved the public release of this report prepared by a working group operating under their auspices. The report, chaired by Randy Quarles of the USA, set out the key features of collective action clauses for sovereign bonds that the G10 Ministers and Governors believed would, if widely adopted, make the resolution of debt crises more orderly (www.bis.org/ publ/gten09.htm). These clauses were widely adopted by the markets, that is both creditors and debtors saw their advantages. The article *Collective action clauses – a review of the international dimension* (Chapter 4) explains in detail this process, its outcome and potential weaknesses. Some follow-up on the value of the collective action clauses (CACs) will be needed to ensure more transparent processes, the reduced role of hold-out creditors and constrained litigation by individuals. It is not clear who will continue with this assessment.

Preceding and concomitant with the introduction of the CACs was the lively discussion of the virtues of a sovereign debt resolution mechanism (SDRM), instigated to a large extent by Anne O. Krueger of the IMF, which aimed at a better grounding or institutionalising of the settlement of sovereign debt in a crisis. Chapter 6, *Debt resolution processes for sovereign debt – current policy issues*, reflects the flavour of that time. The discussion as to whether private-sector processes are superior in sovereign debt settlement to public-sector processes may not have been settled for good.

Mediation between governments of the former Yugoslavia (Socialist Federal Republic of Yugoslavia, SFRY, 2001–2002)

The BIS was asked in 2001 to mediate a financial dispute between the successor states of the former Yugoslavia. These were at that time the governments of Bosnia-Herzegovina, the Republic of Croatia, the Republic of Macedonia, the Republic of Slovenia and the Federal Republic of Yugoslavia. The background work in mediating between these countries is reflected in Chapter 7 (*Successor states of the former Yugoslavia – mediation under Art. 7, Annex C of the Vienna Agreement on Succession Issues – a major review*), a reflective piece that tried to analyse the complex economic, financial and restructuring events that took place prior to the collapse and rebuilding in that region during the period 1988–1992.

In addition to studying the economic and financial background of that time, I faced the major challenge of getting the mediation off the ground. I examined much of the literature on mediation, but it was tainted by private-sector concepts assuming that private parties were ready to assume/start mediation. Concepts of confidentiality of treatment of information and concepts of fair and transparent processes/procedures had to be elaborated as well. Eventually a reasonable agreement on confidentiality was struck between the parties and those (and how many) representing the governments in this mediation. Some countries were represented by their deputy finance ministers, others by their deputy central bank governor, in many cases supplemented by a range of advisors. There were also rules established for the meetings themselves, i. e. who was allowed to speak, for how long, and the sequence of speakers. All parties had to agree on these basic questions before mediation could start in earnest. I researched various legal procedural processes, borrowing heavily from UNCITRAL procedures. There was also the question of existing precedents. On that score, the book by George H. Aldrich[6] provided some helpful insights.

From my point of view, I was deeply concerned about an equal, fair and transparent consideration and process towards all parties; I was even more concerned about not committing any errors. The right legal tone had to be found. It took more than 4 months to contact these countries and settle these more procedural issues. Chapter 13, *Financial intermediation: efficiency, fragility and polices for reform*, reflects the status and views of the countries before the first meeting of the countries' representatives in December 2001 in Basel.

Due to the massive political, economic and legal changes during the period 1988–1992, the underlying financial system in the SFRY came unhinged. The population was holding its entire savings in foreign currency in domestic banks and there was a state guarantee of the SFRY on these substantial foreign currency deposits. These deposits 'disappeared' during that period, and the basic question was who should repay these 'lost' savings. Hans Meyer, who at that time had just retired as governor of the Swiss National Bank, was asked by the management of the BIS to be in charge as an independent advisor in the mediation process. As his right

[6] Aldrich, George H. (1996) The Jurisprudence of the Iran-United States Claims Tribunal. Clarendon Press, Oxford.

hand I prepared the meetings with the successor states in the years 2001–2002. The mediation took place under strict confidence at the BIS. No one besides Hans Meyer and myself had access to the material forwarded to us.

A letter closing down the mediation process was sent to the parties in July 2002, after which the BIS was no longer involved in this process and was not in a position to release documents supplied to the institution on a confidential basis. For further information, however, the reader may contact the individual successor governments of the SFRY.

It remains an open question whether the BIS will be asked in future to play a role in settling this unresolved dispute. The IMF failed in this task in 1996, and the European High Court also unsuccessfully intervened in the years 1999–2000. However, we hope to make a contribution to settling the matter by providing a concrete proposal in fairly precise numerical terms to facilitate a pragmatic, simple and fair solution to this complex issue.

The Central European, Indian and African period (1997–2001)

In an earlier incarnation as economist responsible for eastern Europe, and at one point also Africa and India, I had to keep abreast of current broad macro- and microeconomic and financial trends in such a large and diverse group of countries. I also had to be capable of assessing the key issues in these countries as these issues ultimately formed an integral part of the ongoing and continuing discussions at the BIS meetings. In addition, meeting support had to be provided for governors or deputy governors, the annual report had to be written and special topics and internal queries had to be dealt with. Consequently, little time was left for research.

In those years, I visited the Reserve Bank of India several times, once during the formative stages of the euro, as the RBI was very keen on being kept well informed of the detailed discussions in Europe. The RBI was also very much current on issues surrounding the SDRM and CACs. Asuri Vasudevan was a kind host on several of those visits.

In 2000 I was asked to organise the first BIS meeting with the African deputy governors in Pretoria. Not being a specialist on Africa, let alone monetary policy, in the larger economies of that region. I was fortunate to be able to visit the IMF in preparatory meetings and was impressed by the over 100 IMF economists involved in Africa. I learnt about monetary policy in over 20 large African countries in a very short period of time. There was a wide diversity of economic development among African countries at that time, as well as a paucity of private capital flowing to that region of the world (see Chapter 8, *International bank credit and securities financing in Africa*). While the issue of debt relief in the official sector in Africa is gradually being addressed, it is more relevant to induce sustainable and substantive private capital flows to that region.

In those years, I often visited Budapest, Bucharest, Moscow, Prague and Warsaw. Budapest was indeed one of my favourite cities, especially since Werner Riecke was at that time deputy governor at the Hungarian National Bank. I also visited the central banks in Belgrade, Ljubljana, Sofia and Tallinn. These were demanding trips as an economist from the BIS was expected to be well informed on many key questions, especially as most representatives of these central banks were on a steep learning curve. The key issues always concerned monetary policy, financial stability and financial restructuring and repression. In all those years I was joined once by Philip Turner of the BIS in a visit to Warsaw.

The article comprising Chapter 15, *Capital flows in Eastern Europe: some lessons from the emerging markets in Latin America and Asia*, raises a more general issue that will continue to be on the agenda of economists for years to come as its relevance is not confined to eastern Europe. Do capital inflows into a country raise investment growth and the level of income or is this capital consumed instead?

Chapter 9, *Aftermath of the Russian debt crisis*, digs deep into the debt magnitudes involved in that event and remains a good reference for anybody revisiting the Russian debt crisis. It is one of the few articles that actually analyses in detail the short-term debt data and Russia's creditor position. Chapter 11, *The monetary policy transmission mechanism in Russia*, is included in this book as it reflects an attempt to apply monetary modelling in that country. The article remained unpublished as it got 'lost' in the Russian crisis of 1998. At that time almost identical articles were published elsewhere showing how much in sync the monetary-model economists were in their outlook. These models continue to be relevant as the search for the appropriate role of monetary aggregates in monetary policy continues.

The short article comprising Chapter 14, *The monetary policy transmission mechanism in China*[7], was written when banks in China were still state-owned and had large non-performing loans on their books. To transform these behemoths of the old into modern banks able to assess credit and other risks remained a perennially important topic for observers of the development of China's financial system. Similarly, the article on the *Banking sector reform in transition economies* (Chapter 10) was written at a time when trust in the domestic financial system was still evolving. My writings reflect my work on banking system reform at that time. Very

[7] This article was translated from the German. The original title is "Der geldpolitische Transmissionsmechanismus in China".

early reflective thoughts entered into the piece on *Financial intermediation: efficiency, fragility and policies for reform* (Chapter 13), which was inspired by economists who linked the real and financial sector in one model.

Chapter 12, *Exchange rates and monetary policy in central Europe: a survey of some issues*, presents a solid review of the monetary policy issues facing the economies of central Europe. While these countries have been shareholding members of the BIS since the 1930s, reporting and analysis of these countries was extremely limited for many years until the Iron Curtain fell in the early 1990s. It was only then that the BIS resumed economic and financial analysis with some vigour. At the time of writing this survey essay, the countries had already made their first strides toward reintegrating into the fold of their western European counterparts.

During this latter period I benefited in particular from advice and guidance by Philip Turner of the BIS who kept me on the right analytical path. It has indeed been challenging to work for the Bank for International Settlements.

2 Challenges for governance at central banks

2.1 Introduction

In today's world we demand a lot from our governments. This includes respect for the rule of law; openness, transparency and accountability of democratic institutions; fairness and equity in dealing with the public, including mechanisms for consultation and participation; clear, transparent and applicable laws and regulations; consistency and coherence in policy formulation; and high standards of ethical behaviour. We demand all this, combined with effective and efficient delivery of government services.

Central banks are part of the government sector and face the same challenges, both in terms of governance arrangements and in terms of delivery on their primary tasks. At the same time, they are also asked to exhibit characteristics seen as desirable in the private sector, such as efficient financial performance and transparency in financial accounts.

This paper attempts to highlight the main governance challenges facing the central banking community. These challenges are shaped by the unique position that central banks occupy within the government sector and as an interface between the public and private sectors.

The central banking community intensified its interest in governance developments in the mid-1990s, sometimes leading, but more often following, similar developments in the private and public sectors. Central banks began to compare their internal-governance arrangements amongst themselves, both bilaterally and within the context of meetings of central bankers such as those that happen regularly at the Bank for International Settlements.[1] This peer reinforcement of the importance of good governance has indeed helped make governance one of their key concerns.

External pressures emanating from other public-sector agencies, private-sector firms, international institutions such as the IMF and the public at large have all played a part in nudging central banks towards better governance. But, as this paper demonstrates, central banks themselves have become

---

1 For the role of the BIS in the international financial system, see www.bis.org.

convinced by the merits of improving governance. Good governance assigns a clear, well-defined role to the central bank within the government sector, helping central bankers focus on tasks for which they have undoubted responsibility. Good internal governance arrangements make the central bank more transparent to the public, helping the process of justifying the use of public funds and thereby reducing the risk that future resource restrictions will undermine the effective discharge of policy functions.

The BIS provides one forum for discussions on the governance of central banks. The BIS is also a host to a range of standards-setting bodies, such as the Basel Committee on Banking Supervision (BCBS), the International Association of Insurance Supervisors (IAIS) and the International Association of Deposit Insurers (IADI). These standards-setting bodies have released papers on governance for their constituents. The BCBS (2006), the IAIS (2003) and IADI (draft, 2006)[2] have all established governance principles/guidelines for their worldwide constituents.[3] These initiatives to create standards and guidelines have not gone unnoticed by the central banking community, but beyond general acceptance of the principles embedded in the code of good practices on transparency in monetary and fiscal policy promulgated by the IMF there is no appetite for a singular standard for the governance of central banks. The reasons are explained in this paper.

2.2 A broad perspective on central bank governance

This paper takes a broad approach to the challenges faced by central banks in the area of governance. The key challenges are placed for expository purposes into two large connected domains: 'external' governance, related to factors associated with the political environment in which the central bank operates and over which the central bank has limited control, and 'internal' governance, related to how the central bank conducts its business.

The external-governance challenge mainly deals with the proper role and function of the central bank within society and is accordingly located firmly in the political economy domain relevant to each country. The functions

[2] At this point in time, the paper on the governance of deposit insurance systems by the IADI is only available in draft form. By relying on key elements of operational independence, accountability, integrity and transparency it leans on the principles of the BCBS. Due to its draft nature and the fact that it is based on BCBS principles, the IADI approach is not discussed further.

[3] The OECD (2004) has also released principles of corporate governance for the private business sector (see Sect. III of the paper).

assigned to the central bank normally include monetary policy, currency issuance, payment and settlement system oversight and/or delivery, and acting as the lender of last resort. They may also include promotion of financial stability in general and financial supervision in particular. These functions can each have multiple, and sometimes conflicting, objectives and can overlap and sometimes conflict. Thus, the key issue is to ensure that the external-governance parameters are set in such a way that the central bank can achieve its objectives. As it is typically the legislature's or the current government's responsibility to set these parameters, it is accordingly the legislature or the current government that sets the stage for the function of the central bank, its role within the government sector and vis-à-vis the public.

The internal-governance challenge concerns how the central bank conducts its business, within the broad parameters set by the external-governance arrangements. To a greater or lesser degree, for reasons explained below, central banks are sufficiently independent of direct government control that they can exercise their own judgement on internal governance, management and organisation.

2.3 External governance: challenges of political environment for central banks

How does the central bank sit in terms of the broader political environmental and more formalistic legal structure?

In terms of broad external public sector governance, Kaufmann et al (2003) claim that traditions and existing institutions determine how authority is exercised in a particular country. This includes, firstly, the process by which governments are selected, held accountable, monitored and replaced; secondly, the capacity to manage resources efficiently and to formulate, implement and enforce sound policies and regulations; and thirdly, the respect of the public and the state for the institutions that govern their economic and social interactions.

There would probably be little disagreement if the starting point of public governance for individual public institutions were indeed as described by Kaufmann et al. At the same time, there would probably also be little disagreement that there are large differences on this score between individual countries.

Nonetheless, it is common across all forms of government that politicians need to operate through public-sector agencies in order to implement their wishes. In respect of public services such as tax collection, defence, policing, provision of a social safety net, etc, governments tend to retain close control not only over the selection of objectives but also the manner of their execution. As regards public services such as the provision of a judiciary, governments typically are constrained from, or refrain from, close involvement in the delivery of the service.

In respect of delivery of monetary and financial policies, practice varies across different countries and through time. But there has been a clear trend over the last two decades in particular to restrict government involvement to the selection of the central bank's objectives. Central banks are thus increasingly seen as one of those agents of government that should be granted a degree of autonomy (or independence[4]) from government for decision-making in pursuit of specified objective(s). In turn, the central bank is held accountable for its actions because in an open society a public institution should be ultimately responsible to the public, either directly or as represented by parliaments or legislatures. What lies behind this trend is explained in the next section.

2.3.1 The agency model applied to central banking

The agency model of contracting recognises that in the course of employing someone to execute functions on one's behalf, one needs to be conscious that it will never be possible to fully observe the actions of the agent and that the agent will have their own interests at heart. The challenge then is to devise an arrangement that makes it most likely that the agent will act in the principal's best interest, without negating the benefits of employing an agent by retaining detailed control of the execution of the function.

In the case of central banking and the execution of the monetary policy function, there are in fact two levels of principal and agent. The population elects an agent to represent its interests, i.e. the government. The government, in turn, selects an agent to execute its monetary policy, i.e. the central bank. At both levels, there are problems with conflicting interests and incentives.

Monetary policy has the particular characteristic that the immediate and most observable consequences of monetary policy actions are often different from the lasting but less readily observable results. A tightening of monetary policy, for example, will typically (though not always) lead to a period of economic slack, with slower income growth and elevated unemployment. After some time – perhaps a couple of years – that initial outcome will evolve into a return to normal economic conditions but at a lower rate of inflation. Likewise, a loosening of monetary policy will

[4] This paper does not elaborate on the different concepts of independence and autonomy.

often produce a temporary burst of growth and drop in unemployment, but with the lasting result being higher inflation.

Because of the variability of the scale and timing of this sequence, it is often difficult for untrained observers to connect today's inflation performance with monetary policy decisions made many months, perhaps years, previously.

These characteristics may tempt governments interested in re-election into actions that are detrimental to the country's long-term interest. A monetary policy easing can boost economic activity prior to an election, with harmful inflationary consequences emerging only subsequently. Unless the electorate is able to understand the likely longer-term outcome, such an exploitation of the dynamics of monetary policy could well go unpunished and in fact be rewarded by electoral success.

Central bankers are not immune from incentive problems associated with these policy dynamics either. Although central bankers do not glean electoral advantage from manipulation of monetary policy, they do often garner public opprobrium when tightening policy to keep inflation low. It is not uncommon for central bankers to be criticised for causing unemployment even though the lift in joblessness will be temporary and more than offset in the longer term by gains from low and stable inflation.[5] No one likes to be criticised for doing their job appropriately; such criticism inevitably makes it more difficult to do the right thing.

One solution to these incentive problems involves the creation of a governance arrangement for monetary policy whereby the government delegates responsibility for monetary policy decisions to the central bank, which is in turn obliged to explain and justify its actions in relation to the objective of price stability. In many cases governments retain the right to withdraw or override the delegation or set some other objective. But such an act would alert the public to a renewed potential for manipulation of monetary policy for political ends. Financial market specialists, who for investment-return reasons are more attuned to the risk of such manipulation than ordinary citizens, would probably act early and quickly to withdraw investments. The negative economic consequences of a large-scale withdrawal of investment funds would undermine any political benefit, hence weakening the temptation to withdraw the delegation.

In this solution, the central bank wields a delegated power to implement monetary policy, but it is clear that there is no direct democratic legitimacy

[5] Amongst the important costs of inflation are a corrosive effect on growth through badly chosen and forgone investment and the loss of real income within the poorer strata of society where opportunities for protection against inflation are limited.

of the central bank and the government retains the legitimate role of determining the functions and objectives of the monetary authority via the legislative process.[6] Since the beginning of the 1990s most governments have in fact been following such a policy of 'tying one's own hands' in that they are now basically divorcing the monetary policy function from the political process.[7]

This paradigm shift towards more operational autonomy, and the accountability that is coupled with it, makes it more likely that policies are pursued which contribute to macroeconomic stability. Empirical research tends to support this proposition, as more autonomy has been shown to foster lower inflation.[8]

The more credible the commitment to the objective of price stability and the independence of policy decisions and implementation, the fewer options exist for the government to change the basic tenets of monetary policy. Successive generations of politicians may have different value sets in terms of the dangers of manipulating monetary policy. But a successful policy of 'tying the hands' of governments may effectively reduce this temptation. Operational autonomy of the central bank is thus a means to achieve a favourable macroeconomic outcome and not an end in itself.

2.3.2 Good legal underpinning

This new view of the external-governance arrangements appropriate for monetary policy is now reflected in the legal framework for many central banks.

Amongst other issues, the higher in the domestic legal order that central bank operational autonomy is anchored, the more serious the 'tying of the hands' of the government. For example, central bank independence enshrined in constitutional law is inherently more credible, as constitutional law is more difficult to change than common law. A recent study by Gutiérrez (2003) claims that for countries in Latin America and the Caribbean 'the constitution is likely to be better enforced than ordinary statutes owing to its higher legal rank. Our empirical analysis finds that … those

---

6 In this paper the terms central bank and monetary authority are used interchangeably.

7 Boylan (2004) calls it 'tying successor hands'. She also notes that 'those who favour low inflation should welcome autonomy with open arms, while those who prefer more political control over the economy have incentives to oppose it.'(p. 9)

8 See Cukierman et al (2002). This proposition is not undisputed (Ismihan and Ozkan 2004). More generally, countries with a credible policy commitment where the feasibility of policy change is limited may be better off e.g. in terms of vital infrastructure investments (see Henisz 2002).

countries that entrench the independence of the central bank in the constitution have a better inflation performance.'[9]

Moreover, central bank law does not stand in isolation from the rest of the legal code. With respect to the regulatory functions of central banks, Mullineux (2006) makes the point that '...the independence and effectiveness of financial regulators and supervisors is dependent on the quality of the wider governance system, including the judiciary. A supportive (independent and trusted) legal system is thus a requirement for good governance'. There are parallels elsewhere. IADI (2006) notes that 'governance generally refers to the processes, structures and information used for directing and overseeing the management of an organisation. Importantly, governance also refers to the relationship between the deposit insurance system and the authority from which it receives its mandate or other authority to which it is ultimately held accountable'.

The alignment of legal arrangements and the overall external-governance structure of the central bank will always be main external challenges for central banks. In some countries this means placing the central bank law high in the hierarchy of laws. But legal arrangements are not always the dominating consideration. General attitudes towards central bank autonomy by the government and the public at large will continue to be crucial for central banks. To some extent, central banks themselves can influence general attitudes through the quality of their own performance, and indeed, this is acrucial aspect of the accountability mechanism at work.

It is key to our understanding that operational autonomy is not an end in itself but that it has become a mainstay for central banks for the benefit of the public. The key challenges for central banks on the external-governance front are thus:

1. Continued emphasis on the virtues of operational autonomy so that it remains a solid pillar in the mindset of politicians and is reflected in the central bank law;
2. Continuous justification of the virtue of these arrangements by solid monetary and financial policy performance; and
3. Transparency and accountability as the integral counterpart of operational autonomy.[10]

[9] This is not a dead issue, as the discussions on the envisaged new central bank law for South Africa demonstrates.

[10] The World Bank (2006) notes, 'Transparency is the foundation of good governance, because access to information reduces the incidence of corruption, and transparent institutions earn the public's trust' (p. 6).

2.4 Challenges of internal governance at central banks

Operational autonomy for central banks to pursue agreed monetary policy objectives has profound implications for the internal governance of monetary institutions. More independence implies more accountability towards the public and the government, and accountability requires more transparency about how decisions are being made and resources deployed. Accountability and transparency are fast becoming a standard part of central banking. The IMF's Code of Good Practices on Transparency in Monetary and Fiscal Policies (2000) (see Annex 1) is an example of the newfound orthodoxy.[11] For example, the code requires transparency in monetary policy decision-making and reporting of underlying data and specifies the quality of transparency.

Alan Blinder, a keen observer of monetary policy and central banks, has called the general process towards better governance in monetary policy by central banks 'the quiet revolution' (see box).

The quiet revolution

Blinder, in his book *The Quiet Revolution* (2004), notes: '...thinking about how central banks should conduct their business has undergone changes that can aptly be described as *revolutionary* – although, as befits the discreet profession of central banking, the revolution proceeded quietly and has gone almost unnoticed.'

He has three pieces of advice which a large number of central banks in the world have already followed. These may be interpreted as moves towards better governance in monetary policy: *transparency, group decision-making* and *new communication/interaction with the market.* Transparency is openness towards public scrutiny. A central bank is transparent if its actions are 'easily detected', its policies are 'easily understood', and its pronouncements are 'free from deceit'. Group or committee decision-making leads generally to better decisions in 'monetary policy' than individual decision-making. This realisation is behind the creation of monetary policy committees in a very large number of

[11] IMF (2000): '… transparency for central banks and financial agencies refers to an environment in which the objectives of monetary and financial policies, their legal, institutional, and policy framework, monetary and financial policy decisions and their rationale, data and information related to these policies, and the terms of central bank and financial agencies accountability are provided to the public in a comprehensive, accessible and timely manner.'

central banks. While financial markets are postulated to be efficient and prices to reflect all information, there is also a realisation that the central bank should not necessarily take marching orders from the markets. A market-friendly and competent central bank can remain a leader by setting out its own sensible and comprehensive course.

Central banks have been institutionalising broad internal governance principles in a number of ways: a clear strategy and mission statement, organisational structures that pre-empt obvious conflicts of interest at the board or management level (e.g. an independent compensation committee), a clean oversight structure, an independent and strengthened audit function, a solid compliance function, a move towards comprehensive risk-management strategies, establishment of unambiguous lines of responsibility and accountability throughout the organisation and adherence to corporate principles in the corporate/business sector of the central bank (e.g. in the areas of building, procurement policies and human resources policies, including rules on ethics and codes of conduct for personnel, etc.). In many central banks, there is thus now a transparent and open process of bidding for auxiliary, corporate services. Also, services like the production of notes and coins have in many cases become open for bidding.

Some of these processes are driven by the desire to align the incentives of central bankers with the objectives established for the institution. Some are driven by efficiency considerations, consistent with the need to justify the use of public funds while maintaining operational autonomy with respect to policy making. Some are driven by a desire by central banks as regulators to demonstrate best practice. And some are driven by fear that performance failures with respect to fiduciary duties or ethical standards will undermine reputation and hence the ability to effectively discharge policy functions.

With regard to the last motivation, the central bank community has indeed experienced episodes of weak governance. Some such episodes have fallen short of failure to comply with the relevant rules but have engendered reactions that highlight that perceptions and judgement by the public may drive what is considered to be good governance to a greater extent than explicit rules. This raises the question of whether internal governance arrangements within central banks can be guided usefully by the various standards and codes established for private financial institutions and corporations, or whether the bar may have to be set differently, or higher, for central banks as public policy institutions. The next section describes some of the main private sector standards and codes and considers whether they can be applied to central banks.

2.5 Application of private-sector governance arrangements to central banks

In the private sector, a number of recent episodes associated with weak corporate governance have sharpened sensitivities towards appropriate corporate governance.[12] It is claimed that better corporate governance may have avoided some of these scandals.[13] Legislatures and regulators in many countries have responded by codifying minimum standards – the passage of Sarbanes-Oxley is a case in point. Guidelines by COSO,[14] the IMF, the OECD and the three standards-setting bodies hosted by the BIS are part of this codification process and have also helped to raise the visibility of good governance.

Three such sets of codes and guidelines seem to have greater or lesser applicability to central banks. They are described next.

2.5.1 The Code of Good Practices on Transparency in Monetary and Fiscal Policies

This generic code by the IMF on transparency covers all the relevant areas of monetary policy.[15] The code is structured as a series of recommendations ('should') which, if met, would deliver something close to full transparency. The code provides the authorities with some flexibility in implementation. Its key thrust is transparency vis-à-vis the public. For example, paragraph 2.1. of the code states: 'The framework, instruments, and any targets that are used to pursue the objectives of monetary policy should be publicly disclosed and explained.' In fact, central banks are being asked by this code to establish and maintain public information services (paragraph 3.3).

The majority of the code deals with transparency of the internal governance of the central bank in the area of monetary policy, but transparency is

---

12 See, for example, the Enron, Andersen, Freddie Mac, WorldCom, Parmalat, Refco and Livedoor incidents.

13 De Young et al (2005): 'Although very few commercial banks have failed in recent years, virtually all of these insolvencies were related to improper management behavior and ineffective controls.'

14 The Committee of Sponsoring Organizations of the Treadway Commission (COSO) is a voluntary private-sector organisation founded in 1985 and sponsored by five major professional associations in the USA. COSO is dedicated to improving the quality of financial reporting through business ethics, effective internal controls and corporate governance. It may be seen as a major precursor to the BCBS's corporate governance.

15 See Annex 1.

also required in the areas of financial statements, operation, regulation, organisation and personal conduct.[16]

Even though complying with this code might be a tall order for central banks in smaller countries with limited personnel and financial resources, there can be little doubt as to its applicability.

2.5.2 The OECD principles

The OECD Principles of Corporate Governance (2004) are aimed at the corporate sector. While central bank governance and corporate governance have common features in terms of clear objectives, transparency and accountability, governance arrangements need to be tailored to their substantively different roles in the functioning of the financial system. In corporate governance the profit motive plays a key role, but for central banks making profits is not an objective; the key aim is a public policy goal, like price stability. Corporate governance should empower shareholders to dismiss management if they are not satisfied with the performance; by contrast, a substantial part of the typical central bank law is concerned with ensuring that the major shareholder – the government – cannot dismiss the central bank's management if it disagrees with the bank's conduct of monetary policy (see the earlier discussion under II). In the corporate world, staggered terms for board members are seen as an impediment to shareholders' rights, but for central banks they are viewed as desirable because they prevent any single government from stacking the board with its own candidates.[17]

Adoption of the OECD Principles of Corporate Governance by central banks is thus not an option. However, certain principles are applicable to central banks as well.[18]

---

[16] In terms of external governance, the relevant codes are in subsection 1.

[17] See Knight (2005).

[18] For example, OECD corporate governance principles I, V and VI:
I. The corporate governance framework should promote transparent and efficient markets, be consistent with the rule of law and clearly articulate the division of responsibilities among different supervisory, regulatory and enforcement authorities.
V. The corporate governance framework should ensure that timely and accurate disclosure is made on all material matters regarding the corporation, including the financial situation, performance, ownership, and governance of the company.
VI. The corporate governance framework should ensure the strategic guidance of the company, the effective monitoring of management by the board, and the board's accountability to the company and shareholders.

2.5.3 Basel Committee on Banking Supervision guidance

In 2006 the BCBS issued guidelines to supervisory authorities with respect to the governance of banking organisations. There is no direct reference in the text to central banks. Instead, 'the guidance is intended to assist banking organisations in enhancing their corporate governance frameworks, and to assist supervisors in assessing the quality of those frameworks.'

While broad, the guidelines are tailored to the banking sector and provide general principles which help banking supervisors in their task of evaluating the governance (structure) of banks or banking institutions. Item 10 of the Basel Committee paper reflects the overall thrust:

'From a banking industry perspective, corporate governance involves the manner in which the business and affairs of the banks are governed by their boards of directors and senior management, which affects how they: set corporate objectives; operate the bank's business on a day-by-day basis; meet the obligation of accountability to their shareholders and take into account the interests of other recognised stakeholders; align corporate activities and behaviour with the expectations that banks will operate in a safe and sound manner, and in compliance with the applicable laws and regulations; and protect the interests of depositors.'[19]

These requirements all focus on the role of senior management and the board of directors and have an analogous application to central banks.[20]

As with the governance principles promulgated by the OECD, the BCBS guidelines only apply to the private financial sector. The goals of the private sector and the public sector are different in substance. The OECD principles and the BCBS guidance could, however, be adopted by the central bank where they do not conflict with the public policy role of the central bank.

Transparency, group decision-making processes and communication policies are now all areas of major concern in central banks. Resources are being allocated to these functions and key management is involved. The following section on prevention of conflicts of interest, of which the code of ethics is an example, is an internal governance area where top management involvement has been strong and noteworthy.

---

[19] For more detail, see Annex 1.

[20] Mullineux (2006) notes: 'Banks are special because their managers have a fiduciary duty to (more risk averse) depositors as well as (more risk prone) shareholders and thus a solution to the 'principal-agent problem' aimed at maximising shareholder value is inappropriate.'

2.5.4 Management of conflicts of interest and codes of ethics

The proper management of conflict is especially important for central banks. Clarity in terms of the structure of the central bank, lines of responsibility and processes are an absolute must in avoiding any potential conflict of interest.

Much of the success of central banks hinges on their credibility in markets and their standing among the public. If the public perceives a central banker as lacking good judgement on matters of personal conduct, they may – rightly or wrongly – doubt his or her good judgment on matters of policy. Serious cases of mishandled conflicts of interest are rare in central banking, particularly if one considers that the central bank community spans more than 160 institutions with more than 1000 board members and over half a million staff. Nonetheless, cases have occasionally arisen in the past few years.[21]

Many central banks have thus recently introduced or revised their codes of ethics for staff or the higher echelons of management. A recent review by the BIS across the central bank community shows that codes of conduct have been adopted by an increasing number of central banks in the last few years.[22,23] To some extent these initiatives can be seen as a reaction to events in the private sector,[24] but central banks in general should also be given credit for independently reinforcing high ethical standards within their own institutions. Indeed one may argue that the observance of codes of conduct should even be more stringent for central banks than for private banks.[25,26] The need for an especially strong code of ethics is conditioned

21 See episodes at the Bundesbank (2004), the Banca d' Italia (2005) and the Bank of Japan (2006).

22 The BIS is not an official repository for central bank laws or the codes of conducts prevailing at central banks. However, we fairly regularly update the laws and codes on a global basis.

23 While code of ethics is a first port of call, transgressions may not be avoided. Central banks generally do not have investigative units.

24 While this is an important factor, there is probably also an element of peer pressure as governance structures of central banks are becoming more and more transparent and as many central banks introduced such codes during the last few years.

25 These may be considered a preventive measure to contain risks, but they are, however, not investigative units.

26 Most codes of conduct for central banks contain a statement of principle which asks those covered by the code to observe high standards or ethical behaviour, and (in many cases) also assure officers and staff that the central bank itself is

by the public policy function of the central bank – trust in the monetary authority is of paramount importance to the smooth functioning of the monetary economy and of the financial system. The quest for high standards of ethics is also underpinned by central banks' quest for a high degree of operational independence from the political process (see Sect. II). A high level of independence requires a correspondingly high level of ethics to ensure independence is not threatened. As the governor (or chairperson) is often perceived as the incarnation of the institution itself, his/her actions and behaviour are particularly scrutinised by the public eye.

External pressures on central banks' approach to the management of conflict of interest situations can also be relevant. According to the IMF Code of Good Practices discussed earlier, not only should central banks adhere to monetary policy transparency but also standards for the conduct of personal affairs of officials and staff should also be publicly disclosed. Pressures from freedom of information (FOI) and/or 'government in the sunshine' legislation may also be a factor in some countries. These legislative innovations have sharpened the realisation that transparency vis-à-vis the public is a force to be reckoned with. The public's interest in more information about internal governance arrangements at a central bank will be particularly sensitised to appropriate codes of conduct and the corresponding ethical tone set by management.

Codes of conduct help guide the institution and individuals towards exercising sound judgment. However, many conflicts of interest will continue to be addressed through personal integrity and judgments on what constitutes a conflict. Those judgments may depend on a blend of local customs, trends in other countries or evolving views on best practice.[27] Central banks as a group have generally risen to the governance challenge of more transparency and accountability in the area of ethics, and some central banks have appointed ethics officers in order to monitor the ethics codes more closely. This may be a reasonable approach, especially as the public's view of what might constitute an ethics 'violation' may change.

---

committed to providing them with a working environment where high standards of ethics are maintained. For example, the Reserve Bank of New Zealand's Code of Conduct states that 'the Reserve Bank is committed to being a good employer, and undertakes that, in achieving its mission and statutory obligations, the Bank will treat its staff ethically, honestly and with genuine interest in their individual welfare. Similarly, the Bank expects all staff to behave ethically, honestly and with a genuine interest in the Bank's welfare'.

[27] See BIS (2006).

2.6 Work at the BIS on the governance of central banks

The evolution of interest in governance arrangements is also reflected in developments at the international financial institutions.[28] The Bank for International Settlements (BIS) held its first formal special-purpose meetings on governance topics in the mid-1990s.[29] These were meetings of central bank governors who voiced a particularly strong personal interest in topics of central bank governance. Initially, there were ad hoc meetings, but since 1999 such meetings have been taking place on a regular basis. In order to formalise this process, the BIS adopted a charter for the operation of the 'Central Bank Governance Forum' in 2006 which lays down the governance rules/structure for central bank governors' meetings in this domain (covering, for example, the number of governors, chairmanship, and appointment procedures).

Alongside meetings of Governors on governance topics, the BIS established a central bank governance network. The Governors of about 45 central banks appoint representatives from their institutions to participate in the governance network. Additionally, since 2004, various study groups on issues in central bank governance have been created; the study groups deal with topics such as central bank capital, strategic planning or the governance of risk management.

Most recently, in 2006, the BIS created a Central Banking Studies unit with the aim of providing improved factual, theoretical and empirical underpinnings to the governance issues in the central banking community.

The BIS has thus been an intermediary on governance related questions for the central banking community for the better part of a decade now, bringing together information on how central banks are managed and run. These efforts are not aimed at recommending, let alone prescribing, specific governance arrangements for central banks but are more geared towards describing and analysing existing structures or processes and raising awareness of options.

It is probably true that central banks operate in such a wide diversity of institutional/legal, economic, political, cultural and historical settings that it would be extremely difficult to produce a single set of best practices for their governance. Nonetheless, we believe that it is useful for central banks to compare governance structure, processes and decision-making rules and to learn from their peers.[30] Central banks today are keen to learn

[28] This paper excludes governance issues related to the international financial institutions themselves, such as the IMF, the World Bank, the OECD or the BIS.

[29] The author is not in a position to assess any similar processes at other international financial institutions.

[30] Knight (2005).

from each other (and lean on lessons to be derived from the private sector). The BIS is a facilitator of this process for central banks and keenly assists the central banking community in comparing their scoreboards in the area of governance.[31]

2.7 Conclusion

Like all organisations created to undertake activities on other peoples' behalf, central banks face governance issues related to the attempt to ensure that they act in the long-term interests of their principals. In the central banking case, however, there are striking differences compared with the case of the private corporation, which limit the comparability of specific governance arrangements. Those differences arise from the fact that central banks are creatures of the legislature, usually have their specific objectives set by the government, and account for their performance to politicians. These politicians are themselves agents – with their own interests – of the true principal: the public at large.

For this reason, governance arrangements for central banks are intrinsically bound up with political economy considerations relevant for each country. These considerations set the governance tone for the central bank. Many governments today follow a policy of 'tying one's hands', that is, creating governance structures that leave the monetary policy domain free from political interference. Such a policy of autonomy has proved to be in the best longer-term interest of the public at large.

Central bank autonomy makes transparency and accountability key elements of the governance of central banks. Recently, central bank laws have become more explicit about governance arrangements that promote and utilise transparency and accountability. However, there is usually considerably more depth to central bank governance than that captured by a central bank law. In this regard, good governance guidance currently emanating from the public and private sectors is helping central banks to internalise better governance for their own institutions. International standards-setting bodies hosted by the BIS have released guidance for good internal governance for commercial banks, insurance companies and deposit insurers. This guidance has found wide currency within the central banking community but has to be tempered by central banks' overriding role as public policy institutions.

[31] The BIS itself has recently introduced a new governance framework, and its management is actively pursuing a policy of 'improved' internal governance. However, the central banks themselves are the owners of this process and in a more real sense, the BIS is in fact owned financially by the central banks and thus acts in the common interest of the central banking community.

Table A. stylised governance environment

Level of governance	Goals	Operation	Output	Governance principles	Indicative literature	Related literature	Governance indicators	Governance of governance
International financial institutions	Growth or better income distribution	Efficient cooperation	International financial stability	Literature available but no consensus emerging	Kenen et al (2004); Santor (2006)	International financial architecture	Kaufmann et al (2003); Acemoglu et al (2002)	No direct rules but eg IMF inherent
Central banks (regulators)	Low inflation contributing to growth	Cost conscious (policy driven)	Building integrity and reputation in the domestic financial system	Emerging by and for the central banks (see this paper)	Berger et al (2006)	Optimal decision-making under uncertainty	In process of development	Non-homogeneous legal requirements; new (SRO) rules
Corporate (financial) sector	Growth engines	Profit driven (mainly)	Maximising shareholder value	Have been developed by and for the private sector	OECD (2004); BCBS (2006); IADI (2006); Litan et al (2002)	Principal agent literature	As described by OECD (2004), BCBS (2006)	Exercised by BCBS, IADI, IAIS, OECD supported by FSF

Annex 1

From Code of Good Practices on Transparency in Monetary and Fiscal Policies, IMF, 2000:

1.1 The ultimate objective(s) and institutional framework of monetary policy should be clearly defined in relevant legislation or regulation, including, where appropriate, a central bank law.

1.2 The institutional relationship between monetary and fiscal operations should be clearly defined.

1.3 Agency roles performed by the central bank on behalf of the government should be clearly defined.

2.1 The framework, instruments, and any targets that are used to pursue the objectives of monetary policy should be publicly disclosed and explained.

2.2 Where a permanent monetary policy making body meets to assess underlying economic developments, monitor progress toward achieving its monetary policy objective(s), and formulate policy for that period ahead, information on the composition, structure, and functions of that body should be publicly disclosed.

2.3 Changes in the setting of monetary policy instruments (other than fine-tuning) should be publicly announced and explained in a timely manner.

2.4 The central bank should issue periodic public statements on progress toward achieving its monetary policy objective(s) as well as prospects for achieving them. The arrangements could differ depending on the monetary policy framework, including the exchange rate regime.

2.5 For proposed substantive technical changes to the structure of monetary regulations, there should be a presumption of in favour of public consultations, within an appropriate period.

2.6 The regulations on data reporting by financial institutions to the central bank for monetary purposes should be publicly disclosed.

3.1 Presentations and releases of central bank data should meet the standards related to coverage, periodicity, timeliness of data and access by the public that are consistent with the International Monetary Fund's data dissemination standards.

3.2 The central bank should publicly disclose its balance sheet on a pre-announced schedule and, after a predetermined interval, publicly disclose selected information on its aggregate market transactions.

3.3 The central bank should establish and maintain public information services.

3.4 Texts of regulations issued by the central bank should be readily available to the public.

4.1 Officials of the central bank should be available to appear before a designated public authority to report on the conduct of monetary policy, explain the objective(s) of their institution, describe their performance in achieving their objective(s), and, as appropriate, exchange views on the state of the economy and the financial system.

4.2 The central bank should publicly disclose audited financial statements of its operations on a pre-announced schedule.

4.3 Information on the expenses and revenues in operating the central bank should be publicly disclosed.
4.4 Standards for the conduct of personal affairs of officials and staff of the central bank and rules to prevent exploitation of conflict of interest, including any fiduciary obligation, should be publicly disclosed.

Annex 2

From 'Enhancing corporate governance for banking organisations', Basel Committee on Banking Supervision, February 2006:

Principle 1
Board members should be qualified for their positions, have a clear understanding of their role in corporate governance and be able to exercise sound judgment about the affairs of the bank.

Principle 2
The board of directors should approve and oversee the bank's strategic objectives and corporate values that are communicated throughout the banking organisation.

Principle 3
The board of directors should set and enforce clear lines of responsibility and accountability throughout the organisation.

Principle 4
The board should ensure that there is appropriate oversight by senior management consistent with board policy.

Principle 5
The board and senior management should effectively utilise the work conducted by the internal audit function, external auditors, and internal control functions.

Principle 6
The board should ensure that compensation policies and practices are consistent with the bank's corporate culture, long-term objectives and strategy, and control environment.

Principle 7
The bank should be governed in a transparent manner.

Principle 8
The board and senior management should understand the bank's operational structure, including where the bank operates in jurisdictions, or though structures that impede transparency (i.e. 'know your structure').

Selected bibliography

Acemoglu, Daron, Simon Johnson, James Robinson and Yunyong Thaicharoen (2002), Institutional Causes, Macroeconomic Symptoms: Volatility, Crisis and Growth, NBER Working Paper Series, Working Paper 9124, www.nber.org/papers/w9124.

Bank for International Settlements (BIS) (2006), Conflict of interest for senior central bank officials, Background note for a meeting of the Central Bank Governance Group, 26 November (restricted).

Basel Committee on Banking Supervision (BCBS) (2006), Enhancing corporate governance for banking organisations, February, www.bis.org/publ/bcbs122. htm.

Berger, Helge, Volker Nitsch and Tonny Lybeck (2006), Central Banks around the World: Why Does Membership Size Differ?, www.imf.org/external/pubs/ft/wp/2006/wp06281.pdf.

Bergloef, Erik and Anete Pajuste (2003), Emerging Owners, Eclipsing Markets? Corporate Governance in Central and Eastern Europe, in PK Cornelius and B Kogut, eds, Corporate Governance and Capital Flows in a Global Economy 2003, Oxford University Press.

Boylan, Delia M (2004), Defusing Democracy, Central Bank Autonomy and the Transition from Authoritarian Rule, Ann Arbor, University of Michigan Press.

Carmichael, Jefferey (2002), Public Sector Governance and the Finance Sector in Litan, Robert, Michael Pomerleano, V Sundararajan, eds, 4th Annual Financial Markets and Development Conference by the World Bank, IMF and Brookings Institution, New York, 17–19 April.

Cerra, Valerie, Meenakshi Rishi and Sweta C Saxena (2006), Robbing the Riches: Capital Flight, Institutions and Instability, paper presented at a BIS Seminar, September.

Committee of Sponsoring Organisations of the Treadway Commission, www.coso.org.

Cukierman, Alex and Steven B Webb (1995), Political Influence on the Central Bank: International Evidence, The World Bank Economic Review, vol 9, no 3, pp 397–423.

Cukierman, Alex, Geoffrey P Miller and Bilin Neyapti (2002), Central bank reform, liberalization and inflation in transition economies – an international perspective, Journal of Monetary Economics 49, pp. 37–264, www.elsevier.com/locate/econbase.

De Young, Robert, Patrick Driscoll and Colette a Fried (2005), Corporate governance at community banks: a Seventh District analysis, Chicago Fed Letter, no. 219, October.

Dreher, Axel, Jan-Egbert Sturm and Jakob de Haan (2006), When is a central bank governor fired? Evidence based on a new data set, Version, 18 July.

European Corporate Governance Institute (ECGI), Index of codes, www.ecgi.org/codes/all_codes.php.

Gutiérrez, Eva (2003), Inflation Performance and Constitutional Central Bank Independence: Evidence form Latin America and the Caribbean, IMF, WP/03/53.

Henisz, J Witold (2002), The institutional environment for infrastructure investment, Industrial and Corporate Change, vol 11, no 2, pp. 55–389.

IMF (2000), Supporting Document to the Code of Good Practices on Transparency in Monetary and Financial Policies, Part 1 – Introduction (July), www.imf.org/external/np/mae/mft/sup/part1.htm.

IMF Survey (2005), IMF governance: overcoming reform inertia, Forum, December, www.imf.org.

International Association of Insurance Supervisors (2003), Insurance Core Principles and Methodology, October, www.bis.org.

International Association of Deposit Insurers (2006), Governance of Deposit Insurance Systems, Draft, pp 1–22.

Ismihan, Mustafa and F Gulcin Ozkan (2004), Does central bank independence lower inflation? Elsevier Economic Letters 84, pp. 305–309, www.elsevier.com/locate/econbase.

Kaufmann, Daniel, Aart Kraay and Massimo Mastruzzi (2003), Governance Matters III, Governance Indicators for 1996–2002, The World Bank, Policy Research Working Paper 3106, August.

Knight, Malcolm (2005), Lessons from international corporate governance standards: the ethical perspective in corporate governance, presentation at the 2nd Islamic Financial Services Board Summit, Doha, Qatar, 24 May.

Litan, Robert, Michael Pomerleano and V Sundararajan (2002), Strengthening Financial Sector Governance in Emerging Markets, The Brookings Institution, www.brookings.edu.

List, Christian and Robert E Goodin (2001), Epistemic Democracy: Generalising the Condorcet Jury Theorem, Journal of Political Economy.

Mullineux, Andy (2006), The corporate governance of banks, Journal of Financial Regulation and Compliance, vol 14, no 4, pp 375–382, www.emeraldinsight. com/1358-1988.htm.

Organisation for Economic Cooperation and Development (OECD), Principles of Corporate Governance (2004), www.oecd.org.

Ruffley, David (2005), Accountability – politicians view, Quarterly Journal of Central Banking, vol XVI, no 2, November.

Santor, Eric (2006), Governance and the IMF: Does the Fund Follow Corporate Best Practice?, Working Paper 2006 – 32, Bank of Canada.

Swiss National Bank (2006), Independence, accountability and relationship with the Confederation, www.snb.ch.

The World Bank (2006), Annual Review of Developments Effectiveness 2006, Independent Evaluation Group, www.worldbank.org/ieg.

3 Insolvency laws – a review of the international dimension

3.1 Introduction

From an international perspective, a major international financial meltdown effect appears to be a serious threat when envisaging the bankruptcy of a large complex internationally active financial player or when several large players may be affected in the case of market failure. Given the variety of national laws and the emergence of an international framework for cooperation, where do we currently identify the key risks, and how appropriate are the tool kits for dealing with these risks?

At the same time it remains, of course, relevant from a domestic perspective to assess the risk of insolvency of individual financial institutions. Domestic insolvency laws or regulations may be immediately challenged when a large part or most of the domestic financial sector appears to be subject to the threat of insolvency. This might then have a serious negative impact on real economic activity.

Conceptually there should be a framework in place that copes equitably and efficiently with major cross-border financial insolvencies and is capable of containing larger economic costs. However, equity and efficiency are elusive in both content and measurement terms. Insolvency legislation, which embeds value judgements on these parameters, has recently been subject to major revisions in several key legislations, e. g. the EU,[1] Germany, India, Japan, Switzerland, Thailand and the United Kingdom. These efforts have generally not taken explicit account of cross-border insolvency. In the past, cross-border insolvencies of financial institutions have been solved on a case-by-case basis, and incidences of cross-border bankruptcy of a financial institution have been single and contained episodes. However, the past in terms of the number of bankruptcies and the fact that the financial community was able to contain broader massive damage to the international financial system should not be dwelt on with complacency.

---

1 The EU does not fit neatly into this category, and its directives are explored in some detail in this paper.

This paper looks at the framework currently in place and measures being taken to strengthen it. The key public interests at stake are public confidence, stability of markets and protection of creditors and depositors.

It is the international and domestic set of questions that are the major focus of this paper. It is not obvious how the two sets are linked, as there is no integrated approach to insolvency, which takes account of legal, financial and real variables as well as an appropriate incentive structure for all players in insolvency. One superficial explanation of this lack of a better-integrated assessment is relatively little interest by economists in this domain as they are more concerned with welfare maximisation, whereas insolvency is focused on minimisation of losses (at low/minimum/least cost). More generally, while there is often an absence of ex ante input by economists at the time the insolvency law is developed or revised in a major way, economic aspects of the existing bankruptcy regimes have more recently been studied in a range of papers.[2]

This paper does not provide any insights into the issues involved in setting up a solid framework for domestic insolvency law but attempts to raise awareness of some of the key cross-border questions that might arise due to existing domestic insolvency law and reviews some current initiatives by various concerned parties worldwide. These initiatives mainly aim at creating somewhat similar domestic insolvency laws and focus on the legal parameters for cooperation in a cross-border insolvency situation. This paper is thus in the spirit of a stocktaking exercise and embodies ideas on how crucial international issues might be taken forward. Invariably the starting points are the underlying national insolvency laws (except for the EU) setting the parameters for permissible or regulated behaviour.[3] At the same time, one should note that the cross-border aspect and the domestic aspect are intimately linked.[4]

The paper is thus organised as follows. First, it reviews some of the major issues, assuming bankruptcy of a major, complex, internationally active financial institution. Secondly, it looks at some of the worldwide initiatives dealing with the legal cross-border underpinnings. Thirdly, some key disputed areas are explored in some detail. Fourthly, an approach to tackle some of these issues is ventured, i. e. how the international agenda might move forward.

---

2 For an earlier paper on the direct cost of bankruptcy, see Weiss (1990).

3 The more generic issue of a general insolvency law for all enterprises or a special law for financial institutions is not explored here (see Hüpkes, 2000), nor are issues of sovereign debt default.

4 For a brief review of international insolvency treaties, see Wood (1995, Chap. 17).

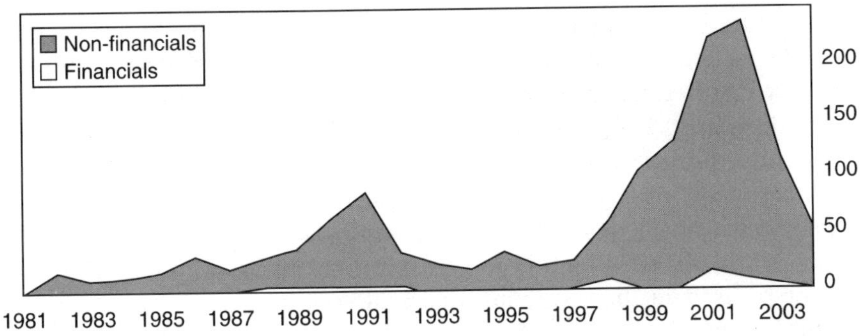

Notes: Based on the default research database maintained by Standard and Poor's. Out of 10,062 companies rated during the period February 1981 to December 2004, 1.410 defaulted in this period. The sample, which includes 90 countries and 10 industries, has been increasing in size over time.

Sources: S&P; CreditPro.

Graph 1. Bankruptcy worldwide (number of companies)

3.2 The key issues identified

The number of bankruptcies[5] in the private commercial area reached peak values in 2001–2002 worldwide and remained substantial in 2003–2004 in historical perspective (Graph 1). Since 1981 about 6% of all bankruptcy cases have occurred in the financial sector; in numerical terms, these are about 84 cases since 1981, with a peak value of 17 bankruptcies in 2001. In the financial sector there were only sporadic individual cases in the past, with relatively little cross-border content.[6]

Insolvency law is no doubt a key underpinning of any domestic economy in resolving the above bankruptcy cases. However, without fair and impartial implementation, the law may not be of much value. A non-corrupt legal system is thus a condition sine qua non. This condition is perhaps to be prioritised above all else.[7]

---

5 This paper does not attempt to define bankruptcy across countries or legislations or for analytical purposes, nor does it attempt to analyse the factors leading to bankruptcy or the efficiency of the bankruptcy procedures as such. For some discussion of these issues, see Claessens and Klapper (2003). This paper also excludes bankruptcy of individuals. At times the term bankruptcy is reserved for individuals while insolvency is the term applied to enterprises. No such distinction is made here.

6 The number of cross-border insolvency cases is well known and documented in detail in various studies (see Herring 2003 for a recent review).

7 Will the underlying legal framework be resilient and strong enough to be implemented in countries with historically weaker legal systems? In Italy, ban-

On a purely individual-firm level, the economic issue of bankruptcy may be couched in terms of two types of errors. The Type I error is to liquidate or dissolve a firm when it has more value as a going concern, i. e. closing too early. The Type II error is not to liquidate when the enterprise is bankrupt, further subtracting value from the economy, i. e. closing too late. Reasonable observers may disagree on how to assess this presumably simple scenario.[8] In this scenario, insolvency law leading to actual bankruptcy is usually seen as an unavoidable final outcome when efforts to save or resuscitate the moribund financial enterprise have not been successful.[9]

The cross-border bankruptcy scenario, from a legal standpoint, may manifest itself quite differently between countries. Financial managers, bankers, supervisors or bankruptcy practitioners are bound in the first instance by their 'own' domestic insolvency laws.[10] In many countries insolvency laws have not been revised for a long time. There are thus limits to or at least grey zones surrounding domestic insolvency laws due, *inter alia*, to the rapidly changing domestic and international financial environment, as evidenced by the emergence of new, complex financial instruments and/or large, new, and complex financial institutions. In many cases, these more recent developments of new markets, new instruments or the complexity of financial institutions, from the point of view of organisation as well as integrated financial services supplied, have not been envisaged by the law. The existing gap between outdated insolvency legislation and today's complex financial world generally adds to legal uncertainty. This perceived gap between the rapidly evolving environ-

kruptcy courts in various regions have interpreted the bankruptcy code in different ways and with different lags, adding to the legal uncertainty in the area of bankruptcies and leading to inefficiencies due to attempts at legal forum shopping. On this, see Glaeser and Shleifer (2003), who argue that a regime of heavier regulation would perform worse in countries operating at lower levels of law and order in the first place.

8 This simple dichotomy ignores the grey zone in between or in terms of time elapsed.

9 Such an economic starting point is not necessarily a given in all economics. In many countries, the bankruptcy of a financial institution is not a viable option as it may undermine confidence, e.g. in the domestic financial system (e.g. bank run) as other resolution mechanisms are sought. Several Asian economies, including India, appear to fall into this category but also countries like Switzerland (although there has been only one minor case), where there is a dominant concern about the withdrawal of the large trust funds held by foreigners in Swiss banks.

10 The G10 Report (2002) states (p. A6): '… many of the cross-border issues related to insolvency have to be investigated against the background of the national … legal regimes applicable in the respective jurisdictions.'

ment in which insolvencies occur and the slower evolution of the local regimes for dealing with insolvency is well documented.[11]

Due to the potential lags between insolvency law and economic/financial developments and thus the emerging gaps of the domestic legal coverage and/or legal outcomes, one key issue is: how is insolvency law to cope?

As some countries' insolvency legislation is more up to date than others', they tend to be out of synch, leading to inconsistencies between countries. But gaps and inconsistency due to the time factor are not the only reasons why insolvency laws in a cross-country setting are incompatible: the underlying philosophy may also be different in terms of the economic trade-offs perceived or the assessment of what is fair and equitable. On cross-border financial insolvencies, the legal profession seems to be haunted by the question of how to square the circle between the principles of territoriality and universality.[12] This is not only a theoretical discussion but has concrete implications. Further, the economic trade-offs perceived in bankruptcy may differ greatly between countries.[13]

In addition, there is little international consensus on the answers to the following questions: What are or should be the broadly accepted rules for netting and carving out? Are the rules on contract enforceability compatible across borders? What are the detailed legal and practical constraints on the principle of comity, that is, how is the principle of comity handled by individual countries?[14]

Do we have mechanisms in place that effectively and efficiently forestall insolvency contagion or spread when a large complex internationally active financial institution/conglomerate goes bankrupt?

The assessments of serious and economically damaging risks emanating from weak domestic legal underpinnings in the insolvency domain have led to a variety of initiatives worldwide to cope with some of the issues raised above. They are described briefly in what follows.

---

[11] See G10 Report (2002).

[12] This issue will be discussed separately (Section III A).

[13] One key element is the assessment of the effects of the bankruptcy of one financial institution on other financial institutions and/or markets and how this risk is evaluated. This holds true on the domestic level as well as on an international level (e.g. as countries/institutions/markets are at different stages of financial development, have different financial structures, etc).

[14] Comity is a complex concept. One way to interpret it is tolerating or cooperating in any way with outside requests for help in bankruptcy proceedings as long as the request and the help/information provided are in conformity with the domestic legal framework.

3.3 What international and domestic efforts are currently under way?

Financial insolvency has been a topic of legal and economic research since the inception of finance, and most legal texts have been written with a view to protecting domestic creditors. Weaknesses of these laws usually become apparent in major financial crises and/or larger cross-border financial insolvency cases.[15]

The lack of alegislative framework in the case of cross-border insolvency seriously undermines cooperation and limits interaction between judges from different jurisdictions. Uncertainty regarding the scope of the existing legislative authority for pursuing cooperation with foreign courts remains amajor stumbling block.[16] However, some progress is being made which may be subsumed under 'soft' law (supervisory progress), the Model Law of UNCITRAL, and in particular the various EU directives that have come into force during the last few years.

3.3.1 G30 study

A study group set up by the G30 following the failure of Barings in 1995 concluded that 'cross-border problems are more likely to be handled on an ad hoc basis, in the first instance by supervisors, rather than by formal procedures set down in law, regulation or memoranda of understanding, which leaves a good deal to chance and they will be handled by supervisors and insolvency practitioners who are trained to be cautious, in situations where rapid judgements about values and outcomes are essential, especially if a firm is to be reorganised short of insolvency'.[17]

Around the same time Wood (1995) concluded: 'Comity therefore appears to be primarily influenced by legal nationalism; cultural attitudes about foreigners; the degree of respect and courtesy; and by the extent of the involvement in international business which generates creditor pressures to satisfy legitimate expectations'.[18]

[15] The case of complex and large international financial institutions need not be made. An extreme example is the Dutch banking system: by end 2002 Dutch banks (ABN AMRO) had on average roughly 65% (80%) of their assets in foreign establishments, either branches or subsidiaries.

[16] IMF (1999).

[17] Group of Thirty (1998).

[18] Wood (1995), p. 230.

3.3.2 UNCITRAL

In terms of providing model laws to be recommended for national lawmakers, UNCITRAL (UN Commission on International Trade Law) completed work on model legislative provisions in 1997. While not directly conceived for financial institutions, UNCITRAL's Model Law on cross-border insolvency has not been superseded by other initiatives. The Model Law fills the gap found in many national laws by expressly empowering courts to extend cooperation in the areas governed by the Model Law. As only a few countries worldwide have subscribed to the UNCITRAL framework,[19] the impact of this Model Law appears to be limited in moving towards an international level playing field. National jurisdiction will continue to apply in each case and thus its impact may be considered modest.[20]

The solutions offered by the Model Law include:

1. Providing access for the person administering a foreign insolvency proceeding ('foreign representative') to the courts of the enacting state and allowing the courts in the enacting state to determine what relief is warranted for optimal disposition of insolvency;
2. Determining when a foreign insolvency proceeding should be accorded 'recognition' and what the consequences of recognition may be;
3. Providing a transparent regime for the right of foreign creditors to commence, or participate in, an insolvency proceeding in the enacting state;
4. Permitting courts in the enacting state to cooperate more effectively with foreign courts and foreign representatives involved in an insolvency matter;
5. Authorizing courts in the enacting state and persons enacting insolvency proceedings in the enacting state to seek assistance abroad;
6. Providing for court jurisdiction and establishing rules for coordination where an insolvency proceeding in the enacting state is taking place concurrently with an insolvency proceeding in a foreign state; and
7. Establishing rules for coordination of relief granted in the enacting state in favour of two or more insolvency proceedings taking place in foreign states regarding the same debtor.[21]

---

[19] The Model Law has been adopted, *inter alia*, by Eritrea, Japan, Mexico, Montenegro, Poland, Romania and South Africa.

[20] Modest as it respects differences among national procedural laws and does not attempt a substantive unification of insolvency law (IMF 1999).

[21] Sekolec (1999).

3.3.3 EU

The EU has for the first time set out procedural rules on how to deal with cross-border insolvency of a financial institution within the confines of the EU. The current rules as propagated in directives have two starting points. The first is the legal set-up of the financial institution: In which country is the main legal seat of the institution and in which countries are the subsidiaries and branches? The second starting point is the home/host distinction along the lines of the Basel Committee on Banking Supervision (BCBS).[22] However, even in the EU context, the national insolvency laws continue to be applied to legal entities in their own territory; there is thus little unhinging of national sovereignty and attempts to harmonise national laws have been abandoned. Yet, rules of cooperation and information sharing in a cross-border insolvency setting have been more clearly specified. This means in particular that the issues of mutual recognition and coordination of reorganisation and winding-down procedures have been tied down in EU member states.

3.3.4 World Bank/IMF

In April 2001, the World Bank approved a first set of Principles and Guidelines for Effective Insolvency and Creditor Rights Systems, for use in ROSCs (Reports on the Observance of Standards and Codes). The Principles now take into account further feedback and lessons from insolvency assessments conducted under the ROSC initiative. The Bank is also working on a paper discussing comparative practices and developmental experience in areas covered by the Principles and is collaborating with other organisations to develop a survey of practices to strengthen international capacity and the international regulatory framework.

The Global Bank Insolvency Initiative (GBII) by the World Bank and the IMF is closely related to the work on effective insolvency described above. It seeks to identify an appropriate legal, institutional and regulatory framework (the Framework), including the context of a systemic crisis, and to develop an international consensus regarding that framework. Significant attention is devoted to participation of the highest possible number of countries. The initiative is being coordinated with other international efforts in related areas. A number of global and regional seminars, as well as a series of consultation meetings with supervisory/legal authorities in different areas of the world, were conducted in 2003-2004. A Core Consultative Group with the participation of 17 systemically important countries

---

[22] Note that the BCBS has not stated this in the context of insolvency.

and the international agencies involved in the initiative has been actively cooperating in the preparation of the main document under this Initiative. This document and its supporting and complementary papers serve as benchmarks for conducting a voluntary evaluation of framework. A small number of pilot studies have started after Board consideration of the main document.[23]

3.3.5 OECD

The Forum for Asian Insolvency Reform takes place under the auspices of the OECD. For example, the third annual meeting took place in November 2003 in Seoul. These fora are sponsored by AusAID and the Asian Development Bank (ADB) in partnership with the World Bank Group and the Government of Japan. At the forum in 2003, participants discussed informal workout procedures and cross-border insolvency.[24]

3.3.6 G10

A consultative Report of the G10 Contact Group on Legal Underpinnings, Insolvency Arrangements and Contract Enforceability was released in December 2002.[25] This Report collected and analysed detailed comparative information on the bank resolution procedures, contract enforceability and insolvency arrangements in principal international financial jurisdictions. The Report contains a cross-country analysis of insolvency arrangements for financial institutions in countries with well-developed economic, financial and legal infrastructures.

Major differences exist across countries in the way distress in financial institutions is resolved. These national differences have been seen as generating tensions among jurisdictions and seriously complicate the working out of financial distress in globally active financial institutions. Recognition of the potential costs has led countries to respect each other's laws and usages without making formal changes in their own. It has also led to efforts at coordination. While not making any policy recommendations, the Report may be seen as an impetus to further reform as efforts thus far appear piecemeal and slow even though efforts to reduce the tensions between insolvency arrangements for financial institutions could yield significant benefits in terms of reduced systemic vulnerability.

[23] It appears that the IMF is currently reviewing the main document of the GBII. The main document has thus not been released as a public document.

[24] The conference proceedings are commented on by Zafft and Vassiliou (2003).

[25] See www.bis.org/publ/gten06.htm.

A follow-up symposium on these issues took place at the ECB on 30 September and 1 October 2003 (Insolvency Symposium 2003).

3.3.7 Basel Committee on Banking Supervision

The Basel Committee on Banking Supervision (BCBS) released a paper on the basic issues arising in the liquidation of a multinational bank from a supervisory perspective. This paper was in response to the closure of BCCI (Bank of Credit and Commerce International S.A.) and is dated December 1992. In 1992, the BCBS also released a paper on 'Minimum Standards for the Supervision of International Banking Groups and Their Cross-Border Establishments'. All the countries subscribing to these minimum standards have adopted these papers. Ab initio, two comments are relevant. In 1992 the Minimum Standards concluded: '…that the nature and extent of information-sharing possible amongst supervisory authorities must continue to be determined largely on a case-by-case basis and cannot, at this time, be usefully expressed in minimum standards. Nevertheless, the Committee believes that supervisory authorities should undertake an affirmative commitment to cooperate, on a best-effort basis, with supervisory authorities from other countries…'. These papers by the BCBS were supplemented in August 2003 to reflect the New Accord.[26] This new paper on 'High-level principles for the cross-border implementation of the New Accord' accentuates the need for supervisory cooperation.[27] The mainly quite generic term of cooperation reflects the need for a pragmatic approach as each banking group differs. Neither the revised BCBS cross-border principles nor the earlier papers by the BCBS provide any explicit guidance or principles with regard to insolvencies.

This appears to be attributable to at least three main reasons:

1. The key role of supervisors is in prudential supervision with emphasis on prevention (not necessarily the resolution) of problems to ensure that proper risk management tools are in place.[28]

---

[26] For a broad review of Basel II, see Himino (2004).

[27] For a broad assessment of the issues arising for supervisors in such a framework, see McCarthy (2004).

[28] Similarly, Himino (2004), p. 41 '… Basel II emphasizes the measurement and management of key banking risks: credit risk, market risk and operational risks among others.' The goal of supervision in most countries may arguably be viewed as some combination of the following: (1) ensure the safety and soundness of individual banks; (2) protect depositors and creditors; (3) ensure stability in the financial system; and (4) ensure smooth operations of the payment system.

2. How insolvency is defined, by whom and who is charged with the execution of insolvency varies greatly between countries. In a range of countries insolvency is declared by the supervisor; in most countries the supervisors are not called upon to liquidate.[29] Sometimes several agencies are involved in these processes. The point at which the legal system is charged with liquidation thus varies greatly between countries.[30]
3. Some countries effectively pursue a policy of no insolvency of financial institutions and will implicitly prevent any insolvency by restructuring, mergers or other means; such an extreme policy is based mainly on the perceived threat (and thus a risk that should be avoided) of undermining confidence in the banking/financial system as a whole or serious contagion effects emanating from insolvency.[31]

However, in practice there may be quite an eminent and imminent role for supervisors to play, as reflected in past cross-border insolvency cases. This may be reflected in Principle 6 of BCBS (2003) even though this principle is referring to oversight of Basel II and not bank insolvency: 'In implementing the New Accord, supervisors should communicate the respective roles of home country and host country supervisors as clearly as possible to banking groups with significant cross-border operations in multiple jurisdictions. The home country supervisor would lead this coordination effort in cooperation with the host country supervisors'.[32] Furthermore, this

[29] The legal framework in which the supervisors work sets the constraints. In terms of coordination the BCBS (2003) notes: 'Supervisors should coordinate their respective work plans as far as possible, taking into account legal and other constraints'.

[30] In other countries, the legal system plays no role at all in liquidation. However, in cases of criminal acts like fraud, before or during liquidation, the legal system will be called upon.

[31] Such financial policies might induce more risk talking than is warranted by competitive behaviour (moral hazard).

[32] The detailed text expands somewhat more (BCBS, 2003, p. 7): '19. It is desirable for home country supervisors, in cooperation with the host country supervisor, to develop a plan well in advance of the implementation date, detailing, as far as possible, the practical arrangements between the home country supervisor and relevant host country supervisors to be followed in implementing the New Accord. This will be particularly desirable for those 'advanced' complex banking structures with significant cross-border operations because the practical supervisory arrangements will depend on how the banking group operates. This plan should be communicated to the affected banking group. In communicating the supervisory plan, supervisors will take care that existing supervisory legal responsibilities remain unchanged.'20. The home country supervisor would lead the development and communication of a supervisory plan. The level of detail

role of banking supervisors is above all confirmed in practice, as evidenced by past incidences of cross-border insolvencies.

Obviously, the past incidences of cross-border insolvencies may not be an indicator or benchmark for any future incidences. Any kind of crisis may be met with a different supervisory response as the degree and nature of cooperation between supervisors may vary across supervisory responsibilities.[33] Past cross-border insolvency cases are usually regarded as not having been too complex. One should also note that the last cross-border insolvency of BCCI occurred at the beginning of the 1990s – that is quite a while back. It appears indeed an open question whether in a cross-border financial insolvency the supervisory and legal questions can be addressed jointly.

3.3.8 Domestic bankruptcy laws

A major strand of progress has emerged after major financial crises. For example, Thailand introduced new legislation in the light of Asian financial crisis. India also introduced new legislation. Do individual country initiatives help in reducing vulnerabilities in the international financial system? Do we have any evidence on this?[34] It is too early to assess any of these new/envisaged laws.

3.4 Serious issues identified

3.4.1 Universality vs. territoriality – theory and practice

There are two prevailing theories governing cross-border issues. Universality advocates that the authorities in the home country of the parent institution should have jurisdiction over all entities in the group. This means that only one authority should decide on the insolvency of a bank. Territoriality permits insolvency procedures to be initiated in any jurisdiction where assets are located.

Universality is more compatible with the principles of consolidated supervision. However, even in supervision, the home supervisor has no direct decisive power over foreign separate entities of the group and must therefore take into account the role and legal situation of the host supervisor, especially

contained within such a plan should be flexible and tailored to the individual circumstances of the banking group.'

[33] See BCBS (2003), p. 4.

[34] This is at most an indicative paragraph.

in cases where the foreign entity happens to be a subsidiary (i. e. a separate legal entity).[35]

Another complication ab initio is the different role played by different agents in bankruptcy across countries. At which point in the process of bankruptcy do regulatory agencies complement or replace judicial action?[36]

Both theories have their pros and cons.[37] In practice the UK is often placed in the universality camp while the USA[38] is often assigned to the territoriality camp. Unfortunately these differences give rise to legal conflict. However, it is now more generally recognised that no country should be placed in any one of these extreme groups but that they tend to differ along a continuum between these extremes.[39]

The USA is often viewed as one of the few countries that permit seizure of assets of any foreign bank branch in the USA in case of bankruptcy. But in the particularly large US financial system branch creditors are generally protected from insolvency. Branches are to be liquidated for the benefit of branch creditors and the residual liquidation proceeds are turned over to home country proceedings.

The USA is also generally wary of the arrangement whereby not only home country supervisors are protected from the systemic consequences of insolvency but also host supervisors. This is, however, one of the key starting points of the principle of universality.[40] The assessment of the host supervisor in judging the risk of the implications of bankruptcy by the home supervisor may not be shared by the US supervisory authorities. The US host supervisory tool kit may also be considered to be more efficient than some home supervisor (or court) initiating proceedings. These tools may range from tougher entry standards and asset maintenance

---

35 It may be disputed whether or not the starting point for this discussion should be based on concepts of legal entity.

36 For the history on this in the USA, see Glaeser and Shleifer (2003).

37 For a recent intervention in favour of the principle of universality, see Sàinz de Vicuña (2003).

38 In very generic terms: The USA has a very broad universality approach in the case of an insolvency of a US bank but pursues a strong territoriality (and outreach positions as US creditors may prove their claims in foreign jurisdictions) approach when branches/subsidiaries of foreign financial institutions are concerned.

39 See Wood (1995), p. 5: '...in practice most developed states adopt a combination of these extremes.'

40 Sàinz de Vicuña (2003, p. 1) argues from a principle of universality point of view: 'The insolvency law of the home country governs the conditions, procedures and effects of the insolvency, and the host country's jurisdiction plays only a complementary role.'

requirements to forced exit, initiation of local proceeding and the ability to act as lender of last resort.[41]

In revisiting the issue recently, Baxter et al (2004) arrived at a compromise solution: 'Financial services are supervised…, general businesses are not. Both prudential supervision and deposit insurance work backward, deriving their mission from the spectre of insolvency. Instead, they have power to modify the insolvency rules that determine the scope of their mission. One of these rules may be the appropriate choice between territoriality and universality…

Our debatable conclusion: everybody is correct. Everybody is advocating the best insolvency rules for their own insolvency system. The UNCITRAL Model Law of Cross-Border Insolvency is appropriate for general insolvency, and correctly permits an exception for financial firms. The more universalistic EU Insolvency Regulation is correct for EU non-financial firms. The fully universalistic European bank insolvency scheme is correct for EU banks. Finally, the mixed United States bank insolvency scheme is correct for jurisdictions like the United States.'[42]

The EU Insolvency Regulation tends toward universality. Where legal frameworks are similar, i. e. authorities have similar abilities and there is a good dose of trust between the states, there may be grounds for universality. Universality proclaims a more equal treatment of creditors,[43] but the underlying interpretation of the *pari passu* clause in international proceedings remains disputed.[44]

Insolvency practitioners are aware of these differences and perhaps the degree of legal certainty will not essentially hinge on whether a country tends towards one or the other model, but rather on the clarity of the law itself and the legal position of the parties.[45]

---

41 Similarly, in some countries the principle of reciprocity is applied when determining whether a foreign judgement is recognised; that is: the prerequisites for recognition and enforcement have to be similar, i.e. mirror the country's own rules (see G10 (2002), p. A20).

42 Baxter et al. (2004) arrive at these conclusions by setting up objective criteria of evaluation.

43 According to Hüpkes (2000) the current US proceedings whereby overseas creditors do not have the right to appear in US proceedings which deal with bank branches of foreign banks in the USA violates the *pari passu* principle.

44 Wood (1995), p. 10: 'In practice even the most cursory examination of bankruptcy internationally shows that the *pari passu* rule is nowhere honoured. On the contrary creditors are paid according to a scale or hierarchy or ladder of priorities.'

45 While this might be true, it remains scant consolation.

The more theoretical discussion on universality vs. territoriality or perhaps underlying memos of understanding in terms of cooperation or the desirable exchange of information is often constrained by domestic legislation, which binds the courts or the supervisors in their ability to act. Furthermore, it could be argued that most countries still aim to maximise their own domestic welfare.[46] Major factors that enter into such an assessment include:

1. An evaluation of the contagion risk and potential damage to real economic activity due to a large cross-border bankruptcy of a large financial institution;
2. Differences in terms of the evaluation of the distribution of assets and liabilities across countries (even though fungibility and mobility across borders exist);
3. Differences in the underlying deposit insurance schemes (and thus who might bear some of the risks);
4. Differences of opinion with regard to the reliability and predictability of the underlying legal system and the enforcement capabilities.

As countries will assess these parameters and other factors and as the assessments will not necessarily be congruent, there is easily room for disagreement, so that statements of cooperative information exchange, beyond mere consultation, may turn out to be hollow shells.[47]

3.4.2 Can we reduce the legal risks relating to the enforceability of netting and collateral agreements?

The defence for netting in bankruptcy is usually as follows: it should be permissible to net financial claims due to time considerations. As the value of claims may change at very short notice, it should be possible to freeze these claims, i. e. settle the gross amounts while the net amount may become part of the liquidation procedure. Thus netting should cut short the potentially large variability in the value of the underlying financial claim.

---

[46] The key question of insolvency law is perhaps not maximising social welfare but minimising losses in arrears. These concepts are consistent.

[47] Even if disagreement exists, this does not imply that countries acting as a group will not be able to have less losses than the sum of the losses due to bankruptcy in individual countries. It may even be true that each individual country will be better off acting on trust/cooperation with the other countries involved; e.g. if a country found a tie-down with another country advantageous, there could be a more general agreement on cross-border bankruptcy.

Netting is admissible as in its absence the underlying collateral or capital ensuring the claims could be unreasonably large. This is true e. g. for the underlying payment and settlement systems. A no-netting prospect would thus be financially inefficient (costly). No netting in payment and settlement systems could lead to immense disorder or liquidity problems in the underlying payment and settlement systems. However, any kind of netting just preceding or during insolvency procedures may be interpreted as changing the priority ordering in insolvency and thus needs to be carefully justified.[48] The permissible concept of netting thus needs to be defined clearly. The EU directive attempts to define when a payment has entered the payments and settlement system and that at that moment the payment needs to be settled without legal interference.

What are the relevant guidelines for other systems (securities, OTC derivatives, swaps, etc.)? Which financial transactions are to be carved out from insolvency proceedings, i. e. permitting special treatment due perhaps to crucial time considerations, and why? As the instruments are a means to manage risk, it should be quite clear what their status is in insolvency. The answer to this question will be a key consideration in determining the type and amount of financial collateral required.

There is a general tendency to exclude financial collateral transactions from traditional collateral rules. The latter assume that one party is the debtor and one is the creditor. In financial transactions, however, this arrangement is often more complex as parties in financial transactions do not always know whether they will ultimately be debtors or creditors. Parties may also enter into many financial transactions with one another, and when they typically net their obligations each day, only then may they discover what one party owes to the other and provide collateral accordingly. Financial collateral transactions are thus two-way transactions, as opposed to commercial collateral transactions. This, coupled with the lack of asset specificity, usually results in an inability to apply conveniently traditional legal rules on collateral transactions. Parties thus typically agree on closeout netting, by which all obligations (both underlying and collateral obligations) are to be netted out if one party gets into financial trouble. Such netting agreements can contain provisions indicating that if one party fails, then all obligations between the parties will be set off and such setting off is valid against third parties and the insolvency administrator.

The subsequent key legal question, however, is whether such closeout netting or related agreement is recognised as valid by insolvency law. If

---

48 IMF (1999, p. 31): '…it is recognized, however, that such a carve-out will complicate the law and will result in preferential treatment for certain types of creditors.'

the validity of closeout netting in private contracts is not clear in a given jurisdiction, this would create even greater uncertainty in cross-border litigation.[49]

While these questions are not new, we have not been able to pinpoint answers in such a way as to arrive at a reasonable level of legal certainty. Unfortunately, answers continue to vary between individual jurisdictions. 'Carving out' transactions raise important questions of equity and efficiency, especially across borders. To the extent that legal recognition of collateral, finality of settlement of funds or securities, netting and offset provisions and financial carve-outs vary between jurisdictions, these differences will create cross-border conflicts.[50]

3.4.3 Insolvency law in a major financial crisis

How creditors are satisfied in terms of time, sequence and priority may change even more dramatically in a major systemic financial crisis. What is the role of insolvency law in a systemically crucial economic and financial crisis like the Asian crisis of 1997?

It appears that, in a major financial crisis where for all intents and purposes the whole financial sector is bankrupt, insolvency law becomes essentially unhinged and is superseded by emergency measures aiming at protecting and ensuring the very existence of the financial system. This may also be interpreted as an attempt to mitigate a major adverse impact on financial stability and contain the concomitant potentially large negative impact on real economic activity. In Asia, specialised bodies were created to handle the wholesale financial meltdown that occurred in 1997 and to preserve or dispose of distressed assets (asset management companies or restructuring agencies). In such an environment governmental rescue laws and informal workouts in order to prevent the collapse of the existing domestic financial system have taken priority over liquidation of financial firms' assets.

While such measures by the state appear quite sensible in order to protect the financial system as a public good, they may at the same time

---

[49] The discussion on financial collateral transactions is based on Kanda (2003). He argues that any financial transaction which transfers future cash flows by private contract could be made subject to netting and thus could generally be considered 'outside' insolvency law.

[50] Wood (1995, p. 101): 'Jurisdictions are sharply divided on the availability of set-off on the insolvency of the debtor.' Hüpkes (2004) and also Mayes (2004) have recently proposed an agreement on critical financial system functionality as starting point for the discussion on immunising (carving out from bankruptcy).

undermine confidence in the stability and reliability of the underlying legal system as legal contracts are not honoured.

In the aftermath of the Asian crisis, some observers noted that, by focusing on rescue law and informal workouts without first putting into place credible liquidation procedures, as well as systems that effectively protect creditors' rights and reform managerial and lending practices, many Asian regimes have postponed rather than confronted the problems that caused the 1997 financial crisis.[51] However, new insolvency legislation has been introduced in several Asian economies. In this context, the key unanswered legal question is under what financial conditions should the domestic insolvency law be superseded by other considerations? Who should introduce emergency legislation/measures through what kind of decision-making/analytical process and when should such incisive decisions be made as they hit at the core of contract reliability and enforceability? While credible and enforceable liquidation procedures effectively protect the creditors' rights, under which financial/economic conditions should the government override/interfere with these rights?

Honohan and Klingebiel (2003) assess the economic implications of the violation/unhinging of insolvency law from a general financial crisis point of view: 'When a crisis breaks, as revealed typically either through audits uncovering widespread insolvency or through liquidity squeezes and depositor withdrawals, government is faced with the task of containment and resolution. Either of two broad approaches can be pursued. One possibility is an accommodating approach, involving such measures as: liberal liquidity support to banks with cash-flow difficulties; depositor guarantees; forbearance by tolerating violations of bank insolvency and minimum capital rules; debtor support schemes that help to prop up bank borrowers who might otherwise default. The alternative is to stick to the rules, requiring banks either to meet standard capitalization requirements or face official intervention that will constrain their operations.'[52]

They find no empirical evidence that accommodating policies will reduce fiscal costs. In fact, their findings tilt the balance in favour of a 'strict' approach to crisis resolution rather than an accommodating one.[53] Their

---

[51] E.g. Zafft and Vassiliou (2003).

[52] Honohan and Klingebiel (2003).

[53] The relevant variables according to Honohan and Klingebiel are Forbearance Type A: banks observed to be in open distress – e.g. those unable to pay depositors rejected at clearing or those with no access to the interbank market or those widely believed to be insolvent (except for public banks) – are allowed to continue to operate without any restrictions for at least a 12-month period; and Forbearance Type B: either Forbearance of Type a or regulations (in particular

findings seem to imply that it is economically preferable to immediately liquidate banks, which are widely believed to be insolvent rather than to allow them to continue to operate.

The Global Bank Insolvency Initiative (GBII) of the World Bank[54] (2003) distinguishes between an isolated insolvency case and systemic crisis: because of the qualitative differences with isolated insolvency cases, the management of a systemic crisis calls for remedial actions on a larger scale and of an exceptional nature.

The World Bank seems, on the one hand, to imply that operational aspects of the legal and regulatory framework of insolvency may be applicable in a systemic crisis. But at the same time it is noted that modifications to the legal framework in a systemic crisis may be necessary and that changes to the institutional framework may be needed in times of crises. Furthermore, the World Bank notes that to address the special aspects of a systemic crisis, the institutional structure for bank insolvency may need to be temporarily adapted.

There is little dispute that in a financial crisis a coordinated effort by the government to step in for the purpose of containing the crisis and restoring confidence is required. As far as insolvency law in such a scenario is concerned, one key question remains: which of the domestically accepted principles of insolvency remain valid?

3.4.4 Potential starting points

3.4.4.1 EU rules to be applied on a broader international basis?

The idea of applying the EU principles of insolvency to a broader range of countries is not novel.[55] The EU has over the last few years not attempted to standardise/harmonise domestic legislation but has espoused principles of resolution for cross-border bankruptcy. These are, in a nutshell, the following six assertions:

1. Assertion of jurisdiction: only one country is principally responsible for bankruptcy. This is the 'home' country in which the financial institution is also mainly supervised.[56]

---

loan classification and loan provisioning) are relaxed or the current regulatory framework is not enforced for at least a 12-month period.

54 World Bank (2003).

55 See Harding (2002).

56 It is rare for clear domestic jurisdictional rules to exist with regard to assertion in a cross-border financial bankruptcy. It is clearly desirable to avoid forum shopping and to define the country of litigation.

2. Assertion of validity of domestic legal framework: the domestic legal rules with regard to insolvency apply consistent with the principle of national sovereignty.
3. Assertion of mutual recognition: the Directives dealing with bankruptcy have laid out procedures for mutual assistance between EU national regulators.
4. Assertion of a minimum level of regulatory standards: this implies a certain harmonisation of regulations.
5. Assertion of financial institutions as a public good: for a variety of reasons such as protecting the underlying financial infrastructure, protecting major markets from collapse and protecting depositors and clients, financial institutions deserve different treatment from other enterprises.
6. Assertion of carving-out/netting of certain transactions: broad agreement on which financial transactions are subject to special rules.

All of the above assertions are contentious. In this paper only the last assertion is discussed (see Sect. 4.2) as being contentious in the international domain.

3.4.4.2 The EU and BCBS cross-border principles

It is speculative to try to map the insolvency principles into the BCBS cross-border principles. A preliminary view indeed reveals parallels. This is probably not too surprising if one sees the legal insolvency protocol as a continuation of the cooperation that takes place within the BCBS. However, this is not to imply that the rules are hand in glove, but that such a perspective might be helpful. At a minimum, a sort of consultative process might be helpful as the BCBS takes a look at insolvency law and vice versa.

Interestingly, the EU in Assertion 1 leans on the BCBS home/host country differentiation in defining who is principally responsible for bankruptcy. The BCBS states 'The home country supervisor will have the final determination on such matters as they relate to the group on an individual basis'.[57]

The BCBS notes clearly that the existing legal responsibilities of national supervisors as laid out in the Basel Concordat framework will continue to apply. This is close to notions of sovereignty in developing countries and applying national law in insolvency recognizing some concept of comity.

Mutual recognition is possible if supervisors opt for formal arrangements such as memoranda of understanding (MOUs). Greater information

57 BCBS (2003). The new rules will be applied to each level of the banking group, so that there is a technical requirement on the part of both home and host country.

sharing is thus possible and crucial according to the BCBS and the home country should lead this coordination effort. The BCBS refrains from more prescriptive rules and notes that these agreements on cooperation and exchange of information should be recorded on whatever basis best suits individual supervisors. The EU is more forthcoming on this point in its directives and even prescribes mutual assistance.

The BCBS in this context then states its preference for a consolidated approach. Home country supervisors will be responsible for consolidated supervision and host country supervisors are responsible for supervision on an individual or subconsolidation basis operating in their countries. The BCBS notes that host countries should consider accepting the methods and approval processes that the bank uses at the consolidated level (to reduce the compliance burden and avoid regulatory arbitrage). The EU does not enter into a debate on principles of territoriality vs. consolidation as the assertion of mutual recognition prevails. It seems that the more there is mutual recognition, the more the dichotomy between territoriality vs. universality/consolidation disappears.

Mutual recognition appears a reasonable way forward if Assertions 4, 5 and 6 are at least partially fulfilled. In Europe the underlying legal systems are somewhat homogeneous, i. e. reliable, predictable and fairly non-corrupt, such that an approach towards more mutual recognition turns out to be feasible. However, it remains an open question whether the ambitious EU Insolvency Directive may gain wider currency.

3.4.4.3 The American Law Institute (Transnational Insolvency Project)

The American Law Institute recently (2002) released 'Principles of Cooperation in Transnational Insolvency Cases among the Members of the North American Free Trade Agreement (NAFTA)'. These are in the form of recommendations for an international agreement initially between the USA and Canada and then to be extended to Mexico. It is noteworthy that General Principle VI clearly states: 'There should be no discrimination against claimants based on nationality, residence, or domicile.' This transnational insolvency project also contains fairly detailed guidelines to be applied to court-to-court communications in cross-border cases.[58] It is certainly worth analyzing this Transnational Insolvency Project in order to determine its usefulness for a broader range of countries.

[58] A more detailed comparative study between the EU directives and the American Law Institute proposal (as well as UNCITRAL and bilateral/multilateral agreements elsewhere) may prove valuable.

3.4.5 The role of rating agencies

Rating agencies assess the obligor's overall capacity to meet its financial obligation. They are thus also in the bankruptcy business. Standard and Poor's issue and issuer credit ratings use definitions which closely match those of the rating agencies. The issue rating definitions are expressed in terms of default risk, which refers to the likelihood of payment – the capacity and willingness of the obligor to meet its financial commitments on an obligation in accordance with the terms of the obligation. This default risk is calculated over the whole life of the debt issue. However, issue credit ratings also take into account the protection afforded by, and relative position of, the obligation in the event of bankruptcy, reorganisation or other arrangements under the laws of bankruptcy and other laws affecting creditors' rights.[59] This implies some estimate of the distribution of the recovery value.[60]

In terms of actual ratings according to S&P:

'C' may be used to cover a situation where a bankruptcy petition has been filed or similar action has been taken but payments on this obligation are being continued.

'D' is used where a default actually occurred. S&P changes the rating to D in the following situations:

- On the day an interest and/or principal payment is due and is not paid. An exception is made if there is a grace period and S&P believes that a payment will be made, in which case the rating can be maintained;
- Upon voluntary bankruptcy filing or similar action. An exception is made if S&P expects that debt service payments will continue to be made on a specific issue. In the absence of a payment default or bankruptcy filing, a technical default (i. e. covenant violation) is not sufficient for assigning a D rating;
- Upon completion of a tender or exchange offer, whereby some or all of an issue is either repurchased for an amount of cash or replaced by other securities having a total value that is clearly less than par;
- In the case of preferred stock or deferrable payment securities, upon non-payment of the dividend or upon deferral of the interest payment.

Rating agencies appear to adjust to the underlying legal parameters in bankruptcy through so-called notching, that is by adjusting their ratings by one or potentially two notches.[61] As this will affect the cost of borrowing,

---

59 Samson (2002), p. 7.
60 For some analogy with sovereign defaults, see Koch (2003).
61 See Samson (2002) of Standard & Poor's: other rating agencies (Moody's, Fitch, etc.) may use different methodologies.

some assessment of the rating agencies' methodology may be enlightening, i. e. according to what criteria does the market price in the underlying legal (cross-border) insolvency parameters despite the issues raised in this paper.

3.5 Conclusion

This paper has identified some key issues: incomplete or completely lacking insolvency legislation, internationally different parameters as starting points of legislation (universality vs. territoriality), different assessments between countries in terms of whether e. g. a bank should go bankrupt or restructure in the first place, internationally incompatible rules on carving out certain financial contracts from bankruptcy, and the little explored assessment of the impact of bankruptcy legislation on financial markets (here represented by the rating agencies) and vice versa.

The paper has identified a range of positive legislative developments, which may be assessed as pockets of progress; however, from a more global point of view the current solution to cross-border issues in practice is still primarily based on comity of law and voluntary cooperation between different national courts and authorities on an ad hoc basis.

1. The World Bank Initiative (GBII) should be fully supported if it aims at a basic level playing field in the area of insolvency law or, even less ambitiously, at identifying the key issues that lawmakers face in imposing/revising/updating their respective domestic insolvency law.
2. The UNCITRAL Model Law should be explored by more countries and perhaps adapted to their country's own legislative and financial/economic framework.[62] However, even if the Model Law were adopted by a sufficient number of countries, interpretation would still be a matter for national courts, and may vary from country to country. Most analysts seem to conclude that the UNCITRAL Model Law is not applicable to the financial sector.
3. Countries should generally attempt to revisit their own bankruptcy laws on a regular basis, not just during or after a crisis. This should prevent the gap between the current financial environment and bankruptcy legislation from widening. Only a few countries have a calendar for revisiting major legislation. From a cross-border perspective, regulation should be clear on jurisdiction, recognition, applicable law and specific provisions on conflict of law.[63]

[62] This conclusion is also contained in IMF (1999).

[63] This paraphrases the key issues of the Insolvency Regulation (European Commission 2000).

4. Netting and carving out remain moving targets. It is not obvious whether legal clarity is helped or hindered by carving out these processes contractually from insolvency (i. e. immunising them). The key issue in a cross-border setting is the validity of these contracts vis-à-vis third parties. As there are many players involved in this area, it is less clear who might move the agenda forward on these critical issues.
5. Bilateral or multilateral memoranda of understanding (MOU) exist between several countries. It would be worthwhile to conduct a study to uncover potentially common ground, how existing MOUs have fared in the past and perhaps draw lessons for jurisdictions in case of a cross-border failure of a financial institution. Ignoring the battle of principles between universality and territoriality, an MOU between two of the largest players, such as the USA and the EU, may be able to address some of the cross-border issues raised.

References

The American Law Institute. 2002. *Trans-national Insolvency Project; Principles of cooperation in trans-national insolvency cases among the members of The North American Free Trade Agreement.* (adopted)

The Banker. 2003. *Thailand regulation moves on.* August: 66–67.

Basel Committee on Banking Supervision. 1983. *Authorization procedures for banks' foreign establishments.* March.

Basel Committee on Banking Supervision. 1983. *Principles for the supervision of banks' foreign establishments.* May.

Basel Committee on Banking Supervision. 1990. *Information flows between banking supervisory authorities.* April.

Basel Committee on Banking Supervision. 1992a. *Minimum standards for the supervision of international banking groups and their cross-border establishments.* Bank for International Settlements. July.

Basel Committee on Banking Supervision. 1992b. *The insolvency liquidation of a multinational bank.* Bank for International Settlements. December.

Basel Committee on Banking Supervision. 1996. *The supervision of cross-border banking.* Bank for International Settlements. October.

Basel Committee on Banking Supervision. 2003. *High-level principles for cross-border implementation of the New Accord.* Bank for International Settlements. August.

Baxter, T., J.M. Hansen and J.H. Sommer. 2004. Two cheers for territoriality: an essay on international bank insolvency law. *American Bankruptcy Law Journal.* 57(1): 57–92.

Birchler, U.W. and D. Egli. 2003. *Ein neues Insolvenzrecht für die Schweiz*, Schweizerische Zeitschrift für Volkswirtschaft und Statistik. 139(2): 125–154.

Bliss, R.R. 2003. Bankruptcy law and large complex financial institutions: a primer. *Economic Perspectives.* Federal Reserve Bank of Chicago. 1st Quarter.

Claessens, S. and L.F. Klapper. 2003. Bankruptcy around the world: explanations of its relative use. *Insolvency Symposium* 2003. European Central Bank. 30 October–1 November. ECB, July.

European Commission, *The insolvency regulation.* No. 1346/2000 (29/5/2000).

Financial Times. 2003. *Old attitudes haunt France's bankruptcy laws.* 19 August.

Glaeser, E.L. and A. Shleifer. 2003. The rise of the regulatory state. *Journal of Economic Literature.* XLI (June): 401–425.

Group of Ten (G10) Contact Group. 2002. *Insolvency arrangements and contract enforceability.* December (www.bis.org/publ/gten06.htm).

Group of Thirty. 1998. *International insolvencies in the financial sector.* A study group report. Washington.

Harding, M. 2002. *The challenges of regulating large, international financial organizations, Proceedings of The 38th Annual Conference on Bank structure and competition on financial market behaviour and appropriate regulation over the business cycle.* Federal Reserve Bank of Chicago. May.

Herring, R. 2003. *International financial conglomerates: implications for bank insolvency regimes*. Prepared for the Second Annual International Seminar on Policy Challenges for the Financial Sector in the Context of Globalisation, sponsored by the Federal Reserve Board, the International Monetary Fund and the World Bank, Washington, D.C. draft. May.

Himino, R. 2004. Basel II – Towards a new common language. *BIS Quarterly Review*. September: 41–49. (www.bis.org/publ/qtrpdf/r_qt0409e.pdf).

Honohan, P. and D. Klingebiel. 2003. The fiscal cost implications of an accommodating approach to banking crises. *Journal of Banking & Finance*. 27: 1539-1560.

Hüpkes, E. 2000. *The legal aspects of bank insolvency*. Kluwer Law International. The Hague/London/Boston.

Hüpkes, E. 2005. 2004–05 Protect functions, not institutions. *Financial Regulator*. 9(3): 43–49.

International Monetary Fund (IMF) 1999. *Orderly and effective insolvency procedures*. Legal Department. www.imf.org/external/pubs/ft/orderly/index.htm)

Kanda, H. 2003. *Financial collateral transactions: what are they?* Insolvency Symposium 2003. European Central Bank. 30 September–1 October.

Koch, E. 2003. *Debt resolution processes for sovereign debt – current policy issues*. 5th Annual Conference on Money and Finance, 30–31 January. Indira Gandhi Institute of Development Research (IGIDR), Mumbai, India.

Mayes, D. 2005. 2004–2005 Planning for cross-border failures. *Financial Regulator*. 9(3): 22–25.

McCarthy, C. 2004. How should international financial companies be regulated? *Journal of Financial Regulation and Compliance*. 12(4): 294–96.

Patrikis, E.T. 1999. *Role and function of authorities: supervision, insolvency prevention and liquidation, in international bank insolvencies: a central bank perspective*, in M. Giovanoli and G. Heinrich. Kluwer (eds.) Law International: 283–292.

Sàinz de Vicuña, A. 2003. *Cross-border aspects of insolvency and the principles of universality and territoriality*, Insolvency Symposium 2003. European Central Bank. 30 September–1 October.

Sekolec, J. 1999. *The UNCITRAL model law on cross-border insolvency*, in Mario Giovanoli and Gregor Heinrich (eds.) International Bank Insolvencies – a Central Bank Perspective: 337–348.

Samson, S.B. 2002. *Corporater Ratings criteria*. Standard & Poor's a Division of the McGraw-Hill Companies. New York. (www.standardandpoors. com/ratings).

Weiss, Lawrence A. 1990. *Bankruptcy resolution, direct costs and violation of priority claims*. Journal of Financial Economics. 27(October): 285–314.

Wood, Philip R. 1995. *Principles of international insolvency*. London, Sweet & Maxwell.

World Bank. 2003. *Global bank insolvency initiative (GBII)*, draft, September (unpublished).

Zafft, Robert and Lampros Vassiliou. 2003. *The unfinished task of Asian insolvency reform*. International Financial Law Review. 12(2) February (www.iflr.com).

4 Collective action clauses: the way forward

Collective action clauses (CACs) are a new element in the international financial architecture intended to ensure the orderly and timely resolution of sovereign default. Before the Working Group of the Group of Ten (G10) was set up in the summer of 2002,[1] no explicit guidelines or framework existed for the formulation of these clauses.[2] The Working Group's proposed guidelines gained wide currency with their endorsement by the G10 Finance Ministers and Governors in September 2002.[3] At the same time, US private sector trade associations (the Gang of Seven) also developed their own proposals for CACs.[4] The International Monetary Fund (IMF) supported the efforts of both the G10 and the Gang of Seven.

---

1 Group of Ten, Report of the G10 Working Group on Contractual Clauses (Sept. 2002), available at http://www.bis.org/publ/gten08.htm. The Group of Ten consists of Belgium, Canada, France, Germany, Italy, Japan, the Netherlands, Sweden, Switzerland, the UK, and the USA.

2 Group of Ten, The Resolution of Sovereign Liquidity Crises: a Report to the Ministers and Governors Prepared Under the Auspices of the Deputies (May 1996), available at http://www.bis.org/publ/gten03.htm. In 1996, the Group of Ten reached the following broad conclusion: '[A] market-led process to develop for inclusion in sovereign debt instruments contractual provisions that facilitate consultation and cooperation between debtors and their private creditors, as well as within the creditor community, in the event of crisis would be desirable. Market initiatives would deserve official support as appropriate.' *Id.*

3 Press Release, Group of Ten, Communiqué of the Ministers and Governors of the Group of Ten (27 Sept. 2002), available at http://www.bis.org/index.htm.

4 Letter from Michael M. Chamberlain et al., to Group of Ten (31 Jan. 2003) [hereinafter Gang of Seven Letter], available at http://www.emta.org/ndevelop/Final_merged.pdf. The letter is signed by the Gang of Seven, which is comprised of the Emerging Markets Trade Association (EMTA), the Institute of International Finance (IIF), the International Primary Market Association (IPMA), the Bond Market Association (BMA), the Securities Industry Association (SIA), the International Securities Market Association (ISMA), and the Emerging Market Creditors Association (EMCA).

In February 2003, such clauses were included for the first time in a sovereign bond issue under New York law by a large major borrower, Mexico.[5] Several other sovereign borrowers followed suit. By the beginning of 2004, it became clear that key elements of CACs, in particular majority action clauses, were routinely included in this new bond documentation on the New York financial market. This feature is expected to contribute to the more orderly resolution of sovereign debt crises by preventing unwarranted creditor holdouts.

Section 1 of this essay provides background on CACs in sovereign bond markets. Sections 2 and 3 review recent developments in adopting CACs in sovereign bond issues and the continued international support for adopting these clauses. Section 4 provides a preliminary legal assessment of these newly adopted CACs. Finally, Sect. 5 reviews some key open issues.

4.1 Background

CACs are an integral part of the bond contract between a sovereign borrower and a private sector lender. These clauses become effective if and when a sovereign borrower defaults on a bond. In the international context, a sovereign borrower may default on its bonded debt for a variety of reasons. From a legal perspective, it is easy to claim *pacta sunt servanda* (contracts have to be honoured), but from a humanitarian, economic or political perspective, a sovereign state may assess debt payments quite differently. CACs have no influence on whether or not sovereign debt is sustainable. CACs are merely a tool in the restructuring of sovereign bonded debt.

From an international perspective, it is desirable to have a fair, orderly and timely mechanism for resolving debt restructuring issues. It should be noted that CACs do not affect the substance of the debt negotiation process itself. Rather, they are primarily concerned with the process through which litigation can be settled within the legal system.[6] Thus, though agreement or settlement procedures concluded outside the courts – such as negotiation, mediation, or arbitration – may be satisfactory, they will not necessarily be

[5] There had been several earlier cases of including CACs in New York sovereign bond issues by a few small borrowers, see *infra* note 14, but these had gone unnoticed by the market. Also, the introduction of majority amendments in note programmes in the United Kingdom and Canada in 2000 had no impact on price or liquidity. See Effie Psalida & Yan Liu, *IMF Promotes Wider Use of Collective Action Clauses*, 32 IMF Survey 153, 166 (2003), available at http://www.imf.org/external/pubs/ft/survey/2003/060203.pdf.

[6] Procedure may, of course, influence substance. Also, we are concerned here with the national legal systems.

covered by CACs.[7] Contractual CACs are intended to address two emerging issues: (1) the distribution of a large number of retail bondholders worldwide on the heels of a large credit appetite by some sovereigns, starting with the 1991–1992 boom periods; and (2) the associated issue that some creditors will attempt to manipulate the process for their own benefit. More recently, in-fighting among creditors themselves in order to reach the assets of sovereign states has emerged as a serious threat to orderly and timely restructuring.

Traditionally, CACs were included in sovereign bonds governed by English, Japanese and Luxembourgian law. Sovereign bonds issued under US, German, Italian or Swiss law did not include such clauses. The largest market for sovereign bonds is in New York State. The adoption of CACs on the New York market was key to providing an internationally acceptable level playing field.[8] While Italy adopted CACs in 2003, under New York law, sovereign bonds issued under German and Swiss law in the last year did not contain CACs.

The role of the official sector is to establish amore transparent and level playing field for debtors and creditors in all major domestic legal systems.[9] Specifically, the goal is to create sovereign debt contracts that reduce legal uncertainty in the international financial architecture.[10] There is also the implicit aim to reduce the time lag between the start of default and final settlement.[11] CACs allow the official sector to become afacilitator of change for the benefit of debtors and creditors. Financial intermediaries may benefit as well because private sector participants would not be able to provide unbiased input to this process easily.

For the most part, the markets have paid little attention to the inclusion of CACs. One is thus inclined to conclude – at least at this point in time – that business concerns over CACs will vanish and that CACs will be

---

7 Assume a world where all outstanding sovereign bonds contained 'standard' CACs. How would this influence actual behaviour of participants in negotiation, mediation or arbitration?

8 See discussion of developments in sovereign bond markets *infra* Box 1.

9 These are primarily the Finance Ministries and Treasuries of major creditor and debtor countries, as well as international institutions like the IMF and the G10.

10 There were substantial differences in governing laws between two major legislations in which substantial sovereign bond issues were released: the United States (New York) and the United Kingdom (London). UK bonds provided for majority action and trustee agreements. In contrast, sovereign bonds on the US market did not constrain in any way an individual's right to litigate and had – and still have – fiscal agency agreements.

11 These lags had been reduced historically during the 1990s. The current case of Argentina will tend to tip the balance in the other direction.

a non-factor in bond pricing of new sovereign issues. However, there is no evidence thus far about how CACs might perform in a case where a major sovereign bondholder defaults on bonds that include CACs. There may also be a realization by markets that sovereign bonds without CACs should have mark-up costs because litigation in default may be longer, more drawn out and subject to higher legal risks than for bonds without such clauses.[12] Also, since the initial public recognition by the Emerging Market Credit Association (EMCA) of Mexico's first bond issue with CACs in February 2003, the Gang of Seven has remained silent on the type of CACs that countries have chosen to employ.

Box 1. Developments in sovereign bond markets

For emerging markets, foreign direct investment is the most important financing source. The international debt securities market has overtaken bank loans and official sector flows over the last 10 years to become the second largest source of capital for emerging market borrowers. By end-2002, bank loans and debt securities (US$485 billion) had roughly equal shares in total external debt.[13]

Table 1 illustrates recent magnitudes. Bonds issued under foreign jurisdictions were asource of finance to sovereign states (mainly emerging market economies) on the order of US$76 billion in 2003. This is back in line with the issuing activity of the 1993–1998 period. By 2003, issuance under New York law had become the most important for such bonds. The

[12] The economic literature seems to demonstrate that the probability of default is independent of CACs. However, the probability of loss-given-default may be influenced by including CACs and may perhaps render bonds with CACs cheaper. Elmar B. Koch, Debt Resolution Processes for Sovereign Debt – Current Policy Issues, at 2–3, presented at the 5th Annual Conference on Money and Finance at the Indira Gandhi Institute of Development in Mumbai, India (30–31 Jan. 2003), available at http://www.igidr.ac.in/~money/koch.pdf. For a review of some recent empirical findings, see generally Barry Eichengreen, Kenneth Kletzer & Ashoka Mody, Crisis Resolution: Next Steps (IMF, Working Paper No. WP/03/196, 2003), *at* http://www.imf.org/external/pubs/ft/wp/2003/wp03196.pdf; Kenneth Kletzer, Resolving Sovereign Debt Crises with Collective Action Clauses, FRBSF Economic Letter, No. 2004–06, at 1 (20 Feb. 2004), available at http://www.frbsf.org/publications/economics/letter/2004/212004–06.html.

[13] Patrick McGuire & Martjin A. Schrijvers, Common Factors in Emerging Markets Spreads, BIS Q. Rev., Dec. 2003, at 65, 68, available at http://www.bis.org/publ/qtrpdf/r_qt0312f.pdf.

English market remains important while most other markets have been fading away more recently, except for Italy.

Table 2 indicates the major shift towards including CACs in the sovereign bond documentation under New York law. Nearly half the issuance value in New York included CACs in 2003. The 'other' group in this table is above all influenced by the shift towards the use of CACs on the Italian market during mid-2003. Since the early 1990s, a range of markets have been relatively small or only had an occasional issue (Austria, Colombia, Denmark, Greece, the Netherlands, Portugal, Sweden and other US states), while others have dried up during the last few years (France and Luxembourg after 1999, Spain after 1998, and Canada after 2001) or have declined (Germany and, to some extent, Switzerland since 1999).

Table 3 shows the breakdown by individual country for 2002 and 2003 under all governing jurisdictions. In 2003, several sovereign states issued bonds with and without CACs. In most cases, this reflects issuance under different governing laws throughout the year; in other cases this may be due to a shift during the year on the New York market itself.

Table 1. Sovereign bond issues, 1991–2003[14] (announced issuance by governing law in billions of US dollars, annual averages)

	1991–92	1993–98	1999	2000–01	2002	2003
New York	2.4	15.6	22.1	36.2	36.9	46.6
English	22.3	27.6	19.0	13.7	15.6	22.5
Italian	3.2	7.4	5.0	6.8	1.5	4.9
German	4.7	9.6	8.6	2.9	0.0	0.5
Japanese	3.2	5.6	0.7	5.2	0.2	0.4
Swiss	1.1	1.4	0.3	0.6	0.1	0.5
Other[1]	2.7	7.6	4.1	0.2	1.0	0.6
Total	**39.6**	**74.8**	**59.8**	**65.6**	**55.4**	**76.1**

[1]Includes Austria, Canada, Colombia, Denmark, France, Greece, Luxembourg, Netherlands, Portugal, Spain, Sweden and other US states.

[14] The data reflected in this table were collected from Dealogic Bondware in January 2004.

Table 2. Adoption of collective action clauses in sovereign bond issues, 2002–2003[15] (in billions of US dollars)

	2002		2003	
	No	Yes	No	Yes
New York	36.9	•	23.9	22.7
English	•	15.6	•	22.5
Other	2.6	0.2	4.6	2.4
Total	39.5	15.8	28.5	47.6
Memo item: *Number of countries*	*24*	*18*	*20*	*28*

Table 3. Sovereign bond issues by country without (no) and with (yes) CACs[16] (in billions of US dollars)

Issuer	2002		2003	
	No	Yes	No	Yes
Bahrain Monetary Agency		0.3		
Bangko Sentral ng Pilipinas (Central Bank of the Philippines)		0.3		
Bank Markazi Jomhouri Islami Iran (Central Bank of the Islamic Republic of Iran)		1.0		
Banque Centrale de Tunisie	0.7			0.4
Commonwealth of the Bahamas			0.2	
Dominican Republic			0.6	
Federation of Malaysia	0.8			
Federative Republic of Brazil	3.5	0.4		5.8
Government of Grenada	0.1			
Government of Jamaica	0.3			

15 The data reflected in this table were collected from Dealogic Bondware in January 2004.

16 The data reflected in this table were collected from Dealogic Bondware in January 2004.

Table 3. Continued

Issuer	2002		2003	
	No	Yes	No	Yes
Government of Romania	0.6		0.8	
Hellenic Republic		0.5	0.7	0.4
Kingdom of Bahrain				0.5
Kingdom of Morocco				0.5
Kingdom of Sweden	3.3		1.3	
Kingdom of Thailand				0.3
LGT Finance Ltd	0.1		0.2	
New Zealand		0.4		0.3
Norges Statsbaner BS – NSB				0.1
People's Republic of China			1.5	
Qatar Global Sukuk QSC				0.7
Republic of Austria	0.1	4.4		4.4
Republic of Belize	0.1			0.1
Republic of Bulgaria	1.2			
Republic of Chile	1.0		1.0	
Republic of China (Taiwan)			0.1	
Republic of Colombia	1.0		1.0	
Republic of Costa Rica	0.3		0.3	0.2
Republic of Croatia		0.6	0.8	
Republic of Cyprus		0.5		
Republic of El Salvador	1.3		0.3	
Republic of Estonia		0.1		
Republic of Finland	1.5			
Republic of Guatemala				0.3
Republic of Hungary				2.2
Republic of Iceland		0.4		0.2
Republic of Italy	12.3		9.9	7.0
Republic of Korea				1.0
Republic of Lebanon	0.8			
Republic of Lithuania	0.4		0.4	
Republic of Panama	0.6		0.3	

Table 3. Continued

Issuer	2002		2003	
	No	Yes	No	Yes
Republic of Peru	1.9		0.8	0.5
Republic of the Philippines	2.6	0.3	2.6	0.7
Republic of Poland	1.4	1.3		4.3
Republic of South Africa	1.3			1.4
Republic of Turkey	2.6	0.7	3.1	2.1
Republic of Ukraine		0.4		1.0
Republic of Uruguay	0.4			
Republic of Venezuela			3.0	0.7
Slovak Republic				0.9
State of Israel		0.3	0.8	
United Kingdom				3.0
United Mexican States	4.0		2.0	5.4
Total	**39.5**	**15.8**	**28.5**	**47.6**

4.2 The adoption of CACs in sovereign bond issues in 2003–2004

The year 2003 may be dubbed the watershed year for CACs. For the first time, they were widely adopted by a range of key sovereign issuers in New York.[17] The official sector continued to play an active role. The European Union (EU) officially recommended including CACs in sovereign bond issues by European borrowers. The IMF and World Bank included a recommendation for the addition of CACs in their revised *Amendments to the Guidelines for Public Debt* in November 2003.[18] Furthermore, towards the end of 2003, the G10 continued its leading role by setting up an informal review mechanism to assess the adoption of CACs.

[17] Bulgaria, Egypt, Kazakhstan, Lebanon and Qatar all issued New York-law bonds with majority amendment clauses prior to the recent initiative. See Anthony Richards & Mark Gugiatti, *Do Collective Action Clauses Influence Bond Yields? New Evidence from Emerging Markets*, 6 Int'l Fin. 415, 421 (2003).

[18] International Monetary Fund & World Bank, Amendments to the Guidelines for Public Debt Management 6 (Nov. 2003), available at http://www.imf.org/external/np/mfd/pdebt/2003/eng/112503.pdf.

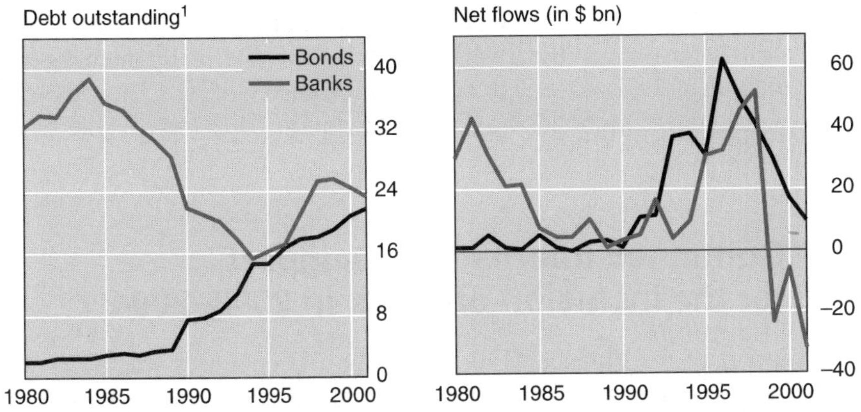

[1]As a percentage of total emerging market external debt outstanding.

Graph 1. Structure of Emerging Market Debt[19]

The breakthrough in terms of actually introducing CACs in sovereign bond issues on the New York market occurred with the Mexican bond issue of February 2003. Other countries followed suit – specifically Uruguay and Brazil in April, Korea and South Africa in May, Belize in June, Italy in July and Turkey in September. In 2004, Chile, Hungary, Panama, Columbia, Costa Rica, the Philippines and Venezuela successfully completed bond issues including CACs for the first time,while Brazil, Turkey, and Mexico's 2004 issues again included CACs.[20] Some sovereign states did not include CACs in their 2003 New York issues, such as China and the Philippines.[21] While there were no sovereign bonds with CACs on the New York market in 2002, in 2003 nearly 50% (on a value basis) of all new sovereign bonds under New York law included CACs (Table 2).

In 2003, there were no CACs included in the sovereign bond issues on the German and Swiss markets. The basic documentation of the only sovereign

[19] McGuire and Schrijvers, *supra* note 13, at 67 (created based on information available from the World Bank).

[20] Press Release, US Dept. of Treasury, Statement of Under Secretary John B. Taylor Regarding Decisions by Countries to Issue Bonds with Collective Action Clauses (CACs) (Feb. 3, 2004) [hereinafter US Dept. of Treasury Press Release] available at http://www.treas.gov/press/releases/js1144.htm.

[21] Bonds without CACs were issued under New York law in 2003, after March, by, inter alia, China, Colombia, Israel, the Philippines, Taiwan (China) and Venezuela. In 2004, only Jamaica reopened a bond without CACs. Bond prospectuses containing this information can be found at the US Securities and Exchange Commission (http://www.sec.gov) under the Standard Industrial Classification (SIC) Code 8888 (Foreign Governments).

bond issue by Turkey on the German market and also the only sovereign bond issue by Greece on the Swiss market remained virtually unchanged.[22] The Japanese and UK sovereign bonds all included CACs.[23] Thus, close to 60% of the sovereign bonds issued worldwide in 2003 (on a value basis) contained CACs.[24]

4.3 Continued international support for the inclusion of CACs in 2003–2004

The support of the Finance Ministers of the EU countries was a key element in promoting inclusion of CACs. In his speech to the International Monetary and Financial Committee (IMFC) in April 2003, Greek Minister of Economy and Finance Nikos Christodoulakis, acting in his capacity as president of the EU's Economic and Financial Council (ECOFIN), announced that

> the EU will use contractual provisions [CACs] based on the framework developed by the G10, and where necessary in accordance with applicable law and adjusted to local practice, in their central government bonds issued under a foreign jurisdiction and/or governed by a foreign law by the end of this year.[25]

Italy subsequently introduced CACs in the documentation of all New York-law-governed bonds issued after 16 June 2003.[26]

---

[22] In both countries some further legal clarification about the status of CACs under domestic jurisdictions is required, and the official sector is in dialogue with the key underwriters.

[23] Only one sovereign bond was issued, by Poland, under Japanese law in 2003 (July). Differences between Japanese and UK bonds continue to exist. One key difference is the permanent bondholders' representative: while the United Kingdom follows a trustee arrangement, there is a fiscal agent in Japan. The Polish sovereign bond issue in Japan follows in the main the newly adopted standards evolving in the USA (New York) market.

[24] The worldwide issue of sovereign bonds in 2003 is estimated to be about US$76.3 billion (based on information available from Dealogic Bondware).

[25] EU Economic and Financial Council, Common Understanding on Implementing the EU Commitment Regarding the Use of Collective Action Clauses (CACs), EFC-ECFIN/ 343/03-fin (Apr. 2003) [hereinafter ECOFIN Statement on CACs], available at
http://www.europa.eu.int/comm/economy_finance/publications/efc/report7.pdf.

[26] Press Release, Ministero dell'Economia e delle Finanze (Italian Ministry of Economy & Finance), Communicato No. 166, Introduction of Collective Action Clauses (CACs) in Global Bond Documentation (16 June 2003) (on file with The Georgetown Journal of International Law).

The IMF continued its supportive role in 2003, as reflected in the April 2003 Communiqué of the IMFC. *The Guidelines for Public Debt Management* now explicitly state: 'When issuing sovereign bonds governed by foreign laws, debt managers should consider including these clauses in new borrowings, in consultation with their financial and legal advisors.'[27] Other publications, like the *IMF Survey*, also continue to support the adoption of CACs, and the IMF has started to encourage the use of such clauses in the context of its annual country and multilateral surveillance efforts.[28]

Towards the end of 2003, the G10 recommended taking stock of developments and continued to monitor changes and emerging problems carefully. The G10 plans to examine the CACs included in sovereign bonds in their recent bond issues and to assess any differences vis-à-vis the G10 template.[29] The follow-up process will take place during 2004. Similarly, in a press release during early 2004, the US Treasury had shown a renewed commitment to include CACs in sovereign bonds under New York law.[30] The Gang of Seven continued to voice support for CACs in their Florida communiqué in February 2004.[31]

4.4 Selected key issues in the introduction of CACs

International institutions continue to monitor closely the role of CACs in sovereign bonds. Whether in fact CACs will be able to deliver a more orderly and timely resolution of sovereign default remains to be seen. Two immediate questions are apparent. First, why have some countries not adopted CACs? Second, should current differences in the nature of detailed CAC provisions raise concerns?

4.4.1 The choice to adopt CACs

One may only speculate why some countries did not include CACs in their New York issues last year. The argument that these countries or their legal advisers may not be aware of these clauses is perhaps now less cogent than

[27] Int'l Monetary Fund & World Bank, *supra* note 19, at 6.

[28] See Psalida & Liu, *supra* note 5, at 167–68.

[29] Group of Ten, Decisions and Points for Action (1 Dec. 2003) (on file with The Georgetown Journal of International Law).

[30] US Dept. of Treasury Press Release, *supra* note 20.

[31] Communiqué, Statement of G-7 Finance Ministers and Central Bank Governors at the G-7 Finance Ministers Meeting, Boca Raton, Florida (9 Feb. 2004), available at http://www.ustreas.gov/press/releases/js1158.htm.

it was at the beginning of 2003. Sovereign bond issues that include CACs are on the rise, and the official sector has been consistently supportive in promoting CACs. Additionally, there has been no evidence of a market impact as a result of the inclusion or exclusion of CACs. Empirical evidence before and after the introduction of CACs has not shown any costs or liquidity constraints associated with the addition of such clauses in bond documentation.[32]

The outlook for the inclusion of CACs in future sovereign bond issues for countries that have not included CACs thus far seems generally positive. This should equally include those countries that plan to tap the market in the near future. Efforts should thus continue to sensitise sovereign borrowers as well as financial intermediaries to the inclusion of CACs.

4.4.2 Differences in CACs across various national legislations

Some key provisions, like the majority action clause, have emerged now as market standards, while other provisions continue to differ between markets, particularly New York and London. Is the current variety in CACs a matter of concern, and should there be further efforts to standardise or harmonise still-existing differences?

There seems to be agreement that no value will be added by pursuing the inclusion of exactly the same clauses in the same format under all relevant governing laws.[33] For example, the IMF Executive Board noted that 'while it might be desirable for CACs to possess [a set of common features] differences in legal systems, market features, or country circumstances may necessitate some variation.'[34] Similarly, ECOFIN's statement regarding the use of CACs recognizes that "flexibility to allow for different legal practices in different countries is necessary."[35] An examination of the variations that

---

[32] It appears that rating agencies have begun to pay some attention to CACs, but even notching by individual rating agencies due to the inclusion/exclusion of CACs is not very likely. Admittedly, this is a preliminary conclusion based on the author's private consultations with Standard & Poor's, and this assessment by the rating agencies may also change over time.

[33] Frank Elderson and Marino Perassi, *Collective Action Clauses in Sovereign Foreign Bonds, Towards a More Harmonised Approach*, Euredia, July 2003, at 259.

[34] Public Information Notice, International Monetary Fund, IMF Continues Discussion on Collective Action Clauses in Sovereign Bond Contracts (18 Apr. 2003), quoted in Elderson & Perassi, *supra* note 33, at 260, available at http://www.imf.org/external/np/sec/pn/2003/pn0353.htm.

[35] ECOFIN Statement on CACs, *supra* note 25.

exist and the significance of those differences demonstrates the impracticability of imposing verbatim clauses in identical formats under differing governing laws.

Broadly speaking, some key provisions of CACs have moved towards an accepted market standard. These include: (1) majority action clauses[36] in amending key terms (thus binding on minorities and holdout creditors); (2) disenfranchisement provisions (which exclude from voting those bonds held directly or indirectly by the issuer); (3) accepted hurdles for acceleration and deceleration (which are the conditions in terms of bondholder shares for pursuit when default occurs and the conditions for reinstatement of the debtor that is rescission of acceleration);[37] and (4) voting on non-reserved matters (which has been consistently fixed at 66 2/3% as recommended by the G10 and the Gang of Seven).[38]

Admittedly, there are a number of individually noted outliers for these provisions. However, a consensus is emerging in bond documentation on these key clauses that broadly follows the G10 recommendations.[39] The standard inclusion of the majority amendment clauses in the New York bonds constitutes a particularly noteworthy step by the United States

---

[36] Most issuers have chosen a threshold of 75% of principal outstanding for votes on 'reserved matters' (such as payment terms). This is consistent with G10 recommendations. However,

> [a] number of early sub-investment-grade issuers (Brazil, Belize, Guatemala and Venezuela) chose a higher 85% threshold, leading some commentators to suggest that sub-investment-grade issuers would need to choose a higher threshold to signal greater commitment to avoiding future restructurings. … But the subsequent inclusion of CACs with a 75% threshold by Colombia, Costa Rica, Indonesia, Panama, Peru, the Philippines and Turkey – all sub-investment-grade issuers – suggests that the distinction between investment and non-investment-grade countries in the design of CACs is becoming more blurred and that issuers are increasingly aligning the threshold chosen for majority amendment clauses with the G10's recommendation.

John Drage and Catherine Hovaguimian, Collective Action Clauses (CACs): An Analysis of Provisions included in Recent Sovereign Bond Issues 4 (2 Nov. 2004), available at http://www.bankofengland.co.uk/fsr/fsr17art9.pdf.

[37] The inclusion of a 25% threshold for acceleration in the event of default has been consistently applied. Rescission of acceleration in New York sovereign bonds requires a threshold of 50% or 66 2/3%. The Gang of Seven had recommended 75% (66 2/3%) as a threshold. See report of the G10 Working Group on contractual clauses, *supra* note 1; Gang of Seven Letter, *supra* note 4.

[38] Chile is the only exception, with 50% of the vote required for non-reserved matters.

[39] See Table 5 *infra* app. B.

toward the UK legislative framework. The majority action provision had been one of the key recommendations of the G10.

However, not all the recommendations by the G10 or those by the Gang of Seven have been embraced by the sovereign issuers of foreign debt and their legal advisers. Some differences remain between the G10 and the Gang of Seven recommended provisions and those the markets are willing to adopt. For example, the G10 Working Group recommended a set of provisions designed to restrict the ability to initiate disruptive litigation, along the lines of the UK trust indenture. Yet the idea of providing the trustee with more power by giving him the power to initiate proceedings has essentially been left out of New York law. This appears to be due to the generally prevailing fiscal structure in current US sovereign bond documentation. It may also reflect the likely preference of sovereign borrowers for adopting a fiscal structure on which they can easily draw and perhaps rely during negotiation. There may also be general market resistance to such a major change due to costs in changing documentation as well as considerations of foregone fiscal fees.

Also, the Gang of Seven had supported the idea of keeping the fiscal agent structure for sovereign bonds issued under New York law. The fiscal agent set-up has thus not been replaced by a trustee agreement in recent New York sovereign bond issues, and only Uruguay has included a trust indenture.[40] Neither the G10 recommendation of an engagement provision nor the proposal for a similar 'engagement clause' by the Gang of Seven has been adopted in New York sovereign bond issues. It is also not surprising that the 'information provision', a milder G10 and a stronger Gang of Seven version, has not been adopted. Such an information provision is difficult to formulate, may be an advantage or disadvantage in negotiation and seems difficult to implement in practice.[41]

The decision not to adopt some G10 recommendations may be interpreted as a preliminary judgment on those recommendations by the market itself. In a more positive vein, it may also be interpreted as leading to certain standards by which the markets are willing to live. In the case of the fiscal agency structure, the Gang of Seven recommendations have been followed. Market practice in New York is now a mix of both sets of recommendations. However, a substantial convergence has been achieved,

[40] While sovereign bonds in Tokyo lean in their CAC provisions predominantly on UK documentation, they include a fiscal agency agreement like those on the New York market.

[41] Most debtors consider this to be imposing undue constraints (e.g. as an obligation to supply certain documents, data, etc.).

even though some proposals by the G10 and the Gang of Seven have not been taken on board by the market at all.[42]

It is not immediately obvious how this current status quo is to be evaluated. Do we need to narrow the gap further between the two main legal centres, New York and London? In addition, should some of the G10 recommendations be pursued further? One starting point for such an evaluation is to revisit the original aims of the G10 Working Group on contractual clauses.

The G10 Working Group noted the following three objectives when promoting contractual clauses:

> Critical to the effort is the desire to create a structure that will build on existing market practices, promote a consistent framework across jurisdictions and benefit the interests of both debtors and creditors. The following three key objectives were identified:
>
> (1) To foster early dialogue, coordination and communication among creditors and sovereigns involved in a sovereign debt problem;
> (2) To ensure that there are effective means for creditors and debtors to re-contract, without a minority of debt-holders obstructing the process; and
> (3) To ensure that disruptive legal action by individual creditors does not hamper a workout that is underway, while protecting the interests of the creditor group.[43]
>
> These three key objectives raise a number of potential responses. With regard to the first objective, the currently emerging version of CACs in New York bonds has not included clauses dealing with information exchange. Fostering early dialogue, coordination and communication among creditors and sovereigns remains an elusive goal. The current long processes involved in Argentina's debt restructuring may be a reminder that this issue remains relevant. Perhaps other international initiatives like the proposals for a 'Code of Good Conduct' may help to fill this gap.[44]

With regard to the second objective, one question that emerges is whether the CACs will be able to deliver on the question of holdout creditors. Majority amendment will bind dissenting creditors, and the wholesale

[42] See *infra* app. A.

[43] Report of the G10 Working Group on Contractual Clauses, *supra* note 1, at 1.

[44] See Statement of G-7 Finance Ministers and Central Bank Governors, Washington, D.C. (12 Apr. 2003) (discussing the growing interest in exploring a voluntary 'Code of Good Conduct' to facilitate good investor relations on the part of the G-7, the IMF, and others), available at http://www.g8.utoronto.ca/finance/fm041203.htm.

adoption of this clause in all markets will ensure that creditors and debtors are able to recontract. Yet, how confident are we that the minority dissenting creditor will not find means and ways to effectively claim payment of outstanding debt later?[45]

Furthermore, with regard to the third objective, the current CACs introduced in New York are also not designed to reign in disruptive legal action. In a few recent cases, *pari passu* clauses have *prevented* sovereign debtors from making payments to newer debtors. This has either resulted in default on the more recent debt or 'forced' a new settlement of the older debt.

In 2000, LP Elliott Associates obtained an order from the Brussels Appeals Court preventing Euroclear from accepting payments or paying out cash from Peru to discharge the interest due on its Brady Bonds.[46] This order was granted without the defendants, Euroclear and Peru, being given the opportunity to present their counterarguments.[47] It was based on a broad interpretation of the *pari passu* provision. According to this interpretation, Peru could not make interest payments on its restructured sovereign debt (Brady Bonds) without at the same time paying holdout creditors (Elliott).[48] Instead of challenging the decision of the Belgian court, Peru decided to settle with Elliott in order to avoid being forced to default on its Brady Bond payments being made through Euroclear.[49] Thus, there was no official ruling on the substance of the *pari passu* clause in that case.

In *LNC Investments LLC v. Nicaragua*, LNC won a US court judgement in 1999 against the Government of Nicaragua for US$87 million as compensation for commercial loans on which Nicaragua defaulted during the 1980s.[50] The creditor opted out of the government buyback of the debt in 1995, in which investors only recouped 8 cents on the dollar.[51] In September 2003, a Brussels court issued an injunction on funds that the government's paying agent, Deutsche Bank AG, was scheduled to transfer to the settlement house Euroclear, headquartered in Brussels.[52] Euroclear would have disbursed the money to the holders of Nicaragua's indemnification bonds.

[45] This is admittedly an *advocatus diaboli* question. This is a hypothetical question which may be answered once sovereign restructuring invoking CACs has occurred.

[46] *See* Elderson and Perassi, *supra* note 33, at 244.

[47] *Id.*

[48] *Id.*

[49] *Id.*

[50] LNC Investments, Inc. v. Republic of Nicaragua, No. 96 Civ. 6360, 1999 US Dist. LEXIS 1846 (S.D.N.Y. 19 Feb. 1999).

[51] *Id.*

[52] See Angela Pruitt, *Nicaragua Creditor Suit Muddies Sovereign Restructurings*, Dow Jones Int'l News, 29 Sept. 2003.

As a result of the ruling, Nicaragua's government was forced into another default, missing a US$1.8 million payment to bondholders that was due on 1 August 2003.[53] Nicaragua had been servicing new bonds since the loan restructuring. However, in March of 2004, the Court of Appeals of Brussels reversed the prior decision and invalidated the order against Euroclear.[54]

The currently adopted CACs will not be able to deliver easily on the G10 Working Group's third objective. All foreign bond issuers in New York (except Uruguay) have used fiscal agency agreements, where the fiscal agent is the agent of the issuer – not the bondholder – and there are no restrictions on individual legal action.

While trust deeds are common under English law, the Emerging Market Creditors Association (EMCA) and the Emerging Markets Trade Association (EMTA) have not endorsed such documentation as it would 'unduly restrict the right of individual bondholder action'.[55] While there is good reason to believe that the inclusion of CACs will effectively bind holdout creditors, the sanguine conclusion is that there are residual legal risks as these are private civil law processes.

The *Italian Bondholders v. Republic of Argentina* cases may be relevant. In one case, the court granted the motion of private bondholders and, moving from the assumption that the issue and the placement of a loan are commercial activities under international private law, denied Argentina immunity from attachment and execution.[56] In another case, an Italian court recently denied a petition of attachment on the basis of the Argentine default because the insolvency of a sovereign state is covered by immunity.[57] In the latter case, the bilateral agreement between the governments of Italy and Argentina prevailed over the (private) contractual agreements in the sovereign bonds.

Regardless of the interpretation of the *pari passu* clause, the fact remains that holdout creditors could stall payments or force sharing of payments, induce further defaults on the part of the sovereign state, or trigger a legal battle between the creditors themselves. The time lags in all these

---

53 *See id.*

54 *See id.* In contrast, *Italian Bondholders v. Republic of Argentina* shows a scale of litigation that is different from past experience, insofar as it includes a large number of retail investors and opens significant debate over the issues of immunity protection for sovereign states. For a discussion of *Italian Bondholders v. Republic of Argentina*, see Elderson and Perassi, *supra* note 33. The litigation among the Italian Bondholders and the Republic of Argentina is still before the Italian courts. *See id.* at 19.

55 Gang of Seven Letter, supra note 4, Attachment 1 at i.

56 See Elderson and Perassi, *supra* note 33.

57 See *id.*

processes have always been several years. This does not augur well for any debt restructuring, as any unsatisfied creditor may be able to affect the settlement of debt.[58]

The current legal playing field is thus full of mines. First, the current uncertainty with regard to the legally 'correct' interpretation of the *pari passu* clause prevails. Buchheit and Pam take pains to trace the meaning of the *pari passu* clause down through US legal history and conclude:

> At no time … did the pari passu clause ever require a borrower to make rateable payments to all of its equally-ranking creditors [as implied by the rulings described above]. Nor did it ever provide a legal basis for one unsecured creditor to enjoin or intercept non-rateable payments to another creditor, notwithstanding the equal legal ranking of their respective claims against the borrower. The rateable payment theory of the pari passu clause is, under the light of history, just a fallacy.[59]

Another legal difficulty is that the seizure of assets in the payment stream may be subject to special bankruptcy laws. 'Carve-out' rules may apply that aim at protecting the payment and settlement mechanism. However, it is not obvious how such rules may be upheld when a legal claim to such assets has already been established.

A final challenge is that payment orders may not be executed. It is not obvious whether and when a holdout creditor may actually be able to collect on such assets in the settlement process. If the payment is being executed by a foreign government, the assets may be subject to some immunity protection. But such immunity protection may not be watertight. Assume, for example, that a country's institution is making a payment via Euroclear and that this country's payment agent resides in the USA. Also assume that the paying institution falls under the US Foreign Sovereign Immunities Act. But what if such US immunity rules are not consistent with rules in other countries, such as Belgium?[60] More generally, there are

[58] This may not bode well for debt restructuring in Argentina, as payments on any old and new debt could be blocked in the future (including payments to international organisations).

[59] Lee C. Buchheit and Jeremiah S. Pam, The Pari Passu Clause in Sovereign Debt Instruments 36 (11 Dec. 2003) (working draft, on file with The Georgetown Journal of International Law), available at http://www.law.harvard.edu/programs/pifs.

[60] As Euroclear's legal seat is in Belgium, the rules of the sovereign State of Belgium may prevail. However, in describing the *Italian Bondholders v. Republic of Argentina* ruling, Elderson and Perassi note:

no internationally accepted rules that would effectively guarantee 'carve-outs' in payment and settlement processes.[61]

In summary, the unresolved question is how we can ensure the priority of new liabilities going forward. The finality to such a question is lodged in the majority clauses of the CACs. However, doubts will continue to exist as this is essentially a private sector process.[62]

4.4.3 Cause for concern

While the adoption of some elements of CACs in New York has narrowed the gap between the issues of bonds in terms of governing laws between the two key countries (the USA and the UK), there may still be cause for concern. Assume a country has bonds under both governing laws and assume a sovereign debt default. Judges in these two jurisdictions may come to different conclusions as to who is allowed to litigate and who might represent bondholders. Admittedly, such different judgements may also result in cases when even the text of the CACs is identical. The risk that a level playing field has not been achieved, because of gaps or because of a different interpretations of the CACs themselves, continues to exist. This may result in legal arbitrage coming into play.

4.4.4 Issues yet to be tackled

There are also some issues that were explicitly not tackled by the G10 Working Group on Contractual Clauses. Two of them are aggregation clauses and sovereign loans. Currently, Argentina is a case in point where such aggregation clauses may have been helpful in coordinating the negotiating position of the creditors. Such coordination is difficult not only due to the

---

The judge had preliminarily considered the Italian Courts as competent, because both the government bond issue and the consequent legal relationship and obligations are activities of a private law nature. As a result, the jurisdiction has to be assessed on the basis of the rules of the private international law and none can invoke the customary principle that guarantees the immunity in favour of foreign States for their activities in Italy, as such principle only applies to activities coming under public law.

Elderson and Perassi, *supra* note 33, at 245. Thus, according to this ruling, immunity considerations are irrelevant.

61 See Group of Ten, Insolvency Arrangements and Contract Enforceability, a Report by the Contact Group on the Legal and Institutional Underpinnings of the International Financial System 27 (Sept. 2002), available at http://www.bis.org/publ/gten06.pdf.

62 The Sovereign Debt Resolution Mechanism (SDRM) was to resolve this uncertainty through tighter international legal agreements.

wide retail holdings of Argentine securities but also because of the lack of existing procedures for aggregating potential claims. Only Uruguay has tackled these questions in its recent bond documentation in New York. Should we conclude that Uruguay sets a good standard for such aggregation clauses to be included in future sovereign bond documentation?

Also, the *Report of the G-10 Working Group on Contractual Clauses* did not include syndicated loan agreements in its deliberations on CACs in sovereign bonds. These loans have become more of a liquid asset and are more widely traded, priced and held. They have become similar to securities as they have become capital market assets in their own right.[63] These developments may call for CACs to be included in such syndicated loans. Already during the Russian crisis in 1998–1999, it became evident that it was no longer as easy as in the past to bind all creditors to the London process. This was primarily due to the diverse holdings of these syndicated loans by banks and a range of different institutional holders. The fact of the diverse holdings of these loans as tradable in the retail sector immediately raises one key issue with CACs: a majority action clause.

4.4.5 Majority action clauses of CACs

As all sovereign bonds include *pari passu* clauses, the recently erupted dispute over the interpretation of the *pari passu* clause also casts a shadow over the key CAC provision on majority action. The wide interpretation of the *pari passu* clause, in terms of *pro rata* sharing in settlement of the debt, has the potential to effectively unhinge CACs. No state will be able to make safe payments if these payments are transferred through another entity and the broader *pro rata* interpretation prevails. Sequestration of such payments would then be both possible and likely.

Due to these risks, markets have already been exploring alternative mechanisms to circumvent such risks, such as collateralising future flow receivables.[64] The evaluation and effectiveness of such new instruments are beginning to be assessed.

Sovereign bonds in the USA do not include effective deterrents to individual holder suits. These are included in UK-style trustee bonds, as the trustee is charged with this right, but are not part of the US fiscal structure. If indeed individuals are able to dispute majority action, this appears to

63 Hugh Thomas and Zhiqiang Wang, *The Integration of Bank Syndicated Loan and Junk Bond Markets*, 28 J. Banking & Fin. 267,302 (2004).

64 *See generally* Int'l Monetary Fund, Assessing Public Sector Borrowing Collateral on Future Flow Receivables (11 June 2003) (for an assessment of the appropriateness of collateralizing public sector borrowing with future receipts), available at http://www.imf.org/external/np/fad/2003/061103.pdf.

unhinge majority action clauses to some extent. Immunity protection of sovereign states may be seen as a deterrent against such individual legal proceedings. Yet, immunity protection itself may not hold, as evidenced by *Italian Bondholders v. Republic of Argentina*.

4.5 Summary and some key open issues

There has been substantial progress in including CACs in sovereign bond documentation on the New York market. The emerging split between sovereign bonds with and without CACs does not appear to be affecting market behaviour or the pricing of new sovereign bonds. CACs have yet to be tested in courts, so a more in-depth evaluation of their merits will have to wait. However, the emerging and unresolved issues may in due course merit a more thorough evaluation of the CACs currently being adopted in the New York market. This summary outlines some areas in which further work could be envisaged and where agreement to move ahead by the G10 or other sponsors may help.

Efforts to include CACs in all major sovereign debt contract laws (New York, Germany, and Switzerland) should continue. It appears that some sovereign borrowers, intermediaries, and creditors are still resisting, indifferent to or unaware of CACs. International efforts to promote the inclusion of CACs should persist.

This essay has explored deviations between the G10 recommendations and the actual adoption of CACs in New York. With the divergence in the legal clauses adopted, there is good reason to revisit individual clauses and assess in more detail why some G10 recommendations have been adopted while others (such as fiscal as compared to trustee agreements) have not. This review of CACs has shown to some extent what the market is and is not willing to accept. Only some of the overall G10 objectives as set out by its Working Group have been achieved. It is particularly relevant to continue monitoring the CACs in the two major markets, New York and London.

Following the evidence in this essay, two major related legal questions arise. First, does the market evolution in 2003 undermine the basic thrust of the CAC policy in such a way that this raises a major concern, as recommendations were not adopted? The G10 may want to explore in some more detail the importance of aggregation clauses, especially as countries have a whole series of different bonds outstanding. The G10 Working Group was unable to reach a consensus on this issue in 2002–2003, but perhaps it is time to reconsider. Second, the G10 may also want to review the question of whether to include CACs in syndicated loan agreements. Syndicated loans have become similar to securities as they are more widely traded and held by more and more diversified financial agents. Collective action under the traditional London approach should thus be considered.

At this point in time, it is not possible to assess the effective contribution of CACs to a more timely and orderly sovereign debt restructuring as their legal role is untested in complex cases. We are looking forward to CACs delivering what they have set out to deliver.

Appendix A

Both the G10 and the Gang of Seven trade associations proposed model features for CACs in sovereign bonds issued under New York law.[65] The key features and how they compare with evolving market practice are summarised in Table 4 below. The main differences are as follows.

- The G10 recommend the use of a trustee (or alternative) as a representative of bondholders and the accompanying restrictions on litigation, while the Gang of Seven prefer use of a fiscal agent who is the agent of the issuer (rather than bondholders) without any restrictions on individual litigation.
- The G10 recommend lower voting thresholds for amendments than the Gang of Seven.
- The Gang of Seven recommend a wider set of reserved matters than those proposed by the G10.
- The Gang of Seven propose more demanding information requirements than the G10.

Market practice is a mix of both. Many of the G10 recommendations have been adopted – most importantly the majority action provisions. But issuers have chosen a fiscal agent structure rather than a trustee, consistent with the Gang of Seven proposals.

Table 4. Comparison of the G10 and Gang of Seven CAC proposals[66]

G10 Recommendations for New York Law Bonds	Gang of Seven Recommendations for New York Law Bonds	Market Practice – in Bonds Issued by Mexico (and Others)
Permanent bondholders' representative (trustee or other)	No – fiscal agent, who represents the issuer	Gang of Seven. Fiscal agent (in all recent NY-law issues except Uruguay's)

[65] See *Report of the G-10 Working Group on Contractual Clause*, *supra* note 1; Gang of Seven Letter, *supra* note 4.

[66] This table was reproduced, with minor editorial changes, from Drage and Hovaguimian, *supra* note 36, at app. B.

Table 4. Continued

G10 Recommendations for New York Law Bonds	Gang of Seven Recommendations for New York Law Bonds	Market Practice – in Bonds Issued by Mexico (and Others)
Bondholders' negotiating representative elected by 2/3 of bondholders	The 'Engagement clause' provides, in the event of default or restructuring, for bondholders to elect a representative committee (or individual) with votes from 50% of bondholders, unless more than 25% object. The representative(s) could engage legal counsel and financial advisors and the issuer would cover the costs.	Neither; no provision for representation (as far as the author is aware)
Bondholders' meeting to be convened at any time upon request of the issuer, permanent representative, or 10% of bondholders	Adds lower 5% threshold for bondholders to request the fiscal agent to call a meeting in the event of default, or if a restructuring is announced	Consistent with both. Slightly closer to G10
Majority action provisions for amendments to reserved matters with 75% vote	Higher threshold of 85% and adds that changes to reserved matters are prohibited if more than 10% object Also includes some matters which require 100% consent to change	Closer to G10 (only Brazil and Belize chose 85%)

Table 4. Continued

G10 Recommendations for New York Law Bonds	**Gang of Seven Recommendations for New York Law Bonds**	**Market Practice – in Bonds Issued by Mexico (and Others)**
List of reserved matters: (i) Change the payment date; (ii) Reduce the principal amount; (iii) Reduce the portion of the principal amount due in the event of an acceleration; (iv) Reduce the interest rate; (v) Change the currency or place of payment; (vi) Change the obligation of the issuer to pay additional amounts; (vii) Change the definition of "outstanding" or reduce the voting requirements; (viii) to (xi) regarding permanent representative and enforcement	Covers (i) to (vii) Also adds changes to the *pari passu* clause (or other speified substantive covenants) as appropriate; and any detrimental changes to the events of default or negative pledge provisions Also adds that changes to the following require 100% consent: governing law, jurisdiction and waiver of sovereign immunity	Elements of both. Most cover G10 reserved matters (i) to (vii) but also add *pari passu*, events of default, governing law and jurisdiction (with 75% threshold)
Majority action provisions for amendments to non-reserved matters with 66 2/3% vote	Higher threshold of 75%	G10
Amendments can be agreed in writing or at a meeting	Yes	Consistent with both
Acceleration instruction by bondholders representing 25% of principal	Yes	Consistent with both

Table 4. Continued

G10 Recommendations for New York Law Bonds	**Gang of Seven Recommendations for New York Law Bonds**	**Market Practice – in Bonds Issued by Mexico (and Others)**
Rescission of acceleration decision by 66 2/3% of bondholders	Rescission by 75% vote	Closer to G10 – mix of thresholds of 66 2/3% and 50% (neither as high as Gang of Seven 75%)
Litigation to be instituted solely by the permanent representative	No	Gang of Seven
Continuation and outcome of litigation – directed by majority of bondholders	No	Gang of Seven
Pro rata distribution of proceeds	No	Gang of Seven
Disenfranchisement provision	Yes	Consistent with both
Information provision – to be included on a case-by-case basis	Requires: SDDS subscription and compliance; publication of 12-month forecasts of central government budget and inflation; Paris Club minutes and terms of agreement; terms of any other restructuring agreements; terms of IMF arrangements; and other information that the fiscal agent, on instruction of 5% of bondholders, may "from time to time reasonably request" Notices and other information provided to bondholders must also be given to the IPMA, EMTA, EMCA and IIF for publication on their websites.	Neither. Only Uruguay has included information requirements, and they would apply only in the event that it seeks amendments

Appendix B

Table 5. Collective action clauses in some recent sovereign bonds: comparison with G10 recommendations[67]

G10 Recommendation (*Other relevant features in italics*)	UK	Italy	Mexico	Uruguay	Brazil	Belize	South Africa	Turkey	Poland	Korea
Governing law	Eng.	N.Y.	N.Y.	N.Y.	N.Y.	N.Y.	N.Y.	N.Y.	N.Y.	N.Y.
Permanent bondholders' representative										
Bondholders' negotiating representative elected by 2/3 of bondholders										
Bondholders' meeting on request of 10% of bondholders										
Majority action provisions for amendments to reserved matters with 75% vote										
List of reserved matters	•	•	•	•	•	•	•	•	•	•
Majority action on non-reserved matters with 66 2/3% vote				•						
Non-material amendments may be made without the bondholders' consent										

[67] This table was reproduced from Drage & Hovaguimian, *supra* note 36, at 7.

Table 5. Continued

G10 Recommendation (*Other relevant features in italics*)	UK	Italy	Mexico	Uruguay	Brazil	Belize	South Africa	Turkey	Poland	Korea
Governing law	Eng.	N.Y.	N.Y.	N.Y.	N.Y.	N.Y.	N.Y.	N.Y.	N.Y.	N.Y.
Acceleration requires support of 25% of bondholders	•			•						
Rescission of acceleration by 66 2/3% of bondholders	•		•				•		•	•
Litigation to be instituted solely by the permanent representative										
Majority action on continuation and outcome of litigation	•									
Pro rata distribution of proceeds										
Disenfranchisement provision		•		•						
Information provision – to be included on a case by case basis				•						
Events of default										

Key:	Same as G10 in Substance	Different from G10	mixed	• Some Minor Variation

5 Note on the consequences of a potential default by Argentina to the IMF

5.1 Introduction

This note basically argues that the IMF will be able to absorb any short-tem non-payment by Argentina by its current burden sharing mechanisms and by its 'reserves'. The impact on both creditors and debtors is small.

While the IMF is able to absorb liquidity shortage, knock-on effects and longer-term legal and political factors may impair its current *modus operandi*. A failure to meet a payment obligation to the IMF has a number of consequences that are quite different from the typical default scenario in the commercial banking world. In the past only a few small countries have been placed into permanent arrears by the IMF. Only a borrower who leaves the IMF is considered in default. The borrower is considered in 'non-accrual' with regard only to the specific payment missed and is expected to return current obligations by paying the due amount even if in arrears. In general, no acceleration or cross-default clauses apply either within a given IFI (International Financial Institution) or across different multilateral lenders. However, approval or disbursement of new funds from other IFIs may be conditional on the borrower country maintaining good standing with the IMF.

5.2 Impact on IMF accounts

5.2.1 Principal

In a normal commercial banking environment, the books of the bank would show non-performing loans (NPL) if a loan is not being serviced, and after a certain period (usually three months) these NPL would have to be written off with an impact on the P&L accounts.

The IMF has never undertaken write-downs on payment arrears as there has so far not been any ultimate failure. There is thus presumably no noticeable impact on the balance sheet of the IMF.

5.2.2 Interest payment

Overdue interest payments would be absorbed by the so-called burden-sharing mechanism. Both the IMF debtor and creditor communities would have to absorb the losses. The debtors would pay slightly higher premiums on the IMF loans and the creditors would receive less interest on the funds made available to the IMF.

As these changes occur on the margin, the actual cost impact or loss in revenue is not easy to quantify precisely. Back-of-the-envelope calculation indicates that the amounts involved appear relatively minor for the creditor countries. For the larger IMF debtor countries (like Brazil or Turkey) the costs are a bit larger when e.g. scaled by GDP.

Assume – *in extremis* – that Argentina 'defaults' on its current total credits to the IMF on the order of SDR 10.7 billion and that interest payments are 10%. The resulting shortfall of SDR 1.07 billion is then to be allocated to the creditors and debtors, i.e. assume SDR .535 billion to the creditors. For the USA, as the largest SDR holder, this amounts to a nearly SDR 100 million implicit loss for the year with quarterly installments of about SDR 25 million. Germany's implied loss as creditor is roughly one third, i.e. a quarterly SDR 8 million.[1] For the largest debtor, Brazil, the 'surcharge' is comparable in size to the implied loss by the largest creditor, the USA. While there may be lags involved, the payment of lower interest to the creditor has an almost immediate positive impact on the liquidity (cash) budget of the IMF.

5.3 Liquidity impact on the IMF

5.3.1 Short term

Unlike a central bank, the IMF cannot create money, borrow on markets and thus provide open-ended access to liquidity. In order to offset losses that go beyond the burden-sharing mechanism, the IMF has in theory several options: mobilisation of precautionary balances[2] (these amount to about SDR 10 billion), take recourse in gold reserves (hypothetical market value about SDR 40 billion) and revert to special assistance (including the GAB and NAB). *In extremis*, the IMF could also consider reductions in operating or personnel expenditures.

---

1 There are lower bounds on how much interest payments are to be reduced.

2 It is not obvious how liquid these precautionary balances (e.g. balances held at the BIS) are.

5.3.2 Longer-term financial flexibility and planning

Non-payment by a debtor to the IMF like Argentina may bring into sharper focus current IMF policies and parts of the current *modus operandi* may be queried. For example, refusal of a major creditor of the IMF to provide reserves to the IMF could thus lead to a major liquidity crisis for the IMF. Such a political liquidity threat cannot be ignored.[3] This could happen even though the amounts involved for the major IMF creditors are relatively small as demonstrated above.

If the IMF started doubting that Argentina will be an isolated case and that several debtors reverted to non-payment (knock-on effects), the IMF may lose its current flexibility in planning liquidity needs for the future and also its flexibility in rolling over current commitments may be impaired. If there is a knock-on effect on other countries, the current roll-over policy, which amounts in practice to longer-term loans, will likely be reviewed (as it is questionable whether that policy is in line with the statutes of the IMF) and this may also lead to a liquidity squeeze of the IMF. Where the knock-on effect would impact other countries in terms of these funds being available to other debtors of the Fund is difficult to assess.

5.3.3 Longer-term prospects

Although the IMF does not have any legal recourse on the assets of a borrower country in default (other than arguably the country's IMF quotas), nor any contractual seniority vis-a-vis other creditors, it has historically been granted by borrowers a *de facto* preferred-creditor status. In fact, apart from a few marginal episodes (Sudan, Libya, etc.), countries have generally kept current on their financial obligations to the Fund even when in default with private creditors.

However, a non-payment of interest or capital by a major country calls into question the preferred creditor status of the IMF and calls for a need to re-assess the role in IFI lending operations. It may be asserted that the IMF's role has shifted from providing funds to cope with temporary BOP misalignments to rolling over loans for a significant number of years to a concentrated pool of borrowers. Even if this new role is accepted by its stakeholders, the Fund's risk management as well as its overall financial policies and strategies would need to be adequately reformed to reflect its new role.

---

[3] See Congress of the United States, Joint Economic Committee, Vice Chairman Jim Saxon: *IMF Exposure in Argentina underlines risk to taxpayers*, March 11, 2004.

6 Debt resolution processes for sovereign debt – current policy issues

6.1 Introduction

6.1.1 The recent political and institutional backdrop to the Sovereign Debt Resolution Mechanisms (SDRM) discussion

Over the last few years, sovereign debt restructurings have often been difficult and somewhat disorderly. Agreement on how to best undertake such restructuring and involve the private sector in the process has also been elusive. However, support for a market-oriented contractual approach to debt restructuring has recently gathered considerable momentum while the statutory approach to sovereign debt resolution continues to be challenged by the private sector.

Currently both the contractual and statutory approaches are being pursued in parallel. The US Treasury has been one of the major forces in promoting the contractual approach while the IMF is moving the statutory approach forward.[1] The *statutory* approach would provide a final settlement agent the power to bring any disputes about sovereign debt between the debtor country and private debtors to an end by a legally binding adjudication.

A working group of the G10,[2] established in June 2001, has been working on the legal provisions underlying the *contractual* approach. The remit of the Group is to make concrete drafting proposals or arrive at underlying principles for model clauses which would pave the way for a level playing

---

1 More recently, the idea of a third road has been launched by Claude Trichet (governor of the Banque de France) and others (see Banque de France, Financial Stability Review, Nov. 2002, p. 23). This avenue of a "Code of Good Practices" is not covered in this paper.

2 This Group was called the Quarles Group named after Randal Quarles of the US Treasury.

field for all sovereign debt restructurings under all legislations where sovereign bonds are issued. Obtaining ownership on the part of both debtors and creditors is key to the adoption and activation of collective action clauses (CACs). To this end, a well-designed framework in terms of appropriately balanced debtor and creditor roles would be critical and should in itself facilitate the adoption and implementation of the legal provisions in a voluntary manner as it would be in the interest of both parties.

Part 2 provides a brief review of the current thrust of policy, i.e. the motivation behind current efforts. Part 3 elaborates the broad consensus that has emerged on moving forward but also shows some of the further challenges ahead. Part 4 looks at some of the issues of CACs, while Part 5 attempts to summarize the status of the SDRM discussion. This is followed by a summary.

6.2 The nature of the underlying problem and a possible solution

Difficulties in achieving an orderly sovereign debt workout in recent years derive from both administrative/behavioural as well as economic/legal aspects. A vast and diverse creditor base for sovereign debt has made collective decisions administratively difficult due to coordination problems, a situation often referred to as a collective representation problem. In addition, and sometimes not independently, there are behavioural problems or what are generally referred to as collective action problems. These generally occur when there is a difference between individual (private) and collective (social) returns related to a given course of action. The main economic issue is in how markets will value CACs.[3] Individual emerging market issuers are hesitant in adopting these clauses, as they fear potential first mover costs. The key legal issue is to craft clear procedures that cannot easily be undermined legally.

In suggesting solutions for sovereign workouts, analysts have drawn on the analogy with corporate bankruptcy, where the framework attempts to maximise the value for all interested parties and thus prevent the wider economic costs of a disorderly workout. The proposed contractual approach framework would allow for differences between a firm and a sovereign, and – analogous to maximising the *ex post* value of assets in the corporate workout – would aim to enhance the *ex post* income and growth prospects for the debtor country. It would also attempt to encourage the

[3] This paper does not deal with the exact nature of CACs (the 'required' legal covenants) but only alludes to what CACs are aimed at achieving.

adherence to the ex *ante* provisions of the contract. Collective action clauses would play a useful role as an integral part of such a framework.

Insolvency procedures only exist at the level of national legislatures. Insolvency procedures for sovereigns are undefined worldwide. The SDRM is an attempt to plug this gap. As we are dealing here with sovereign states, which will continue to exist, and as any collateral, as in domestic bankruptcy procedures, may not be seized domestically, there is a need to have some basic understanding of how a default of a sovereign borrower should be dealt with. A major impetus to move the SDRM decisively forward is due to a series of key speeches of Anne Krueger, Deputy General Manager of the IMF starting toward the end of 2001. She proposed a two-pronged approach: the statutory and contractual approaches to the bankruptcy of a State. This initiative was broadly supported by the G7 as well as the G10.

The deputy governors of the G10 were asked to spearhead the effort on the *contractual* front. The G10 set up a Working Group on Contractual Clauses in June 2002, and the first public statement of the work of this group was reflected in the 27 September 2002 communiqué of the G10 ministers and governors.[4]

Box 1. Recent sovereign bond restructurings

Sovereign bond restructuring was important recently e.g. in Russia, Pakistan, Peru, Ukraine and currently in Argentina. The role of CACs/no CACs is particularly illuminating in three cases: Ukraine, Peru and Argentina.

In Ukraine in 2000 the threat of a more orderly resolution, and in particular a better co-ordinated approach by the creditors, led the sovereign debtor to pre-empt such a move by creditors and a well-argued and well-marketed exchange offer was accepted by the bondholders. That is, the potential threat of CACs led to an exchange offer, which was accepted by the bondholders.

The case of Peru in 2000 has been reviewed widely (Box 2) and demonstrates that a country can be held to ransom by some holdout minority in restructuring. This case has been called upon repeatedly to justify collective action clauses, which bind a minority to majority action and prevent holdout creditors to upset the process of restructuring.

In the current Argentine crises, some Argentine bonds have CACs others not. A look at outstanding bonds by Argentina subject to New York or English law revealed no difference in pricing. A preliminary look at bond prices revealed, of course, difference in prices, but these

[4] See Annex.

could be attributed either to the size of the issue and more or less liquid markets and/or the currency of issue. For example, there appeared a slight premium on issues in Italian lire.

The financial crisis in Argentina, however, which involves a large number of bonds which are issued under different jurisdictions and spread over numerous creditors, underscores the relevance of the current process of including so-called collective action clauses (CACs) in sovereign bonds by ensuring that creditors are dealt with fairly, ensuring intercreditor equity.

What is the logic and work behind this communiqué? Today there is less discussion about the question of why we need CACs; the emphasis has shifted to equity and fairness towards all parties involved in potential bankruptcy, that is official debtors, private creditors, the markets and the official sector, and how such procedures could be crafted. It is widely accepted that CACs are a market-based instrument for overcoming obstacles to debt rescheduling and there is a wide-ranging consensus that such clauses should become the global market standard.[5] It is widely accepted that holdout rogue creditors should not be permitted to hold countries to ransom (Box 2).

The Group of Ten released a *Report of the G10 Working Group on Contractual Clauses* to the ministers and governors of the G10 countries and the same report was also discussed informally by the G10 plus Brazil, China, Korea, Mexico, Poland, Russia and Turkey.[6]

6.3 Broad agreement on underlying motivation

The motivation for moving these initiatives forward are based on (1) underlying changes that have taken place in world capital markets, in particular widespread/diffused holding of sovereign bonds; (2) the realisation that the time lags involved in restructuring foreign debt are too long and thus costly for debtors and creditors and that underlying resolution processes have been opaque and disorderly; (3) legal uncertainty about where and who is able to litigate worldwide as reflected in the fact that rogue creditors have been able to implicitly hold some debtors to ransom.

[5] Newspapers, Ackermann (2002).

[6] India had also been asked to participate. However, as this informal meeting was taking place on fairly short notice during the IMF meetings in Washington in September 2002, the Indian delegation was unable to attend due to earlier commitments.

1. Capital markets have become the principal source of external finance for emerging market economies. While the 1980s may be called the era of syndicated loans, the beginning of the 1990s saw a shift to increased bond issuing by sovereign borrowers, a tendency which was reinforced with the beginning of the Mexican crisis in late 1994 and the subsequent Asian and Russian crises in 1997–1998. These crises led to a reduction in bank lending to emerging markets generally and boosted borrowing by bonds. There was thus a fundamental shift in emerging market debt away from syndicated loans towards bonds. The issuance of sovereign foreign debt in terms of bonds has led to a worldwide holding of this debt by institutional as well as diversified retail bondholders. While such diversified holdings are perfectly sensible from a diversified portfolio point of view, i.e. from the investors' perspective, they are also generally desirable from the debtors' point of view as it becomes easier to place new debt on a broader investor base and as diversification may lead to desirable liquidity in these markets, thus avoiding erratic price swings in these instruments.

If these international bond markets for sovereign debt are to play this international financing role, there must be an effective means to deal with debt distress. Without such a process one important route of financing may be seriously constrained for any sovereign borrower, be it an industrial or emerging market issuer. Orderly workouts of sovereign debt would thus be a desirable underpinning for both parties. Orderly essentially refers to an efficient bundling of claims, rules that clearly specify who is to represent the interests of the creditors and some consensus where litigation is to take place.

Box 2. Elliot Associates vs. Peru

1. In 2000 LP Elliot Associates obtained an order from the Brussels Appeals Court preventing Euroclear from accepting payment or paying out cash from Peru to discharge the interest due on its Brady bonds. This order was granted without the defendants, Euroclear and Peru, being given the opportunity to present their counter arguments. It was based on abroad interpretation of the *pari passu* provision. According to this interpretation, Peru could not make interest payments on its restructured sovereign debt (Brady bonds) without at the same time paying holdout creditors (Elliott). Instead of challenging the decision of the Belgian court, Peru decided to settle with Elliot in order to avoid being forced to default on its Brady bond payments being made through Euroclear.

2. This case raises anumber of issues. One of the most important is the threat it poses to the orderly workout of sovereign debt problems. If holdout creditors are able to use the *pari passu* clause to induce debtors to pay them in full, other creditors will be reluctant to reach agreement with adebtor on restructuring terms that will make the debt sustainable. Another is the risk that payment systems could be disrupted when holdout creditors seek to enforce their claims.
3. There are a number of avenues for solving this problem. A first avenue would be to achieve a more definitive *interpretation of the* ***pari passu*** *clause*, through a legal opinion, an amicus brief or a declaratory judgement. A second possibility would be to modify national *legislation on settlement systems* in order to forbid any freezing of accounts held on the books of settlement systems or of settlement systems' cash correspondents. And a third solution would be, through *collective action clauses (CACs)* or the establishment of a *sovereign debt restructuring mechanism (SDRM)* to make it impossible for minority creditors to hold out in a debt restructuring agreed upon by a required majority.

The aim of the process is thus to arrive at an orderly and timely resolution of sovereign debt restructuring in default for all bondholders for bonds, which are subject to legislation other than their own.

2. Recent restructurings have invariably been messy and somewhat protracted. Due to the long time lags involved and also the associated uncertainty with regard to the question of the finality of the settlement, bankruptcy procedures have imposed large economic and legal costs on debtors and creditors. While there are only a few sovereign bonds restructuring cases, they all have suffered from various degrees of disorderliness due to underlying legal uncertainty. The most blatant case of the intervention of rogue creditors has been in settling the debt of Peru (Box 2). There is some early evidence that the move towards CACs has helped in the case of Ukraine.

3. The current **legal underpinning** is different. Sovereign bonds are traditionally only offered in a few markets (mainly New York, London, Germany, France, Luxembourg and Japan).

Especially sovereign bonds issued under New York law are currently different from those issued in other jurisdictions as covenants of the US bonds do permit the individual bondholder to hold out against all other bondholders. Quite a few countries have issued bonds under New York law during the last 12 years (Table 1). The US Trust Indenture Act of 1938 enshrined the

Table 1. Sovereign bond issues in New York by country, 1991–September 2002

Asia	China, Indonesia (Kazakhstan), Korea, Malaysia, Philippines, Thailand
Europe (EU)	Austria, Finland, Greece, Iceland, Ireland, Italy, Portugal, Spain, Sweden
Central and South America	Argentina, Barbados, Belize, Bermuda, Brazil, Chile, Colombia, Costa Rica, Ecuador, El Salvador, Grenada, Guatemala, Jamaica, México, Panamá, Peru, Trinidad & Tobago, Uruguay, Venezuela
Other countries	Bulgaria, Canada, Egypt, Hungary, Israel, Lebanon, Poland, Qatar, South Africa

Source: Bondware.

legal right of the individual to litigate, a right that could not be rescinded by legal covenants. While the Trust Indenture Act was to apply to domestic debt, it was also traditionally (that is by standard market practice) implanted in foreign debt issues under New York law. Under current proposals, the USA is about to make a major move by allowing majority representation and action rules in sovereign bonds issued in New York.

However, the aim of the initiative on contractual clauses is in the limit to achieve more: to harmonise or standardise as far as possible the legal contractual texts in all sovereign bonds in all major legislations. Such clauses would be an attempt to move toward a level playing field in a debt resolution crisis for all sovereign bonds[7] by reducing legal uncertainty and by providing for equitable processes and procedures in debt resolution. In moving ahead, the 'new' legal covenants will lean on current established market practice, especially in London.

6.4 Inside CACs: economic, legal and political issues

During 2002 there were noticeable shifts. While at the beginning of the year there was much resistance to including CACs in sovereign bonds, some consensus seemed to emerge in the private as well as official sector by about the September 2002 IMF meetings that such clauses could be beneficial to debtors and creditors, i.e. a positive sum game.

[7] There have also been early discussions whether other instruments like syndicated loans might be subject to similar covenants.

6.4.1 Economic issues

The *economic dimension* has been one of the serious stumbling blocks. This dimension is primarily concerned with the question: Are CACs costly? This section will review the available evidence. Will markets adopt CACs?

While CACs may not change the probability of default, as this is primarily the characteristic of the issuer, it would facilitate quicker and more orderly debt restructuring. During the restructuring process, therefore, the recovery value should be higher for bonds with CACs.[8] Whether the above arguments hold some merit can only be tested by empirical investigation. Recent studies consistently conclude that there are no additional costs involved from the inclusion of CACs, but that there may be additional net benefits (Box 3).

The thrust of the cost arguments is quite clear: there are no first-mover disadvantages but there are probably first-mover advantages. This will be the overriding consideration by finance ministries/treasuries when considering CACs. The CAC route should thus appeal to the enlightened self-interest of lenders and investors. Accordingly, the tone of the comments by emerging market issuers and the (primary) market makers has become much more conciliatory as the nature of the underlying CACs is becoming clearer and better explained and as the underlying paradigm has been shifting over time from concerns about costs to the potential benefits to be reaped.

Box 3. Recent empirical studies on the costs of CACs

While the econometric evidence cannot be definitive in this matter, there is a growing literature that confirms that the introduction of CACs will have no direct negative impact on emerging market borrowing costs. Indirectly, by promoting market depth and continuity, it can be expected to improve the flow of finance and lower risk premia.

Tsatsaronis (BIS 1999) using regression analysis proxies CACs in bond markets by comparing sovereign bond yield spreads for bonds with (UK) and without (US) CACs. He concludes, 'The results suggest that while the flexibility in the renegotiation process afforded by the governing law of international sovereign bonds may give rise to higher spreads, this influence is not very systematic'.

[8] Current pricing differences of Argentine bonds seem to hinge on concepts of liquidity (size of issues) and currency.

Eichengreen and Mody (1999, 2000), using a multinomial logit approach, note that the impact of contract structure is discernible only when borrowers are disaggregated by credit quality. They find that 'more credit-worthy emerging-market borrowers value their capital markets access and are unlikely to walk away from their debts. For less credit-worthy borrowers, in contrast, the presence of collective-action clauses significantly aggravates moral hazard and increases borrowing costs. Still, the fact that collective-action clauses allow such borrowers to restructure in a more orderly fashion is attractive to creditors. The two effects tend to work in opposite directions, resulting in a relatively small and insignificant overall impact on borrowing costs'. (1999, pp. 18–19)

In a more recent paper, Eichengreen and Mody (2001) are somewhat more positive about their empirical results: '...we found that opting for collective action clauses raised spreads for borrowers with low credit ratings but reduced them for borrowers with high credit ratings. The impact was particularly strong at the extremes.'

In contrast, a study by Becker et al. (2001) finds no evidence that the presence of collective action clauses increases primary or secondary markets yields for either higher- or lower-rated issuers. It concludes that the perceived benefits from easier restructuring are at least as large as any costs from increased moral hazard.

The introduction of CACs in sovereign bonds by Canada and the UK apparently had no impact on markets (in terms of yields or behaviour).

Bond markets[9] are by their very nature heterogeneous. This is mainly because the underlying product is not very standardised, and so the international bond markets are still quite segmented. The bond markets for sovereign debt of emerging markets are perhaps even less homogeneous[10] and bond characteristics may change from one issue to the next. In fact the markets for sovereign debt are segmented along a variety of lines as sovereign borrowers issue debt in a range of legal jurisdictions, using a variety of instruments, to a diverse and diffuse group of creditors.

9 While what follows is focused on loans, the motivation for CACs is to be applied to all sovereign debt (instruments).

10 As the number of sovereign issuers is relatively small, the move towards a common CAC platform appears to be potentially easier.

6.4.1.1 CACs at issue of sovereign debt

According to market makers in sovereign debt, the question of including CACs or not has not been relevant in selling sovereign bonds.[11] This seems to imply that the value of CACs thus far has been considered negligible. Issuers and underwriters in selling sovereign bonds have thus tended to be indifferent towards inclusion of CACs or they have been negative as they are unable to assess the value of CACs at issue. Because of the current uncertainly regarding CACs in future bond contracts one might even argue from the point of view of risk aversion that the range of outcomes, as some instruments may include CACs and others not, may have widened the probability distribution of future negotiation outcomes, and this may have increased the risk. Admittedly, this latter argument might be a temporary phenomenon. If the sovereign borrower were quite indifferent towards inclusion of CACs, then the intermediary will probably also not raise the question of inclusion of CACs at issue. However, current evidence does not vindicate such arguments, as is shown later.

6.4.1.2 CACs during default

A different market scenario may arise just before or during restructuring. In historical sovereign debt restructurings thus far a country will default on its sovereign bonds regardless of whether the bonds include CACs or not. It appears thus that the probability of default will be the same with or without CACs for the same issuer. The probability of default is unlikely to be different for the same sovereign borrower under the impact of either no differentiation between sovereign bonds on account of CACs during restructuring or due to the existence of acceleration clauses. Recent history of sovereign debt restructuring has not provided any firm indication that CACs have indeed provided all the benefits during restructuring. This is partly due to the fact that some parts of the restructured debt included CACs and other parts did not (Argentina is currently a case in point). As restructuring tended to encompass both types of instruments, benefits of including CACs in sovereign bond contracts have thus far been muted.

6.4.2 Legal issues

Next to the economic issues in introducing CACs, arriving at legal clauses in the major legislations where sovereign bonds are issued has not been accomplished. A lot of progress has already been made by involving private sector lawyers of all the major jurisdictions in the formulation of the

[11] See Becker et al. (2001).

CACs. The aim is to provide clauses that are fair to debtors and creditors and contain multiple litigations. The clauses are thus to meet the following requirements:

- To foster early dialogue, co-ordination and communication among creditors and a sovereign experiencing debt problems;
- To ensure that there are effective means for creditors and debtors to re-contract, without a minority of debtholders obstructing the process; and
- To ensure that disruptive legal action by individual creditors does not hamper a workout that is under way (Box 1).

The envisaged contractual clauses would make possible a restructuring agreement that was binding on all bondholders. The clauses would also be quite clear on who is allowed to litigate, providing legal certainty.

6.4.3 Political and other issues

The political dimension is understandably multifaceted. Who has and who is going to introduce these clauses? Canada and the UK have included CACs in their bond issues for some time now without any noticeable impact on pricing. EU member states announced in September 2002 that they intend to include appropriate contractual provisions in their new government bonds to be issued under foreign jurisdiction[12] (Table 1).

The following challenges may hamper faster progress in introducing CACs for sovereign bonds issued in major markets:

First, the process at arriving at fairly standard CACs in terms of definite/final formulations that are valid in all major legislation (France, Germany, Japan, Luxembourg, UK, USA) is not yet finished.

Second, even if there were such clauses, these were only introduced over time and the old large stock of sovereign debt would be without such clauses. The data in Table 2 may provide some indication of the time frame involved. Similarly, CACs only apply to one issue of homogeneous bonds. A country usually has several classes of bonds outstanding and the question whether or not the calling upon the CACs in one-bond issues affects the others is largely unresolved (i.e. the question of accelerating clauses).[13]

Third, many emerging economies and some market participants still fear that there may be costs involved or that they may provide a greater incentive to default when introducing CACs. While this may contradict the facts and

---

12 Wall Street Journal *Finance Ministers in Europe Back New Bond Clauses*, 9 September 2002.

13 The group of eminent lawyers elaborating CACs proposes that majority be counted across instruments no broader than individual issuances of sovereign bonds so that each issue would have its own majority.

Table 2. Sovereign[1] bond issues by emerging markets under various governing laws, end-September 2002

Laws	Amounts (billions of US dollars)	Average maturity[2]
New York	135.3	10.5
English	58.8	9.6
German	33.7	7.7
Japanese	19.8	6.9

[1]Central governments.
[2]Average term weighted by size of issue.
Source: Bondware.

current empirical evidence, poor communication or fear alone may act as a deterrent. The challenge is to ensure that emerging market economies are actively involved in moving this process forward (to ensure ownership). CACs will have (to continue to be) adopted by some larger emerging market economies as several industrial economies have already led by example.

Fourth, CACs may prove a toothless tiger if something like a bankruptcy court is not threatening in the end. The big stick may have to be somewhere, especially if both debtor and creditors conclude in negotiations that it might be better to hold out as the 'official international community' may come to the rescue. Or, we may come up with other mechanisms which will effectively cope with the current motivations for introducing CACs. The challenge to bind the progress on CACs or on the statutory SDRM approach is consistent with the evolutionary thinking on lender of last resort, bailing in the private sector, early intervention and assessments of debt sustainability remains.

6.5 SDRM – taking stock

The progress on the statutory approach to SDRM faces a long time horizon especially as national legislatures will have to adopt it. At this point in time it is still an avenue which is actively pursued by the IMF, and further work has been endorsed by the G7 and the G10. For many there is no contradiction in pursuing a contractual, market-oriented approach and a more rigorous statutory approach. The two approaches are not opposed, but one should perhaps continue pursuing more vigorously the contractual approach, as the statutory approach is a longer-term proposition given the complications that its implementation would entail. The CAC approach and the statutory SDRM are thus not seen as being mutually exclusive but complementary.

Involvement in producing a set of standard CACs worldwide and perhaps the threat of a more incisive statutory approach have led to a much more positive attitude by the private investment community in the course of 2002 towards CACs.[14]

The IMF has over time modified and further elaborated its view on the SDRM. The private sector remains sceptical due to the fact that the IMF will keep its preferred creditor status in resolution, that the SDRM might reduce the prospects of large financial support in case of future crises and that the underlying question of debt sustainability remains largely unresolved.[15] Furthermore, the threat of loss of business as fees may be lost in bond workouts also reinforces opposition by some underwriters and investors.

It is also not quite clear which sovereign debt should be subject to the SDRM mechanism and whether there should by a hierarchy of claims (priority): exclude IMF and World Bank claims (due to preferred statue), exclude also the bilateral official claims as they are currently effectively dealt with by the Paris Club, exclude or give priority to claims based on short-term trade credit and include domestic debt claims as well? Are certain other short-term financial claims for liquidity reasons to be dealt with outside the SDRM mechanism? Is there a fairly clear concept of sovereign debt in particular as subgovernment issuers come in different cloaks (e.g. states/districts, municipalities, quasi-government institutions, etc.).

There are, however, also a range of strong arguments in favour of the statutory (compared with the contractual approach) approach as it explicitly addresses the problem of the outstanding stock of all debt, as this would better facilitate aggregate voting across instruments (it aggregates creditors), while preserving seniority of certain private claims. It might also provide a mechanism for a super majority of creditors to vote to subordinate their claims to new money enabling the private sector to participate in ways that so far had not been possible. Furthermore, the process of resolution itself would become more transparent and standardised for all countries and perhaps also more equitable.

It is also clearly argued that the threat of a more official SDRM may induce cooperative behaviour by the debtor and the creditor in the 'shadow of the law', i.e. before the actual SDRM process is being started. The SDRM is only a means at the end of an impasse that should only exceptionally occur.

[14] In the USA this is notable in the formation of the 'Gang of Six', the Emerging Markets Creditors Association (EMCA), Emerging Markets Traders Association (EMTA), the Institute of International Finance (IIF), the Institute of International Primary Market Association (IMPA), the Securities Industry Association and the Bond Market Association (see International Financial Review, 5 Oct. 2002).

[15] Euromoney, SDRM finds few friends in the markets, November 2002.

6.6 Summary

Progress on the current worldwide debate on contractual and statutory approaches to improving resolution mechanisms of sovereign debtors in default will not be easily forthcoming. As sovereign financial crises will continue to occur, a better understanding of processes and procedures involved may hopefully result in less output lost to the debtors and also a better restructuring deal for the creditor (a positive sum game for the parties involved). Market mechanisms will be part of the process, as the official sector will aim more at avoiding any moral hazard issues. Current proposals are not seen as the futile search for the Holy Grail or a silver bullet that could provide clockwork like solutions to sovereign financial restructuring. Be reminded that this paper only deals with issues in sovereign debt resolution while issues of prevention and prediction should probably rank much higher on the international agenda. Governor Ortiz of Mexico has frequently remarked that it is much more important to have an efficient emergency ward when a patient arrives at the hospital than to take pains to treat the patient when he is in the morgue.

The progress on developing contractual clauses has been very substantial and such clauses could be included in some emerging market debt during 2003. To implement some statutory approach will take substantially longer.

As it is widely accepted that collective action clauses are a useful means of dealing with rogue creditors and more generally as there are benefits to be gained by debtors and creditors as the debt resolution process becomes more transparent and efficient as well as equitable, the G10 will pursue making further progress on the contractual approach to sovereign debt workout mechanisms. Obviously this is only possible with close involvement of sovereign debtors and market participants.

Annex: Pricing of bonds

This Annex takes the *pricing of bonds* calculations by Dixon and Wall (2000) one step further.

Their starting point is for a one-period bond: if investors are risk neutral,[16] the yield (y) on a single-period risky (zero coupon) bond may be calculated by assuming that its expected return is equal to the risk free rate, r:

$$(1 + r) = (1 - \pi)\,(1 + y) + \pi \cdot \delta(1 + y)$$

$$y = \frac{r + \text{p}(1 - \text{d})}{1 - \text{p}(1 - \text{d})}$$

where π is the cumulative probability of default over the lifetime of a bond and δ is the (expected) recovery rate in the event of a default defined as the fraction of the face value of the bond.

In anumerical example by Dixon and Wall the values were set as follows: $\pi = 0.20$, $\delta = 0.4$ and $r = 0.05$. In order to provide abetter feeling for possible outcomes, we looked at the results for $r = 0.02$, $0.20 < \pi < 0.0025$ and $0.3 < \delta < 0.5$. These ranges were broadly mapped from historical patterns of domestic bonds assuming for simplicity that the ranges are somewhat similar.[17] If one iterates these parameters over all the values, one is led to conclude that at fairly low probabilities of default even large changes in expected recovery have very little impact on expected yield. For example, if the recovery value is expected to drop over the whole range from 0.5 to 0.3 (i.e. the face value of the bond is expected to drop from 50% to 30% of face value) the yield will only change by 5 basis points when the expected default probability is estimated at 0.005.

Table A1. Expected changes in basis points of a bond under various assumptions

	$r = 0.02$					$r = 0.05$				
$\Delta\delta =$	π					π				
-0.02	0.20	0.10	0.05	0.01	0.005	0.2	0.10	0.05	0.01	0.005
	530	230	105	21	5	550	237	112	21	5

---

[16] The risk neutrality assumption may always be challenged.

[17] These ranges were chosen as the underlying parameters change over time. Of course the assumption of risk neutrality is somewhat weak.

It is probably unrealistic to assume a default rate of 20% when a sovereign bond is issued. In such a case the price of the bond would be too low and the rating too low to permit placement (one could, of course, envisage many sovereign bond issues at junk bond levels). Yet even at an expected default level of 10%, the massive expected decrease in the recovery value would require the expected yield at issue to be higher by around 230 basis points.[18] At lower levels of changes in the expected recovery value, the impact would still be there but likely not be as discernible. On the basis of these calculations and on the basis of the assumption that CACs indeed shorten the time to resolution (during which period bond prices generally fall), we might posit that CACs lower required yields at issue.[19]

[18] It may be demonstrated that the level of the risk-free rate has little impact on the following assertions.

[19] Pricing the orderliness in restructuring may also be captured by this approach. What is not captured are the legal fees due when introducing CACs as well as the (probably much larger) legal fees during restructuring.

References

Bank for International Settlements (1999), *The Effects of CACs on Sovereign Bond Spreads*, Box by Tsatsaronis, Quarterly Review, November.

Banque de France (2002), *The ongoing debate on the restructuring of sovereign debt*, Financial Stability Review, November.

Becker T., Richards A., and Thaicharoen Y. (2001), *Bond Restructuring and Moral Hazard: Are Collective Action Clauses Costly?*, IMF Working Paper 01/92.

Beddington, Francis (2002), *Reform of International Financial Architecture Back on the Agenda*, Emerging Markets Research, JPMorgan.

Bretton Woods Committee (2002), *Round Table Discussion of Sovereign Debt Strategy*, Washington, D.C., 23 September.

Buchheit L. C. and Gulati G. M. (1999), *Sovereign Bonds and the Collective Will*, Georgetown University Law Center, Working Paper No. 34.

Crossman, Alexander (2000), *Restructuring gains foothold*, International Financial Review, Special Report, May.

Dixon L. and Wall D. (2000), *Collective Action Problems and Collective Action Clauses*, Bank of England, Financial Stability Review, June.

Dooley, Michael P. (2000), Can Output Losses Following International Financial Crises Be Avoided, NBER, Working Paper 7531, February.

Eichengreen B. and Portes R. (1995), *Crisis? What Crisis? Orderly Workouts for Sovereign Debtors*, CEPR, September.

Eichengreen B. and Mody A. (2000), *Would Collective Action Clauses Raise Borrowing Costs*, NBER, Working Paper 7458.

EU/Economic and Financial Committee (2002), *Collective Action Clauses: Should the EU lead by example?*, Brussels, 26b July (EFC/ECFIN/351/02/rev2).

Folkerts-Landau, David and Garber P. M. (1999), *The New Architecture in Official Doctrine, Global Markets*, Deutsche Bank, April.

Group of Ten (2002), *Communiqué of the Ministers and Governors of the Group of Ten*, Washington, D.C., September.

Haldane A. and Kruger M. (2001), *The Resolution of International Financial Crises: Private Finance and Public Funds*, Bank of Canada Review, November.

International Financial Review (2000), *Ukraine defies debtors with U.S.$2.7bn debt swap success*, 18 March (1325).

International Monetary Fund (2002), *The Design and Effectiveness of Collective Action Clauses*, Board Paper SM/02/173.

International Monetary Fund (1999), *Involving the Private Sector in Forestalling and Resolving Financial Crises – Collective Action Provisions in International Sovereign Bonds*, SM/99/207.

International Monetary Fund (2002), *IMF Board Discusses Possible Features of a New Sovereign Debt Restructuring Mechanism*, Public Information Notice, September 24.

Krueger, Anne O. (2002), Preventing and Resolving Financial Crises: The role of Sovereign Debt Restructuring, IMF lecture at the Latin American Meeting of the Econometric Society, Sao Paolo, Brazil, 26 July (www.imf.org/external/np/ speeches/2002/072602.htm).

Krueger, Anne O. (2002), *Sovereign Debt Restructuring Mechanisms: One Year Later*, IMF First Deputy Managing Director, presented at the Banco de Mexico's Conference on "Macroeconomic Stability, Financial Markets and Economic Development", Mexico City, 12 November.

Miller M. and Zhang L. (1999), *Sovereign Liquidity Crisis: the Strategic Case for a Payments Standstill*, CSGR Working Paper No. 35/99.

Rogoff, Kenneth and Zettelmeyer J. (2002), *Early Ideas on Sovereign Bankruptcy Reorganizations: A Survey*, IMF Working Paper, WP/02/57.

Taylor J. (2002), *Sovereign Debt Restructuring: A U.S. Perspective*, Institute for International Economics, April.

Wall, David (2000), *Ukrainian Exchange Rate Offer – Use of Collective Action Clauses*, Note for the Record, Internal Document, Bank of England, International Finance Division, 9 March.

Wirz M. (2002), *Market gangs up on SDRM*, International Finance Review, 1454, 5 October.

Newspapers

Euromoney "SDRM finds few friends in the markets", November 2002.

Financial Times "There is a better way to manage debt crises" by Josef Ackerman, 25 September 2002.

Financial Times Deutschland "Regeln für den Staatsbankrott", 30 September 2002.

Frankfurter Allgemeine "Streit über Insolvenzordnung für Schwellenländer", 30 September 2002.

Handelsblatt "Banken lehnen geplantes Konkurssystem strikt ab", 30 September 2002.

Les Échos «Anne Krueger: La diversité du financement des Etats nécessite un nouveau cadre de résolution des crises», 30 septembre 2002.

Wall Street Journal "Finance Ministers in Europe Back New Bond Clauses", 9 September 2002.

7 The successor states of the former Yugoslavia – mediation under Art. 7, Annex C of the Vienna Agreement on Succession Issues – a major review

The following note reviews some of the potential issues facing the group in their negotiations. It may provide a starting point for the negotiation. The financial expert, also called mediator in this note, does not, at this point in time, exclude from consideration any reasonable arguments in supporting an individual country's position. The starting point for the negotiations is the 'Agreement on Succession Issues' signed by all five successor States of the former SFRY.

7.1 Some background

The dramatic political changes in Yugoslavia (FRY) in October 2000 have been of major significance for the integration of the State into the international financial community. In the early 1990s, the former Socialist Federal Republic of Yugoslavia (SFRY) fell apart and then Yugoslavia (Serbia and Montenegro) claimed to be the sole legal successor to the SFRY. At the same time, the other SFRY successor states, Bosnia and Herzegovina, Croatia, Macedonia and Slovenia, had become members of the IMF and World Bank (1992–1996) and had been recognised as independent states. The political changes in the year 2000 in the FRY paved the way for recognition of the new political realities in that region and within a fairly short period led to the acceptance of the FRY into the fold of the IMF, World Bank and the Bank for International Settlements.

Equally importantly, the political sea change in the FRY also led to a path-breaking 'Agreement on Succession Issues', issues that were unsettled since the break-up of the SFRY. The agreement was signed by the five successor states on 29 June 2001 in Vienna ('Agreement on Succession

Issues' or 'Vienna Agreement' for short).[1] The Vienna Agreement was arrived at in a very short time after the October 2000 events in the SFRY and underpins the willingness of the parties involved in coming to terms with the history of the early 1990s.

7.2 The issue at hand

One issue[2] that has been left open in the Vienna Agreement is reflected in its Article 7 of Annex C which states:

> *'Guarantees by the SFRY or its NBY [National Bank of Yugoslavia] of hard currency savings deposited in acommercial bank and any of its successor state before the date on which it proclaimed its independence shall be negotiated without delay taking into account in particular the necessity of protecting the hard currency savings of individuals. This negotiation shall take place under the auspices of the Bank for International Settlements.'*

Subsequently, in July 2001, the BIS was approached and nominated the former president of the Swiss National Bank, Hans Meyer, as financial expert, usually referred to as mediator, to proceed in tackling this unsettled issue.

7.3 The content of this note

The following is prepared by the Secretariat to shed some light on some of the potential issues involved.

1. Part 4 is a preliminary review of information/documentation that is available in the public domain on this issue. This involves some fact-finding and some assessment of information that might be relevant to the question of the guarantee of the hard-currency savings (HCS) of individuals in the former SFRY.
2. Part 5 is a first attempt to arrive at principles or arguments in seeking any kind of resolution being cognisant of the issues alluded to under Part 4 and without implying any preferred road for settlement among the parties.
3. The last part summarises and attempts to state the issues in the forthcoming negotiations.

---

[1] The Vienna Agreement clearly reflects this. It starts as follows: 'Representatives of Bosnia and Herzegovina, the Republic of Croatia, the Republic of Macedonia, the Republic of Slovenia and the Federal Republic of Yugoslavia, being in sovereign equality the five successor States to the former Socialist Federal Republic of Yugoslavia, ...have agreed as follows: ...'

[2] This appears to be the only still unresolved issue in the Vienna Agreement.

Annex 1 is an attempt to summarise the measures taken by the governments after succession. Annex 2 reviews the Basel process, which is potentially relevant to the negotiating parties. Annex 3 contains some boxes from IMF reports dealing with HCS in some countries. The appendix contains some SFRY laws.

7.4 The setting

7.4.1 Hard-currency savings in the former SFRY

The importance of hard-currency savings (HCS) as a resource for commercial banks and for savings/investment formation has been amply demonstrated from the early experience of the SFRY. In contrast, dinar deposits played a negligible role in these processes due, *inter alia*, to continuous depreciation threats and negative domestic real interest rates for many years.[3]

The government thus looked favourably upon access to HCS (and its use); individuals profited by receiving interest payments in foreign currency, and many individuals were thus able to smooth their consumption behaviour over time. When the guarantee of these deposits was initially conceived (around the mid-1970s) the idea of safeguarding the HCS was perhaps at the forefront of deliberations and such confidence strengthening measure was to cement the status quo, i.e. a continuation of HCS in the future. Implicitly, the guarantee of HCS may have also implied that the depositors were assured that they could always get back their HCS and that there was thus no foreign exchange rate risk.

The Croatian submission[4] states:

> *'In an attempt to prevent this regular source of funds for the domestic foreign exchange market and its foreign exchange reserves from one day drying up, the government promised complete legal protection, guaranteed by the Federation, to foreign exchange depositors. This protection came through regulations on foreign exchange operations and various government decisions.*

As practically all banking textbooks will indicate that a bank's role is to convert short-term deposits into long-term claims (i.e. maturity transformation); it is also quite clear that any run on practically all HCS could probably never be expected to cover all potential claims (at least not within a very short period of time). The situation of a more or less simultaneous

---

[3] Circovic and Jovic (1985).

[4] There are 'submissions' by all five successor states. They are referred in what follows as Bosnia and Herzegovina, Croatian, Macedonian, Slovenian and FRY Submission.

run on these HCS was probably not envisaged by the original guarantee and almost certainly not the situation of a breaking up of the SFRY.

While the economy (commercial banks and enterprises) profited from access to these HCS deposits, by 1988 it had become clear that repayment of these deposits to the depositors was practically impossible and the National Bank of Yugoslavia (NBY) became more reluctant to accept these deposits as it was not willing to face the ever mounting exchange rate risk. At that time aplan was discussed to convert the potential foreign-currency liabilities on the books of the NBY into state debt; however, this plan was never executed and was overcome by subsequent developments.[5]

It appears that around March/April 1991 deposit holders were effectively prevented from drawing on their HCS accounts. The rights to use these savings became increasingly restricted and limited to small amounts. Commercial banks were often unable themselves to purchase foreign currency from the NBY. However, there was never a legal act to freeze these deposits.

The freezing and 'unfreezing' (restitution) of the savings deposits has 'obvious' implications for the budgets of any of the successor states and may also have implications for the future savings behaviour of the public in terms of amounts and instruments used and thus may have implications for the public's consumption behaviour. Furthermore, the HCS process may also influence monetary policy and considerations of financial stability (e.g. runs on banks, attitudes towards financial safety nets or deposit insurance schemes).

7.4.2 The question of timing

Article 7 of Annex C of the Vienna Agreement states: 'Guarantees by the SFRY and its NBY of hard-currency savings deposited in a commercial bank and any of its branches in any successor State *before the date on which it proclaimed independence* shall be negotiated without delay…'

The attached Table 1 aims to cope with question of timing, i.e. when independence was proclaimed. While one might disagree with some of the dates in Table 1, the verb 'proclaim' in this context was looked upon as an official public announcement.[6] It may be worthwhile to note that the dates

[5] There are more detailed accounts in the Croatian and Slovenian submissions.

[6] According to Stanič (2001), the date of independence is usually regarded in international law as the date of succession. Her Table 1 contains the following (disputed) dates: Bosnia & Herzegovina: 6 March 1992 (date on which the results of the referendum were officially announced); Croatia: 8 October 1991 (date on which the moratorium on independence ended); Macedonia: 17 November 1991 (date of the adoption of the new constitution); Slovenia: 25 June

Table 1. Successor states of the SFRY

	Independence from SFRY 'proclaimed'	First elections	New constitutions
Bosnia & Herzegovina	1 March 1992	–	December 1995
Croatia	30 May 1991[1]	April–May 1990	December 1990
Macedonia	8 September 1991[2]	Nov–Dec 1990	November 1991
Slovenia	25 June 1991[1]	April 1990	December 1991
Federal Republic of Yugoslavia	–	–	April 1992

[1]See Whitaker (Croatia); 30 May is also 'Independence Day'. However, 25 June 1991 is the declaration of independence day according to Whitaker (Yugoslavia) and the Europa World Year Book 2001 (Croatia and Slovenia).
[2]See Whitaker (Macedonia) and the Europa World Year Book (The Former Yugoslav Republic of Macedonia). However, Whitaker (Yugoslavia): 'Macedonia declared its independence on *18* September 1991.' The date 26 April 1992 is seen as 'monetary independence and sovereignty proclamation of the Republic of Macedonia' in the submission of Macedonia to the Parliamentary Assembly within the Council of Europe on 26 September 2000, which was also submitted by Nikola Todorcevski by letter to Dr. Hans Meyer dated 28 September 2001.
Source: Whitakers Almanac 2001 and the Europa World Year Book 2001.

are different among the successor states.[7] However, according to Stanič there seemed to be some convergence of opinion on 25 June as the date on which the SFRY ceased to exist.[8]

It is less clear what this difference may imply for the savings deposits in the commercial banks. Measures taken by individual governments after the proclamation of independence are not *directly* relevant for settling under Article 7 Annex C.[9]

A quote from Stanič (2001) may illustrate the positions countries took at the beginning of 2001:

1991 (date of the proclamation of independence); FRY: 27 April 1992 (date on which the FRY as presently constituted was established).

7 According to many publications, Croatia and Slovenia declared independence on the same day, 25 June 1991. For the slightly different view of the Badinter (Arbitration) Commission please consult e.g. Trifković (1999).

8 This issue will continue to be disputed.

9 See, however, Sect. 4.9: "Events after Succession".

> 'Secondly, the lack of agreement on a single date of succession will complicate the valuation of the SFRY's net assets and their apportionment since, if the above listed dates are adopted, at least five different balance sheets will have to be adopted. The 31 December 1990 has informally been agreed upon by all parties as the date at which the first accounts will be drawn and accounts made since on such date the last approved SFRY budget was drawn up. However, according to Sir Arthur Watts, it is unlikely that this date will also be adopted as the date of the passing of assets and liabilities. In fact, in his last draft Sir Arthur Watts suggested 30 June as the date for accounts to be drawn up, that is five days after Slovenia and Croatia declared independence.'

At the meeting in Ljubljana in February 2001, Slovenia reiterated Sir Arthur Watt's proposal for 30 June 1991 as the date for drawing up the SFRY's accounts. However, the parties reached no agreement, although it seems that Bosnia, Croatia and Macedonia will endorse this position. However, it is likely that different succession dates will be agreed for different types of assets'.

The subsequent Vienna Agreement of June 2001 confirmed such different timings: the crucial date for distribution of archives is 30 June 1991 (Annex D, Article 1), for pensions residency on 1 June 1991 matters (Annex E, Article 2 (ii)) and for legal titles to private property the 31 December 1990 is decisive (Annex G, Article 2).

The question of timing may not have any relevance in finding an agreement under Annex C, Article 7 as long as such timing does not violate this article outright. Indications are that any date beyond 30 June 1991 may not easily qualify as 'before the date on which it claimed independence'.[10]

The Bosnia and Herzegovina Submission proposes the date of the HCS outstanding set as of 31 December 1990. On the basis of the foregoing, such a date would comply with the requirements of Annex C, Article 7 of the Vienna Agreement and the date seems also reasonable in light of the preceding discussion.

7.4.3 The question of size

Timing as well as size are crucial for Annex C, Article 7. As savings deposits are fungible, that is they move about each day, the date on which these savings were frozen may become crucial. As indicated earlier, freezing means that effectively the access of individual citizens to their hard-currency savings deposits were blocked.

---

[10] Such a cut-off date may have importance, for example, for hard currency deposits which occurred after that date. It may not be necessary to agree on *one* final date.

'In 1978 the equivalent to US$5.7 billion was deposited in foreign-currency savings accounts in the SFRY and at the end of 1990 that amount had increased to US$ 13.5 billion. Based on 1989 figures, the foreign currency savings of people in the Bosnia and Herzegovina Republic could be estimated at US$1.7 billion.'[11] Some other sources note that up to $11 billion of funds deposited in the Yugoslav banking system up to the end of 1991 may have been lost to depositors.

According to some observers at that time when the deposits were frozen by the SFRY/NBY, there was no major disagreement on the size of the savings deposits that were effectively frozen.[12]

For the ensuing negotiations, the data above represent only an upper limit of all the potential claims involved. As each successor state has already started to pay the HCS back to their own citizens or on its own territory, only the potentially unsatisfied claims, e.g. those that fall in the legal national gaps of the five successor states, are being considered under Annex C, Article 7.

The structural changes in the banking system that occurred after 1989 thus also cover the following cases and hence will not be included under Article 7: the former Ljubljanska Banka – Prodavska Banka Koprivnica is covered under Croatian Law under the successor bank Prodavska Banka d.d. Koprivnica and the former Ljubljanska Banka – Main Branch Beograd is covered by FRY law under the successor bank – Slavija Banka d.d. Beograd.[13]

In one case a bilateral solution was introduced: the Republic of Croatia regulated the guaranteeing of citizens' hard-currency deposits in Bosnia and Herzegovina in a manner *identical to regulating guarantees for Croatian citizens' savings.*[14]

---

[11] Human Rights Chamber for Bosnia and Herzegovina. Item(?) 38. See, however, item 59 where the amount is stated at DM 1.8 billion for 1989. Item 82 mentions DM 2.36 billion as of 31 March 1991.

[12] If one were to assume that this is true, one might nevertheless ask if there were no instances where individual deposit holders were paid back some deposits during the period of freezing the deposits. In cases where there were repayments made by banks on the 'old' HCS it is assumed that this claim has been settled finally.

[13] The Secretariat is not sure whether this is correct as stated. When Milosevic came to power, the branches of Ljubljanska Banka in Serbia were nationalised and became part of Slavija Banka. This happened before 'freezing' of HCS accounts. All hard-currency deposits were at that time transferred to Slavija Banka. This implies that potential claims of Serbs on Ljubljanska Banka have ceased to exist and are covered under the existing laws on restitution of the FRY.

[14] This was the case of the Republic of Croatia – Splitska Banka d.d. Split with branch offices in Bosnia and Herzegovina. Such a bilateral agreement may raise issues vis-à-vis other successor states.

The Bosnia and Herzegovina submission claims the following amounts: US$184,890,000 (SLOVENIA, Ljubljanska Banka d.d. Ljubljana, Sarajevo Branch Office) and US$94,173,000 (FR YUGOSLAVIA, Beogradska Banka, Invest Banka d.d. Beograd, business units in Bosnia and Herzegovina).

The Croatian submission concerning Ljubljanska Banka – Main Branch Zagreb notes:

> *'At the end of December 1989, 76% of its total liabilities, amounting to USD 611.6m, were household foreign exchange deposits.'*

In the Macedonian submission no specific amounts are mentioned of the size of a potential claim of the Republic of Macedonia on other successor states including the Republic of Slovenia.

7.4.4 The commercial banks

Throughout the period under review there were no restrictions on commercial banks of the former SFRY accepting hard-currency deposits. Commercial banks were also allowed to have branch banks throughout the whole former Yugoslavia. Only commercial banks with their main seat in one part of the Republic and branch offices in the other parts (or one other part) of the Republic effectively accepted such hard-currency savings deposits. There were only a few large banks with extensive branch networks throughout the SFRY. The existing structure of the banking system at that time determined to a large extent which bank was in a position to collect hard-currency deposits.[15] The 1989 banking law provided more independence to commercial banks and the commercial end of banks took a more prominent role. A commercial bank essentially followed consolidated financial reporting procedures, i.e. reporting of financial data of branches were included in the reporting by the head office.

[15] The FRY contribution states: '*Pursuant to the Law an Banks and Other Financial Organisations, Yugoslav commercial banks were up to 1990 authorised to operate in all the republics of the former SFRY. Two banks had the greatest banking nets in the territory of other republics: Ljubljanska Banka d.d. Ljubljana, and Jugobanka d.d. Beograd. Up to 1989, these two banking systems (actually 'associated banks' with the seats in Ljubljana and Belgrade respectively) comprised about 20 'basic banks' each. Other 'associated banks' – Beogradska Banka d.d. Beograd; Privedna Banka, Sarajevo; Stopanska Banka, Skopje and others, had only a few basic banks (member banks) included in their systems outside the territory of their mother republics.'* It appears that the HCS deposits in the 'other' associated banks were either non-existent or very small not to deserve mention?

Table 2. Selected economic indicators

	Population in thousands	GNI $ million	GNI per capita	Trade as % of GDP	Export shares of Europe	Trade shares with the Balkans
	1999			1992		
SFRY	–	–	–	–	0.79	3.0
Bosnia-Herzegovina	3,881	4,706	1,210	–	0.79	3.0
Croatia	4,464	20,222	4,530	36.5	0.79	3.0
Macedonia	2,021	3,348	1,660	33.1	0.79	3.0
Slovenia	1,986	19,862	10,000	58.5	0.79	3.0
FRY	10,616	–	–	–	0.79	3.0
Bulgaria	8,208	11,572	1,410	22.9	0.29	18.3
Greece	10,583	127,648	12,110	25.5	0.54	3.9
Turkey	64,385	186,490	2,900	16.2	0.83	3.0
Portugal	9,989	110,175	11,030	38.9	1.03	–

Sources: World Bank Atlas (2001) and Marvin Jackson (2001).

According to some observers, Ljubljanska Banka of Slovenia was collecting large hard-currency deposits in some of the other successor States (especially Croatia and also Bosnia-Herzegovina and Macedonia).[16] Bosnia and Herzegovina as well as Macedonia note[17] the 'freezing' of their citizens' money in Ljubljanska Banka, which had its main seat in Slovenia. This would also include HCS deposits of a Croat citizen living abroad or in Croatia placed with the branch of Ljubljanska Banka in Croatia. Slovenia had and still has a much higher income than the other successor states (Table 2) and had relatively few guest workers abroad and so was able to attract deposits from other regions of the former SFRY.[18]

[16] The latest European Commission on Slovenia's Progress Towards Accession (2000) states: 'Slovenia's relations with its neighbours remain good. ...However, there are still some outstanding issues to be settled between the two countries (*Croatia and Slovenia*) including...the debt of the Slovenian Ljubljanska Banka to its former Croatian account holders at the bank's former branch in Zagreb also need to be tackled.' (Italics added.).

[17] In their respective submissions to Dr. Mayer both dated 28 September 2001.

[18] See the story of Ljubljanska Banka as commented on by the IMF in Box 4 of the annex.

Jugobanka of Beograd's branches in other republics also had large HCS deposits. The FRY contribution explains in some detail why claims on Jugobanka are not being made:

> *'...After the break up of the SFRY and after deriving economic and financial balance sheets on the level of newly created states, Croatia appraised that the aggregate (both dinar and foreign currency one) net balance sheet of the branches of Jugobanka d.d. in Croatia was positive for Croatia, meaning that this republic lost nothing through these branches, actually that it obtained certain assets. Consequently, Croatia claimed nothing on the basis of that either from Jugobanka d.d. Beograd, or from the FR Yugoslavia. The Government of the Republic of Croatia enacted special decrees on July 31, 1991 and February 27, 1992 by which all the branches of Jugobanka d.d. Beograd in the territory of Croatia were liquidated, whereas new Croatian banks (founded in this Republic) undertook the total assets and liabilities of the branches of Jugobanka d.d.'*

Subsequently, Croatia prescribed that the total dinar and foreign-currency assets collected by branches (including citizens' foreign-currency assets) should be placed at the disposal of the clients from the territory of the subject branch. The legal succession of domestic banks taking to all the assets and liabilities of branch banks ensured there would be no open outstanding HCS claims on Jugobanka or perhaps due the deposit guarantee on the FRY.

Croatia was the republic with the largest amount of HCS deposits by households, and branches of banks of other republics located in Croatia were able to attract substantial HCS deposits as well.

In Bosnia and Herzegovina there were presumably five banks with head offices outside Bosnia and Herzegovina collecting HCS.[19] In the Bosnia and Herzegovina submission it is, however, noted that no parent banks from Bosnia and Herzegovina had business units in other newly created states during the period of independence-acquiring processes.[20]

It is not clear whether other commercial banks (in addition to Ljubljanska Banka and Jugobanka) at that time with branches in other parts of the former SFRY were also collecting foreign-currency deposits at their branches on a substantial scale. There appear no other banks apart from Ljubljanska Banka and Jugobanka for which such a claim is being made.[21]

---

[19] Human Rights Chamber for Bosnia and Herzegovina (item 111).

[20] The Secretariat is not entirely sure about the facts in this case. Did Bosnia and Herzegovina not have any bank offices outside its territory?

[21] See footnote 15.

Commercial banks appear as the main initial beneficiaries as they could transfer these hard currency funds abroad (e.g. to correspondent banks in New York) or provide foreign exchange financing for customers. Branch banks, of course, were able to support the operations of the main offices.

7.4.5 The commercial banks and the NBY

Once a foreign currency deposit was received by a commercial bank, what kind of rules were in force to deal with this inflow? There seem to be two important questions in this context: First, how large was the redepositing requirement with the NBY? And second, was this rule being enforced/ignored/circumvented?

The redepositing requirement was changed over time during the 1980s. It appears that it was never 100%, but varied between 30 and 90%.[22] This view may be disputed (or is perhaps not explicitly discussed by) the Macedonian submission:

> *'It is known that the problem regarding the deposited foreign savings of the citizens is inherited from the time when the Republic of Macedonia was an integral part of the former Yugoslav community. The history of this problem dates back to 1977 when, according to the Law on Foreign Exchange and Foreign Credit Relations and the appropriate Decisions of the Federal Executive Board of Governors of the National Bank of Yugoslavia, the commercial banks deposited the foreign exchange of the citizens' foreign currency accounts at the National Bank of Yugoslavia.'*

It is not evident which kind of effective redepositing practice was in force.[23] It appears, however, that by 1988 the NBY had become reluctant to accept the then existing redepositing rules as redepositing of the hard currency with the NBY effectively meant that the commercial bank acquired an asset on the NBY as a 'claim on the NBY' and the NBY had in

---

[22] Human Rights Chamber for Bosnia and Herzegovina, item 39: 'The commercial banks would transfer their foreign currency to the National Bank of Yugoslavia. During the period 1978–1990 roughly 90 per cent of the entire foreign currency savings in the SFRY was deposited with the National Bank, according to Mr. Omicevic.'

[23] Mr. Piljak in testimony before the Human Rights Chamber for Bosnia and Herzegovina, item 47: 'Mr Piljak expressed doubts as to whether the commercial banks had been under an obligation to deposit foreign currency with the National Bank of Yugoslavia. Rather the commercial banks deposited part of their foreign currency because, in return, the National Bank was obliged to grant the banks interest-free loans in dinars according to the official exchange rates. The commercial banks used the dinars they received mainly for their own investments or to give loans to companies'.

fact acquired foreign currency (an asset) but also a foreign-currency liability to the banks. This effectively meant that the NBY had become the national carrier of the foreign exchange rate risk.[24] Recognising the situation as unsustainable due to the mismatch between foreign-currency liabilities and actual foreign currency assets on the books of the NBY[25], the Law on Foreign Currency Transactions was amended in October 1988 and the former policy of transfers from the commercial banks to the NBY was to be abolished. The SFRY was to take over, as internal debt, the individual claims for disbursement of their foreign-currency savings. All savings were to be reimbursed by April 1992. However, these plans were never realised.[26]

These bookkeeping entries at the NBY may show how much of the funds were kept with the commercial banks and how much was transferred. However, complicating this scenario may be the fact that commercial banks used part of these deposits directly to satisfy their customers' demand for foreign currency. These funds were used with the consent of the NBY and it is less clear whether these funds were (partly) not registered in the books of the NBY. The hearings to the Human Rights Chamber for Bosnia and Herzegovina note (item 48) that 'only a smaller part of the foreign currency held by the commercial banks (probably one third of the total amount) was *de facto* transferred to the National Bank; the rest remained in the respective Republics and was spent there. It was mainly used for the import of equipment, food and other goods'.[27] In the same hearing, similar comments were made later (item 58):

> 'The commercial banks in the Yugoslav republics deposited their foreign currency with the National Bank of Yugoslavia on a voluntary and contractual basis. In exchange they were granted interest-free credits in dinars which they could then lend, at interest, to their clients. The interest thereby drawn was higher than the profit that banks could make by depositing foreign currency in accounts abroad. The banks used their dinar credits within the territory of the respective republic with the direct knowledge and involvement of the national bank of the republic, which *de facto* provided the credits from its foreign exchange quota with the National Bank of Yugoslavia.

---

[24] As some of these assets were not kept as reserves but presumably spent, the NBY had good reason to get worried.

[25] This is a very loose statement, as, of course, in a bookkeeping sense total assets have to equal total liabilities plus equity (see later).

[26] Similarly, the Croatian Submission and Mr. Omicevic's testimony in front of the Human Rights Chamber of Bosnia and Herzegovina. Similarly also the Croatian and Slovenian submissions.

[27] Statement by Mr. Piljak.

> The deposit of foreign currency with the National Bank was normally only a *pro forma* or ledger transaction. Thus a large part of the foreign currency remained with the commercial banks."[28]

The most detailed explanation of the processes involved in dealing with HCS is given in Vujacic. The two main driving considerations were financial: who was to carry the exchange rate risk and how could the foreign exchange rate commissions to be paid to foreign banks be reduced?[29]

Before 1977, the exchange rate losses incurred by banks, including the foreign exchange differences on the basis of foreign exchange accounts, had to be borne in principle by the commercial banks; yet these were usually able to recover exchange rate losses form the SFRY (by temporary special decrees). Attempting to find a more permanent solution, a position was taken that exchange rate gain/loss at banks would be eliminated if the foreign exchange in the private foreign exchange accounts were deposited with the NBY. This meant that the banks would not be obliged to bear the expenses for exchange rate gain/loss, and therefore the idea appealed to them. This idea was imposed upon the NBY since the concept of regulating the exchange rate gains/losses emanating from HCS was not discussed at regular NBY internal meetings/proceedings. The NBY obligation to accept foreign exchange deposits was a legally imposed obligation, which the NBY had to accept/implement. The legal obligation is based on Article 51 of the Law on Foreign Exchange Operations and External Credit Relations ("The Official Gazette of SFRJ", No. 165/77). The law stipulated the following:

> Banks' authority to deposit foreign exchange on the basis of private foreign exchange accounts at the NBY and the obligations of the NBY to accept such foreign exchange deposits.
>
> The obligation of the NBY to grant interest-free loans to banks on the basis of foreign exchange deposits at the level of dinar equivalent according to the exchange rate effective on the dates when foreign exchange deposits were made.

These general rules were followed by a special Decision on Procedures of Depositing and Returning the Private Foreign Exchange Savings held by NBY ("The Official Gazette of SFRJ", No. 13/78) which specified that banks may deposit foreign exchange on the basis of private foreign exchange accounts at NBY only by effective transfer of foreign exchange from their accounts abroad. On the same basis the legislation also specified that the national banks of the republics and national banks of the autonomous

[28] Statement by Mr. Stojanov.

[29] The Croatian and Slovenian Submissions are similar on this account. (Also, see Vujacic (1991?)).

provinces may approve the banks' interest-free loans in the amount determined by the NBY in the amount of the dinar equivalent to the foreign exchange deposits, according to the foreign exchange rate effective on the dates when foreign exchange deposits were made. This special decision effectively transferred the future exchange rate gain/loss to the NBY.

As banks incurred high foreign exchange commissions to foreign banks, an amendment was adopted ("The Official Gazette of SFRJ", No. 26/78) according to which the banks could deposit foreign exchange on the basis of private foreign exchange accounts at the NBY in two ways:

> On the book – pro forma procedure, foreign exchange generated in the previous period, as well as the total inflow that relates to the accrued foreign exchange interest rate to the private foreign exchange account; and
>
> By effective transfer of foreign exchange from foreign exchange accounts at banks abroad, total net monthly inflow on the basis of private foreign exchange accounts – according to the banks' monthly accounts.

There is thus some reasonable doubt about how much of the HCS deposited at commercial banks was actually passed on to the NBY according to the Law on Foreign Exchange Transactions, Article 103. The NBY was obliged to accept foreign-currency deposits by the commercial banks but commercial banks were not obliged to redeposit at the NBY HCS deposited with them. Commercial banks were given the option of redepositing HCS and thus passing the foreign exchange risk on to the NBY. Also, there is some reasonable doubt about the bookkeeping mechanisms in place to capture the flow of foreign-currency deposits through the financial system. The bookkeeping entries between the commercial banks and the NBY may not adequately reflect the underlying real financial flows.[30]

The Slovenian Submission concludes slightly differently:

> *'...the obligations of the former NBY towards the banks in individual republics and autonomous provinces...in respect to the deposited foreign exchange savings by banks with the former SFRY... correspond in general to the liabilities of the banks towards their savers in the period of dissolution.'*

---

[30] The Bureau of Accounts and Payments, often called by its local acronym ZOP and formerly known as SDK in SFRY, was the institution in charge of providing control over virtually all financial transactions and related information in FRY. As its predecessor did across all former SFRY republics, ZOP has a vast physical network with highly standardised methods and computer systems that interconnect all of the FRY's territory. ZOP plays a key role in ensuring government control over virtually all financial flows among economic entities – including individuals – and possesses vast amounts of information. (See World Bank, Federal Republic of Yugoslavia, 2001). Perhaps it is possible with the help of ZOP (formerly SDK) to unravel the movements of HCS, if required.

However, the Slovenian submission itself issues a serious caveat as commercial banks reimbursed their foreign exchange savers also in dinars and as some servicing of liabilities was funded from the current foreign exchange receipts in individual banks without recourse to the NBY. Also, the submission of the Slovenian government admits that linking as HCS deposits claims of each successor state territory to territorial liabilities of the NBY is a fragile exercise as these 'territorial liabilities' can shift rapidly in a short period of time.

The Croatian submission also deals with this question in some detail:

On the behaviour of the banks:

'The banks used foreign exchange collected from households to make external placements, settle their own external liabilities, meet the demands of clients for their external payments, or for sale on the domestic foreign exchange market...This was why banks lacked sufficient free foreign exchange to deposit with the NBY, and instead had to buy these funds from the NBY through the foreign exchange market.'

On the foreign exchange rate risk:

'Redeposit of foreign exchange from banks to the NBY de facto created a transfer of negative exchange rate differentials on foreign exchange household deposits from commercial banks to the NBY. This transfer was realised de jure at the moment when foreign exchange was deposited with the NBY. This provided an additional stimulus to banks to collect foreign exchange household savings, and insured...However, the problem of negative exchange rate differentials was not thereby solved, but only transferred from the banks' balance sheet to the balance sheet of the central bank.'

Starting with the second half of the 1970s until the break-up of the SFRY, economic considerations appeared to have dominated the behaviour of the financial system. The foreign exchange rate risk was imposed upon the NBY, which was expected to cover eventual losses from general budget funds. In addition, measures were taken to reduce the payment of foreign exchange commissions to foreign banks, and banks played an increasingly prominent role in placing the HCS to use according to their own business criteria. From the submissions it is clear that the option of banks to redeposit HCS with the NBY and the evolving nature of the relationship between the banks and the NBY render it very difficult to assess how much or how little of the HCS in reality flowed to the NBY.

It appears that during all this time of changes in the financial structure and system the nature of the guarantee of the HCS was not actively discussed but assumed as a given, and that this was the underpinning of confidence in the overall financial system.

7.4.6 The nature of the depositors in the former SFRY

A large part of the hard-currency deposits were from guest workers living abroad and sending their remittances to the former SFRY. In the five successor sates, the living standard was the highest in Slovenia and the need for remittances was less pressing in that region and thus remittances to Slovenia were the lowest.

The Vienna Agreement in Annex C, Article 7 does not distinguish between resident and non-resident (those living abroad, i.e. outside the former SFRY) hard-currency deposits. The Article aims at protecting hard-currency savings by individuals. One might therefore be inclined to conclude that any discussion should also not differentiate along nationality lines, i.e. national vs. foreign. This might imply that none of the four following groups of hard-currency depositors should be excluded from discussion a priory by each successor state: Croatians living at home and abroad as well as foreigners living in or outside Croatia.[31]

Foreign natural and juridical persons were permitted to maintain accounts in foreign exchange (as well as dinars) in the SFRY according to the following rules: foreigners residing outside Yugoslavia may freely open accounts in convertible currencies with fully authorised banks in Yugoslavia; and foreign missions and foreigners residing in Yugoslavia may freely open accounts expressed in foreign currencies with any authorised bank.[32]

7.4.7 Freezing of accounts and the foreign exchange market

Freezing of the hard-currency savings deposits means that a depositor cannot (at all) get hold of the deposits even when respecting the rules and regulations which were in force when he deposited his funds.[33]

[31] The same should hold true for Bosnia-Herzegovina, Macedonia, Slovenia and the FRY.

[32] IMF (1991), Exchange Rate Arrangements and Exchange Restrictions, Annual Report.

[33] See Appendix 1 Law on Contractual Relations, Article 1035 and Article 1038 paragraph 2. In this note I have used the words 'claim' or 'potential claim' on a commercial bank interchangeably. According to Aldrich (1996 p. 97) a liability of the commercial bank exists only when the claimants demand for withdrawal of funds had been refused: 'It is axiomatic that the duties of a banker to honour its customers' cheques only crystallise into a specific obligation once a cheque is presented or a request is made with respect to particular funds'. And later he states (p. 217): '12. Refusal by a bank owned by the State

The use/transfer of hard currency deposits had not been completely 'free' for some time before 1991. For example, transfers from foreign exchange accounts in convertible currencies by non-residents were free when made in the currency in which the account was kept; outward transfers could be made in other convertible currencies provided that the bank holding the account was prepared to make the necessary conversion.

Residents had been allowed to buy unlimited amounts of foreign exchange until 20 December 1990. While the purchase of foreign exchange henceforth was restricted to specific purposes[34], cash withdrawals were limited to DM 1,000.00[35] and balances were not transferable to other persons or accounts. As the rules applying to the use of hard-currency deposits were gradually made more restrictive, it may be difficult to ascertain the precise moment in time when deposits were effectively frozen.

The EIU's analysis at that time appears fairly correct but places the date of freezing probably too late[36]: 'The Serbian government effectively froze most hard currency savings (FCD, foreign currency deposits) at the start of 1992 when it introduced a dual exchange rate: for savings deposited before the outbreak of hostilities in September 1991, withdrawals were only possible in dinar at a rate of just 15–20 per cent of the official rate. If depositors are not paid the full value of their claims immediately, some or all of the deposits are effectively temporarily frozen. Savings deposited since then may, however, still be withdrawn at the official rate, which is reasonable, although less than the parallel market rate. There were limited exceptions for both categories, allowing withdrawals in hard currency, for example to pay for education.'[37] Obviously, the legal framework also had become successively tighter in terms of justifying withdrawals and the time limits

to seek permission from the appropriate authorities for foreign exchange when an alien account holder has requested the transfer of funds from his account creates liability'. The reason for this is that the Tribunal in the US-Iran dispute was reluctant to hold that a legal cause of action existed against a bank that it found had done nothing wrong and stated its willingness to honour properly drawn requests on the accounts. The ensuing note does not pursue these arguments further.

[34] These were expenses incurred in hospital treatment abroad; payment of court and other administrative fees; expenses for legal assistance abroad, and payments of traffic and other fines; relocation costs, fees for membership in international associations, and burial-related expenses abroad. (See IMF, Exchange Rate Arrangements and Exchange Restrictions, Annual Report, 1992).

[35] Not more than DM 1,000 per person could be taken abroad in the form of bank notes.

[36] The timing was discussed earlier (see 1.2. of this note) with regard to the question of succession.

[37] The Economist Intelligence Unit (1992) "Yugoslavia", No. 1.

imposed upon withdrawals.[38] The unilateral action of Serbia at the time would tend to date the latest moment of freezing at September 1991.[39] However, according to witnesses at that time, people were effectively blocked from access to their savings already by March/April 1991.

There is one way to cut through these rules by arguing that what matters are not these rules but whether or not the hard-currency depositor could in fact somehow claim the deposit from the bank. It appears that in retrospect, freezing was a gradual process.[40] While commercial banks were to honour the depositors' claim in foreign currency or in dinar, banks were often willing to pay the deposit holder in dinar but when the claim was made in hard currency, the commercial banks did not honour the claim. The non-honouring of the claim was a gradual process as the banks themselves experienced shortages of foreign exchange.[41] The commercial banks at that time did not have sufficient hard currencies themselves and could hardly get hold of funds from the NBY.[42] While the dinar was pretty stable against the

---

[38] See Appendix 1 on the Legislation of the SFRY *under Decisions on Methods and Conditions for the Deposition and Withdrawal of Citizens' Foreign Currency at the Deposit of the National Bank of Yugoslavia (OG SFRY no. 73/85)* and amendments.

[39] It is noteworthy that the Serbian measure occurred after the dates when individual successor States proclaimed independence (except for Bosnia-Herzegovina, see Table 1). By the way, all successor States "froze" foreign currency deposits after independence. In Croatia, for example, the balances I foreign exchange accounts were frozen on April 27, 1991 in accordance with the decree law of December 23, 1991 and were being released only in special cases with the permission of the Ministry of Finance (see IMF, Exchange Arrangements and Exchange Restrictions, Annual Report, 1993).

[40] In the Human Rights Chamber for Bosnia and Herzegovina (item 113) the Federation of Bosnia and Herzegovina argues similarly: 'The Federation states that, at the time when the applicants deposited their foreign currency, the use of such savings was restricted by the old SFRY legislation. The restrictions, which increased over time, included limitation on the purposes for which the savings could be used and on the amounts that could be withdrawn from the accounts. Also, withdrawals could only be made if they had been announced in advance. The applicants were aware of these restrictions when they made their deposits in the banks. Although no legislation completely blocked the savings accounts, the accounts were blocked *de facto* already in 1991 and 1992.

[41] See Human Rights Chamber for Bosnia and Herzegovina (9 June 2000) concludes similarly: '…the withdrawal of money from these "old" foreign currency savings accounts was progressively restricted by legislation enacted during the 1980s and the early 1990s'.

[42] Human Rights Chamber for Bosnia and Herzegovina, item 79: 'The OHR stated that it was not aware of any legislation by which the old foreign currency accounts had been blocked. Thus, no responsibility for the blocking of foreign

DM during 1990, by the end of 1990 the forex market broke down, accelerating the public's demand for hard-currency deposits made earlier with the commercial banks. A look at forex market developments at that time would confirm that freezing effectively occurred at the latest by March/April, that is at a point in time which does not coincide with the timing issues of succession under Article 7. Earlier dates like December 1990 also appear quite feasible on this account.

7.4.8 Hard-currency savings defined

There appears to be little or no disagreement on what is meant by *hard-currency* savings. Accounts at that time could be denominated in any of the following currencies: Austrian shillings, Canadian dollars, Danish kroner, deutsche mark, Finnish markka, French francs, Italian lire, Japanese yen, Netherlands guilder, Norwegian kroner, pounds sterling, Spanish pesetas, Swedish kronor, Swiss francs, and US dollars.

7.4.9 Events after succession

A relevant question may be whether developments after succession are allowed to feed back on the time before succession?

First, the existing social, economic and political landscape may condition to some extent the attitudes and thought processes entering into the negotiation process. Obviously, the most recent history throughout the 1990s will condition to a large extent 'official' government policy.

The successor states all aim to join the EU. They are willing to tie their economic and, to some extent, political future to the EU. The political support of this process varies between successor states, and the distance on the road travelled towards the EU is also quite different. In more general terms, the speed of transition among the successor states varies quite a bit. Some authors have also elaborated on the generally faster transition in the Baltic States and Central Europe compared with developments in the Balkan region.[43]

The resolution of the guarantee of hard-currency savings is not directly part of the *acquis communautaire*. However, as mentioned in the EU Commission Report on Slovenia '...the debt of the Slovenian Ljubljanska Banka to its former Croatian account holders at the bank's former branch

savings accounts could be attached to either respondent Party. Rather, the blocking originated in events in the SFRY and, as a consequence of those events, the banks had stopped disbursements from the accounts on their own motion.'

[43] For some of the reasons, see Dobrinsky (2001).

in Zagreb also need to be tackled.' From an EU perspective it is quite clear that an agreement on outstanding financial issues inherited from the SFRY should be forged before entry into the EU.

Secondly, it is often argued that the amounts to be reimbursed to HCS depositors cannot be paid back from the budget (or constitute too large a drain) as the amounts involved would effectively undermine any budget process. This may be true but appears irrelevant to the issues faced in settling the question of the 'old' HCS. If it were possible to find 'solutions' to the HCS claims recognised by each successor state, there would also be solutions found to the residual or gap claims.[44]

Thirdly, the measures taken by the individual successor states with regard to the HCS after succession cannot be ignored as economic reality. This implies that some disagreement with regard to Annex C, Article 7 of the Vienna Agreement was preprogrammed as countries dealt with the restitution question of HCS deposits differently (Annex 1). Each country now, of course, feels obliged to defend the measures taken in the past as being in line with international law or being fair and equitable. Without implying judgement, the fact that successor states have taken different approaches in dealing with HCS is one of the compelling reasons to find a compromise so that each government may save face and may be considered fair by its own citizens, by the other successor states and by the outside world.

7.5 Is there a solution (solutions) in sight?

One may discuss which principles should be applied and how to the guarantees of the HCS deposits of the former SFRY. These principles might be gleaned from international law and other considerations may be valid as well. The following discussions do not necessarily claim to be consistent nor do they implying that the mediator is taking the position of any one particular successor state. Some potential principles are stated.

It may be relevant what the exact wording of the guarantee was at the time and whether this wording has changed over time.[45] All successor states have started (or have almost finished the process) of reimbursing their own citizens for their 'old' HCS. In the Human Rights Chamber for Bosnia and Herzegovina it was clearly stated there is no legislation cancelling

[44] These are simply all potential claims based on HCS minus the claims currently being settled.

[45] This is a question of the legal acts/directives involved at that time. It appears that this point will need special further investigation.

claims related to such HCS.[46] Similarly the other successor states have recognised the obligation to repay the HCS according to their own law, as they have also never explicitly frozen the HCS in banks.

7.5.1 Final beneficiary

The final beneficiary rule may apply here. It is commonly applied to loans given to individual countries by international organisations. For example, the World Bank had granted the SFRY US dollar loans. These were guaranteed by the federal government, but had been granted to finance specific projects in individual republics. Consequently, when apportioning the loans, the World Bank adopted the final beneficiary rule, whereby a loan is deemed to be owed by the entity that actually benefited from it, rather than by the entity which entered into the loan contract. In other words, it treated the debts as localised (allocated) debt even though the SFRY was the contracting party. Accordingly, the World Bank apportioned the debts to the republics in which the specific projects were located.

If it could be ascertained who used and benefited from the frozen deposits, that institution or successor state could be asked to restitute/reimburse these deposits. Such an argument does not necessarily include any consideration of guarantee as it was ignored in the case of the World Bank loans alluded to.[47] While such a principle may be a good starting point, it may be less clear who benefited: the financial intermediaries, enterprises or perhaps the NBY or others. They all may have used the funds for different purposes. So the beneficiary may have to be defined not as final beneficiary but perhaps as beneficiary who had the power of actually disbursing these funds.

The EIU at that time stated: 'These funds were placed with the National Bank of Yugoslavia in exchange for dinars at the then prevailing exchange rates.'[48] However, it is not clear what shares of HCS deposits were forwarded to the NBY at that time. There was no obligation on the part of the commercial banks to redeposit the HCS deposits with the NBY at that time. Some observers also noted that these redepositing requirements

---

[46] Human Rights Chamber for Bosnia and Herzegovina, item 42.

[47] This may be disputed. One line of argument may refer to the ancillary character of the guarantee or whether such a guarantee was an integral part of the contract concluded between the bank and the depositor. However, the social benefit of the guarantee may also have benefited the financial system and final beneficiaries at large.

[48] The Economist Intelligence Unit (1992), Yugoslavia, No. 1, p. 13 states, 'The National Bank is unable to account for an amount of the money, and what it can locate has anyway been effectively impounded for a period of time.'

changed during the 1980s and it is not clear what regulation was in effect at the time the deposits were frozen. Redepositing rules provided commercial banks with options for dealing with excess HCS. (See Sect. 1.5.) There are also some unconfirmed statements hinting at individual agreements or temporary rules being struck between individual commercial banks and the NBY, rendering quantification more difficult.

Even if one were to acknowledge that a portion of the HCS were redeposited with the NBY according to book-entry records with the NBY, these entries were pure bookkeeping entries, i.e. 'pro forma' bookkeeping entries with the sole aim of covering the foreign exchange risk.

These arguments seem to effectively exclude the NBY from being considered beneficiary. This conclusion probably holds true, apart from the question whether the NBY and SFRY can be considered beneficiaries at all in a narrow sense as they were presumably the institutions which furthered the common good not as an end in themselves but for the whole State.[49]

Admittedly, a HCS deposit at a commercial bank in Zagreb may not have flowed to the Republic of Croatia. Admittedly, it is even less likely that HCS deposited in a branch banks of another republics would have been 'used' in Croatia.[50] Therefore, to allocate these HCS to commercial banks as beneficiaries may be an option. Commercial banks themselves contribute to GNP growth, but banks are mainly seen as intermediaries in allocating funds efficiently. Due to the fungibility of these flows of HCS, their use on the books of the commercial banks cannot realistically be traced. Assume e.g. that part of the funds was redistributed by the commercial banks on the foreign exchange interbank market. While one may see a benefit in having such a market, it will not be possible to name any direct economic financial beneficiaries – again, there were broader economic benefits. The beneficiary rule applied to commercial banks cannot be made operational, but it may be fair to consider in the negotiations that branch banks imported more 'benefits' to the main bank and thus perhaps to the successor state which was the legal host than to the republic in which the branch was physically located.

---

[49] Obviously, this latter argument is being refuted on grounds that the NBY misused funds for 'war purposes'. While not defending any misuse of funds, that particular argument appears misplaced and may only have political currency.

[50] The FRY contribution states unequivocally: '…it was a characteristic of Ljubljanska d.d. that it directed a significant part of the foreign currency – collected from citizens in main banks (later on branches of these banks) which operated in the territory of the former SFRY other than Slovenia – to foreign-currency accounts of the Head Office of Ljubljanska Banka. These collected foreign currencies were used for imports and payment abroad, mainly on the basis of decisions and instructions of the head office…'

The beneficiary of the initial redepositing appears to be the NBY, but the NBY only acted as an agent for the government in redistributing these funds as the government's intermediary. The banks could have used these funds in various ways. If a link could be drawn between hard-currency funds deposited by individual citizens in branch banks and hard-currency loans given by commercial banks (or the NBY) to the benefit of enterprises in a successor state, a case for final beneficiary rule could be deduced. Such an argument, however, appears highly artificial, as any financial/economic links are much too vague.

Definitions of who the beneficiary might be, fungibility of funds, changes over time in potential beneficiaries and vague bookkeeping procedures are among the many issues in asserting and/or implementing a 'final' beneficiary principle or rule. Fighting for a redistribution of 'federal' funds to the individual republics is in a sense a 'normal/regular' claim on funds which one finds in all countries with similar constitutions.[51] In this process funds are almost never received and distributed one to one. Other criteria, as, for example, developing weaker geographical parts of the country or developing certain industries or reducing unemployment, may drive a wedge between collection of funds and their distribution. The political nature of the distribution of funds should thus not be part of any negotiation deliberations as the SFRY was at that time a single state. While it might be fair to look at the question who benefited from the HCS (in branch banks), no reasonable operational conclusion appears to emerge *prima facie* from these deliberations.

7.5.2 The nature of the guarantee – the inheritance principle

It appears that when the savings deposits of the individuals were frozen in the former SFRY, these were indeed covered by a SFRY state guarantee.[52] In fact, this guarantee had emerged before the 1980s with the original aim of safeguarding the public's savings but also with the thought in mind that such a guarantee might be an additional tool of attracting further funds to the banking system. The SFRY and the commercial banks both had an interest in receiving additional hard-currency deposits.

However, it also became evident over time that any substantial run on the banks could not be covered by the commercial banks even with the help of the government. By the time the deposits became inaccessible to the depositors it had become clear that the state guarantee had become

[51] This redistribution of funds has been very prevalent and serious in Russia and Argentina.

[52] See Appendix 1, the *Law on Foreign Exchange Transactions*, Article 14.3.

effectively an empty shell. There was never any explicit funding envisaged by the SFRY, nor were any kind of reserves (provisions) accumulated at commercial banks in order to face a potential systemic run on the banking system. A clear differentiation between the NBY and commercial banks probably made little sense at that time, as all the commercial banks were in fact state owned.[53] If one were to follow this argumentation, one might want to admit that the nature of the state guarantee is less from obvious as it probably had lost its original meaning, or at least part of it. Regardless of how one might interpret the nature of the guarantee, it is obvious that at the moment of setting up/creating this guarantee there was no thought given to the possibility of a disintegration/dissolution of the SFRY and what that would mean.

According to Feilchenfeld's maintenance theory on the succession of debts, debt passes while 'auxiliary rights' do not necessarily pass onto the successor states. The fact that the successor states are proposing and willing to renegotiate the guarantee of HCS according to Annex C, Article 7 of the Vienna Agreement may be interpreted as indicating that only an auxiliary role is being accorded to this guarantee and that this guarantee is thus not automatically inherited. Thus the case of inheritance of the guarantee must be (re) stated?

As all the successor states were part of the SFRY, which provided this guarantee, inheritance would fall on all successor states again. The review of the contributions of the successor states appears to indicate a willingness to settle any legitimate HCS claims. This seems to imply that inheritance as a principle is not disputed. In dispute is the meaning of such an inheritance principle.

If one were to adopt a pure inheritance-of-debt point of view, all newly created states assume obligations of their legal entities for which the former SFRY was a guarantor and these could also include obligations for HCS deposits at branch banks. At that time only the parent banks (main office) had its own legal identity. Thus the obligation to repay the HCS according to the pure inheritance principle of debt may indicate that the attached guarantee may have been inherited by the successor states covering all commercial banks with legal identity in the former republics of the SFRY. This conclusion appears possible.

However, the counter-arguments are strong:

> If all financial assets and liabilities were inherited by the successor states it seems that they should all share in these according to perhaps some equitable key.

[53] This is probably why these guarantees are being dealt with at the state level and not at the individual bank level.

If the guarantee had indeed been inherited by the successor states, there is no *a priori* rule on how this guarantee should be handled in case of a break-up of the SFRY. As the guarantee itself is silent, any rule appears thus to some extent arbitrary.

As will be shown later, the territory and equity principles may lead to perhaps different conclusions.

7.5.3 Equitable division of foreign assets and liabilities as principle

In the Vienna Agreement the successor states agreed to divide external assets and external liabilities according to certain guidelines.

In a very general sense the deposits of the population in the commercial banks presented a potential claim on the banking system which was essentially government driven. As all potential (financial) claims were guaranteed by the SFRY (or the NBY), all (financial) state assets potentially secured these claims. As these claims were not satisfied and were generally supposed to be backed up by the assets of the state, one might consider applying the principle of equitable division of foreign assets and liabilities also to domestic assets.

If one were to follow this line of reasoning, then a way would have to be found to apportion all these financial claims. On this basis, there is also no intuitive counter-argument to exclude HCS in any commercial bank regardless of the legal status of the bank. Thus all remaining HCS gap claims are to be added up and an agreement drawn up according to which these HCS are to be paid back.

This point of view would thus essentially argue that successors to the former SFRY are the five new states in that region. As they have decided to inherit all financial assets and liabilities, this might also mean that they inherited the guarantees of the former SFRY, including the guarantee of all the HCS deposits. As financial assets were split up according to some weights (keys) assigned to the successor states, this weighting may also be applied to the (guarantees of) HCS deposit claims. Such an approach may claim internal consistency, and this more mechanical approach may be easy to implement, for example, the IMF key[54] may be applied.

Such a mechanical approach violates the (narrow) geographical territory principle; but with some goodwill a broader territorial principle might also be interpreted as follows: all the commercial banks which had a legal identity on the territory.

[54] The BIS assets were divided according to the IMF key (see Vienna Agreement, Appendix). However, this case may appear different again.

Such an approach applied to liabilities also violates the pure legal inheritance principle as it extends some obligation to branch banks, which are not legal independent entities in the territory.

Obviously such an approach would also ignore considerations of the source or the use of funds deposited with the commercial banks. Even though one would conclude that the beneficiary principle is impossible to implement, it is nevertheless probably correct to assume that the beneficiaries of HCS of branch banks mainly benefited the host/main bank and its successor state.

If one were to approach a resolution to the problem of HCS in this way, the agreement could be interpreted as compromise and restitution to individuals could potentially proceed impartially and fast.[55]

7.5.4 Equity as principle for the apportionment of assets and liabilities

The UN Convention as well as recent practice and doctrine indicate that equity is the principle of international law for apportionment of both assets and liabilities. Thus finding an equitable solution is one of the few well-established principles of international law applicable to state succession.

The Vienna Convention on State Succession in Respect of State Property, Archives and State Debt of 7 April 1983 introduced some important rules mirroring the contemporary developments of international law. According to this Convention, the successor states shall acquire an equitable share of debts of the predecessor state (Articles 37.2, 40.1 and 41); however, the priority of settling by agreement the problems of state property and debts of a predecessor state was reserved (Articles 14, 17.1, 18.1, 37.1, 40.1 and 41).

Czaplinski (1999) points out two important reservations: 'the equity and the understanding of equitable principles are relative and can change over time' (p. 65) and 'the results of applying equitable principles must be equitable….It is, however, the result which is predominant; the principles are subordinate to the goal….The equitable result achieved by applying the equitable criteria should be evaluated *in casu*' (pp. 66–67).[56]

---

[55] While it is beyond the scope of this note to discuss the various restitution mechanisms, it is important that the procedure be clear and transparent to all concerned. Individual HCS depositors should know exactly to whom the claim should be made.

[56] Unfortunately, Czaplinski does not draw any strong conclusions. He notes, however, "The usual practice to be followed is that the rights acquired as a result of state succession should correspond to the shares of debts to be under-

What appears equitable in terms of the HCS in the case of the former SFRY may thus be debated. It appears that all successor states have started to repay the HCS according to rules which they considered fair and equitable. Furthermore, it appears equitable to be equally fair to repay all HCS deposit holders. It thus appears as a violation of international rules of equity to distinguish between HCS according to any criteria if this results in arbitrary groupings.

Thus, *prima facie*, any restriction to access to HCS savings which were part of the 'normal' savings behaviour appears to violate the principle of equity (perhaps in the sense of one's own use of property). International law would not distinguish between a domestic or foreign source of a HCS deposit. The principle of equity thus appears to indicate that all HCS deposit holders should be reimbursed. It does not appear that any higher principles might upset this conclusion as e.g. the 'general good' of the state as such an assertion was never made and, as demonstrated earlier, the outcome of the freezing of the HCS was the result of the succession history. It is probably equitable to conclude that all HCS deposit holders in the former SFRY should be compensated. This principle of equity is thus also to be applied to those HCS holders who are currently not part of any reimbursement scheme.[57]

It is, however, less obvious what equitable criteria are to be applied *in casu*, that is which result would be equitable. The result in terms of who is to reimburse the deposit holder must also be equitable. Perhaps the idea of an equitable solution may drive some of the negotiation processes.

Equal treatment appears to be quite an equitable proposition. As the repayment schemes in individual successor states started at different times and as the repayment mechanisms are different among successor states,

---

taken. Such a solution would certainly satisfy the criteria of equity, reasonableness and proportionality" (p. 72).

57 One way to move forward is to let these HCS holders have access to one of the existing reimbursement schemes. This may sound fair, as everyone will receive the same treatment. Of course such a simple 'solution' may raise other issues as the rules and regulations applied by each successor state in its own jurisdictional area are different. Assume the hypothetical situation that a Croatian HCS holder in Ljubljanska Banka in Zagreb was to be reimbursed and assume further reimbursement under the Slovenian scheme. Assume further that this reimbursement is more (or less) generous than the reimbursement scheme in his own country, Croatia. Either way, equal treatment could not be achieved. Assume on the other hand that that person was reimbursed by his own Croatian government, that is one provides access to the Croatian reimbursement scheme but with possible (partial) compensation from the Slovenian scheme (paid to the Croatian scheme?).

equal treatment of all former SFRY HCS holders is only a hypothetical proposition.

Bosnia and Herzegovina also put the equal-treatment argument forth in striking an agreement with Croatia. The Republic of Croatia regulated the HCS deposits collected by the Croatian Splitska Banka in Croatia as well as HCS deposits collected by the Splitska Banka's branch offices in Bosnia and Herzegovina in the same manner. No differentiation was drawn between domestic citizens' deposits and deposits by citizens from Bosnia and Herzegovina.[58]

The equal treatment is this case appears to be based on the principle of the inheritance of debt and thus generally suffers from the same criticism as was raised earlier. One may also ask whether Croatia has applied equal treatment to all successor states or not. The equal-treatment argument is made *ex post* and as an argument seems to hold equally with other underlying principles of international law.

7.5.5 International law and domestic law

International law plays an important role in the June 2001 Vienna Agreement. The preamble includes the following sentence: 'Demonstrating their readiness to co-operate in resolving succession issues in accordance with international law, Have agreed as follows:'

Article 9 of the Vienna Agreements states:

> 'This Agreement shall be implemented by the successor States in good faith in conformity with the Charter of the United Nations and in accordance with international law'.

International law is referred to both in the spirit of the agreement and in the implementation of the agreement.

It appears that all the successor states have agreed that international law represented the legal basis of the negotiations, and *prima facie* there appears no reason to deviate from the principles of international law in this part of the negotiations.[59] Yet, what this means in terms of Annex C, Article 7 is subject to this negotiation process.

As the potential settlement is to be of a binding nature, it will imply that all the governments concerned comply with any kind of agreement being struck. There is a risk, however, that differences in treatment under domestic

[58] This equal-treatment rule is also invoked by the potential claims of Bosnia and Herzegovina vis-à-vis Slovenia and the FRY. The equal-treatment rule is also invoked by the potential claims of Macedonia vis-à-vis Slovenia.

[59] See Stanič (2001) for the history of this.

law will subsequently appear. Questions in this domain may concern, *inter alia*, jurisdictional issues or lack of jurisdiction, nature of the claim or claimant, burden of proof or size of the claim, etc.[60]

There may also be a 'choice of law' question involved. While we may want to consider any agreement as conclusive and binding, we may want to be explicit on what kind of recourse any claimant may have. Are the successor states happy with the assertion that any legal suit will be treated equally under any agreement being struck even if it is being contested in the domestic legal system? Certainly we would exclude any claim being brought in two different domestic jurisdictions.[61]

7.5.6 The attitudes of the parties involved

In general all successor states are willing to co-operate, especially in the spirit of Article 7, i.e.'taking into account the necessity of protecting the hard-currency savings of individuals'. By submitting views on Annex C, Article 7 to the Treaty on Succession Issues, all countries have shown a willingness to negotiate. Bosnia and Herzegovina stands ready to strike an agreement in good faith and under appropriate dynamics. The Macedonian delegation is prepared 'in the spirit of co-operation to search for a common solution to this issue, which is of common concern both to the government of the Republic of Macedonia and to many Macedonian citizens who have deposited their foreign-currency savings in accordance with the law'.[62]

All successor states hope to find final and appropriate solutions which will be fair and just to each individual successor state.

7.6 Summary of open questions, concerns and first impressions

1. The negotiations under Annex C, Article 7 of the Vienna Agreement are a natural continuation and extension that led to this treaty. It is essential that the same spirit of cooperation that led to this treaty also prevail in finding a solution to the unsettled question of HCS of the population under this article. We are working on the assumption that the succession states enter into a direct exchange of ideas in good faith.

[60] A good case is the US-Iranian disputes (Aldrich 1996).

[61] Even though the parties may come to an agreement, the outcomes in legal proceedings may not always be completely congruent for a variety of reasons.

[62] Submission of Macedonia.

We do tend to agree with the submission of the Slovenian government:

'Redistribution among Successor States of public debt, originating in former foreign exchange savings and accepted by the Successor States according to their legislation, should not be a matter of discussion. Such debt should be considered finally accepted and not subject to the negotiations under Article 7 Annex C'[63]

and

'No double treatment of the same issues should be allowed in respect to the solutions already accepted as final in the Treaty on Succession Issues acceptance of the former SFRY guarantee for savings.'

It may, however, be unavoidable that some of the issues resolved earlier will have to be revisited in order to find a fair and reasonable solution under the article in dispute.

While we support the application of rules of international law in this process, we also realise that without a strong political will to reach an agreement, any settlement under Article 7 will be difficult and negotiations may be protracted and futile. We therefore urge you to proceed on the road of compromise.

2. As a first impression, it is probably futile to enter into any discussion of the exact date of succession. This area remains complex and controversial and any agreement on this may not help in finding feasible solutions to the problem at hand. An initial review of the time period preceding the declaration of independence of the successor states of the former SFRY seems to indicate that the restrictions to access to HCS became progressively

[63] There may be a special case or an exception in the bilateral relationship between Croatia and the FRY. The FRY submission states: '*...after the proclamation of independence, Croatian banks changed the foreign currency savings books of the "old foreign currency depositors" in a very short period of time during 1991. In the circumstances of the known and military events in the Republic, a huge number of old foreign currency depositors (mainly Serbs) were not informed of that in time, which prevented them from changing the old foreign currency savings books. Afterwards, most of these citizens were forced to leave Croatia and go to Serbia, so that the issue of their "old foreign currency savings" remained unsolved.'* This issue alluded to does not appear to fall under the gap approach taken in this note. The claims were recognised by Croatia but the time frame allotted to state such a claim is considered too short or was not clear/evident to the claimant. Could this issue be dealt with bilaterally or should it be included in the current negotiations? In a sense, the events after (?) succession have created this unplanned gap – i.e. unsatisfied HCS deposit claims of FRY citizens on Croatia.

tighter just before the first declarations of independence were made, i.e. around March/April 1991. On this basis it would probably not be impossible to agree on a date of freezing – if this is needed in order to proceed. Any time between December 1990 and June 1991 appears feasible.

Secondly, it appears too complex and unreasonable to try to unravel what happened to the HCS once deposited in commercial banks. These deposits had too many options to travel and the underlying financial records may not capture real transfers adequately. Thus to assign any final beneficiary by successor states is, for all practical purposes, a hazardous exercise. However, it can probably not be denied that the local economy benefited to some extent from these deposits; it will probably not be possible to quantify what is meant by 'to some extent', or should we say 'to a large extent'? Admittedly, for branch banks probably the opposite holds true, confirming the difficulty of this line of argument. Also, the beneficiaries – if we were to define these as local enterprises – changed over time in the SFRY.

Thirdly, a crucial issue concerns the nature of the guarantee. It appears that regardless of how one interprets the nature of this guarantee, an obligation of the successor state to repay HCS only appears to come into existence with the new laws passed by the successor states in this regard. All successor states felt obliged to implement such laws. It appears that this would have probably happened with or without the guarantee.

We do not believe that depositors deposited HCS with commercial banks because of the guarantee. When introducing the guarantee, there was also nobody thinking of succession issues. That the question of the guarantee is now being negotiated under Annex C, Article 7 also seems to indicate uncertainty about the nature of the guarantee. There is thus no intuitive reason from looking at the guarantee that certain 'obvious' international law principles are to be applied.

One may also dispute whether a 'hollow' guarantee can be inherited and whether the inheritance of the guarantee was only an ancillary right that is linked to the underlying claim. Would a citizen's claim have been successful in court while referring to the guarantee? Perhaps one should not overstate the possible responses to these questions.

Fourthly, while we might argue about the nature of the guarantee, it appears that the five successor states are willing to reinstate all HCS holders who had 'legitimate' deposits in the former SFRY. The emphasis is here on the word 'all'. Such a 'wide' resolution would certainly be looked upon favourably by all the deposit holders at the time of the dissolution of the SFRY, and it would provide a very strong signal to current and potential savers, create a lot of goodwill towards the governments in the region providing the benefit of trust in the current government, and certainly also be looked upon favourably by the larger international financial community.

Fifthly, the reason to reinstate all HCS deposits is primarily based on the contract between the commercial bank and the deposit holder. This contract obliges the commercial bank to pay back the HCS upon demand. It appears that is was not primarily due to the non-willingness of the commercial banks to fulfil their obligations to the deposit holders but that the political events at that period in the time of the SFRY prevented repayment and led to the freezing of the deposits. In the SFRY the non-payment of deposits was essentially due to interference of the state and the ensuing historical break-up and succession. It is true that individual commercial banks have the obligation to honour the deposits, but as the non-payment was due to events outside their control and as these events were driven by government action, it is appropriate that the settlement be done by the governments.

If one assumes that the private contracts were inherited by the successor states, the bone of contention might be: on what basis? On this point differences of opinion exist. If one were to apply a concept of domestic legal inheritance only a legal person, i.e. the parent bank and not the branch of a bank, could inherit such a claim with the state being a legal successor. This appears to be a very formalistic domestic legal argument. Furthermore, as all the commercial banks were government owned, did it matter by whom and where HCS were collected? If one were to apply the pure 'narrow' territorial principle, the rights and obligations of entities on the territory of the successor states are passed on. Branches of banks outside the territory of the successor state were thus excluded. This note has explored some arguments in this context.

3. The mediator's search is for justice and equity, even when local law or individual principles of international law seem to oppose justice and equity. Furthermore, the search is for a politically acceptable solution to all five successor states bearing in mind the actual economic and political realities of today. The Secretariat thus prefers to analyse the question of compensation in accordance with general fair principles. The depositors had generally made their hard-currency deposits in the belief and trust that they could withdraw these funds at one point in time. Thus a contract implying such repayment was struck between the bank and the deposit holder. It is difficult to establish who benefited the most from these funds. It appears, however, that generally some of these deposits benefited the local economy while for branch banks it is probable that the opposite holds true and that the final benefactor changed over time. However, it was not due to the non-willingness of the commercial banks to fulfil their obligations to the deposit holders and the natural commercial behaviour of the banks but due primarily to the political events in the history of the former SFRY. As the commercial banks behaved at the behest of government and as they were gov-

ernment owned, it appears that it is in the end government which is the correct party to address for any reimbursement claims.

The potential argument that the freezing of these accounts was motivated by worthy economic or social objectives is found to be of no defence against liability – the mediator thus prefers that all potential justified claims of deposit holders (at end December 1990) be satisfied. All the holders of hard-currency deposits whose access to these funds was frozen acquired a claim (or some kind of an obligation to repay) on the government.[64]

In a nutshell, in the succession debate, the three successor states (Bosnia-Herzegovina, Croatia and Macedonia) claim essentially that the head office of banks in these states are liable to the savers and that the former SFRY guarantee thus applies to these deposit liabilities of the head offices. On the other hand, Slovenia and the FRY favour the territorial principle in the distribution of the former SFRY guarantee. The national laws following succession reflect these differences.

Not surprisingly, each successor country has chosen the line of argument most favourable to his own ends, i.e. reducing any claims on the successor state. Slovenia and the FRY can be generous by including foreign (other successor states) branches of banks in their territorial principle as there were practically no such banks in their territory. Bosnia-Herzegovina, Croatia and Macedonia essentially invoke the principle of citizenship. The result is a gap in coverage of all private deposit holders in the former SFRY. It appears that the guarantee is silent on the appropriateness of the principle to be applied in succession. Insisting on pure principles thus does not appear to help in arriving at a compromise of views.

[64] Do we want this claim to be explicitly stated by the holder? If so, then one needs to be clear to whom and during which time period?

Annex 1

The following table is a stylised breakdown of how successor states have dealt with the HCS after succession:

Table. Stylised breakdown of HCS

	A Type of bank	B Type of depositor	C Type of citizen
1	Domestic bank	Resident	Citizen
2	Head office or subsidiary of foreign bank	Non-resident	Foreigner
3	Branch office of foreign bank		

Bosnia-Herzegovina (1999): acknowledges claims of persons who were citizens of the former Socialist Republic of Bosnia and Herzegovina on 31 March 1991 as well as citizens living outside the Federation of Bosnia and Herzegovina on 31 March 1991 having HCS in banks with head offices in its territory (A1, 2, B1, 2, C1).

Croatia (1991): converted foreign-currency deposits in 'domiciled' banks into public debt. Croatian citizens who had foreign-currency deposits in non-domiciled banks were allowed to transfer their foreign-currency deposits to Croatian banks (A1, 2, 3, B1, 2, C1).

Macedonia (1992): regulated HCS deposited in banks with headquarters in Macedonia and HCS deposited in bank branches operating in Macedonia with their head office outside its territory. On request those latter deposits were transferred to one of the banks with headquarters in Macedonia. (A1, 2 (limited), B1, 2 (limited), (1, 2 (?)).

Slovenia (1991): grants claims for all foreign currency deposits deposited in banks established in its territory. This includes branches of banks in Slovenia with headquarters in the territories of other successor states without exception. All savers in the territory of Slovenia are treated equally, without regard to nationality, citizenship or any other factor (territorial principle) (A1, 2, 3, B1, C1, 2).

Federal Republic of Yugoslavia (1988): the scheme provides for the recovery of savings to savers in individual banks of the FRY. The law enumerates the banks on the territory of the FRY. Any savers are entitled to this scheme (A1, 2, B1, 2 and C1, 2).

Annex 2: The Basel process and procedural aspects

In a more and more internationally integrated framework, the Basel decision-making framework has proved to be fairly effective. Country representatives meet in Basel out of their own free will. Any kind of agreement struck in the Basel meetings is usually the result of a (long) process of international negotiation in which country representatives import their own country perspective. The agreement of national experts has to be defended on the country's own home turf. As most of these agreements find their way into documents, final decisions to implement these decisions resides at the national sovereign level.

'...while final decisions must still be taken at the national level where sovereignty continues to reside, these national decisions are increasingly the final act in a long process of international negotiation and agreement among national experts meeting in Basel and elsewhere. Therefore, while national sovereignty remains in an internationally integrated financial world, it does so in a form that is materially constrained.'[65]

Admittedly, there is some peer pressure once the national experts have struck some kind of agreement on the nature of the text.[66] On the other hand, there is usually the general realisation that no agreement is perfect from one's own country's perspective.

In the case of the former SFRY, the negotiations now being held under the auspices of the BIS are first of all a continuation of the preceding process which resulted in the Succession Agreement of June 2001.[67]

The role of the appointed financial expert is essentially one of mediator, similar to the role played by Sir Arthur Watts who had been appointed a special negotiator for succession issues in March 1996. The opinions of the mediator expert are thus exploratory and advisory in nature and are not binding upon the negotiating parties.

A1 The role/nature of the BIS's involvement

The successor states of the former SFRY have entered into a process which deals with the issues of the HCS of individuals which were frozen at one point in time and which are now to be restituted to the individuals concerned.

---

[65] White, William R. (1999). p. 19.

[66] White (1999) argues that 'while national sovereignty remains in an internationally integrated financial world, it does so in a form that is materially constrained' (p. 19).

[67] A review of the history of these negotiations is found in Stanič (2001).

The process aims at resolving disputes between the successor states on these issues (this issue). The mediator is to actively support this process.

It is therefore necessary that the mediator be authorised to have access to any underlying facts and be able to appraise/evaluate these. It is less clear whether or not the mandate includes making specific recommendations for a voluntary settlement. This could be done orally or in written form. One view on this particular aspect of the role of the mediator might be that any recommendations or more affirmative acts would require the prior consent of all the parties involved.

The mediator's task is to – hopefully – seek to persuade contending parties to agree (by logic and negotiation skills and perhaps other means) by compromise. However, it is clearly not in his remit to render any decisions binding on the parties to the proceedings (in other words it is a mediation process and not an arbitration process). This does not preclude, of course, that the parties enter into an agreement by themselves with his help.

In order to proceed in this regard, three questions may be relevant: What is the nature of the process called the Basel process and could there be any help/insights from this process? What do the current negotiating parties expect from the mediator? Are there key concerns in terms of procedural aspects for the envisaged negotiation procedures?[68]

A2 The Basel process specified

The exact role of the BIS by 'assisting' the successor states of the former SRFY in resolving this issue is less than clear. The phraseology 'assisting the parties involved to negotiate their own agreement acceptable to all of them' appears to be a statement which is acceptable to all five countries.[69]

Obviously the role should be impartial/neutral. Neutrality in this process might easily be questioned if the mediator were to take a position or support only one of several points of view. On the other hand, taking a position might help the negotiation process.

Also it is quite obvious that the role is one of mediation[70] as it is in the end the five successor states that have to come to an understanding and

[68] Negotiation procedures have not been agreed upon, but one can assume that these are to follow essentially the same principles which led to the Vienna Agreement.

[69] See letter of Sir Arthur Watts, Office of the High Representative, addressed to Mr. André Icard, Deputy General Manager, Bank for International Settlements, Basel, dated 29 June 2001. The representatives of the five successor states signed this letter.

[70] Mediation is a process whereby a neutral person, the mediator, assists the parties in reaching a mutually acceptable resolution to their dispute. The mediator

agreement on this issue.[71] Mediation should certainly comprise fact-finding, but it is less clear whether assistance might also include a more proactive role (e.g. recommendations/proposals/innovative resolution) of the mediator. The American Arbitration Association, for example, notes as one of the advantages of mediation that the mediator, as a neutral third party, can view the dispute objectively and can assist the parties in exploring alternatives which they might not have considered on their own.

One crucial issue is not to violate the equality of treatment in argumentative positions or in procedural aspects. There is thus a very strong prior presumption that the process itself has to be transparent for the five successor states involved. This means e.g. that any relevant information is distributed to all parties at the same time. It is less clear whether or not and to what extent the five countries involved are also looking for a more proactive role of the mediator. It appears that any initiatives taken by him which go beyond procedural aspect should have the (implicit[72] or) explicit agreement of the five states involved. One crucial element in this regard is the trust and confidence placed in the mediator and those acting (even if only indirectly) on his behalf.

Breathing life into the above considerations (that is 'under the auspices of the BIS') the BIS has asked the former president of the Swiss National Bank to function as financial expert; the BIS provides logistical support.[73] The persons chosen as mediators have a judicial temperament and patience. They are respected in the international financial community for their integrity and have a commitment to resolving this dispute.

A3 Expectation of the negotiating parties

The Vienna Agreement has made it quite clear that succession of state issues are a question of government policy. For the issue at hand – which was treated in the Vienna Agreement – the parties have implicitly agreed that the resolution and treatment of the issues is a question of government policy. Further negotiations on HCS guarantees do not involve the decision

---

does not have the authority to make a binding decision, unlike arbitration, where the arbitrator renders a decision that is final and binding (see the website of the American Arbitration Association, www.adr.org)

71 This is not an arbitration process as such a process – whether voluntary or involuntary – results in a binding agreement imposed upon the parties involved.

72 For example, if the reaction time to some proposal is fixed at one month, a 'no response' may imply implicit agreement.

73 The financial expert is Hans Meyer, the former president of the Swiss National Bank. Elmar B. Koch of the BIS assists in this process and provides logistical support.

of the central banks but the governments of the five successor states.[74] The BIS accepts that any potential agreements with regard to Annex C, Article 7 of the Vienna Agreement are a question of government policy. Governments are sovereign.

It is further assumed that the Vienna Agreement is also applicable by analogy to any agreement that may be struck with regard to Annex C, Article 7 under the auspices of the BIS.

A3.1 The Basel process and current negotiations under the Vienna Agreement on succession issues, Annex C, Article 7

The Basel process does not lead immediately to any kind of final agreement of the participating parties, nor are the standards/principles or rules discussed in Basel binding upon the negotiating parties. It is up to each individual country to introduce the relevant legislation in this regard. One crucial element of this process is peer pressure. Countries may also adhere to certain principles without having a more formal legislative process.

Czaplinski (1999) discusses the notion of agreement under general international law. He notes that it is disputable whether a general duty to negotiate and more so to conclude a specific agreement exists under general international law. However, on numerous occasions the Hague Courts have expressed the opinion that the duty to negotiate consists exclusively of the obligation to enter into direct exchange of ideas in good faith; the states involved should conduct their talks with a view to concluding an agreement based on equitable premises. This does not mean that the duty to negotiate automatically amounts to *pactum de contrahendo*.[75]

A3.2 Are some other legal aspects relevant before negotiations?

It is probably a mute point to speculate why individuals or other entities whose savings deposits were frozen at that time were unable to take the commercial banks to court. Up until now it has not been established what the guarantee of the savings deposits of the former SFRY implies today. It appears to some extent logical that it was thus far from clear to whom such a claim should be addressed. Article 8 of the Vienna Agreement at least establishes the principle of a potential claim:

---

[74] Even if one assumes an agreement on how to treat the guarantees of the savings deposits, each individual successor state will decide on its own how such a potential agreement is to be implemented. (This is in analogy to Article 5 (4) of the Vienna Agreement: 'The procedure…shall in no circumstances permit the expert to determine the practical application of any of those agreements. …')

[75] See Czaplinski (1999), p. 70.

> 'Each successor State, on the basis of reciprocity, shall take the necessary measures in accordance with its internal law to ensure that the provisions of the Agreement are recognised and effective in its courts, administrative tribunals and agencies, and that the other successor States and their nationals have access to those courts, tribunals and agencies to secure the implementation of this Agreement.'

At this point, however, Annex C, Article 7 is under discussion and it appears that only after an agreement on the resolution of this article will potential claimants be a step closer to pursuing their claims in court. A lot will therefore depend on the nature of the potential agreement struck.

It appears that in a court case in Slovenia, where an individual attempted to sue the Ljubljanska Banka in order to restitute the HCS deposits, it was claimed that legally a 'new' Ljubljanska Banka was created under Slovenian law and that this new Slovenian bank was a new entity which was legally different from the 'old' Ljubljanska Banka. Thus legally Ljubljanska Banka could not be sued. Furthermore, the HCS of that time had been hived off to a special entity and these deposits would remain frozen until an intergovernmental agreement between the successor states (discussed here) had been struck.[76]

A4 Procedural aspects

The mediator appointed by the BIS has asked the successor states to state their position with regard to Annex C, Article 7. A letter to this effect was sent to the successor states on 25 July requesting them to state their positions by the end of September 2001.[77] This letter was sent to the responsible minister of foreign affairs in the five successor countries on 25 July 2001 with a request to respond by the end of September 2001. By 26 October 2001 all five successor states had responded.

The mediator shall fix the date and time for the mediation session(s). The sessions may be held at a location which is convenient to the parties and the mediator. As the BIS in Basel provides adequate meeting facilities, a first meeting is to take place in Basel.

The mediator may require any successor state to supply additional information. This additional information is to be supplied at the latest within 1 month of the request.

---

[76] This might imply that such a legal claim would have some success in future.

[77] The time allotted for a first response is more than 2 months, perhaps more time than usually allowed due to the summer vacation period during that time of the year.

The mediator is authorised to conduct joint and separate meetings with any of the successor states and, when requested, to make oral and written recommendations for the resolution of the dispute. There will be no official stenographic record of the mediation process.

There should be some reasonable time horizon set during which the mediation process should be concluded. The successor states may agree on such a deadline (after which time the mediation process might be considered as having failed).

A4.1 Confidentiality

The process of compromise relies heavily on open discussions within the group concerned, and the proceedings of those discussions are often quite confidential. The presumption is that we shall only have a frank and sincere discussion if there is some guarantee of confidentiality involved. 'Compromise' is of course a very vague word and may not adequately describe the potential dilemmas which the national authorities are facing, e.g. domestic vs. international considerations, legal vs. economic or political considerations, etc.

Obviously, different groups meeting in the BIS attach different value to the confidentiality elements, as confidentiality may be somewhat in conflict with transparency requirements. Each group is, however, free to set its own disclosure parameters. Frequently the process of negotiation/power interplay/compromise is kept fairly confidential while the final 'document/agreement' is subsequently released (i.e. will be in the public domain). In this regard is may be useful to have some guidance with regard to dealing with the press.

The mediator shall not divulge confidential information disclosed by the successor states. The submissions are thus kept in a confidential file within the BIS Registry. However, in the attached note some quotes were taken from the submission to the mediator which were considered helpful in the forthcoming negotiations. It is assumed that the note is for the time being considered restricted[78] as well and that negotiations will take place 'behind closed doors'. It is probably also essential to the negotiation process that the representatives of each successor state keep any information exchanged during the negotiation process confidential, i.e. that they not divulge information to outside sources.

It appears that only if confidentiality can be assured individual parties will be willing to speak freely and to settle without losing face. It should be borne clearly in mind that all negotiators will in the end have to take the

[78] As stated earlier, this note is not aimed at proposing specific solutions but serves as background to the ensuing discussions.

results home and defend their agreement in their own country and potentially also on their own political platform. It is also understood that the appointed negotiators will keep in close contact with their own governments.

Annex 3

Box 1. Frozen foreign-currency deposits

At the time of the dissolution of the former Socialist Republic of Yugoslavia (SFRY), commercial banks in FYRM had significant claims on the SFRY National Bank, both from foreign exchange actually redeposited with the SFRY National Bank and for exchange rate losses against which the SFRY National Bank had guaranteed the commercial banks. As of December 1999, outstanding foreign exchange deposits were DM 1.1 billion, equivalent to about 17.5% of GDP, reduced by payment transactions from the original stock of CA. DM 1.7 billion as of April 1992.

After the dissolution of SFRY, the FYRM passed a law on the 'guarantee of the Republic of Macedonia of foreign exchange deposits of citizens.' This law effectively froze the foreign currency deposits of Macedonian citizens, as these deposits could be used only for the limited payments specified in the law. The law provides that the FYRM guarantees the foreign exchange deposits of its citizens with the National Bank of the SFRY. The law also determines that, as guarantor, the FYRM provides banks with foreign or local currency for the purpose of repaying citizens' foreign exchange deposits. Under the law, the deposits accrue interest and commercial banks are currently permitted to pay local currency to depositors, up to the specified amounts, for some limited purposes specified in the law; commercial banks may also provide foreign exchange to depositors for certain kinds of limited payments abroad. However, no other payments or transfers are permitted to be made with the foreign-currency deposits guaranteed by the FYRM.

The government is currently preparing a new draft law to address the issue of servicing frozen foreign deposits within a fiscally sustainable framework.

Source: Drummond, Paulo p. 6.

Box 2. Frozen foreign-currency deposits

In 1991, the Yugoslav government suspended withdrawals from households' foreign exchange balances with domestic banks. The deposits were redeposited with the NBY, whose foreign reserves were run down. A 1998 law converted the deposits into public debt, capitalised the interest (based on a government-set interest rate of 2% per annum) and established an ambitious repayment schedule for these deposits, without giving due consideration to the fiscal implications. The total public debt assumed by this law amounted to DM 7.4 billion, which is equivalent to 35% of GDP in 2001. Based on this law, the repayment started in 2000 and the federal government issued a decree in January 2001 on two special state bonds to be issued to the holders of such deposits.

The servicing of these bonds would have placed a heavy burden on the budget starting in 2005. With a view to alleviating these pressures, the federal and Serbian governments have decided to modify the original repayment schedule to ensure that annual payments will be limited to no more than 0.9% of projected GDP in 2005–2011 on average under the original repayment schedule. In light of uncertainty about the overall size of the obligation – as indicated by the limited withdrawals in 2000 and so far in 2001 – the government will issue bonds only up to amounts corresponding to repayments of DM 10,000 per account in 2001 and will discuss with the Fund staff the revised repayment schedule for 2005 and subsequent years in the context of the second review under the stand-by arrangement.

Source: IMF Country Report, Federal Republic of Yugoslavia, June 2001.

Box 3. Frozen bank deposits

In December 1991 the government of Croatia modified the terms of certain foreign-currency deposits, effectively retroactively to 27 April 1991, and transformed them into deposits to be repaid in 20 semi-annual instalments starting 30 June 1995. These measures were taken in order to protect Croatian banks from collapse after the foreign exchange counterpart to these deposits had been blocked by the National Bank of the former SFRY. Since then, the stock of such frozen deposits has fallen considerably, partly due to the fact that banks have been permitted to reduce the deposits more rapidly at their own discretion, but mainly due to budgetary payments which still amount to about 0.75% of GDP per annum. Moreover, interest payments on these deposits have been made twice annually, and in a timely fashion. However, because the frozen balances may include revenues from current international transactions which were generated prior to the 1991 freeze, the measures give rise to an exchange rate restriction subject to approval under article VIII, 2(a) of the Fund's Articles of Agreement.

Source: IMF, Country Report, Republic of Croatia, March 2001.

Box 4. The case of Ljubljanska Banka

Before the break-up of Yugoslavia in 1991 and 1992, a large number of Croats, Bosnians and Serbs had deposited foreign exchange savings with the Ljubljan-ska Banka. Since 1992, these accounts had been inaccessible and the funds have effectively been frozen. The Slovenian parliament subsequently passed legislation establishing relations between the old and the new Ljubljanska Banka. The new bank has not taken over the old bank's obligations. The old bank now only existed in order to fulfil its sole function of the administrative management of accounts. All account holders with the old bank who were resi-dent in Slovenia had received compensation; however, nothing had been done for those who lived abroad and had held accounts at the branches of Ljubljan-ska Banka outside Slovenia, for example in Zagreb or Sarajevo. It appears that 130,000 Croats with deposits totalling DM 300 million and 165,000 Bosnians with assets totalling DM 276 million were affected. They had deposited their money in foreign currency. The names of those concerned and the amounts they had deposited are known.

It is not clear what happened to these deposits. Presumably all or part of it was channelled to Ljubljanska Bank's main seat in Ljubljana or perhaps some funds may have remained in Belgrade as the deposits were redeposited there?

Source: Account based on minutes of the Committee on Legal Affairs and Human Rights, Strasbourg, 24 January 2000.

Appendix 1

A1 Legislation of the Socialist Federal Republic of Yugoslavia

The *Law on Contractual Relations* (Official Gazette of the SFRY – hereinafter 'OG SFRY' – nos. 29/78 and 39/85). The following provisions are relevant:

Article 1035:

1 A contract on a monetary deposit is concluded when the bank obliges itself to accept and the depositor obliges himself or herself to deposit in the bank a certain amount of money.
2 By this contract the bank has the right to dispose of the deposited money and the obligation to return it in accordance with conditions determined in the contract.

Article 1038 paragraph 2:

'Unless otherwise agreed, ...the depositor has the right to dispose of the whole or a part of the balance [of the deposit] at any moment.'

The *Law on Foreign Exchange Transactions* (OG SFRY no. 66/85; last amendment in OG SFRY no. 96/91) regulated the foreign-currency deposits. The relevant provisions, as amended, stated:

Article 14:

1 Domestic natural and legal persons may keep foreign currency in a foreign-currency savings account or foreign currency savings deposit at an authorised bank and use it for making payments abroad, in accordance with the provisions of this law.

...

3 The foreign currency on foreign currency savings accounts or foreign currency savings deposits are guaranteed for by the SFRY.

Article 71:

1 Domestic natural persons may sell convertible currencies to an authorised bank or other authorised exchange office or they may deposit them in a foreign-currency savings account or foreign-currency savings deposit with an authorised bank.
2 Foreign currency kept in a foreign currency savings account or a foreign currency savings deposit may be used by domestic natural persons for payment of imported goods or services for his or

her personal needs and the needs of close family members in accordance with the federal law governing foreign trade operations.

...

4 Foreign currency referred to in paragraph 2 of this article may be used by domestic natural persons for the purchase of convertible bonds, for endowments for scientific and humanitarian purposes in Yugoslavia and for payment of a life insurance policy with an insurance company in Yugoslavia.
5 The National Bank of Yugoslavia shall regulate the operation of foreign-currency savings accounts and foreign-currency savings deposits of domestic and foreign natural persons.

Article 103:

1 The National Bank of Yugoslavia is obliged, following a request from an authorised bank, to receive into deposit foreign-currency funds which have effectively been deposited by domestic and foreign natural persons in foreign-currency savings accounts or foreign-currency savings deposits after the entry into force of this law.
2 The methods and conditions for the deposition and withdrawal of foreign currency at the deposit of the National Bank of Yugoslavia shall be regulated by the Federal Executive Council on the proposal of the National Bank of Yugoslavia.

A *Decision on Methods and Conditions for the Deposition and Withdrawal of Citizens' Foreign Currency at the Deposit of the National Bank of Yugoslavia* (OG SFRY no. 73/85) was issued in accordance with Article 103. Paragraph 5 of the decision provided:

1 On the basis of the deposited foreign currency…the national banks shall authorise credits to banks in dinars in an amount equal to the deposited foreign currency, which shall be established on the basis of the average daily exchange rate applicable at the end of the respective month when the foreign currency is deposited.
2 When withdrawing foreign currency from the deposit, the bank is obliged to repay the national bank the used dinar credit in an amount equal to the amount of foreign currency withdrawn from the deposit, which shall be established on the basis of the exchange rate as applied when the same foreign currency was deposited.'

On the basis of Article 71 of the Law on Foreign Exchange Transactions, a Decision Regulating the Operation of Foreign Currency Savings Deposits of Domestic and Foreign Natural Persons was promulgated on 25 January

1991 (OG SFRY no. 6/91). Paragraph 8 of the decision confirmed the purposes for which foreign currency could be used, as prescribed in the amended Article 71. Paragraph 10 of the Decision added the following:

> Domestic natural persons may withdraw from their accounts foreign money, cheques and letters of credit for travelling to a foreign country in accordance with applicable regulations.

The 1991 decision was amended on 25 April and 16 May 1991 (OG SFRY nos. 30/91 and 36/91) by the addition of certain provisions, of which paragraph 17c established the following rules on advance announcement of withdrawals:

> 'Authorised banks shall execute orders to pay to domestic natural persons foreign currency deposited in their foreign-currency accounts...if such persons previously announced to the authorised banks, within the following time limits, that they will use foreign currency in the following amounts:
> 1. An amount not exceeding 500 German marks: within 15 days for the first withdrawal...and within 30 days for any subsequent withdrawal...
> 2. An amount not exceeding 1,000 German marks: within 30 days for the first withdrawal...and within 45 days for any subsequent withdrawal...
> 3. An amount not exceeding 3,000 German marks: within 90 days; and
> 4. An amount not exceeding 8,000 German marks: within 180 days.'

The *Law on Banks and Other Financial Institutions*, published on 17 February 1989 (OG SFRY no. 10/89), provided, *inter alia*, the following:

Article 1 paragraph 1:

> 'A bank is an independent self-governing financial institution which administers deposits, credits and other banking business in accordance with the law.'

Article 2:

> 1 A bank conducts its activities independently with a view to making profit based on the principles of liquidity, security and profitability.
> 2 Banks and other financial institutions are holders of all rights, obligations and responsibilities in legal payment operations with respect to both social and other funds at their disposal which they use in accordance with the nature and purpose of financial funds.

3 Banks and other financial institutions decide independently on the manner and form of organisation and association as well as on their activities in accordance with market conditions and profit-making, pursuant to the provisions of this and other laws.

Article 61:

The liability of banks shall be settled out of the bankruptcy estate in the following order:

1 Claims of individuals;
2 Claims of the National Bank of Yugoslavia, the SFRY and other creditors who are not the founders of the bank;
3 Claims of the founders of the bank.'

Selected references

Aldrich, George H. (1996): "The Jurisprudence of the Iran-United States Claims Tribunal", Oxford University Press.

American Arbitration Association (AAA) website: www.adr.org.

Czaplinski, Wladyslaw (1999): "Equity and equitable principles in the law of state succession", in Succession of States, ed. by Mojmir Mrak, Martinus Nijhoff Publishers, The Hague, London, Boston.

Circuvic, Milutin and Srboljub Jovic (1985): "Savings of Households in Yugoslavia", in Financial and Banking System of Yugoslavia, ed. Milutin Circovic and Negoslav Ostojic, Research Centre for Cooperation with Developing Countries, RCCDC, Ljubljana, Yugoslavia.

Council of Europe, Minutes of the Committee on Legal Affairs and Human Rights, Strasbourg, 24 January 2000.

Drummond, Paolo (2000): "Former Yugoslav Republic of Macedonia – Banking Soundness and Recent Lessons". IMF, Working Paper/00/145.

Economic Commission for Europe (UN): "Economic Survey of Europe", 2001, No. 1 (pp. 97–101 "Reforming Yugoslavia's economy").

European Commission (2000): "Slovenia's progress towards accession (Slovenia 2000)", 8 November 2000 (http://europa.eu.int/comm/engargement).

Human Rights Chamber for Bosnia and Herzegovina (2000), Decision on admissibility and merits, Case nos. CH/97/48, CH/97/52.CH/97/105, and CH/97/108 Milovan POROPAT, Senija POROPAT, Murdifa SEREMET, and Muhamed HRELJA against BOSNIA and HERZEGOVINA and the FEDERATION OF BOSNIA AND HERZEGOVINA (9 June 2000); (www.gwde.de/~ujvr/ hrch/0000-0999/0048).

IMF, Country Report 01/50 on the Republic of Croatia (March 2001).

IMF, Country Report 01/76 on the Republic of Slovenia (May 2001).

IMF, Country Report 01/93 on the Federal Republic of Yugoslavia (June 2001).

IMF, Country Report 01/106 on Bosnia and Herzegovina (July 2001).

IMF, Country Report 01/07 on the Federal Republic of Yugoslavia: Membership and Request for Emergency Postconflict Assistance – Staff Report, and Press Release on the Executive Board Discussion (January 2001).

IMF: "Exchange Arrangements and Exchange Restrictions", Several Annual Reports.

Kapstein, Ethan B. (1992): "Between power and purpose: central bankers and the politics of regulatory convergence", International Organisation 46, 1, winter 1992.

Kapstein, Ethan B. (1994): "Governing the Global Economy, International Finance and the State", Harvard University Press, Cambridge, MA, London.

Kaufman, Georg G. and Steven A. Seelig (2001): "Post-Resolution Treatment of Depositors at Failed Banks: Implications for the Severity of Banking Crises, Systemic Risk and Too-Big-To-Fail", IMF, Working Paper/01/83 IMF Country Report 01/76 on the Republic of Slovenia (May).

Mrak, Mojmir (1999): "Apportionment and Succession of External Debts: The case of the Socialist Federal Republic of Yugoslavia", Research Reports No. 259, The Vienna Institute for International Economic Studies (WIIW), August.

Petrakos, George (2001): "Fragmentation or Integration in the Balkans? Strategies of Development for the 21st Century" in The Development of the Balkan Region, ed. By George Petrakos and Stoyan Totev, Ashgate.

Petrovic, Pavle, Zeljko Bogetic and Zorica Vujosevic (1999): "The Yugoslav Hyperinflation of 1992-1994: Causes, Dynamics, and Money Supply Process", Journal of Comparative Economics 27, pp. 335–353.

Stanič, Ana (2001): "Financial Aspects of State Succession: The Case of Yugoslavia", EJIL, Vol. 12 No. 4. pp. 751–779.

Submissions received by Dr. Hans Meyer: Bosnia and Herzegovina (28 September 2001), Republic of Croatia (24 October 2001), Republic of Macedonia (28 September 2001), Republic of Slovenia (28 September 2001), Federal Republic of Yugoslavia (26 October 2001).

Trifković, Miloš (1999): "Fundamental controversies in succession to the former SFR Yugoslavia", in Succession of States ed. by Mojmir Mrak, Martinus Nijhoff Publishers, The Hague, London, Boston.

White, William R. (1999): "Evolving International Financial Markets: Some Implications for Central Banks", BIS Working Papers, No. 66, April, (www.bis.org).

World Bank (2001): "Federal Republic of Yugoslavia: Breaking with the Past: The path to stability and growth", Volume I: The Economic, Social and Institutional Reform Agenda.

8 International bank and securities financing in Africa

Improvements in Africa's macroeconomic performance and prospects have in recent years led to a modest turnaround in private capital flows to the continent (Graph 1). Privatisation, financial sector reforms and macroeconomic stabilisation programmes contributed to an increase in international investment beginning in the mid-1990s. Foreign direct investment accounted for the bulk of the increase, rising to $9 billion in 1999 from less than $2 billion annually during the first half of the 1990s. Securities financing also picked up, exceeding $1 billion in most years since 1994. Bank lending has yet to turn positive, but net repayments to banks in the BIS reporting area slowed substantially in the late 1990s.

The international financial crises of the late 1990s dampened bank and securities flows to Africa but, in contrast to Asia or Latin America, the crises did not result in a retrenchment across the board by foreign creditors. Bank lending to many smaller countries remained stable during the

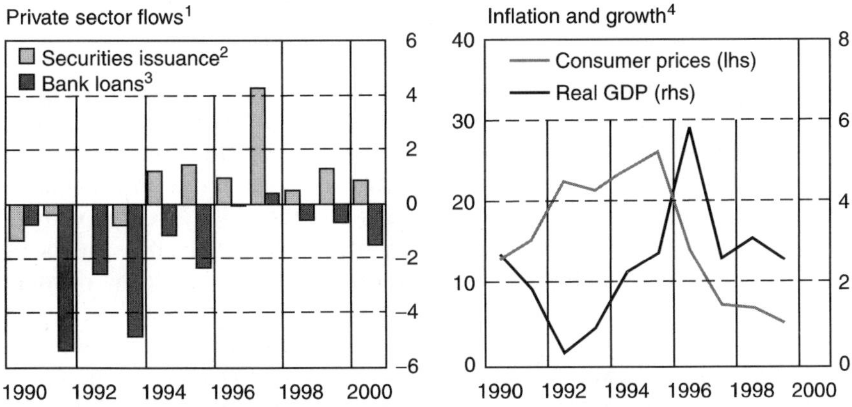

[1]In billions of US dollars. Data for 2000 refer only to the first two quarters. [2]Gross issues minus repayments. Data include money market instruments and long-term bonds and notes. [3]Exchange rate adjusted changes in cross-border bank loans. From 1990 to 1995, data include changes in banks' holdings of securities and other assets. [4]Annual percentage change.

Sources: Bank of England; Capital DATA; Euroclear; IMF; ISMA; Thomson Financial Securities Data; BIS.

Graph 1. Private sector flows, inflation and growth in Africa

Table 1. Bank credit to selected countries in Africa

	Locational banking statistics				Consolidated banking statistics			
	Loans[1]				Banks' total claims[2]	Short-term claims[3]	Claims held by[3]	
	1997	1998	1999	2000 H1			EU banks	US banks
Algeria	–2,054	–1,451	–1,148	–242	5,110	32	79	5
Cameroon	–25	–74	80	204	2,022	69	99	0
Côte d'Ivoire	40	–948	203	240	2,563	41	94	1
Egypt	628	1,138	97	446	7,222	57	66	8
Morocco	250	558	169	–85	6,886	32	76	3
Nigeria	–461	121	–76	–316	1,670	50	58	18
South Africa	1,295	–608	–959	–849	18,739	63	55	15
Tunisia	331	80	215	–138	2,855	41	78	4
Total Africa[4]	**392**	**–611**	**–676**	**–1,492**	**61,550**	**53**	**72**	**8**

[1]Exchange-rate-adjusted changes in cross-border bank loans, in millions of US dollars.
[2]Data include banks' holdings of debt securities and other assets.
[3]As a percentage of total claims.
[4]Excluding Liberia, which is grouped with offshore centres.

late 1990s, and even increased to Egypt, Morocco and several other countries (Table 1). Nevertheless, owing to significant outflows from Algeria, where political uncertainty weighed heavily on investors, and South Africa, total bank lending turned negative in 1998 and 1999 following the first year of net inflows – $0.4 billion in 1997 – in over a decade. South Africa was able to refinance a portion of its bank outflows in capital markets; indeed, the country was the only African issuer active in the internationaldebt securities market in 1998. Bond issuance by African borrowers in 1998 and 1999 was down substantially from 1997 levels, but issuance in 1997 had been abnormally high because of $3.4 billion raised by residents of Mauritius.

In the first half of 2000, net repayments to international banks accelerated sharply, with South Africa, Angola and Zimbabwe experiencing the largest cutbacks in lending. Banks in the reporting area also drastically reduced their claims on Liberia, the only offshore centre in Africa.[1] Political strife has racked Angola, Zimbabwe and countries bordering Liberia for much of this year. Bank lending to Côte d'Ivoire increased in the first

[1] Data for Liberia are not included in the graph or the table in this box.

half of the year despite uncertainty about whether the government would meet payments due on its Brady bonds. In contrast to bank lending, securities issuance by African borrowers is on track to exceed 1999 levels.

Although Africa's economic and financial weaknesses might be expected to limit its access to longer-term debt finance from private creditors, in fact maturities are not unduly concentrated at the short end. The maturity distribution of bank claims is similar to that of other developing regions: as of June 2000, 53% of banks' claims on Africa matured within 1 year, compared to 47% in the Asia-Pacific region and 49% in Latin America (Table 1). South Africa faces a heavy repayment schedule, with nearly two-thirds of its international bank debts maturing within 1 year. Morocco and Algeria, respectively the third and fourth largest bank debtors in Africa after South Africa and Egypt, have more favourable maturity profiles, with 32% of claims on them due within the next year. In the international debt securities market, African issuers tend to issue long-term bonds rather than money market instruments or other short-term securities. Nevertheless, issuers, especially those not regularly tapping markets, remain vulnerable to swings in market sentiment because payments tend to be bunched and the investor base for African securities is narrow.

As a result of strong trade and historical links, the bulk of lending and securities flows to Africa originate in Europe. The European Union accounts for nearly three-quarters of total bank claims on Africa (Table 1). France alone accounts for almost 30% of total claims, with French banks' exposure concentrated in Algeria, Morocco, Tunisia and the CFA franc zone. US banks are responsible for only 8% of all bank lending to Africa, of which more than half is to South Africa. The majority of outstanding bonds issued by African borrowers are denominated in US dollars, although South Africa is one of very few developing countries able to find a market for international debt securities issued in its own currency.

Notwithstanding the turnaround in private capital flows in the mid-1990s, Africa remains on the fringes of international banking and financial markets. The region accounts for ca. 7% of international banks' (consolidated) claims on developing countries and only 3% of the outstanding stock of international bonds and notes issued by developing country borrowers. Loans and securities flows to Africa are highly concentrated in the larger and financially more developed countries of northern and southern Africa. Moreover, aside from South African borrowers, very few other African issuers are active in international capital markets. Political uncertainty (and the consequent risk of policy reversals), high debt levels, poor payment records and underdeveloped domestic financial systems are some of the obstacles to improved market access for many African countries.

9 The aftermath of the Russian debt crisis

9.1 Introduction

In August 1998, the Russian Federation floated the rouble and declared a 90-day moratorium on its debts. The ensuing crisis led to a significant depreciation of the rouble and insolvency of most of the Russian banking system.

The basic shortcomings that led to the August 1998 moratorium included an unfavourable external environment for Russian raw material exports, especially oil and gas, as well as a range of real and financial weaknesses on the domestic side. In particular, the federal budget deficit remained high as the collection of taxes was poor and revenues could not be adjusted accordingly. The IMF and other lenders, under the impression that some monetary and price stability had been achieved, agreed in July 1998 to provide Russia with US$22.5 billion in loans to help stabilise the country's finances. After the first tranche was disbursed, the Russian government declared a moratorium on its domestic debt and prevented private sector institutions from servicing certain foreign-currency obligations, including non-deliverable forward FX contracts.[1] The rouble/dollar peg and debt prices collapsed. IMF credits were frozen, domestic banks went insolvent and foreign banks scrambled to cut their exposure (see Appendix 1: Chronology of the Russian financial crisis).

This paper assesses questions related to the debt moratorium. First, we look at the debt situation immediately following the crisis and then how payment arrears mounted. We next turn to Russia's oft-strained relations with its creditors and briefly survey the debt situation of Russian regions and cities. One commonly overlooked aspect of the Russian crisis is that Russia was and is also a creditor nation. In the sixth section, therefore, we look at Russia's financial relations with other CIS countries. Russia's default on its domestic debts and restructuring of its debt instruments are surveyed in Sect. 7. Section 8 looks at issues that surfaced in the aftermath of

---

[1] The broad macro and micro factors leading up to the crisis are described in the IMF's 'World Economic Outlook and International Capital Markets,' December (1998) and Bank for International Settlements, Annual Report, June 1999.

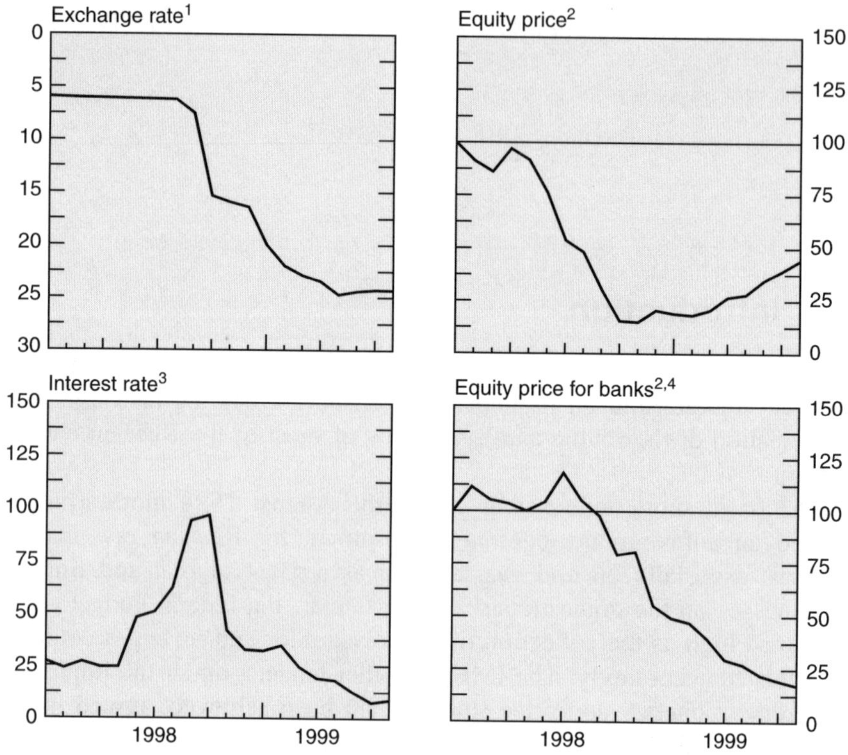

[1]Rouble/US$; inverted scale. [2]End-1997 = 100; in US dollar terms. [3]Overnight rate. [4]Relative to total index.
Sources: Datastream and national data.

Graph 1. Financial indicators in Russia

the Russian moratorium and the possible lessons for Russia learned from the Polish and Mexican experiences. The last section provides a conclusion.

9.2 Economic developments since the crisis

At the time of the Russian default, many capital-market participants viewed it as a catalytic event. It forced them to rethink the reliability of the official safety net they took for granted when purchasing emerging market debt (or at least the debt of geopolitically important countries). Moreover, it induced investors to question the willingness of major countries and international organisations to support credit-strapped sovereigns.[2] The resulting deleveraging of portfolios in autumn 1998 had a global impact.

[2] Report by a BIS Working Group of the CGFS (October 1999) on the events of the fall of 1998 (the Karen Johnson Report).

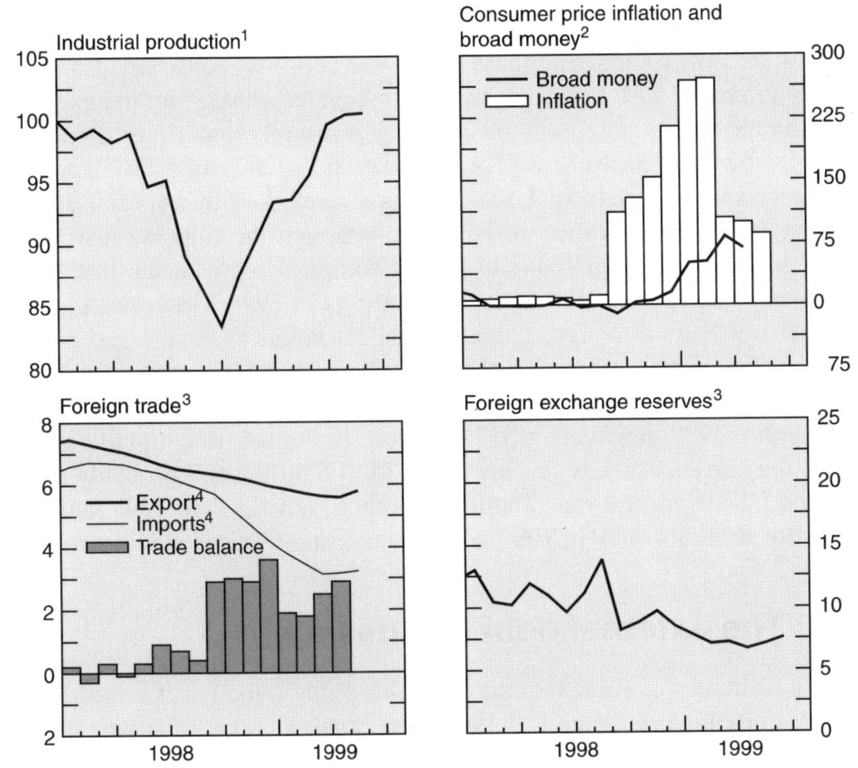

[1]End-1997 = 100. [2]Percentage change over 6 months at an annual rate. [3]In billions of US$. [4]3-month moving average; seasonally adjusted.

Sources: IMF, International Financial Statistics and national data.

Graph 2. Economic indicators in Russia

In 1999, Russia's government faced an external debt servicing obligation of around US$20 billion. Because liquid foreign exchange reserves dropped to a level of about US$7 billion, successful debt servicing had to rely on improved tax collection, higher commodity prices and/or financial support from external (official) creditors. The March–April 1999 budget plan for the same year envisaged payment of only about US$9.5 billion for principal and interest on foreign-currency-denominated debt. In addition, as the year's total debt payments equalled the entire revenue of the 1999 federal budget (US$19 billion), additional budget allocations to meet external debt payments seemed unlikely. Critically, there was no provision for payment of inherited Soviet-era debt. The budget further assumed that foreign financing would be forthcoming. In the contingency of no foreign funding, complete restructuring or default on Soviet-era debt seemed obvious outcomes.[3] Nevertheless, Russia chose not to draw on its already low reserves. Its ability and willingness to pay was seriously constrained.

By summer 1999, the stock markets recovered somewhat, the exchange rate more or less stabilised, inflationary pressure receded and fiscal balances showed improvement. Towards the end of July, the IMF approved the long-awaited credit of US$4.5 billion earmarked in a special account for payment of funds due to the IMF. Although the improvement in the trade balance was mostly due to import compression, it meant that Russia enjoyed a substantive current account surplus in 1999. However, the large capital outflows also meant that Russia's foreign exchange reserves remained low during 1999 (Graph 2). At the end of 1998, Russia's foreign exchange reserves (excluding gold) stood at US$7.8 billion. At the end of November 1999 they were US$7.6 billion. In the first three quarters of the year, the current account surplus was US$14.6 billion and probably rose to around US$18 for the year. Industrial output grew 8.1% in 1999, and forecasts for Russia's GDP in 1999 were also constantly revised upwards.

9.3 The external debt of Russia

While estimates of Russia's external debt, Table 1 likely reflects the magnitudes involved at the end of 1998. The nominal value of sovereign debt incurred after 1991 stood around US$55 billion, while Russia's outstanding debt inherited from the Soviet Union amounted to US$102 billion. This yields a total debt stock of around US$158 billion. In addition, non-sovereign debt (virtually all incurred by banks and corporations) amounted to approximately US$32 billion. (See Appendix, item 2 'Taxonomy of Russian debt instruments').

The terms of Russian moratoria on the domestic and external debt were opaque at the time they were declared on August 17. With time it became increasingly clear that around US$40 billion in domestic Treasury debt was not to be serviced[4] as well as all Soviet-era for which the 1999 budget had not made explicit provision. Thus, servicing debts outstanding to the London and Paris Clubs was skipped. Servicing of interest on some of the MinFin bonds was also skipped (see item 2 'Taxonomy of Russian debt instruments').

Technically, Russia defaulted on its Soviet-era debt to the London (commercial creditors) and Paris (sovereign creditors) Clubs some time ago. At stake were some US$35 billion owed to commercial creditors and US$40 billion owed to Paris Club countries (Table 1). The Russian government

[3] Russian Economic Trends, 13 April 1999.

[4] The amount of US$40 billion is based on the rouble/dollar exchange rate when the crisis occurred, i.e. 6.3 roubles to the dollar.

Table 1. Estimated debt stock of Russian Federation at year-end 1998, US$ billion

		Debt
Russian era	IMF	19.4
	Other IFIs	6.6
	Official creditors	9.7
	Eurobonds & MinFins	19.6
	Other	0.2
	Total	55.4
Soviet era	Paris Club	40.0[1]
	COMECON	14.7
	Other official creditors	4.7
	Commercial creditors (mainly London Club)	35.2
	MinFins	7.6
	Other	0.5
	Total	102.8
Total		**158.2**

Note: Above does not include forward contracts (estimated at around US$5–7 billion) of Russian banks. The liabilities of the former GDR (transfer rouble) amount to about US$14 billion.
[1]Of which, an estimated US$18 billion is owed to Germany.
Source: Various non-Russian sources.

missed a US$362 million Prins (see item 2 in the appendix) payment to the London Club on 2 December 1998. By June 1999, Russia had missed another payment of US$855 million, so that arrears to the London Club banks amounted to about US$1.2 billion.[5] Already in August and September of 1998, Russia skipped interest payments of DM 751.5 million and US$49.8 million due to Germany as part of the Paris Club agreements.

By mid-1999,[6] Russia was slightly over US$2 billion in arrears to the Paris Club. Because neither creditor group was ready to declare Russia

[5] Bank of Finland, Institute for Economies in Transition, Russian and Baltic Economies (BOFIT), Russian and Baltic Economies, the Week in Review, 18 June 1999.

[6] Wall Street Journal: "Russia's MinFin Default Leaves Only Eurobonds Sacred," 21 April 1999.

officially in default, Russia had some breathing room to agree on a compromise.[7] In August 1999, the Paris Club creditors agreed to postpone Russia's debt payments of some US$8 billion until the end of 2000, by which date the exact terms of restructuring would be negotiated. In February 2000 Russian Federation and the London Club creditors reached an agreement on the restructuring of Russia's debt. Under this agreement the Prins issued by Vneshekonombank would be changed to eurobonds of the Russian Federation at 37.5% of their nominal value. The IANs (item 2) will be changed to eurobonds at 33% of their nominal value. The payment terms of these eurobonds ensure that Russia will receive approx. 50% debt reduction on this part of the old Soviet debt, if at least 75% (by value) of the holders of these debt instruments accept the deal.

MinFin dollar-denominated bonds were issued to cover foreign-currency deposits frozen by Soviet banks and amount to about US$14 billion. Private Western creditors hold about US$8 billion of this total. Russia missed a US$1.3 billion payment on MinFin principal due 14 May 1999. Additionally, some US$300 million on MinFin interest was due at that time. In December 1999, the Russian government offered holders of a specific MinFin tranche (the one which Russia did not pay in May) a chance to convert their bonds into rouble-denominated four-year bonds or dollar-denominated bonds with a maturity of 2 years.

In the debt restructuring talks in Paris concerning sovereign debt, an inclusion of MinFin bonds[8] may be one way for the private sector to be included in the adjustment costs (see section on bailing-in) as a large portion of MinFins are held by institutional private investors.

On 10 June 1999, Russia did meet an interest payment of US$73 million on its eurobond series maturing in 2003 (Table 2), and the Russian Federation has been current on its interest payments on eurobonds ever since. While Fitch IBCA and Standard and Poor's warned in mid-January that Russia's deteriorating finances threatened its ability to service its post-1992 eurobonds,[9] the Russian Federation has so far diligently serviced its eurobonds. This approach clearly stressed the difference between the old Soviet debt and debts incurred by the Russian Federation. The schedule of eurobond interest payments is displayed in Table 2. However, one prominent financial group, Uneximbank and the Rossiisky Kredit bank, have missed the latest payment on their eurobonds.

---

7 See Financial Times, 25 January 1999.

8 BOFIT, Russian and Baltic Economies, the Week in Review, 16, 23 April 1999.

9 See Financial Times, 14 January 1999.

Table 2. Russian eurobond amounts and interest payments as of June 1999,[1] (US$ million)

Issuer	Amount	Due	Payment dates	1999	Next payment[2]
Central government					
Russian Federation	1000	2001	27 Nov	27 May	46
Russian Federation	1250	2003	10 Jun	10 Dec	73
Russian Federation	2500	2028	24 Jun	24 Dec	159
Russian Federation	2969	2005	24 Jul	24 Jan	130
Russian Federation	3467	2018	24 Jul	24 Jan	191
Russian Federation[3]	1069	2004	25 Mar		95
Russian Federation[3]	668	2005	31 Mar		63
Russian Federation[4]	405	2003	30 Apr		36
Russian Federation	2400	2007	26 Jun		240
Local government					
City of Moscow	500	2000	30 Nov	31 May	24
City of St. Petersburg	300	2002	18 Jun	18 Dec	14
Region of Nizhny Novgorod	100	2002	3 Oct	3 Apr	4
City of Moscow[3]	267	2001	9 Apr		24
City of Moscow[4]	216	2001	18 May		21
Banks					
Vneshtorgbank	200	1999	26 Jun	26 Sep	4
Alfabank	175	2000	28 Jul	28 Jan	9
Uneximbank[5]	250	2000	1 Aug	1 Feb	12
Rossiisky Kredit[5]	200	2000	29 Sep	29 Mar	10
SBS-Agro	250	2000	21 Jul		26

Table 2. continue

Issuer	Amount	Due	Payment dates	1999			Next payment[2]
Companies							
Sibneft	150	2000	15 Aug	15 Nov	15 Feb	15 May	3
MGTS	150	2001	19 Sep	19 Mar			9
Lukoil	230	2002	6 Apr				8
Mosenergo	200	2002	9 Oct	9 Apr			8
Irkutskenergo[3]	67	2001	20 Apr				8
Tatneft	300	2002	29 Oct	29 Apr			14
LUKoil	350	2003	3 Nov				4

[1]Including eurobonds held by residents.
[2]Amount due.
[3]DM-denominated bond, valued at current exchange rate.
[4]Italian lira-denominated bond, valued at current exchange rate.
[5]Restructuring, missed most recent payment.
Source: IIF; Russian Federation Economic Report, 11 June 1999.

9.4 Russia's relations with its creditors

9.4.1 Russia and the IMF

Russia is one of the largest debtors of the IMF, owing US$15.9 billion at the end of November 1999 or about one-fifth of the IMF's outstanding loans.[10] Payments due in 1999 were US$4.3 billion, but the net payments are smaller, because Russia also received money from the IMF in 1999. Russia had to pay about US$300 million to the IMF each month except in July when payments jumped to more than US$1 billion.[11] Since IMF loans cannot be rescheduled, receiving new credits to pay for old ones is one way to stay current on one's payments to the IMF. The new end-July 1999 IMF agreement hinged on a wide range of measures, while moral hazard for the IMF was great. This time, the new stand-by credit was clearly earmarked for repayment to the IMF and the money was kept in a special escrow account in Washington. Now, partly thanks to higher oil prices, the Russian government has been able to service its debts to the IMF (and to the World Bank) despite the fact that the IMF has withheld the remaining tranches of the July debt program.

[10] Russia's IMF quota is about US$8 billion.
[11] Wall Street Journal, 23 February 1999.

Table 3. Some of the IMF's requested prior actions

1. Increasing budget revenues
   - Postpone VAT cut from 20% to 15%
   - Raise taxes on alcoholic beverages
   - Introduce taxes on luxury cars and gasoline stations
   - Enforce better tax collection from large oil companies
2. Bank restructuring
   - Pass bank restructuring and bankruptcy legislation
   - Strengthen ARCO (agent for bank restructuring)
   - Withdraw licences of banks to be liquidated
   - Authorise the CBR to issue its own debt paper
3. Foreign exchange restrictions
   - Abolish the two-tier foreign currency market
   - Lift restrictions on foreign bank participation in the foreign exchange market

Source: BOFIT, June 1999.

The IMF thus attempted this time in its negotiations from March through July 1999 to set rigorous terms (conditionality) on the release of funds to Russia. Disbursement was contingent on Russian actions that included tax hikes, a new bank restructuring law, relaxation of foreign exchange restrictions (Table 3) and a special audit of the foreign reserve management of the Central Bank of Russia (CBR). By mid-July 1999, Russia had made substantial progress on most of these conditions, thereby moving closer to an IMF agreement.[12] At end-July, the IMF concluded Article IV consultations with Russia.[13]

Like many countries subject to debt negotiations, Russia's new agreement with the IMF was critical in multiple respects.[14] The agreement unlocked funds from other official lenders (the World Bank and Japan) and allowed Russia to reschedule payments on its Soviet-era debts. The Paris

[12] For a status review, see JP Morgan (1999) and BOFIT, June 1999. For example, on 17 June the Duma rejected a draft law that would have imposed a new tax on gasoline stations.

[13] IMF, Public Information Notice No. 99/67 (IMF concludes article IV consultations with Russia). By end-September 1999, several structural benchmarks remain to be completed (IMF, News Brief No. 99181, December 7, 1999).

[14] See Group of Ten (1996), p. 23.

Club and the London Club both made the IMF agreement a precondition for negotiations on debt rescheduling.

In general, if IMF participation increases the expected value of any existing official or private debt contract, lenders benefit. This externality effect of the IMF's role not only benefits the borrower but also the rational lender as the probability of default on the external debt is reduced. While this may be true in general, however, the evidence for Russia is difficult to assess. The difficulty lies in the fact that markets invariably assess the likelihood and size of a forthcoming IMF agreement over time. The final IMF agreement is thus only one point of a sequence of events. This time sequence appears particularly difficult to assess for Russia because the conditions attached to the IMF loan were more stringent than usual and the preconditions had to be met over an extended period of negotiations with the IMF.

9.4.2 Russia and the Paris Club

The Paris Club took the lead in debt restructuring. While the G-8 meeting in late June 1999 urged the Paris Club to start renegotiations quickly, the G-8 had failed to agree on a firm commitment for an outright write-down of Russia's inherited Soviet-era debt.

In the run-up to the agreement with the Paris Club of 3 August 1999, payments to the Paris Club were stalled, as Russia was in arrears (see above). The total debt to the Paris Club countries is US$40 billion of which US$18 billion is owed to Germany (Table 1). There were some early indications that the main creditors, particularly Germany, would not agree to a general write-off of the Paris Club debt,[15] even though the official attitude appeared to have softened. This attitude was essentially conditioned by the basic principle of *pacta sunt servanda* – a deal's a deal. Debt forgiveness is warranted only in exceptional circumstances. It appears that the United States may have taken a somewhat more lenient approach to official debt forgiveness to Russia, partly perhaps prompted by the country's relatively small exposure to Russia and perhaps partly influenced by more global geopolitical considerations. On the other hand, Russia itself initially proposed a 75% reduction of its official debt.[16] However, Russian officials at the June 1999 G-8 meeting seemed to indicate that they were no longer demanding an outright write-down of this magnitude. Both sides appeared to be ready for compromise. If precedents for Poland and Egypt were any indication, debt reduction of up to 50% should have been possible. At any

[15] BOFIT, 24 June 1999: "Germany, Russia's biggest creditor, firmly opposes Russian proposals for forgiveness on Soviet-era debt."

[16] Financial Times, 22 April 1999.

rate, it is clear that Russia expected a far-reaching restructuring of its Soviet-era debt. Possible compromises may include willingness on the part of creditors to accept partial payment in goods. Russia reportedly also proposed that some of the debt to the Paris Club be 'exchanged' for some of its outstanding claims on other countries, which the Soviet Union had accumulated and which were subsequently inherited by Russia.[17]

One issue in the run-up to the debt renegotiations within the Paris Club was whether or not outstanding eurobonds should be part of the rescheduling of debts Russia owes. Not surprisingly, bondholders objected vehemently.[18] As long as this threat reigned, the value of eurobonds plummeted. However, by July 1999 it had become clear that the Paris Club would not allow Russia to restructure its post-Soviet dollar eurobonds.

Now the Paris Club has begun to insist on the principle of burden sharing between private and public creditors. This consensus seems fairly broad and firm, but the question on how to achieve this in a fair and equitable way for all players without creating undue volatility in the markets appears less settled. The Paris Club recently also appears to have required that Pakistan and Turkey include eurobonds in their debt restructuring, but as yet no eurobonds have been officially included in any country's restructuring.[19]

Traditionally, negotiations with the Paris Club only start after a loan agreement with the IMF. The Russian case was no exception. As the Paris Club is only a secretariat without legal power or the resources to conduct an independent economic assessment of a country, the current assumption of a valid agreement between Russia and the IMF as a precondition for entering Paris Club negotiations is an accepted part of debt restructuring.

Paris Club rules are differentiated and tailored to individual countries while respecting the principle of fair and equal treatment. There is no automatic mechanism for being included under Paris Club rules as the whole procedure violates the principle of *pacta sunt servanda*. Initially, the Paris Club dealt with low-income, highly indebted economies. The Houston terms of 1990 subsequently also allowed lower middle-income countries to be considered for restructuring. Egypt and Poland were lower middle-income countries when their debt was restructured. Russia falls into this income category.

In principle, Russia also had to meet two further requirements to be eligible for a Paris Club rescheduling. One requirement was that Russia would default on its external obligations in the absence of relief. One indicator of this condition is, for example, the existence of substantial external

[17] See Buch et al. (1999), p. 19 where the claims of the former Soviet Union are assessed as essentially worthless (Section 6).

[18] Financial Times, 22 March 1999.

[19] A more in-depth discussion of these issues is found in the section on bailing-in.

payment arrears. This situation is sometimes labelled 'imminent default.'[20] As shown above, willingness apart, Russia was *de facto* in a situation of 'imminent default'. The second requirement is that before proceeding to the Paris Club debt rescheduling negotiations, the debtor must have first accepted an economic adjustment program with the IMF.

There was also the lingering question as to how Russia's position as 'creditor' nation might affect its eligibility as debtor in the Paris Club and the ensuing negotiation position. While this situation is unusual (being both a debtor and creditor at the same time), this position does not appear to have a direct bearing on eligibility to the Paris Club renegotiation process. However, as indicated earlier in this paper, Russia may have wanted to offer some credits of the other former Soviet Union countries as payment of its debt. However, as indicated later in this paper, Russia as a creditor nation may have to renegotiate some of its agreements with former Soviet Union countries depending on the outcome of the negotiations with its own Paris Club creditors. If forgiveness had been part of the Paris agreement, Russia could have been asked to pass on some of these benefits to its debtor countries.

In the event, Russia and the Paris Club agreed to reschedule roughly US$8 billion of arrears of Soviet-era debt falling due between August 1998 and the end of 2000. The US$8 billion would be repaid over 15 to 20 years. Discussions about the final fate of this debt would start in the autumn of 2000.[21]

9.4.3 Russia and London Club

After the debt moratorium the Russian Federation negotiated with the private creditors represented by the London Club on the restructuring of Prins ('principal notes', see item 2) and IANs ('interest arrears notes'). Russia demanded partial debt forgiveness and offered in exchange to upgrade the remaining debt into sovereign eurobonds. Previously, these debt instruments were liabilities of the state-owned foreign payment agent Vnesheko-nombank. The situation was further complicated by the fact that the ownership of the debt securities is quite dispersed, making an agreement more difficult to reach. However, in February 2000 the negotiators did reach a preliminary agreement, which would reduce the value of old Soviet debt by approx. 50%, if accepted by at least 75% of the bondholders. As a part of the deal, the debt of Vneshekonombank will be exchanged for eurobonds of the Russian Federation. This deal means that private creditors are forced

[20] See, for example, Hackney and Shafer (1986), p. 479.
[21] Financial Times and Wall Street Journal, 3 August 1999.

to bear some burden of Russia's debt restructuring and will most probably pave way for a roughly similar deal with the Paris Club.

9.5 The debt situation in regions and cities

Russia's regions are also facing difficulties in paying their foreign loans. The immediate cause of these difficulties is the depreciation of the rouble, rather than excessive indebtedness. Tatarstan defaulted on its eurobonds in October 1998 and its regionally administered oil company, Tatneft, also ran into problems. In April 1999, the city of Moscow announced that it would seek restructuring of its foreign loans. The Leningrad region narrowly avoided default on an interest payment by announcing that it had negotiated a restructuring of its entire US$50 million syndicated loan. Only after considerable effort did Nizhny Novgorod region manage to make timely repayment of interest on its eurobonds in April 1999, and in October of the same year it failed to make a US$100 million interest payment. Subsequently, the loan was restructured. Numerous other Russian regions are currently in talks on restructuring their loans. Regions also presently do not service a considerable share of their domestic borrowing.[22]

9.6 Russia as creditor nation

By mid-1998, all former Soviet Union states, except the Baltics, were debtors to Russia (Table 4). These debts stemmed from credits extended by the CBR to these states after 1992. Most of these countries also ran trade deficits vis-à-vis Russia.[23] Belarus, Ukraine and Moldova, in particular, received large credits for energy (mainly natural gas) supplied. These debts can be repaid by delivery of goods, shares in industry (or other financial asset transfers) as well as in roubles or freely convertible currencies. As some countries were unable to pay, Russia agreed to restructure their debts. However, among these countries the principle also holds that new credits are only granted if the country is current on its service obligations.

In addition to the CIS countries, Russia is still a creditor to Cuba, Vietnam and many African countries. The Soviet Union extended credits to these countries, and their restructuring talks began in the Paris Club when Soviet-era debts were first restructured.

---

[22] BOFIT, Russian and Baltic Economies, The Week in Review, 14 May 1999.

[23] This section relies heavily on information reported by Surubovic and Usakova (1999). It only deals with the former Soviet Union and not with former CMEA countries or other economies.

Table 4. Debt of former Soviet Union states to Russia as of mid-1998, US$ million

	Total debt	Of which overdue:	
		Principal	Interest
Armenia	95	0.1	1
Azerbaijan	96	43	14
Belarus	54	–	1
Georgia	181	–	0.2
Kazakhstan	1720	568	380
Kyrgyz Republic	154	–	20
Moldova	100	30	6
Tajikistan	301	–	11
Turkmenistan	150	146	–
Ukraine	2042	111	1
Uzbekistan	538	–	33
Total	**5432**	**898**	**465**

Source: Surubovic and Usakova (1999).

A restructuring agreement was signed with Kyrgyz Republic in 1996 in the amount of US$128 million to be paid back from year 2000 to 2009 with 10% due each year. At the beginning of 1997, Russia and Georgia agreed that the repayment of US$179 million was to occur in equal instalments over the 6-year period from 2000 to 2005. Similar agreements also exist with Armenia, Moldova, Ukraine and Uzbekistan. A zero-repayment agreement was signed between Russia and Belarus in February 1996.

While the Russian policies towards other former Soviet states may be considered quite generous, they appear to be in the longer-term interest of Russia and do not imply debt forgiveness. As payment of debt is often not of a monetary nature, they are usually not considered an important factor in boosting Russian reserves.

Debt forgiveness or the reduction in the former Soviet debt may, however, raise the issue of the old Soviet (net) debt between Russia and other former Soviet Republics. At the time of the break-up of the Soviet Union, Russia inherited all the assets and liabilities of the former Soviet Union. This agreement was based on an understanding that assets and liabilities were netted, which implied that the assets (e.g. embassy buildings abroad) were also transferred to Russia. If Soviet-era debt is to be reduced (as now seems probable), there may be grounds for other former Soviet republics to reopen negotiations on this agreement, for example, on recovering assets on a *pro rata* basis.[24]

9.7 Payment on domestic debt

In August 1998 Russia declared a payment freeze on about US$40 billion of GKO/OFZs, of which around US$13–15 billion were held by foreigners. The initial Russian offer to restructure these instruments in November 1998 was for around 4 cents on the dollar.[25] While the initial offer was for around US$550 million, the last offer amounted to around US$200 million. This latter amount was to be paid in equity.[26] A subsequent new offer was even lower at around 1.5 cents on the dollar.[27] The unilateral decision by several foreign banks to accept the Russian restructuring proposals of November 1998 rendered a coordinated effort to seek improved terms unlikely.[28] By April, some 90% of Russian and 40% of foreign holders of GKOs and OFZs had agreed to the restructuring package where they received 10% of the face value of the bonds in cash, 20% in short-term debt securities and 70% in long-term debt securities. The foreign holders could repatriate their rouble holdings in special currency auctions held by the central bank. The CBR offered only small amounts of foreign exchange in these auctions (in the first auction US$50 million) at an exchange rate that was clearly disadvantageous for the participants. Incidentally, the short-term debt securities held by the CBR were exempted from this restructuring.

While it may be difficult to allocate losses to final holders of the Russian T-bills, BIS statistics indicate that about US$7.7 billion of these papers were held by foreign banks in June 1998 (Table 5). The remainder of the US$13–15 billion was held by other financial institutions. About 85% of banks' holdings were concentrated in banks operating outside of London.

The CBR has been buying back some GKO/OFZs from Russian banks as part of a debt swap, under which the domestic banks received short-term central bank bonds known as OBRs. This program discriminates between investors as smaller domestic banks and some foreign creditors were

---

[24] See Handelsblatt, 8 July 1999.

[25] Financial Times, 26 November 1998. Foreigners had invested US$13–15 billion, of which US$550 million were to be repaid.

[26] The story has been somewhat simplified here. For more detail, see Kolleeny et al. (1999).

[27] Wall Street Journal, 22 March 1999.

[28] International Institute of Finance, Russia, March 1999.

Table 5. Banks' adjustment to exposure in Russia[1] (US$ billion)

	1998			1999	
	June	September	December	March	June
Amounts outstanding	64.9 (28.3)	56.0 (29.8)	54.7 (29.5)	49.1 (25.6)	46.9 (24.7)
Loans	57.2 (27.8)	52.7 (29.2)	50.9 (29.0)	46.4 (25.4)	44.4 (24.6)
Securities	7.7 (0.5)	3.3 (0.6)	3.8 (0.5)	2.7 (0.2)	2.5 (0.1)
Changes (exchange rate adjusted)	2.7 (0.7)	–10.8 (0.2)	–1.6 (–0.5)	–2.0 (–0.9)	–1.5 (–0.2)
Loans	2.0 (0.6)	–6.2 (0.2)	–2.1 (–0.5)	–1.0 (–0.6)	–1.2 (–0.3)
Securities	0.7 (0.1)	–4.6 (0.0)	0.5 (0.0)	–1.0 (–0.3)	–0.3 (0)

[1]Data in parentheses refer to banks in Germany.
Source: BIS International Banking Statistics.

excluded.[29] Meanwhile, the Russian Finance Ministry is restructuring the GKO/OFZ papers as it paid RUB 7 billion to holders of these papers on 16 June 1999.[30] At the beginning of December 1999, the Russian Ministry of Finance extended the deadline for agreeing to the restructuring terms to the end of the year.

9.8 Selected issues

9.8.1 Banks and other institutional investors

By mid-1998, when the Russian crisis broke, the exposure of foreign banks to Russia was about US$65 billion. By year-end 1998, banks had reduced their overall exposure by US$12.5 billion, a trend that continued in the first quarter of 1999 with a further retrenchment of US$2 billion. Two-thirds of the (exchange-rate-adjusted) US$15 billion decline since mid-1998 is attributable to non-renewal of loans (including sales to hedge funds), while one-third is estimated to represent changes in the dollar price of 'defaulted' T-bills and bonds dominated in roubles. The bulk of the banks' adjustment occurred immediately following the crisis in the third quarter of 1998 (Table 5).

[29] Russian Economic Trends, March 1999.
[30] BOFIT, Russian and Baltic Economies, The Week in Review, 18 June 1999.

The exposure of German banks in Russia was much larger than that of any other country, and the exposure of US banks was comparatively small (around US$7.8 billion in June 1998). By year-end 1998, it was clear that the banks in the USA had written down the losses in the Russian market, while banks in Germany had increased their provisions but appeared more hesitant to write down their loan losses. Perhaps German banks hoped to recover part of the loans to Russia, a position held by the authorities (who guaranteed many of these loans). Although a large write-down represents tacit acknowledgement that assets could not be recovered, most international banks went ahead and wrote-down the value of Russian domestic securities in their portfolios (US$4.5 billion in the third quarter of 1998).[31] Some have argued that this settlement may have weakened banks' resolve to fight for better repayment terms (which in the end amounted to 2 to 3 cents on the dollar).[32]

Holdings of the GKOs/OFZs were more widely dispersed. Non-banks (e.g. investment and mutual funds) held about 40% of the US$13.5 billion stock of rouble paper held abroad at the beginning of the crisis.[33] Whereas in the past, London Club banks handled such claims, the presence of non-banks has made it more difficult to implement a common approach to restructuring. By the beginning of August 1999, however, a group that represented the hedge funds became known as the London Club of Portfolio Managers, apparently coordinating some actions with the traditional London Club.[34]

The devaluation of the rouble dramatically reduced the value of government paper held as part of the required capital of foreign banks operating in Russia. In response, the CBR urged these Western banks to recapitalise their subsidiaries. This pressure was resisted by the main offices of foreign banks, which proposed solutions such as revaluation of real estate investments or other assets or a special valuation of the GKO/OFZ papers (as was done for some Russian banks). With the Russian financial system

[31] German banks did not make a large write-down initially.

[32] Merrill Lynch and Co, for example, declined to take a seat on the London Club of bank creditors involved in Russia's Soviet debt restructuring talks (Reuters, 24 June 1999).

[33] This is a rough estimate as about US$7.7 billion of the Russian papers were held by banks (Table 5); the remainder of the US$13.5 billion of these papers held abroad appears to be in the hands of other non-bank financial institutions (as they were not in private hands). Note that at the beginning of the crisis in August 1998 foreigners held about RUB 84 billion of GKOs/OFZs which amounted to about one-third of the total value of the papers outstanding. At that time, RUB 84 billion amounted to about US$13.5 billion at a rouble/dollar exchange rate of 6.3.

[34] Wall Street Journal, 3 August 1999.

collapsing, Russian depositors fled from Russian to Western banks and Sberbank.[35]

9.8.2 Bailing-in calls and the role of the private sector

The bailing in of the private sector in a financial crisis of a country has been an issue for some time. In the past, it appeared that when the IMF provided new funds or the Paris Club rescheduled debt, the country often promptly used these resources to meet its international obligations, in particular, bond repayments. In the end, the international community primarily shouldered the external debt burden. Now, there appears to be broad agreement that this situation implicitly sheltered the private sector to the detriment of the public sector. The private sector was seen as implicitly taking advantage of the official sector's role as lender of last resort. One burden-sharing proposal has focused on the holding of international bonds.[36] The idea of 'bailing in' bondholders in sovereign debt rescheduling was recently explicitly addressed by a report of the G-10 countries.[37] The group noted specifically that there should not be a presumption that any type of debt would be exempt from payment suspension or restructuring and that it was desirable to develop contractual provisions facilitating cooperation between debtors and creditors. Many emerging market economies have now become significant issuers of international bonds, which implies a shift in capital flows from the official to the private sector. Likewise, calls for including the private sector in debt rescheduling have become more persistent.

Changing the role of the private sector in sharing the debt burden involves a major rethinking of current IMF, Paris Club and London Club procedures. In the 1982 debt crisis, the IMF informally, but actively, persuaded banks to continue lending to certain countries in eastern Europe and Latin America. It was essentially attempting to expand its role beyond 'informal persuader' to prescribing involuntary lending by private banks. This expansion of the role of the IMF occurred first in November 1982, when the IMF informed bankers with major exposure in Argentina and Mexico that it would not commit its resources to stabilisation programs until the banks increased their exposure by complementary amounts.[38]

---

[35] Sberbank is the dominant savings bank of Russia, holding more than two-thirds of all bank deposits. Unlike at other banks, the government insures these deposits.

[36] Contingent credit facilities are another mechanism but are not discussed here.

[37] Group of Ten (1996).

[38] Hackney and Shafer (1986), p. 476.

The calls for improved covenants in international bond contracts should not undermine the principle and resolve of debt repayment. The widely proposed idea that the terms for international bonds should include covenants that would facilitate rescheduling in a crisis addresses the principles of transparency and efficiency in resolving the crisis in a fair and equitable way to all concerned. Three clauses that might prove useful in this regard provide for (i) collective representation of debt holders, (ii) qualified majority voting to alter the terms and conditions of the debt contract, and (iii) the equitable sharing of proceeds among creditors.[39] While there are doubts as to the potential impact of these clauses on borrowing costs of emerging market economies, these clauses could improve the quest for transparency and render the process of foreign debt settlement more efficient.[40] Unwinding a bond contract under American law, for example, is currently a major undertaking.[41]

The above considerations would only apply to future bond contracts, as modifying the terms of outstanding bond issues is generally rejected. Nevertheless, there were some attempts recently by the Paris Club to consider Pakistan's as well as Russia's currently outstanding international bonds in the debt renegotiation process. This quest appeared to comply with several official statements suggesting that international bondholders should, as a general rule, surrender their privileged position in debt restructuring. Although this is seen as an important step in principle, the potential impact on international bond markets (i.e. overruling existing legal covenants in current international bond contracts) has been a matter of controversy. Besides the obvious legal implications, some believe that such a strong international move would introduce uncertainty into a range of existing contracts and potentially serve to exclude high-risk emerging economies from the market. Moreover, it might be detrimental to a range of emerging market countries or lead to significant increases in risk premia.

On the other hand, many believe that the preferential treatment thus far given to eurobonds has created pricing distortions, leading to excessive debt accumulation in certain countries.[42] We have already seen recent cases of quasi bail-ins. In the fall of 1998, for example, the IMF asked the Ukrainian government for assurances that it would not use IMF proceeds to pay off the holders of expiring euronotes. The Paris Club also told Pakistan that the willingness of official creditors to reschedule debt interest

---

[39] For details, see Petas and Rahman (1999).

[40] For some of the issues and legal complexities involved, see Group of Ten (1996).

[41] Mayer (1999).

[42] Bank for International Settlements (1999) "International Banking and Financial Market Developments," Quarterly Review, Monetary and Economic Department, June 1999.

payments was contingent on negotiating 'comparable' arrangements with private creditors, including bondholders.[43]

9.8.3 The role of credit rating agencies in the Russian crisis

The role of credit rating agencies has been particularly criticised in the wake of the Asian crisis: they were seen as cheerleaders when times were good and morticians when trouble came.[44]

In Mexico, credit rating agencies failed to anticipate Mexico's 1994–1995 economic crisis. While the December 1994 devaluation of the peso rocked the world financial markets, Standard and Poor's put Mexico's sovereign debt only one notch below investment grade with a positive outlook. At that time, moreover, Mexican domestic paper had been selling as investment grade since the early 1990s. Moody's, in contrast, maintained its non-investment grade across the board. Thus, the Mexican crisis to some extent already produced the notion that credit rating agencies reacted to events rather than anticipated them.[45]

In Russia's case, credit rating agencies appear to have lagged in anticipating the sequence of events as debt arrears occurred and the markets absorbed new information. In general, downgradings occurred after the event. In June 1998, for example, Standard and Poor's cited the persistence of fiscal deficits and increased reliance on external finance as reasons for its downward revision from BB– to B+ (Table 6). The Duma's rejection of implementing key elements of the government's anti-crisis package agreed with the IMF, prompting a further downgrade in August. A downgrade to CCC followed the debt moratorium and the default on the local currency bills on 17 August. A further downgrade in September was sparked by concerns about the impact of the central bank's intention to settle wage arrears by printing roubles and its default on Paris Club debt, paralysis of the banking system and lack of a meaningful plan for structural change.[46] In January 1999, Russia's country risk changed to selective default (SD) from a rating of CCC–. A rating of SD implies that Russia is in default on some of its obligations but expected to meet the rest of them. It was no surprise that only at that point in time did the rating agency warn against defaults on MinFins which were payable in roubles and which were subject to Russian law. The non-servicing of MinFin bonds occurred subsequently.

---

[43] Mayer (1999).
[44] Mayer (1999).
[45] Larrain et al. (1997).
[46] Economic Survey of Europe, 1998 No. 3, p. 120.

Table 6. Foreign currency rating histories of Russia and Mexico

Russia			Mexico		
Long-term	Outlook	Date	Long-term	Outlook	Date
BB–	Stable	4 Oct 96	Adequate		14 Nov 91
BB–	Negative	19 Dec 97	BB+		30 Jul 92
BB–/CW	Negative	27 May 98	BB+	Stable	3 Nov 92
B+	Stable	9 Jun 98	BB+	Positive	18 Nov 98
B–	Negative	13 Aug 98	BB+/CW	Negative	23 Dec 94
CCC	Negative	17 Aug 98	BB	Stable	10 Feb 95
CCC–	Negative	16 Sep 98	BB	Negative	23 Mar 95
SD	NM	27 Jan 99	BB	Stable	3 Sept 96
			BB	Positive	2 Sept 97
			BB	Stable	2 Oct 98

Source: Standard and Poor's.

Ratings can provide additional information (presumably incorporated in market yields) beyond that contained in standard macroeconomic statistics. In addition, credit ratings appear to influence yields independently – over and above their correlation with other publicly available information. In particular, Cantor and Packer (1996) found that rating announcements had immediate effects on market pricing for non-investment-grade issues. Larrain et al. (1997) similarly concluded that the rating announcements on emerging market sovereign bonds were highly significant in explaining the relative bond yields. These conclusions were based on short-term 'windows', where the effect of arating change was seen to have an effect on credit risk spread within afew days after the event. This effect appears to have been in place for the August 1998 period in Russia.

It is also important, however, not to infer too much from credit ratings. After all, rating strategies tend to be conservative because credit rating agencies must avoid being overly influenced by cyclical developments and because their credibility depends on rating stability. Hence, a country's rating naturally tends to be far more stable over time than actual domestic conditions or spreads on international bonds.[47] In addition, the level of the spread may not indicate much about the level of the ratings. Sharp movements in international bond prices, like the July/August 1998 interlude in Mexico and, to a lesser degree, the September/October 1998 blip in Poland

[47] Similarly, Bank for International Settlements (1997).

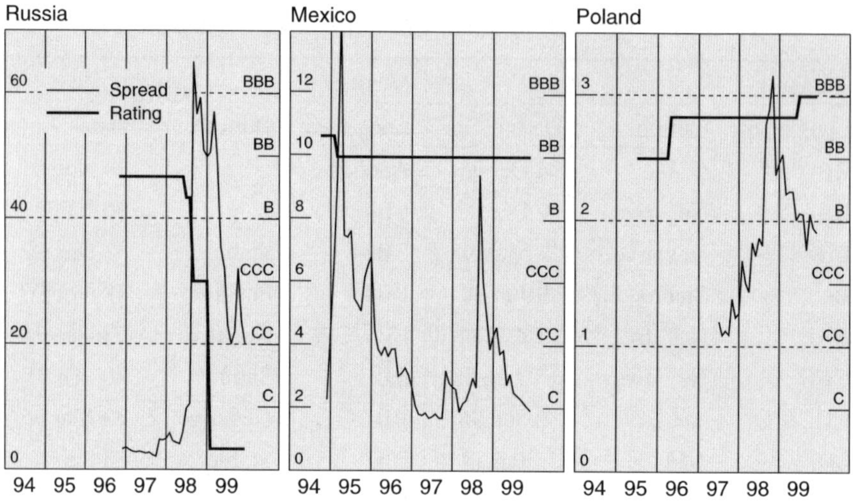

Sources: Bloomberg; Standard and Poor's.

Graph 3. Emerging market spreads and ratings (in percentage points and by rating category)

underscore how spreads can vary over time without rating changes or substantial shifts in the fundamental conditions of the issuing country. The rating changes for Russia clearly indicate that the probability of default of Russian government obligations has increased during the period under review. Each downgrading was preceded by a spate of negative information.

Ratings are generally intended to address the likelihood of default, whereas yield spreads reflect a broader range of factors, including the prospects for recovery in the event of default. This can differ across classes of bonds,[48] which explains some of the movements of the Russian government bond spreads. As bond spreads rose to over 6,000 basis points in the immediate aftermath of the crisis in Russia in August 1998, the country was effectively denied access to further borrowing from the market. At year-end June 1999, the spread remained prohibitively high at 2,300 basis points, yet this relative improvement may have reflected the increased probability of some repayment.

[48] Ammer (1997).

9.8.4 Lessons from the Mexican and Polish debt scenarios

9.8.4.1 Mexico

Mexico tried in 1993–1994 to overcome a sudden outflow of capital by converting its national-currency-denominated debt into foreign-currency-denominated debt. At the end of 1993, some 94% of the Mexican government (T-bills) debts were concentrated on *cetes*, which are denominated in the national currency, the peso. In the spring of 1994 the situation on Mexican financial markets worsened as political instability and the beginning of the tightening of US monetary policy increased the vulnerability of the economy. With the Mexican current account deficit at 7.5% of GDP by early 1994, devaluation became an issue and expectations drove up interest rates on domestic debt. The government responded by beginning an exchange of its peso-denominated debt (cetes) into dollar-denominated *tesobonos* (dollar-linked securities payable in pesos) with maturities of no more than a year. By end 1993, tesobonos accounted for only 4% of government securities held by the public while this share reached 71% by November 1994. Of the purchase of US$20 billion in tesobonos during this time, three-quarters were attributable to the adjustment of the portfolio of non-resident holders of Mexican government debt securities.[49]

The Mexican conversion may have delayed devaluation, but it failed to avert it. Indeed, the large volume of dollar paper may have made the devaluation larger when it finally came in December 1994. Economists stated in May 1994 that the peso was overvalued and that Mexico needed devaluation. They proposed a devaluation of 10 to 20%.[50] In December, when foreign investors refused to roll over their tesobonos, Mexico had to abandon its fixed exchange rate policy, and the peso quickly lost about half its value.[51] IMF and US Treasury credit helped to stabilise the situation on the financial markets months later, but the real costs of the crisis were enormous. In 1995, Mexico's GDP fell nearly 7%.[52]

---

[49] OECD Economic Survey (1995), Mexico, p. 26.

[50] Dornbusch and Werner (1994).

[51] It is difficult to assess, even *ex post*, whether or not an 'earlier' devaluation of the peso would have come at less cost and, in particular, how markets would have reacted.

[52] In the resolution of the short-term liquidity crisis which was based on a US$48.8 billion multilateral financial assistance package, Mexico used the funds disbursed by the authorities of the United States to redeem tesobonos (largely held by US investors). Mexico was thus able to avoid default on its debt obligations. See Banco de Mexico (1996), Chap. IV.

Russia tried to avoid a liquidity crunch by converting its short-term domestic debt into longer-term debt in June–July 1998. This maturity lengthening appeared possible since at the time most Russian foreign debts were long-term with relatively low yields to maturity. Some observers thought, however, that foreigners would have been happier to exchange their risky GKOs into less risky eurobonds, which would have also been more attractive in case of devaluation. By easing market pressure, the measure would have given the government enough time to put its finances in order and devaluation would have been avoided.

Foreign holders of GKOs were reluctant to participate in the swap and only a small volume of GKOs were ever converted into long-term bonds. There were no big gains in debt servicing and market pressure increased again 2 weeks after the swap. Lengthening of the maturity of domestic debt may have helped postpone the devaluation, but the interest costs of the swap were large, as were capital losses arising after devaluation through the increase in the share of dollar-denominated debt.[53] Both the Mexican and Russian experiences of debt conversion suggest that structural economic problems such as an overvaluation of the real effective exchange rate or persistent budget deficits cannot be solved by financial engineering measures. In particular, the conversion of domestic debt into foreign debt can create a small-time gain for government, but the costs further down the road may outweigh the benefits.

In Mexico's rescue programme, the ensuing debt restructuring program supported by the IMF and US government credit reduced fiscal spending by 1.3% of GDP. A national accord among workers, business and government assured that wage and price increases did not cancel out devaluation, thus assuring a significant real devaluation of the peso. Structural reforms allowed private investment into e.g. railroads, opened the telecommunication sector to competition and increased foreign competition in the domestic banking sector. These measures helped Mexican firms increase their competitiveness and achieve stable growth once the crisis had abated.[54] No such support came to pass in the Russian situation as a one-sided moratorium was declared. Indeed, no comprehensive program of restructuring has yet materialised in Russia.[55]

[53] Wyplosz and Yudaeva (1999).

[54] This section ignores the close trade links between Mexico and the USA and the buoyant US economy after the crisis.

[55] See also IMF Survey, 2 August 1999.

9.8.4.2 Poland

Poland stopped servicing its debt to commercial bank creditors in the last quarter of 1989. By the end of 1993 US$6.3 billion in arrears had accumulated. A Brady-style restructuring operation was reached in March 1994, paving the way for Poland's access to international capital markets.

The Polish situation in 1991–1992 may have some relevance for the Russian case. At that time Poland had difficulty in attracting spontaneous private market capital into the real sector of the economy. The country faced large debt payments and reached an agreement with the London Club creditors after protracted negotiations in 1994 implying a comprehensive debt and debt service reduction of the roughly US$14 in billion commercial bank debt. In view of Poland's compliance with the IMF program, the Paris Club also agreed on official debt reduction. The debt reduction exercise significantly improved its creditworthiness and paved the way for subsequent healthy private capital inflows, at first mostly as foreign direct investment.[56] Poland gained favourable restructuring terms because of its strong, consistent macro and structural reforms.

Poland's external debt indicators improved substantially after the London and Paris Club agreements. Although the country remained moderately indebted, it appears that the constraints on policy in the years following the debt settlement were relatively small. The very favourable rescheduling terms deferred repayments for a long time – to the early years of this millennium. The traditional strategy of helping the country to grow out of its difficulties appears to have worked in Poland.

Russia may also grow out of its external debt servicing difficulties as it has been running historically substantial current account surpluses and is endowed with rich natural resources. Nevertheless, Russia continues to experience large capital outflows. A consistent policy package on restructuring terms would probably be advantageous here.

9.9 Lessons from the Russian crisis

If we learn anything from the Russian crisis, it is that prevention is the first and most fundamental element in crisis management. The best preventive measure is the pursuit of sound domestic economic policies. Unfortunately, political processes have often stymied the implementation of basic structural economic policy elements. More fundamentally, Russia lacks an overall political consensus on the general thrust of economic policy. While

[56] The World Bank, "Trends in Developing Economies," Washington, D.C., 1995.

the attempt to lengthen the debt profile just before the crisis may have been able to buy some time, it came too late. Russia declared a one-sided external and domestic debt moratorium in August 1998. Such a dramatic step was avoided in Mexico in 1994–1995 with external help. In the aftermath of the crisis, foreign private creditors incurred large losses while any attempts at 'bailing in' the private sector in official debt restructuring failed.

The current external debt process of Russia will remain on the agenda for some time. The preliminary considerations point to some compromise in the Paris and London Clubs. German banks (and German taxpayers) will have to absorb the largest part of the anticipated reduction of Russia's debt payment. The developments after the moratorium show that restructuring of the external and domestic debt remains a fairly opaque, messy process. Attempts to increase transparency in these processes or to improve the sequencing of the processes have so far been unsuccessful. The preliminary deal with the London Club may help the Russian Federation to gain access to international capital markets at some point in time. No matter how the debt restructuring problems are ultimately solved, the Russian Federation faces sizeable external debt payments in the next few years (see item 3 in the appendix). This reduces its flexibility in fiscal policy after the current mild upturn in the Russian economy ends.

Rating agencies have played a subordinate role in the Russian debt scenario. Most of the time, agencies have adjusted their ratings downwards after market developments, so it seems unlikely that they exacerbated crisis. The market price of Russian debt has been highly volatile, reacting to any relevant news immediately. In particular, the markets seem to embrace any potential positive new information with enthusiasm.

The Polish experience of the early 1990s may be relevant to further debt renegotiations, while the follow-up after the crisis in Mexico suggests that a fairly consistent and comprehensive economic policy package is now needed in Russia.

Appendices

Item 1. Chronology of the Russian financial crisis

1997

November	The central bank refinancing rate is raised from 21 to 28%; anew central rate of RUB 6.2 per US dollar is announced; the intervention band is widened from ±5% to ±15% for the period 1998–2000.

1998

May	Following liquidity problems, a large bank, Tokobank, is temporarily placed under central bank administration. The refinancing rate reaches 150% on 27 May and fluctuates widely thereafter.
July	Russia and the IMF agree on a stabilisation package of US$22.6 billion for 1998–1999. A first IMF credit tranche of US$4.8 billion is made available on 20 July. It includes emergency fiscal measures to raise tax revenues and reduce government spending.
August	Two major banks stop payments in early August. To forestall a run on the assets of other credit institutions, the authorities extend RUB 4.1 billion to a number of banks (using their T-bills as collateral). Limits on foreign exchange purchases by commercial banks are imposed. On 17 August, authorities allow the rouble to float to a new limit of RUB 9.5 per US dollar; payment in rouble-denominated short-term state debt is put on hold and a 90-day moratorium is declared on commercial entities' foreign debt payments. On 23 August, the government is dismissed.
September	After spending more than US$9 billion in July and August to support the rouble, the central bank abandons its upper limit of the rouble corridor on 1 September. Six major banks are required to transfer their retail deposits to state-controlled Sberbank, and exchange controls are imposed. On 11 September, parliament confirms a new government. The rouble stabilises temporarily at around 16 roubles to the dollar. The central bank announces it will bail out the major Russian banks and buy back most of their outstanding T-bills. The IMF states on 30 September that any further lending to Russia under the July agreement hinges on a strong programme of tax collection and bank reform.

1999	
January	The government debt market reopens; the central bank sets a 120% yield cap.
February	Renewed negotiations with the IMF fail.
April	Preliminary agreement with IMF to disburse US$4.5 billion over 1.5 years on conditions that include explanation of past use of IMF resources and a implementation of a range of economic measures.
May/June	The rouble stabilises at around 24 to the dollar.
July	Russia receives a US$4.5 billion stand-by credit from the IMF. US$640 million is immediately available.
August	The Paris Club agrees to postpone for a period of 15 to 20 years US$8 billion in payment on Soviet-era debt falling due before the end of 2000.
September	The first large Russian bank, Menatep, is declared bankrupt. Menatap's debts are reported to be at least US$1.2 billion. At the end of August, Russia had 1,390 banks, only one hundred less than the year before. IMF continues to withhold the second tranche of the stand-by credit.
November–December	Russia and London Club fail to agree on restructuring terms for the Soviet debt. At the beginning of December Russia misses another interest payment to London Club creditors, bringing the total arrears to the London Club to US$1.4 billion. The rouble continues to depreciate, so that at the end of November it stands at 26 to the dollar. IMF continues to withhold further tranches of the stand-by loan.
2000	
February	Russia reaches a preliminary restructuring agreement with London Club creditors. The old Soviet debt previously handled by Vneshekonombank will be exchanged for eurobonds of the Russian Federation, and at the same time the details of the deal mean that Russia will receive an approx. 50% reduction in the value of this debt. The deal still requires an approval of 75% of the debt holders.

Item 2. Taxonomy of Russian debt instruments

Eurobonds: Payment terms being met
Russia issued its first $1 billion eurobond in November 1996 and has since issued eurobonds with a total dollar value of about $16 billion. Denominated in various currencies, eurobonds are the highest class of Russian debt. Rescheduling is very difficult to negotiate, since eurobond holders are dispersed around the globe.

London Club debt: in default
In late 1997, Russia completed a deal to restructure about $28 billion of Soviet-era debt to the London Club, which represents more than 600 Western commercial lenders. The debt was split into two types of securities. About $20 billion became 'principal notes', or *Prins*, which represent loans that the state-owned foreign payment agent, Vneshekonombank, defaulted on in 1991. The remaining $8 billion became 'interest arrears notes', or *IANs*, which represent interest accrued since the default. Russia effectively defaulted on the Prins by the end of 1998.

Paris Club debt: restructured temporarily
In 1996, Russia rescheduled nearly US$40 million in Soviet-era debt to the Paris Club, a group of Western governments that have lent money to emerging market economies. In 1998 Russia missed payments on this debt, but in August 1999 Russian Federation and Paris Club creditors agreed to postpone the US$8 billion in debt servicing falling due before the end of 2000. Details on the restructuring are to be agreed upon later.

MinFin bonds: payment due
Also known as Taiga bonds, these dollar-denominated securities were issued in 1993 to cover about $8 billion in corporate accounts that Vneshekonombank froze after the Soviet Union's collapse. In 1996, Russia's Ministry of Finance issued two new tranches. MinFin bonds are technically domestic debt under the jurisdiction of Russian law, making it very difficult for foreigners to make claims in the event of a default. Russia has presumably paid $1.3 billion of the MinFins in 1999. In May 1999 Russia missed a payment on the MinFins. They may ultimately be swapped into equity or new MinFin series 98 bonds or exchanged for OFZs at a sliding interest rate starting at 15%.

Treasury debt: mostly restructured
Also known as *GKOs* and *OFZs*, this rouble-denominated debt has been issued by the Russian government since 1993 to finance its budget deficit. By mid-1998, the dollar value of Russian Treasury notes had reached about $70 billion. On 17 August 1998, the government stopped payment

on notes set to mature before the end of 1999. Foreigners held about $13.5 billion of that debt. Owners of GKOs and OFZ had to settle for very disadvantageous restructuring terms, and their initial compensation (at market prices) was approx. 1.5 cents to the dollar.

Source: Wall Street Journal, Central Europe and author.

Item 3. Forecasts of Russian Federation's external debt servicing burden, US$ billion

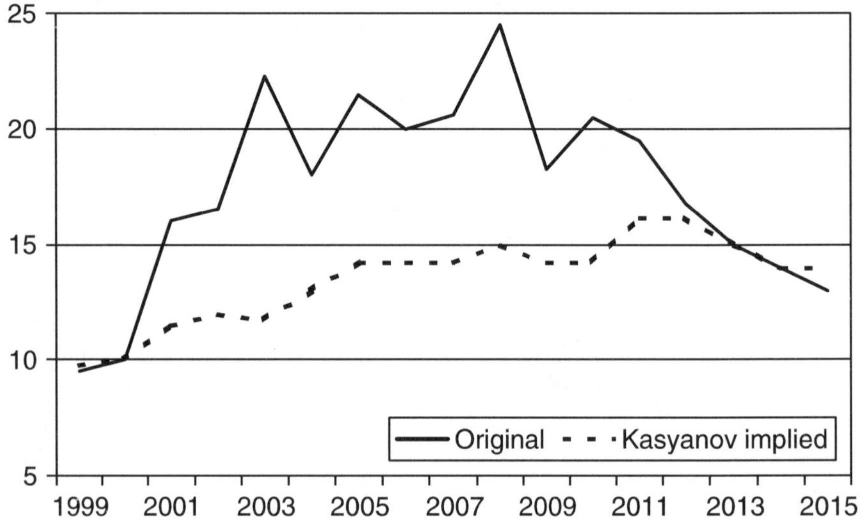

Note: The forecast given by Finance Minister Kasyanov assumes that both London and Paris club restructure their debts. Some studies estimate the original debt burden lower than Troika Dialog.

Source: Troika Dialog.

References

Ammer, John (1997), Pilot Study: Sovereign Credit Ratings and International Debt Markets, Board of Governors of the Federal Reserve System (document prepared for the Euro-currency Standing Committee, BIS), December.

Banco de Mexico (1996 and 1997), The Mexican Economy.

Bank for International Settlements (1997), Annual Report, Chapter VI, June.

Bank for International Settlements (1999a), Enhancing transparency regarding the authorities' foreign currency liquidity position, Committee on the Global Financial System, April.

Bank for International Settlements (1999b), Annual Report, Chapter III, June.

Bank for International Settlements (1999c), A Review of Financial Market Events in Autumn 1998 (the Karen Johnson Report), October.

Bank of Finland, Institute for Economies in Transition (BOFIT), Russian and Baltic Economies in Transition, The Week in Review, several issues.

Bowe, Michael and James W. Dean (1997), Has the market solved the sovereign-debt crisis?, Princeton Studies in International Finance, No. 83, August.

Buch, Claudia et al. (1999), Die wirtschaftliche Lage Russlands; Schuldenstreichung statt Reformen?, Kiel Discussion Papers 340, May.

Cantor, Richard and Frank Packer (1996), Determinants and Impact of Sovereign Credit Ratings, Federal Reserve Bank of New York, Economic Policy Review, September.

Claessens, Stijn (1990), The Debt Laffer Curve: Some Estimates, World Development, Vol. 18, No. 12, pp. 1671–1677.

Dornbusch, Rudiger and Alejandro Werner (1994), Mexico: Stabilisation, Reform and No Growth, Brookings Papers on Economic Activity, 1.

Easton, Stephen T. and Duane W. Rockerbie (1999), Does IMF conditionality benefit lenders?, Weltwirtschaftliches Archiv 1999, Vol. 135 (2).

Ebenroth, Carsten-Thomas, Chris Maina Peter and Matthew James Kemner (1995), Rescheduling of sovereign debt: a new role for the Paris Club, 7 JIBL.

Group of Ten (1996), The resolution of sovereign liquidity crises, A report to the Ministers and Governors prepared under the auspices of the Deputies, Basel and Washington, May.

Hackney, James V. and Kim Leslie Shafer (1986), The Regulation of International Banking: An Assessment of International Institutions, North Carolina Journal of International Law and Commercial Regulations, Vol. 11, No. 3, Summer.

Holman, Michael and Quentin Peel (1999), Too much to bear, Financial Times, 12/6/99.

International Monetary Fund (1998), World Economic Outlook and International Capital Markets, December.

JP Morgan (1999), Russia: Winning a battle in the war against default, Morgan Guaranty Trust Company, Economic Research note, Global Data Watch, June 25.

Kolleeny, Glenn, Mira Davidovski and Brenda Horrigan (1999), Damage limitation, Central European, May 1999.

Kroszner, Randall (1999), Is it better to forgive than to receive? Repudiation of the Gold indexation clause in long-term debt during the great depression, draft, University of Chicago and NBER, April.

Larrain, Guillermo, Helmut Reisen and Julia von Maltzan (1997), Emerging market risk and sovereign credit ratings, OECD Development Centre, Technical Papers, No. 124, April.

Mayer, Martin (1999), The ratings game, The International Economy, July/August.

Meisner, Norbert (1998), German bank exposure to Russia, DCD Marchés, Research Department, Flash, 28 August.

Mundell, Robert A (1997), The Great Contractions in Transition Economies, in Macroeconomic Stabilisation in Transition Economies, ed. by Mario I. Blejer and Marko Skreb, Cambridge University Press, Cambridge, UK.

OECD Economic Surveys (1995–98), Mexico.

Petas, Peter and Rashique Rahman (1999), Sovereign Bonds-Legal Aspects that Affect Default and Recovery, Deutsche Bank, Global Emerging Markets, May 1999.

PriceWaterhouseCoopers (1999), Report evaluating the activities and operations of Financial Management Company (FIMACO), prepared at the request of the Central Bank of Russia, IMF website, August 4.

Reddy, Y.V. (1999), External debt policies in emerging market economies, speech at the Seminar on Corporate External Debt Management in Kathmandu, Nepal, 11/6/99.

Russia Portfolio, The Russian Securities Newsletter, Cambridge, MA, US, numerous issues.

Russian Economic Trends, Russian European Centre for Economic Policy, Moscow, several months.

Sachs, Jeffrey D. (1999), Release the Poorest Countries From Debt Bondage, International Herald Tribune, 14 June 1999.

Surobovic, Aleksej and Natalija Usaskova (1999), Die Praesenz der russischen Wirtschaft in der GUS, Tel II: Finanzbeziehungen, Berichte des Bundesinstitutes fuer ostwissenschaftliche und internationale Studien, Cologne, 10 February.

Tietmeyer, Hans (1999), Systemic Risk and Lender of Last Resort Facilities, speech by the President of the Deutsche Bundesbank at a conference organised by the Centre for Financial Studies, Frankfurt, June.

Troika Dialog (2000), Russian Economic Monthly January 2000. Troika Dialog Research, Moscow.

United Nations (1998), Economic Survey of Europe, No. 3.

World Bank (1995), Trends in Developing Economies.

World Bank (1999), Global Economic Prospects, Beyond Financial Crisis, Washington, DC.

Wyplosz, Charles and Ksenia Yudaeva (1998), The cost of debt conversion. Russia and Mexico compared, The Centre for Economic Reforms, Russian Economic Trends Quarterly No. 4.

10 Banking sector reform in the transition economies – a central banking perspective

10.1 The relevance of the topic

Banking sector reform cannot be seen in isolation from the broader question of financial sector reform. The financial sector itself is based on three pillars: the payment and settlement system, financial institutions and financial markets.[1] Developments in the banking sector and any reform of the existing structure should thus ensure that these three pillars remain sound.

The OECD stated recently that the creation of transparent, flexible financial systems open to worldwide capital flows is essential if underdeveloped countries are to achieve strong economic growth in the years ahead.[2] The EBRD[3] summarises the key elements as follows: 'The weaknesses in banking systems in transition economies stem from a combination of legacies of bad loans, political interference and lack of skills and capital, with large macroeconomic shocks resulting from rapid disinflation and remonetisation. Most countries of the region have not so far been affected by systemic crises on account of the relatively small role played by financial intermediation in their economies, although most have experienced a process of bank consolidation as regulatory frameworks have been tightened. However, the establishment of sound banking principles and appropriate bank supervision has far to go. The financial sector weaknesses in the region hold more potential upsets in store for both forecasters and policy makers'.

---

1 This structure is standard. More recently, finance theory has placed more emphasis on, *inter alia*, the proper incentive structure for financial agents, risks in all markets, instruments, balance sheet items and the 'CIA' (contracts, information and agents). The main question is what drives the financial system. See, for example, Bisignano (1995), Berthelemy and Varoudakis (1996) and Crockett (1996).

2 OECD (1997c).

3 EBRD (1997).

The OECD proposes aiming for a flexible and open domestic financial system to underpin growth. The EBRD clearly identifies the typical immanent weakness of the domestic financial system in economies in transition. Both these topics, the *relationship between a stable financial system and growth and the immanent systemic weaknesses in the banking sector*, are relevant for this paper.

Most central banks are charged with some responsibility in the area of financial system stability. If bank restructuring is to lead to a sounder banking system, then central banks will be involved and perhaps asked to play an active role in this process. For example, in a February 1998 lecture, the governor of the Bank of England, Mr. George, clearly stated that the bank's second core purpose was the maintenance of financial stability. As put recently in more general terms by Mr. White, the economic adviser of the BIS: 'Weak financial systems can have long-lasting and insidious macroeconomic implications (the problem of 'financial fragility') that are naturally of concern to central bankers'.[4]

From an international perspective it should be clear that the role of the BIS is to share the central banks' concerns about financial stability. It is one of the world's leading institutions in promoting financial stability, particularly strengthening banking supervision and payment and settlement systems. Recently, in a joint initiative with the Basel Committee on Banking Supervision, the BIS established an Institute for Financial Stability, which will respond to the increasing demands for assistance in implementing sound principles and policies in all areas bearing on financial stability.[5] The role played by individual international organisations in strengthening financial systems was detailed in the Report of the Working Party on Financial Stability in Emerging Market Economies released in April 1997 by the Group of Ten.[6]

---

4 White (1998).

5 'The BIS Institute will be engaged in three principal activities: the organization of high-level seminars directed at key policy making officials in central banks and supervisory agencies; the provision of training on a regional basis for groups of senior officials that implement policies; and acting as a clearing house for the co-ordination and provision of technical assistance by central banks and supervisory bodies.' BIS, *Press Communiqué*, 12 March 1998.

6 The constituent members of this Group of Ten Working Party attest to the broad approach taken in the strategy for the formulation, adoption and implementation of sound principles and practices to strengthen financial systems: representatives from the finance ministries and central banks of industrial and emerging economies and from the Basel Committee on Banking Supervision, the International Accounting Standards Committee, the Bank for International Settlements, the European Commission, the International Monetary Fund, the

The role of the BIS in particular was outlined in a recent paper by its economic adviser. What is of concern to central banks worldwide is naturally of concern to the BIS as the coordinator of central banks' cooperative efforts. The topic of this paper – banking sector reform in the transition economies – is therefore very much germane to the concerns of central banks and particularly of the BIS.[7] In the final analysis, however, it is the responsibility of the national government and the financial authorities in each individual country to develop and ensure financial stability domestically.

10.2 Some major caveats[8]

What do we mean by bank restructuring? The concept applies not only to rebuilding after a crisis. There should be continuous efforts to monitor and strengthen the financial sector, paying due respect to the ever changing economic and financial environment.[9]

10.2.1 Interdependence, comprehensiveness and complexity

What is important to note at the outset is that whatever will lead to a strengthening of the banking system will not occur in a vacuum or in isolation. This implies that the macro- and micro-environment will have to be taken into account[10] when assessing bank restructuring and, equally importantly, interdependencies between the various economic reforms. One aspect of this complexity is captured by the literature on the sequencing of reforms.[11] The notion of interdependencies also leads to the acceptance of

---

Organisation for Economic Co-operation and Development and the International Bank for Reconstruction and Development (World Bank).

7 White (1998) outlines the BIS's important contribution to international financial stability. His paper is also relevant for the countries in central and eastern Europe. The specific functions of the BIS are not developed further in this paper.

8 Similarly, Crockett (1994).

9 The Group of Ten, in considering the sequencing of the financial liberalisation process, notes: '...whether a rapid comprehensive liberalization ('Big Bang') is better or worse than a more sequenced or gradual process depends critically upon the state of financial markets and their environment at the outset' (p. 48).

10 The interdependencies between macro and financial instability are documented, for example, in Goldstein and Turner (1996) and the Group of Ten (1997).

11 Harwood (1997), in a summary of a Brookings Institution Conference on financial sequencing, concludes that there is no optimal path to financial sector development.

the concept of the comprehensiveness of the approach taken, be it in terms of the legal framework or of financial (including banking) supervision.

My second preliminary remark is that one should not underestimate the complexity of the problems involved. This is clearly indicated by the above quotations from the EBRD and OECD. It is also reflected in the fact that the integration of the financial block in economic modelling, on theoretical as well as empirical grounds, remains largely elusive. There is, for example, comparatively little work on the inclusion of the banking systems' intermediation function in growth frameworks.[12]

10.2.2 Eastern Europe – a diverse group of countries

What is probably a less contentious statement is that central and eastern Europe is by no means a homogeneous area as far as domestic banking systems[13] are concerned. This is perhaps an obvious observation but certainly needs reiterating and indeed is borne out by the fact that most conferences or books on this area include country studies, an approach which is also reflected in the structure of this seminar. This implies, *inter alia*, that more general statements on particular developments for a range of countries may be somewhat contentious from an individual country perspective. On the other hand, one could probably agree that other countries' experiences provide useful insights and guidance in the quest for a balanced, stable, efficient and secure financial system.

10.2.3 Sound banking – a vision emerging

The importance of a sound banking system has come under scrutiny of late, a situation unfortunately exacerbated by the Mexican and, more recently, the Asian crisis. There now appears to be much more agreement on the broad principles than ever before.[14] The broadest framework is found in a milestone paper by the Group of Ten.[15] That paper's stylised list of the major elements to be considered on the road to financial stability is reproduced here as an

[12] On this point, see Pagano (1993), King and Levine (1993), Fry (1995) and Andersen and White (1996).

[13] There is quite a bit of literature emerging on the role of non-bank financial intermediaries. While this trend is to be observed carefully, especially in countries more advanced in the transition process, the role of these institutions is quite small as measured, for example, by the share in total financial assets.

[14] See Goldstein and Turner (1996), Lindgren et al. (1996), White (1997), Basel Committee on Banking Supervision (1997), Group of Ten (1997) and Folkerts-Landau and Lindgren (1998).

[15] Group of Ten (1997).

annex. 'Sound' in this context means that a systemic collapse is not very likely. It is the risk of contagion which is the major reason for official involvement, in one form or another, in the regulation and protection of the financial industry.[16] Of course, individual banks should still be able to go bankrupt. But to find the delicate balance between eliminating unsound banks and ensuring the continued soundness of the rest of the financial system is perhaps the most challenging task.

10.3 Growth and finance – the important link

10.3.1 Introduction

The crucial link between growth and finance sets the framework for the ensuing discussion. While it is well documented that remedying financial instability is costly,[17] there is less evidence of a positive relationship between finance and growth. Most economists acknowledge the interaction between a solid financial system and the growth path. In general terms, a developed financial sector can raise the productivity of capital by improving its allocation. The elucidation of the empirical link between financial intermediation and economic growth has invariably been plagued by at least three major issues: the complexity of existing financial systems, the continuous changes taking place in the financial system as the borders between markets and agents become blurred and overlap, and changing 'concepts' of growth.[18] However, some general conclusions have evolved from this empirical work[19] to influence our thinking on the state of the financial system. In the following section I have picked out four very important factors which have broadly been identified in these studies as being relevant for growth: excessive government involvement, low monetisation, macroeconomic instability and unhealthy banks.[20]

While central bankers are essentially concerned about price stability, a second major goal of theirs may be broadly called financial stability. The four key variables identified above as being crucial for economic growth are assessed in fairly general terms in the following sections.

---

[16] Crockett (1996).

[17] Lindgren et al. (1996).

[18] Koch (1997a).

[19] See, for example, World Bank (1989), King and Levine (1993) and Johnston and Pazarbasioglu (1995).

[20] Possible statistical proxies for these factors are, in order of priority, claims on the private sector/GDP, broad money/GDP, the real effective exchange rate and/or the real interest rate, and the lending minus the deposit rate.

10.3.2 Selected factors in stimulating growth

10.3.2.1 The crucial role of the government – too much?

The government will have to set the proper framework within which the financial system can prosper. The German concept of *Rahmenbedingungen* ('framework principles') captures the essence of what is required. The creation, life and death of a bank need to be properly institutionalised. In the area of banking supervision the core principles are the analogous concept. The 'framework' for conducting banking business has to be ensured. Sound public finances are one of the cornerstones. There are many ways in which lax fiscal policy may undermine banking sector reform efforts, ranging from the over-taxation of banks through their preferential treatment in receiving government deposits (either interest rate free or free of reserve requirements) to their being obliged to hold government paper in their portfolios at below-market rates. Continuous 'drip-feeding' of loss-making state enterprises by banks still represents a major problem in many countries (see below, 'Creating healthy banks'). While direct credits and directed credits are being phased out in general, governments may influence the allocation of credit to particular sectors, extend favourable loan-discounting privileges to certain borrowers, prevent private banks from engaging in certain profitable banking activities and direct banks to borrow in foreign currencies.[21] In a broader sense, confusing public and private interests strikes at the very nature of democracy and reduces transparency and accountability.

It may also be important to limit government spending. The government sectors in many transition economies are still very large and may run sizeable deficits even in growth periods. Hungary's public sector, for example, accounts for 47% of GDP. Large governments are more exposed to revenue shortfall in times of recession, and a large public debt leaves economies vulnerable to interest rate shocks. Government may also command the lion's share of credit, constraining the development of the private financial sector. Fragility in the public finances may thus have disastrous consequences for attempts at restructuring the banking system, either by blocking or retarding a smooth process of adjustment.

10.3.2.2 Low monetisation – but how to remedy it?

The central bank will have to be able to supply 'final' liquidity to financial agents and is usually sought out to provide or act as agent for the payment

---

[21] Goldstein and Turner (1996).

and settlement system. In performing these major tasks the central bank should treat all participants and financial institutions equally.

The central bank is also often entrusted with the development of financial markets. This appears to be perfectly natural, and the process usually starts with foreign exchange markets, followed by government securities markets and then the interbank market. It is fairly consistently and rightly argued that fostering government debt markets is one of the financial priorities in emerging economies. The process, however, is fraught with pitfalls, takes time and requires constant monitoring. One of the main problems is to strike and maintain a delicate balance between government involvement and the evolution of the private markets. The awareness of the proper 'exit' strategy for the government emerges as the individual financial markets develop resilience, depth and liquidity.

Monetary policy may provide wrong or biased signals during the process of banking sector reform. Russia, for example, singles out certain larger banks for closer supervision, thus presumably creating a circle of 'better' banks which enjoy a 'less risky' bonus. In Poland and Russia, state banks still appear to derive a privileged position from their extensive network of branches and state guarantees, a situation which reduces the efficiency of monetary policy. Such idiosyncrasies will have to be removed in the longer run. In a broader sense, monetary policy and government agencies have to ensure that the core functions of money are accepted by society. Low monetisation (measured by the ratio of broad money to GDP) in almost all the transition economies in general reflects low levels of confidence in the traditional core money functions, namely a store of value, an acceptable unit of account and a medium of exchange.[22] The development of reliable financial markets will overcome some of these transitory problems.

Dollarisation still represents a major macro- and microconstraint in those economies where confidence in the domestic currency is low. Open dollarisation, i.e. the measurable component of dollars usually held in the form of deposits at commercial banks, may not capture the importance a foreign currency may play in the traditional functions of money. Dollarisation presents a particular problem for the monetary authorities and may undermine the efficacy of policy. Moreover, a high level of dollarisation may also jeopardise the development of the banking sector. Domestic residents holding large amounts of dollars 'under the mattress' or conducting financial transactions among themselves without using money (barter, non-payment of bills) not only introduce inefficiencies into financial transactions but also weaken the growth of deposits at commercial banks (one component of national savings) and facilitate the avoidance of tax payments. Russia, for example, has taken

[22] For Slovenia, see, for example, OECD (1997a).

firm measures in the past to boost the use of its domestic currency, the rouble, by prohibiting the use of foreign currency (in particular the dollar) in transactions. It appears that further dollarisation of the economy has effectively been halted.[23]

Banking sector reform may be hampered if the underlying structural framework, in terms of the payment and settlement systems or an inconsistent or weak institutional policy, reinforces a low rate of monetisation. The infrastructure found in more advanced economies is clearly extensive and will take time to develop. In addition to laws and regulations, it will include financial intermediaries such as banks, securities firms and insurance companies. Proper market transaction mechanisms are required for each market, ranging from such markets as repo and the other short-term money markets to capital markets and institutions such as stock exchanges, trading systems, clearing houses and registrars. Information sources such as credit systems may be desirable. Accounting systems are needed to provide standard, useful information on all market participants. While countries are at different stages in meeting these infrastructure requirements, and while it may not be possible or desirable to bring together all these ingredients in a preset framework, a sequence of steps has been evolving. In terms of institutions, this pattern may be characterised by the following stylised sequence: central bank, commercial banks and other non-bank financial intermediaries. In terms of markets, a frequently observed sequence has been: central bank liquidity facilities, foreign exchange market, interbank market, repo market, short-term government paper market, longer-term government paper markets, short-term private money markets and longer-term private markets.

10.3.2.3 The macroeconomic framework

Serious macroeconomic distortions will, of course, also undermine banking sector reform. History has shown time and again that the macroeconomic parameters have to be under reasonable control for any reforms in the banking sector to yield tangible results. Recent works by many authors consistently conclude that an unstable macroeconomic environment is a principal source of vulnerability in the financial system. Significant swings in the performance of the real economy, and volatile real interest rates, exchange rates, asset prices and inflation rates make it difficult for banks to assess accurately the credit and market risks they might be incurring.[24] However, since macroeconomic stability is a necessary but insufficient condition for

---

[23] Brodsky (1997). For a detailed account of barter and financing by non-payment, see OECD (1997b).

[24] Goldstein and Turner (1996) and Folkerts-Landau and Lindgren (1998).

ensuring financial stability, the implication is that more specific measures for ensuring financial stability are still warranted and are indeed urgently required.[25] a positive aspect in the current scenario is that in central and eastern Europe there is some convergence towards macroeconomic stability.

There are a couple of points to be made about macroeconomic policies. First, it is important to adopt policies that preserve monetary discipline. When faced with insolvent banks, many governments have in the past yielded to the temptation of relaxing monetary policy so much as to generate high inflation, negative real interest rates and devaluation. By eroding the real value of bad bank loans, this tactic can appear to pay short-run dividends. But such policies typically provoke capital flight, shrinking the domestic deposit base of sound as well as unsound banks. Moreover, the memory of expropriation through inflation endures long after lax monetary policies have been reversed.

The second warning about macroeconomic policy is that governments need to be wary of allowing exchange rate misalignment to persist for too long. In many Latin American countries, tight monetary policies and/or fixed exchange rates led to significant reductions in inflation in the 1990s, but at the price of real exchange rate appreciation and widening current account deficits. Significant real effective appreciation until the first quarter of 1997 was also a factor in the economies most affected in the Asian financial crisis. Several eastern European countries may now face a similar dilemma. In Russia, the real effective exchange rate has risen by a factor of two during the last 3 years.

Current economic developments in many countries in central Europe may contain the seeds of a weakening of the banking sector. Rapid credit growth may indicate potential problems, since rapid real credit extension has been identified as a leading indicator of many banking crises. Across much of the central European region there has been a surge in real credit growth to the private sector, often matching increased consumer demand (Chart 2). In Estonia, vigorous economic growth has gone hand in hand with the growth of credit to the private sector on the order of 70% annually. In Poland in 1997, the central bank twice raised bank reserve requirements, nudged up the interest rate by about 2% and started to take deposits from the general public in a bid to stem the credit boom. The latter has fuelled imports, which in turn have pushed trade and current accounts into deficit. The Czech koruna was forced to float and banking fragility was revealed in May 1997; again, the external scenario was a large and fast-growing current account deficit. Several other countries in the region are currently running high current account/GDP ratios.

---

[25] White (1998).

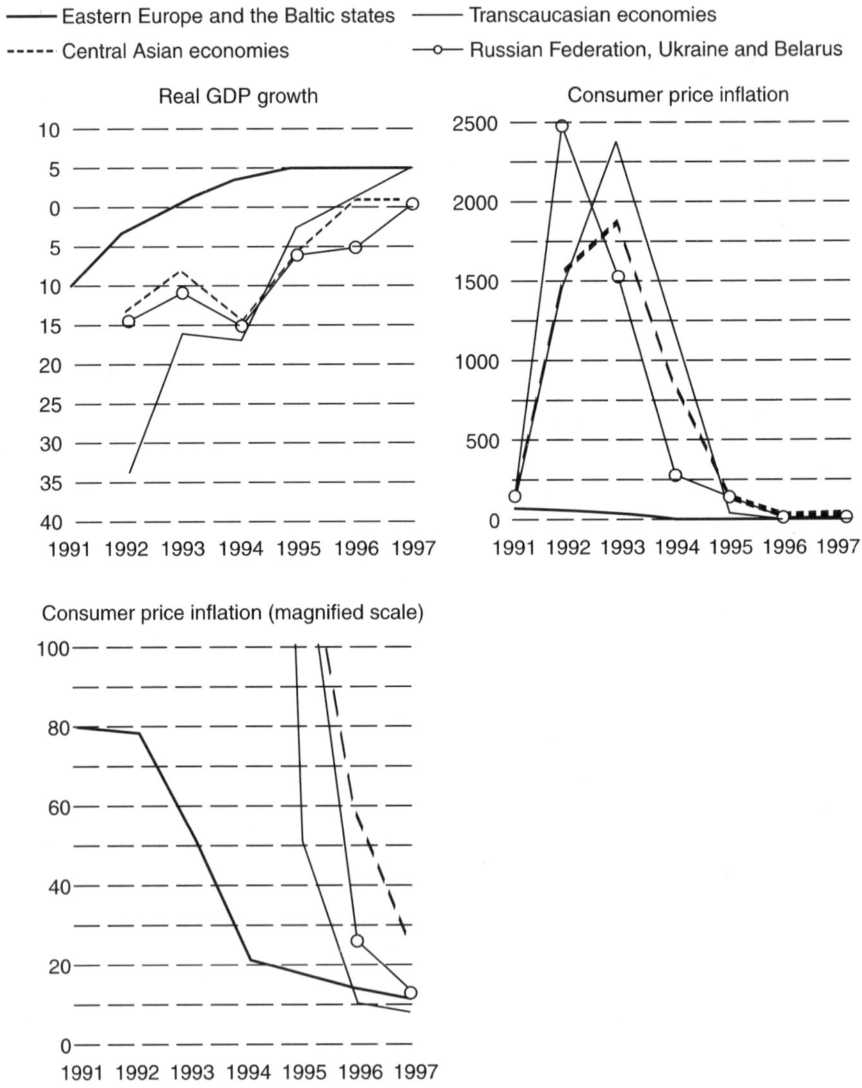

[1]Calculated using weights based on 1990 GDP and PPP exchange rates.
Source: National.

Chart 1. GDP growth and inflation in transition economies,1 1991–1997 (percentages)

An example of the distortions created by 'weak' macroeconomic parameters is provided in Russia. The initial financial liberalisation and loose entry requirements implied that the banks were able to speculate easily on the further depreciation of the rouble. They took advantage of this and earned large profits on their foreign exchange trade while at the same time benefiting from high inflation rates. This profitable speculation came to an end with the introduction of the rouble corridor in June 1995. With the subsequent development of the government securities market, the banks again reaped easy profits as the nominal interest rates received on loans were much higher than the rates paid on deposits (i.e. the margins were very high). The upshot of these distorted macroeconomic parameters was that banking sector reform did not start in earnest. Owing to the existing macroeconomic environment, the incentive structure was distorted in favour of the banks, and the core elements of banking such as credit assessment and allocation and maturity transformation were not even established.

10.3.2.4 Creating healthy banks

Privatisation – what do we mean?

If the banking system is to contribute to growth rather than impede it, there must be a proper system of incentives to encourage productive lending and, even more importantly, to avoid lending that may lead to subsequent credit problems. This underlines the importance of credit analysis and the monitoring of banks together with appropriate supervision. However, when governments pre-empt a disproportionate share of private savings, the amount that is left to go through the financial system may be too small to stimulate effective financial intermediation and market development.[26]

If it is agreed that banks should be essentially private sector entities, then they should be run as private sector entities. Large government holdings of bank capital may indicate that banks are not in fact being run along commercial lines. Data on the privatisation of banks in the central European economies, in terms of bank assets, loans, deposits and capital, demonstrate a willingness on the part of the state to privatise at least some of their state banks. Hungary has become the first country to declare explicitly that banks are no longer considered 'strategic' assets and can be satisfactorily monitored without the state having an ownership stake.[27]

In Russia, the new law on the divestment of ownership in banks came into force in March of this year. According to this law, the central bank will maintain majority stakes in Sberbank, Vneshtorgbank, Moscow Narodny Bank, London, Eurobank, Paris and Ost-West Handelsbank, Frankfurt. The literature dealing with privatisation on a theoretical basis as well as the results of practical experience does not, according to some economists,

[26] Crockett (1994); similarly, Kapoor (1997) and Keuschnigg (1997).
[27] See Borish et al. (1997) for the underlying data; for the privatisation struggle in central European economies, see Kapoor (1997).

provide conclusive evidence as to the merits of the change in ownership from the state to the private sector.[28] Regardless of this discussion, it appears quite clear that the private side of banking needs further strengthening. This will remove any threat of government interference in what are essentially private sector decision-making processes, as foreign investors will almost inevitably wish to collaborate with the private sector and moves towards joining the EU will also advance this process. The EU accession process is likely to be a major driving force as a more competitive banking system will be a requirement of entry.[29] The recent parliamentary decision in the Slovak Republic to postpone privatisation of the major state-owned savings bank (as well as a dominant insurance company) until 2003 is likely to slow down adjustment in this sector.

While the timing and method of privatisation are controversial issues, most would agree that demonopolisation is a prerequisite for privatisation: otherwise the new owners would simply be able to extract monopoly rents. Furthermore, the evidence from United Kingdom privatisation programmes is that the major gains in labour productivity in state-owned enterprises came from commercialisation (i.e. enterprises being subjected to competitive pressure and run commercially) rather than privatisation. Similarly, privatisation when key prices are still controlled will mean that the new managers' decisions will be guided by a distorted set of relative prices and the opportunities for corruption enhanced.

Allowing 'insiders' (managers or workers) to obtain control of state companies creates the risk that they will resist any change that worsens their own position. Moreover, methods of privatisation that lead to a very dispersed ownership structure (e.g. voucher-based privatisation) may in practice leave the old management with a free hand to resist adjustment. This is a particularly sore point if the providers of funds are overindulgent (as state banks have been) or if the state retains a controlling interest.

Effective privatisation should thus go hand in hand with demonopolisation and with banking business being conducted along commercial lines. The question of installing an adequately balanced incentive structure for managers, owners and employees remains crucial.

Continued bad loans and large margins between borrowing and lending

In their pursuit of operational efficiency, banks face a host of serious problems: an asset portfolio that hinges on short-termness, bad loans, little experience of credit standards, the existence of many new firms and undercapitalisation. They may therefore appear to be more risk averse than their

[28] OECD (1997c).
[29] Similarly, Keuschnigg (1997).

Western counterparts. At the same time, large banking infrastructure investments are a necessity in today's world. The inheritance and accumulation of new bad loans may have also made banks more cautious. They appear much more reluctant to assume their traditional role of maturity transformation. In particular, the lengthening of asset and credit portfolios may have to be addressed more seriously.

The aim has therefore invariably been to lengthen the maturity profile of the financial assets in the economy. This may be a long-term process; macroeconomic stability probably needs to have been established for some time before such longer-term markets can evolve, as illustrated by developments in Russia and the Czech Republic: by the end of 1997 only 2% of total credits outstanding were for more than 1 year in Russia while the equivalent figure was nearly 30% in the Czech Republic.

The inheritance of bad (or non-performing) loans[30] and the accumulation of 'new' bad debts, to some extent perhaps unavoidable at the beginning of the transition, may have also led to more cautious behaviour by banks. Progress has been made in particular in Poland and Hungary as the average bad loan/total loan ratios have fallen from their peak levels of about 3 years ago (Chart 2). In these two countries, the bad loan constraint has largely been resolved. Dealing with the bad loan problem, however, still remains one of the most serious constraints on the performance of banks in the region. The literature on bad loans is already quite vast and individual country experiences in terms of solutions have been widely covered, especially the different approaches chosen by the Czech Republic, Hungary and Poland. While individual country approaches and the many problems encountered in implementing a given strategy have not been discussed, it has become clear that the process of containing bad loans will take a long time. When bad loans reach 70 or 80% of total loans held by individual banks, whose asset portfolios contain a large share of credits, as was the case with many Bulgarian banks before the crisis and some smaller Czech banks recently, urgent action is required. In the Czech Republic, the bad loan/total loan ratio has hardly changed.[31] The persistent 'drip-feeding' of loss-making companies is tantamount to undermining the hard budget constraint on companies.

[30] There is no international standard for the definition of a bad loan. In all cases, however, a loan is considered bad if it has not been serviced for a specified amount of time. Time elapsed may not be a good indicator of a loan's 'quality'. Definitions of time elapsed differ between countries. One major way to circumvent a loan being classified as 'bad' is the capitalisation of interest before the due date.

[31] The closing down of some smaller Czech banks with a very high proportion of bad loans on their books seems to explain the slight improvement in the situation there during the last 3 years.

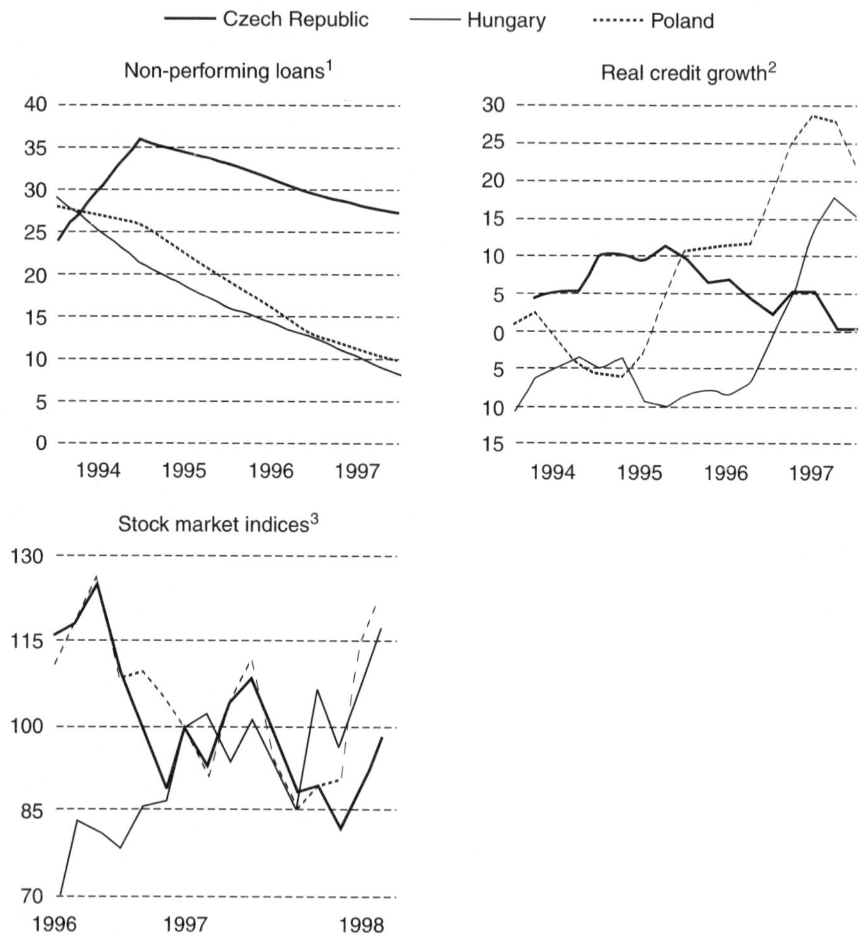

[1]As a percentage of total loans.
[2]Four-quarter changes in credit to the private sector deflated by the annual rate of inflation (percentages).
[3]June 1997 = 100.

Source: National.

Chart 2. Financial indicators in eastern Europe, 1993–1998 (percentages)

This phenomenon is prevalent not only in the Czech Republic, but also in Croatia, Romania and the Slovak Republic.

It is not evident that government involvement in efforts to solve these problems has been successful. In Hungary, where state involvement has been heavy, the problem of moral hazard in bailing out banks has been quite prominent and there was hardly any real progress in clearing up bad loans in the initial phase of liberalisation. It was the deliberate policy of letting foreign banks compete on the domestic market that was probably one of the main factors contributing to an improvement in the bad loan portfolio of the banking system. Banks with too much bad debt could not keep up with their competitors. Positive real economic developments may have helped to ease the bad loan problem in Poland, so that it may be difficult to attribute the fairly successful Polish experience to more 'hands-off' government policies.

In spite of the success stories in some countries, in general bad loans still constitute one of the major problems of the region. To partly offset this drain on the asset side of banks' balance sheets, margins between borrowing and lending have remained high in comparison with banking systems in the traditional industrialised economies, even though they have narrowed in some countries. While in the industrial economies the margin is on the order of 2 to 3%, it is twice as high in central Europe and even higher in some countries further east. The higher lending rates entail a cost to the economy, especially if they are high in real terms, thus potentially slowing down investments. At the same time, economic doctrine requires positive real deposit rates in order for savings to be created. The high margins thus give rise to a potential dilemma on both the asset and liability side of bank balance sheets. However, there may be some justification for these higher margins on account of the large investments required to boost the banks' financial infrastructure. Furthermore, higher interest rate margins may make the banking system as such profitable – an argument not easily dismissed. Generally interpreted as indicators of inefficiency in the banking system, large margins may nevertheless be justifiable at least for a limited period.

Bad-loan categories should be reflected in loan-loss provisioning on the asset side of bank balance sheets. In principle, provisioning should reflect the recoverable value of the underlying asset, the recoverable value being the actual market value. While reported provisioning levels have gone up in central Europe, there are doubts as to whether they are adequate. If a loan is collateralised, its recoverable value will be reduced if the collateral cannot be legally enforced. The experience in the Czech Republic, for example, seems to indicate that, although collateral may appear sufficient, it does not *de facto* provide security to the lender if the lender's claim is not enforceable.[32] Unfortunately, this situation may lead to a sense of false security on the part of the lender. Loan-loss provisions based on non-performing loans also do not take account of expected losses in loan portfolios. For example, the Swiss banks recently increased their loan-loss provisioning due to the Asian crisis. Banks' capital is frequently overstated, as charges are not taken for loans that have become non-performing.

---

[32] Similarly, Kapoor (1997). This paragraph raises issues of transparency for the authorities as well as banking supervisory issues.

Strengthening the capital base and credit assessment

Strengthening the capital base, like reducing bad debts, will increase confidence in the banking system. Banks are generally asked by their respective central banks (or supervisory authorities) to respect the BIS guidelines on capital adequacy. Whereas the 8% capital adequacy ratio was out of reach for all countries at the beginning of the transition, some countries now require ratios that are marginally higher than the Basel Committee recommendations. Estonia, following Latvia and Lithuania, raised the capital adequacy ratio from 8% to 10% in October 1997 (Table 1). This higher requirement acknowledges that the banking systems in central and eastern Europe are still more fragile than in the Western economies.[33] Banks operating in riskier environments need higher capital or liquid asset ratios. In crisis-hit Asia, capital adequacy ratios have only been significantly higher than prescribed by the BIS guidelines in Hong Kong (18%) and Singapore (19%), two countries that weathered the Asian storm relatively well.

Credit assessment and, in more general terms, the proper assessment of all balance sheet risks remain difficult issues. This applies in particular to the establishment and running of internal and external financial auditing procedures. However, the institutionalisation of such risk assessment systems covering, *inter alia*, operational, credit and interest rate risk and the interlinkages between these various risks is a challenge for all commercial banks, not only for banks in eastern Europe.

Development of the markets and the tax environment

The development of individual money and capital markets should remain high on the transition agenda. It will not only accustom governments to borrowing at market rates but will also facilitate monetary policy implementation by allowing open market operations. This should foster the move away from direct monetary policy instruments to placing the interest rate mechanism at the centre of policy. Domestic borrowers may make use of these markets and foreigners may hold part of the related assets in their portfolios. Furthermore, longer-term markets provide a source of funding for domestic banks, reducing the maturity transformation risk faced by all banks. Progress in establishing more complete markets is at different stages in individual countries.[34] Even in the more advanced economies of central Europe, there are few instruments with long maturities.

---

[33] This is not undisputed; see, for example, Keuschnigg (1997).

[34] An attempt at a cross-country view of the size of the foreign exchange market is made in Koch (1997b). For a discussion of the cautious approach to developing a foreign exchange market in Poland, see Malecki (1997).

It may be necessary to take a fresh look at the fiscal treatment of banks. The tax environment does not appear dramatically different from that of some western economies, for example in terms of profit tax. However, tax evasion or the simple non-payment of tax is still much more widespread. High reserve requirements also place additional strains on the financial performance of banks.

Corporate governance – largely unresolved

The issue of corporate (including banking) governance is vast and complex. It has a bearing on the behaviour of individuals in relation to any incentive structure existing within their bank. Managers, owners and employees have to play their part in the delicate balance of power in corporate control. Mismanagement of funds, opportunities for fraud, asset stripping and connected lending may be better contained if an adequate incentive structure is in place. The adequacy of such structures is a key element in bank restructuring. These issues are also the subjects of intense discussion in the industrial economies. Legal structure and actual control and/or behaviour may not coincide, rendering a legalistic/administrative approach useful but limited.

In summarising the four crucial factors discussed above in promoting growth, it is probably fair to assert that the government's role should not be to squash private initiatives. Higher monetisation is probably also a key precondition for any sensible restructuring of banking. The interaction between the macroenvironment and, in particular, the performance of the enterprise sector and the health of the banks hardly needs stressing. Most transition economies have thus initially sought to provide a stable macroframework. The paper also confirmed the general microfinancial weakness in many banks in the transition economies: a large share of non-performing loans, underdeveloped risk assessment and auditing systems in banks, and a weak capital base. However, here the intercountry differences in developments are particularly pronounced.[35]

[35] See the caveats mentioned at the start of this paper.

Table 1. Banking supervision

	Bulgaria	**Czech Republic**	**Estonia**	**Hungary**	**Latvia**	**Lithuania**	**Poland**	**Romania**	**Slovak Republic**
Supervisory authority	Central bank	Central bank	Central bank	Supervision agency and central bank	Central bank	Central bank	Central bank	Central bank	Central bank
Establishing a bank:									
Types of licence	General/ limited BGL 450 million	General/ limited	General	General/ special HUF 100 million HUF 500 million	Banking/ foreign exchange	Full/ limited	Full/ limited	Preliminary/ operational	Preliminary/ operational
Capital requirement[1]	BGL 800 million	CZK 500 million	EEK 25 million	HUF 1 000 million	ECU 5 million (new banks)	LTL 10 million	ECU 5 million	ROL 12 billion	SKK 500 million
Capital requirement in dollars[2]	US$6 million US$11 million	US$19 million	US$2.2 million	US$1 million US$4 million US$7 million	US$6 mil- lion	US$2.5 million	US$6 mil- lion	US$4.7 million	US$17 million

Table 1. Continued

Current business:									
Capital adequacy	8%	8% by end 1996	8%	8% by end 1994	10%	13%	8%[3]	8%	8% by end 1996
Risk-weighted assets	Yes	Yes	Yes	Yes	Yes	Yes	Yes	Yes	Yes
Large credit exposures[4]	25% of capital	25% of capital	25% of own funds	25% of capital	25% of capital	30% of capital	15% of capital	20% of own funds	40% of capital[5]
Liquidity ratio	Not specified	Not specified	Not specified	10% of weighted assets	Not specified	>30% of liabilities	Not specified	Minimum reserves	Not specified
Total open foreign exchange position	Limited	20% of capital	No special limits	60% of own funds	20% as from early 1996	30% of capital	30% of capital	10% of own funds	25% of capital
Total non-bank participations	May not exceed equity capital	25% of capital	–	60% of capital	60% of own funds	10% of capital	25% of capital	20% of capital of non-banking entity	25% of capital
Deposit insurance	Under consideration	≥CZK 100 000	In preparation	≥HUF 1 million	None	LTL 5 000	ECU 3 000	Under consideration	Under consideration

Table 1. Continued

	Bulgaria	**Czech Republic**	**Estonia**	**Hungary**	**Latvia**	**Lithuania**	**Poland**	**Romania**	**Slovak Republic**
Reserves/ provisions for bad debts	General: 1.25% loans Provisions: unlimited	General: 1% of loans Provisions for different risk categories	Yes	General: 1.25% loans Provisions for different risk categories	Yes	Yes	Provisions for different risk categories	General: 2% of loans	Provisions for different risk categories
Reporting requirements	Annual report	Annual report	Annual report	Annual report	Annual report	Annual report	Annual report	Annual report	Annual report
Audit	≥2 external auditors	External auditor	External auditor	External auditor	External auditor	≥1 external auditor	Chartered accountants	External audit not a legal obligation	International audit
On-site inspection	Possible	Possible	Yearly	Yearly	Yearly	Regular	Regular	Aim: yearly	Possible

[1]Multiple figures indicate different types of bank.
[2]At end-1995 exchange rates.
[3]New banks 15%/12%.
[4]Maximum per economic unit.
[5]25% starting late 1996.
Source: Bank for International Settlements, *Handbook on Central Banks of Central and Eastern Europe* (Basel, BIS, 1997).

10.4 Banking supervision – status and core principles – a must in avoiding crashes

A fragile domestic financial system may constrain the central banks in their pursuit of more stable policies. One factor, which needs to be addressed in the restructuring process, is banking supervision. In almost all the countries in transition, supervision is considered to be fairly weak. On the legal side, a large number of countries has already introduced adequate legislation, often leaning on EU legislation and BIS recommendations. For example, the legal framework created by the Czech Republic in 1995 is quite impressive. In Russia, the approach has been different, namely more pragmatic, as only selected larger banks are subject to close inspection. a summary of the status quo in June 1997 is shown in Table 1.

Given that weak banking supervision has been identified as playing a major role in almost all banking crises, it needs to be seriously addressed. It is therefore advisable to implement the Core Principles of the Basel Committee on Banking Supervision without undue delay.[36] In practically all countries, the implementation of banking supervision will thus need to be accelerated. While a necessary condition of financial stability, banking supervision is neither a surrogate for nor a guarantee of such stability. Banking supervision will be most effective if it is seen as a corrective mechanism preventing systemic crises while preserving market discipline.

Transparency and prudent regulation in financial markets covers a wide range of issues, from the timely release of reliable economic statistics to effective enforcement of conservative banking regulations, and capital market and company accounting rules that meet international standards. In the Asian crisis, the Republic of Korea turned out to have much more short-term debt than had previously been disclosed. Thailand for a long time withheld the true level of its foreign exchange reserves. In transition economies there are scores of conglomerates, companies and banks that do not reveal the true nature of their balance sheets. In some countries, such as Romania, archaic accounting rules are employed. Several of the region's stock markets remain poorly regulated. The 'bad loans' also illustrate the problem. Invariably these were under-recorded in the initial phases of banking fragility. This has been well documented in central Europe, Japan and, more recently, in the Republic of Korea. All this leaves markets unable to price assets accurately and so deters investors. Reporting requirements in the economic and financial domain were increased in a wholesale fashion after the Mexican crisis in all the emerging economies.

---

[36] Basel Committee on Banking Supervision (1997).

The quest for timely and more complete information on banks and the banking system is an ongoing process. As a result of the Asian crisis, the Hong Kong Monetary Authority (HKMA) has issued tighter guidelines to banks, requiring more detail on exposure to counterparties, the maturity profile of assets and liabilities, the sectoral composition of loan portfolios, and capital adequacy ratios with effect as of late 1997. More recently the HKMA also raised the minimum capital requirements.

Next to these more short-term financial data it should not be overlooked that some basic structural data by economic agent and by instrument, for example a flow of funds survey and corresponding balance sheets, is needed. These major gaps in current financial reporting in eastern Europe hamper the assessment of whether or not bank restructuring is moving in the right direction.

10.5 The supportive role of foreign banks

Foreign banks provide not only capital to weak banks but also expertise in bank management and the technical know-how for creating a competitive environment. Perhaps their greatest advantage is that they can expose the unsound credit business of their domestic counterparts, notably connected lending and lending to loss-making enterprises.[37] Yet many policy makers continue to worry that few domestic banks are strong enough to withstand competition, and possible foreign domination of the banking system remains an issue of acute political sensitivity.

The Hungarian authorities decided to allow foreign banks into the country before domestic banks had been fully restructured. Foreign banks, initially more profitable than domestic banks, have quickly integrated into the Hungarian domestic financial system. Non-residents, who owned 12.5% of the share capital of all banks in 1993, now own more than three-quarters. In the Czech Republic, foreign banks now account for about one-fourth of banking assets. Poland opted for a more gradual opening. Foreign banks were allowed to buy or merge only with certain domestic banks designated by the government, which sought foreign help in restructuring problem banks. The foreign response was not very enthusiastic because the banks on offer were mainly the weaker banks and because the lags involved in entry requirements (a 2-year presence in the domestic market before foreign exchange business could be conducted) deterred potential entrants. At present, foreign banks hold only about 10% of total banking assets. However, further liberalisation is intended within the next two years as the country aims to

[37] Goldstein and Turner (1996).

join the European Union. Even so, competition in the banking sector already appears to be intense enough to pose achallenge to the dominance of the state banks. The Hungarian and, to alesser extent, the Polish experience indicates that the financial sector should be open to qualified new entrants, including those from abroad. Various studies have shown that the fairly strong banking sector in these two economies owes alot to the influx of these banks.

In Hungary and Poland foreign banks have initially been earning higher profits than domestic banks. As time elapses, however, and foreign banks become involved in retail banking, the difference in profit margins between foreign and domestic banks will tend to disappear and domestic banks should emerge strengthened from this process.[38]

Enhancing competition through further privatisation, strengthening banking supervision, tightening disclosure standards and accelerating the entry of foreign banks (one aspect of reducing bad loans) are important milestones on the road to a sound financial system. The microfragility of many banks in terms of risk assessment systems and financial auditing remains high in many countries. What is more, low monetisation, continued high dollarisation, generally low savings and the high number of inefficient (loss-generating) enterprises render banking sector reform a hazardous task.

10.6 Non-bank financial intermediaries and conglomerates – high on the watch list

While it is true that non-bank financial enterprises in the majority of countries account for only between 2 and 5% of total financial sector assets, they should also be carefully monitored from the beginning.[39] The restructuring of banks would not be complete without a look at the relationship between banks and other financial institutions. Financial restructuring should encompass banks and other financial institutions.

Two cases illustrate why the relationship between banks and other financial/industrial entities may have to be carefully monitored. The connections between banks, investment funds and enterprises in the Czech Republic were a major factor in the financial crisis in 1997. Evolving FIGs (financial industrial groups) in Russia have been identified as one of the

[38] For Hungary, see Karvalits (1997); for Poland, see Mondschean and Opiela (1997).

[39] One important aspect is the evolution of pension funds (Vittas and Michelitsch 1995). The public/private sector split and the move from a pay-as-you-go system to a funded system are major points of discussion.

major concerns, particularly abroad. The main problem is that the newly emerging FIGs may threaten the transition to a more market-driven economy. It is estimated that six to eight FIGs account for up to half of Russia's hard-currency earnings. FIGs are usually centred on a bank, and their vast holdings normally include raw material enterprises and media outlets. The main immediate worry is that they are not operating on a 'level playing field' but enjoy state privileges such as 'free' government deposits and special tax breaks. The principle of 'fair competition' is thus at risk. Adequate corporate governance, openness, competition and banking supervision may all be more easily compromised in the presence of such a financial structure.[40]

10.7 Conclusion

In the final analysis, there is no ideal way of conducting a reform of the banking sector. While some 'Big Bang' reforms have been successful, as in the United Kingdom in the late 1980s, in many countries serious thought was given to financial restructuring only under duress. Since the banking crises in individual countries tend to be resolved at a high cost, there seems to be general agreement that preventive action is essential. That cautious approach would place a premium on the stability and safety of the evolving financial system.

Some of the core elements in this process are sound government institutions, effective legal mechanisms, broad financial supervision and the requirement that each individual market have a sound infrastructure. The Group of Ten's Working Party on Financial Stability in Emerging Market Economies (1997) recently developed a broad framework, the major elements of which are listed in the annex to this paper.[41] In fact, international financial institutions have used up substantial, sometimes pooled, resources in moving towards such a framework of financial stability. Questions of interdependency, sequencing and the resulting complexities are also important. One widely accepted conclusion is that to liberalise financial markets, and especially the capital account in the balance of payments, is not sensible if the supervisory and regulatory framework is inadequate or weak.

A country's particular circumstances – its macroeconomic, financial, legal and political systems and particularly the government's behaviour towards the market – will influence the steps it should take in creating

[40] For more details on these concerns, see OECD (1997b).

[41] While each country can take stock of its financial system on the basis of the framework, reference should be made to the caveats in Sect. 2.

a sounder banking system.[42] This paper has elaborated on only a few of the critical elements of this broader framework. Three of the current barriers on the path to successful bank restructuring are worth repeating here: government involvement, which throttles financial developments in the private sector; low monetisation, which prevents serious intermediation efforts by banks; and the fact that most banks in the region remain weak and need strengthening.

There are several areas in which more immediate determined action is possible. The bad-loan problem needs further attention, as it is one of the major constraints on banking reform. The role played by foreign capital in the development of the banking sector requires reassessment in several countries. Financial supervision and its implementation need to be further strengthened in nearly all countries along the lines of the core principles for banking supervision. The gaps in financial reporting should also be addressed immediately.

A clearer path towards a stable financial sector has been laid during the last few years by the international financial institutions. The responsibility for reaching the destination, however, is placed squarely with the national authorities and needs constant attention in each individual country.

[42] Similarly, Harwood (1997).

Annex: Illustrative list of indicators of robust financial systems

(i) Legal and juridical framework
- Well-defined property rights and contract law
- Market contracts easily enforceable in practice
- Ability to pledge and seize collateral
- Well-developed bankruptcy code

(ii) Accounting, disclosure and transparency
- Loan valuation, asset classification and provisioning practices reflecting sound assessment of counterparties
- Effective and regular auditing mechanisms
- Information on the creditworthiness of financial institutions made publicly available on a regular, frequent basis
- Timely publication of relevant aggregate financial data (macroeconomic indicators, reserves, banking sector statistics, etc.)
- Availability of impartial credit-rating or credit-information facilities

(iii) Stakeholder oversight and institutional governance
- Capital adequacy requirements commensurate with risk
- Replacement of management for poor performance
- Enforceable legal liability of managers
- Pervasive use of effective systems of risk management and internal control

(iv) Market structure
- Financial sector open to qualified new entrants, including those from abroad
- Share of foreign participants in total assets
- Financial sector concentration ratios
- Liquid interbank money and capital markets
- Regulations permitting a full range of financial instruments
- Sound and effective payment and settlement systems
- Share of banking system assets held by public sector financial institutions

(v) Supervisory/regulatory authority
- Independent of political interference in the daily conduct of supervision and appropriate accountability for achieving clearly defined objectives
- Power to force disclosure, impose penalties, etc.
- Adequate resources for staffing, training, compensation
- Conducts supervision on a consolidated basis
- Sharing of information with other supervisors

   - Verification of information on risk management and internal control systems and on asset quality by regular examinations or external audits
   - Adherence to norms established by international consultative bodies (Basel Committee, etc.):
   - In principle
   - In practice
   - Measures to address particular types of risk:
     - Evaluation of risk management systems
     - Connected lending
     - Risk exposure and loan concentration
     - Special attention to foreign currency and interest rate risk management and exposures
     - Heightened scrutiny of asset quality and capital adequacy in the face of sharp asset price movements
   - Strategy for addressing financial insolvency:
     - Procedures for prompt corrective action or the equivalent
     - Appropriate exit policy

(vi) Design of the safety net
   - Explicit rather than implicit deposit insurance, paid for by banks and targeted especially towards protecting small depositors
   - Appropriate allocation of losses among stakeholders
   - Stringent conditionality for the use of public money

Source: Group of Ten (1997), Annex 1.

References

Andersen, P. and W. White (1996), The macroeconomic effects of financial sector reform: an overview of industrial countries, paper presented at the Conference on Interactions between Structural Reform, Macroeconomic Policies and Economic Performance, OECD (Paris), January.

Bank for International Settlements (1997), *Handbook on Central Banks of Central and Eastern Europe* (Basel), June.

Basel Committee on Banking Supervision (1997), Core principles for effective banking supervision, Bank for International Settlements (Basel).

Berthelemy, J.-C. and A. Varoudakis (1996), Models of financial development policy and economic growth, in Hermes and Lensirik (eds.), *Routledge Studies in Development Economics* (London and New York).

Bisignano, J. (1995), Paradigm for understanding changes in financial structure: instruments, institutions, markets and flows, paper presented at the Conference on Structural Change and Turbulence in International Financial Markets, International Centre for Monetary and Banking Studies (Geneva), November.

Borish, M., W. Ding and M. Noel (1997), The evolution of the state-owned banking sector during transition in central Europe, *Europe-Asia Studies*, Vol. 49, No. 7, pp. 1187–1208.

Brodsky, B. (1997), Dollarisation and monetary policy in Russia, Bank of Finland, *Review of Economies in Transition*, No. 6.

Crockett, A. (1994), The achievements and challenges with respect to financial sector reform in transition economies, remarks made at the Joint Vienna Institute, 3 November.

——— (1996), The theory and practice of financial stability, *De Economist*, Vol. 144, No. 4.

European Bank for Reconstruction and Development (EBRD) (1997), *Transition Report 1997* (London).

Folkerts-Landau, D. and C.-J. Lindgren (1998), *Toward a Framework for Financial Stability* (Washington, D.C., International Monetary Fund), January.

Fry, M. (1995), *Money, Interest and Banking in Economic Development* (Baltimore and London, The Johns Hopkins University Press).

George, E. (1998), The role and structure of the New Lady of Threadneedle Street, Vital Topic Lecture, Manchester Business School, 24 February.

Goldstein, M. and P. Turner (1996), Banking crises in emerging economies: origins and policy options, *BIS Economic Papers*, No. 46 (Basel), October.

Group of Ten (1997), Financial stability in emerging market economies: a strategy for the formulation, adoption and implementation of sound principles and practices to strengthen financial systems, Report of the Working Party on Financial Stability in Emerging Market Economies, BIS and IMF (Basel), April.

Harwood, A. (1997), Financial reform in developing countries, in A. Harwood and B. Smith (eds.), *Sequencing, Financial Strategies for Developing Countries* (Washington, D.C., Brookings Institution Press).

Johnston, B. and C. Pazarbasioglu (1995), *Linkages Between Financial Variables, Financial Sector Reform and Economic Growth and Efficiency*, IMF Working Paper WP/95/103 (Washington, D.C.).

Kapoor, M. (1997), Banking survey: heading for the sun?, *Business Central Europe*, October.

Karvalits, F. (1997), The Hungarian banking system: ten years of two tier banking, paper prepared for the Euro-Forum Seminar (Budapest), March.

Keuschnigg, M. (1997), Banking in central and eastern Europe, *Moct-Most*, No. 3.

King, R. and R. Levine (1993), Finance, entrepreneurship and growth, *Journal of Monetary Economics*, No. 32.

Koch, E. (1997a), Financial intermediation: efficiency, fragility and policies for reform, paper presented at the Seminar of the Central Banks of the Baltic States (Tallinn), May.

——— (1997b), Exchange rates and monetary policy in central Europe – a survey of some issues, Austrian National Bank, *Working Paper*, No. 24.

Lindgren, C.-J., G. Garcia and M. Saal (1996), *Bank Soundness and Macroeconomic Policy* (Washington, D.C., International Monetary Fund).

Malecki, W. (1997), Polish zloty foreign exchange market, Institute of Finance, *Working Papers*, No. 52 (Warsaw).

Mondschean, T. and T. Opiela (1997), Banking reform in a transition economy: the case of Poland, Federal Reserve Bank of Chicago, *Economic Perspectives*, March/April.

OECD (1997a), *Economic Surveys: Slovenia 1997* (Paris), April.

——— (1997b), *Economic Surveys: Russian Federation 1997* (Paris), October.

——— (1997c), The new banking landscape in central and eastern Europe: country experience and policies for the future, Centre for Co-operation with Economies in Transition and the Vienna Institute for Comparative Economic Studies (WIIW), proceedings.

Pagano, M. (1993), Financial markets and growth, *European Economic Review*, No. 37.

Vittas, D. and R. Michelitsch (1995), Pension funds in central Europe and Russia, World Bank, *Policy Research Working Paper*, No. 1459 (Washington, D.C.), May.

White, W. (1997), Pitfalls and policy options particular to the financial systems of emerging markets, paper presented at the 12th Pacific Basin Central Bank Conference (Singapore), 18–20 November.

——— (1998), Promoting international financial stability: the role of the BIS, paper presented at the conference Coping with Financial Crises in Developing and Transition Countries: Regulatory and Supervisory Challenges in a New Area of Global Finance, Netherlands Bank (Amsterdam), 16–17 March.

World Bank (1989), *World Development Report 1989: Financial Systems and Development* (New York, Oxford University Press for the World Bank).

11 The monetary policy transmission mechanism in Russia

11.1 Introduction

Russia's financial system is currently experiencing a phase of endemic weakness. The Central Bank of the Russian Federation (CBR) is stemming the rising tide by limiting the creation of new banks through a progressive tightening of entry requirements, liquidating or restructuring banks or placing CBR officials at the helm of those in distress as well as exercising the new regulatory and supervisory powers invested in it in the spring of 1996. The current difficulties tend to bring the responsibilities and tasks of the CBR into sharper focus, making the demarcation line between the central bank and other official bodies, such as the ministry of finance, less blurred.

At this juncture, the leverage of any monetary policy measures is heavily constrained. Transmitting any message to the markets, which cover only a short-term horizon and in which the CBR has as of yet no history of building any confidence, is severely hampered by the current financial situation. Interenterprise arrears and non-performing loans continue to blunt any effectiveness which credit and monetary policy may otherwise have, while the results of a more genuine financial squeeze would be unpredictable as such a process might hit viable or negative value-added enterprises. Many banks are in general not only suffering from the 'connected' enterprise problem and a payment and settlement system less reliable than in other countries but are also groping their way through a fast-changing and fast-growing thicket of rules, regulations and decrees while having to deal with a central bank whose policies are often in a state of flux, in particular as far as its short-term lending and borrowing facilities are concerned.

11.2 The CBR – moving forward

While the CBR faces such a fragile financial environment and while the current upheaval in the banking system is in a sense inevitable, the great strides made, in general, in financial liberalisation are remarkable in that any serious reversal has thus far been avoided. Price liberalisation and administrative price adjustments, exchange rate unification, privatisation and generally improved budgetary processes[1] have gone hand in hand – as will be shown – with a more forceful tightening of the monetary reins by the CBR. What was particularly satisfying from the central bank's point of view was that inflation became more clearly identified as a monetary phenomenon as a fairly stable relationship evolved between it and broad monetary aggregates.[2] The CBR targets M2 as intermediate objective for monetary policy.[3] The CBR also moved forward decisively in promoting Treasury bills[4] and providing greater impetus to the notion that government financing has to be justified on economic grounds other than in terms of the expediency of the fiscal authorities. In fact, domestic bonds covered 55% of the budget shortfall in 1996, compared with a share of less than 20% for bond financing in 1994, when the difference was made up essentially by CBR credits. Direct credits from the CBR to the government were completely eliminated by March 1995,[5] after having covered 50% of the deficit in 1994. For 1997, the major part of the projected shortfall will be covered by the sale of bonds[6] and the remainder by foreign credits. While the domestic securities markets are in general in an evolutionary phase, their presence might accelerate the transmission of

[1] While fiscal imbalances remain a major current threat to monetary policy and operating procedures and thus inflation, the assessment in this paragraph looks at the matter from an historical point of view. We have seen, *inter alia*, an improvement in the budget process, a more sober assessment of the macro-situation underlying that process, the improved timing of the process and a decrease in public sector arrears. On the problems involved in measuring budget deficits, see OECD (1997).

[2] The appendix to this paper tests the link between M2 and prices.

[3] See Khandruev et al. (p. 118): '…at the early stages of market reform the mechanism of monetary transmission was largely unknown and could not be accurately determined on the basis of historical data, which made it difficult to work out if there was too little or too much money in the economy. However, despite some deviations from the established final targets, the economy demonstrated the desired reaction to monetary restriction, i.e. inflation has fallen. However, the Bank of Russia has been able to determine the major characteristics of the transmission process with increasing accuracy and monetary policy has become increasingly effective in attaining the final objectives of price stability.'

[4] The government securities market is probably the most technologically advanced sector of the Russian financial market. All trading in government bonds is done on the MICEX (Moscow Interbank Currency Exchange).

[5] The last direct credit was granted in February 1995.

[6] As these 'bonds' are short-term rising interest rate fed rapidly into the budget.

monetary policy. In principle, well-developed and competitive capital markets respond more flexibly to changes in policy rates than do bank-administered loan and deposit rates.

The introduction of the rouble corridor in mid-1995 made the success on the macroeconomic front somewhat more apparent as there were no major setbacks to maintaining the gentle nominal depreciation of the rouble.[7] A further firming of the exchange rate policy has been announced for 1998: the rouble/dollar rate has been redenominated to 6.1, with the rouble being allowed to fluctuate 15% on either side of this new central rate.

11.3 The money channel – strengths and weaknesses

The main tenet of Russian monetary policy is that inflation is essentially a monetary phenomenon. Russia has thus adopted an intermediate monetary target in pursuing its monetary policy. The central bank is attempting to control inflationary processes on the assumption of a fairly rigorous link between the intermediate monetary target, measured by M2, and inflation. The notion that money creation is the ultimate cause of inflation has tended to become more widely accepted in Russia. To quote from Khandruev et al. (1996): 'The main aim of the government's policy has been to reduce inflation' and 'The most effective means of controlling inflation is controlling the growth in the money supply... .'

The theory behind this proposition is the quantity theory of money, which implies that in the long run prices will be determined by the money supply. The complexity of this simple theory may be captured by just listing some of the underlying assumptions: full employment, stable velocity and reasonable estimates for productivity developments. If real output (y) can be assumed to be determined by the supply side of the economy – the size and productivity of the labour force, capital equipment, land and technology – and if velocity (v) is assumed to be stable, then the theory implies that changes in the money supply will be fully reflected in changes in prices. In a dynamic context this means that changes in monetary growth will be fully mirrored in changes in the inflation rate (money is neutral in its effect on real output). This approach by the CBR appears to follow essentially the 'traditional' monetary targeting methodology pursued by the Deutsche Bundesbank.[8] Acknowledging the potential complexities of the

7 The move from a sloping corridor in 1995 to a 'sliding band' in May 1996 did not appear as a change in exchange rate policy.

8 Hoggart (1995).

simple quantity theory of money, it is basically an empirical question whether or not and in which form the quantity theory of money may hold in Russia. One important consideration is that the usefulness of monetary aggregates appears to be in general less eroded in those countries where financial innovation or financial market reform is rather less advanced.

The anti-inflationary policy pursued by the central bank is reflected in the low average growth rates of base money and M2, which expanded by 2.0% and 2.4% per month respectively in 1996.[9] However, by the autumn of 1997 a gap had opened up between the movements of M2 and the CPI (Graph 1). The CBR's October 1997 statement to the Duma acknowledges the rapid expansion of M2 in 1997 as its growth in the 8 months up to the end of August amounted to 28% while it had been predicted to increase between 22 and 30% over the entire year.[10] The development of the broader monetary aggregates in 1995–1997 has largely mirrored the behaviour of base money as reflected in the relatively modest changes in this period in the money multiplier.[11]

Rapid structural changes may have caused breaks. One of the more auspicious breaks came at the beginning of 1995.[12] While it is difficult to ascertain a deep-rooted macroeconomic policy shift, decisive measures were taken at that time, perhaps reflecting a more serious resolve on the part of the authorities yet probably also a reaction to the serious fundamental weaknesses in the Russian economy.[13] The redirection of policy was seen in the planning of deep cuts in federal spending with the aim of reducing the budget deficit, and increased reliance was to be placed on the issuance of short-term government securities to finance that deficit. The recourse to direct central bank credits to cover the budget was also discontinued in February 1995. These measures eventually halted the slide of the rouble, and the announcement of a US$6.8 billion loan from the IMF in March generated further confidence, reflected in a quick increase in reserves, which doubled to US$10 billion during the second quarter of 1995. Around that time the more restrictive monetary policy pursued by the then acting governor of the CBR, Tatyana Paramonova, took hold. Appointed in

---

9 The setting of policy is described in Bank of Russia, Annual Report, 1995, pp. 46–48.

10 The CBR predicts a slowdown in M2 for the remainder of 1997.

11 The money multiplier is the ratio of M2 to H, where M2 is the monetary aggregate and H is the monetary base consisting of currency in circulation and commercial banks' reserves held at the CBR. It has remained fairly stable around 2.2 in 1995–1997, rising slightly only towards the end of 1996 mainly owing to the CBR's lowering of reserve requirements.

12 The appendix looks in rather greater detail at the relevance of breaks.

13 Bank for International Settlements, 66th Annual Report, June 1996, p. 49.

October 1994, she shifted from a moderately tight to a tight monetary policy; reserve requirements were also raised in steps, and a new central bank law was signed in April 1995. She also introduced the exchange rate corridor in July 1995.[14] The decisive change in underlying macroeconomic developments and coinciding measures may have induced some confidence in the holding of domestic roubles, accounting for the shift in the holding of real balances around February 1995.[15]

For some time now the CBR and international institutions have insisted on a low rate of expansion for M2 in Russia. The appendix to this paper shows that the link between the expansion of the monetary aggregate (M2) and changes in prices is fairly strong and direct. The preliminary result of a simple parsimonious model supports the policy currently pursued by the CBR. The main dangers facing the policy of pursuing a 'not too rapid' expansion of the money supply appear to come from autonomous sources, capital inflows and fiscal laxity. Capital inflows and the possibility of subsequent rapid capital outflows are a general threat to the foreign asset position of the central bank and thus the liability side of the central bank's balance sheet. The most recent episode, in which foreign investors withdrew US$5 billion from the government debt market over a few weeks in October-November 1997, appears to indicate that integration in world capital markets may come at a price. Uncontrolled variations in government deposits on the liability side of the central bank's balance sheet, however, are seriously threatening to undermine control of the monetary base. As a large number of government and quasi-government institutions hold deposits with the central bank, it is a Herculean task to keep track of major withdrawals from these accounts. This undertaking is complicated by the fact that withdrawals may also be made at branches of the CBR and that it is difficult to ascertain the daily central bank positions if such withdrawals are recorded at the head office with lags.[16]

While the daily management of the central bank's liquidity position remains a serious challenge, a determined policy shift around the beginning of

[14] See Khandruev et al. (1996) for more details.

[15] Similarly, De Broek et al. (1997).

[16] It seems that fiscal discipline is particularly slack when the fiscal decision-making process is highly fragmented, with many ministries and government bodies at various levels themselves determining how to spend a common pool of resources. This aspect of fiscal laxity may easily undermine the good intentions of the CBR. What appears to be called for is perhaps better coordination between the finance ministry (if so desired) and the CBR. Coordination could, for example, imply a clear budgetary pact at the outset of the budgetary process or a clear delegation of the supervision and use of available funds to the finance ministry.

1995 appears to have accounted for an improved 'bite' in monetary policy. Market players realised that the CBR had become a determined and powerful force in the economy. The gain in confidence was reflected in a turnaround in the holdings of real rouble balances.

11.4 The credit channel – a challenge

The banks at the centre of the Russian financial system (the role of non-bank financial institutions is negligible as they hold only about 2% of total financial sector assets) felt the impact of the reduction in inflation and the fairly stable rouble in their balance sheets. The high-inflation period in Russia resulted in an underemphasis on credit analysis and an overemphasis on exchange rate speculation. The tightening of the monetary conditions reversed the gains in foreign currency positions and made default by marginal borrowers more likely as loan principal and arrears were no longer eroded by inflation. In addition, non-performing loans continue to permeate the system.[17] The introduction of Treasury bills, in contrast, helped commercial banks as their rates were comfortably above those of inflation, thus cushioning the impact of the changing environment faced by the banks. In fact, from 1994 to 1996 the share of securities in banks' balance sheets rose from 6% to over 20% of total assets. At the same time, the banks' balance sheets reflected that they were only hesitantly performing their traditional function of transforming short-term liabilities into long-term assets: only about 3%[18] of the banking system's credits are in the form of long-term credits to the economy (i.e. longer than 1 year). In real terms credit allocation to the private sector fell by more than 10% annually in 1993–1995 and 2% in 1996. These credits predominantly finance inventories and receivables. This short-term nature of credits makes the "evergreening" of loans almost unavoidable. In addition, the failure of banks to properly assess credits is still prevalent, partly owing to inadequacy on the part of the banks themselves, but also to the tendency of potential clients to submit obscure financial statements in the absence of internationally accepted accounting standards and practices. An informed analysis of the borrower's capacity to repay still seems an elusive goal. Yet similar problems appear to be germane to almost all countries in transition.

---

[17] When arrears on bank credits and overdue interest were added, they amounted to nearly 20% of total credits in April 1997.

[18] See Bank of Russia (1997): "Bulletin of Banking Statistics", 5(48), Table 24, Moscow.

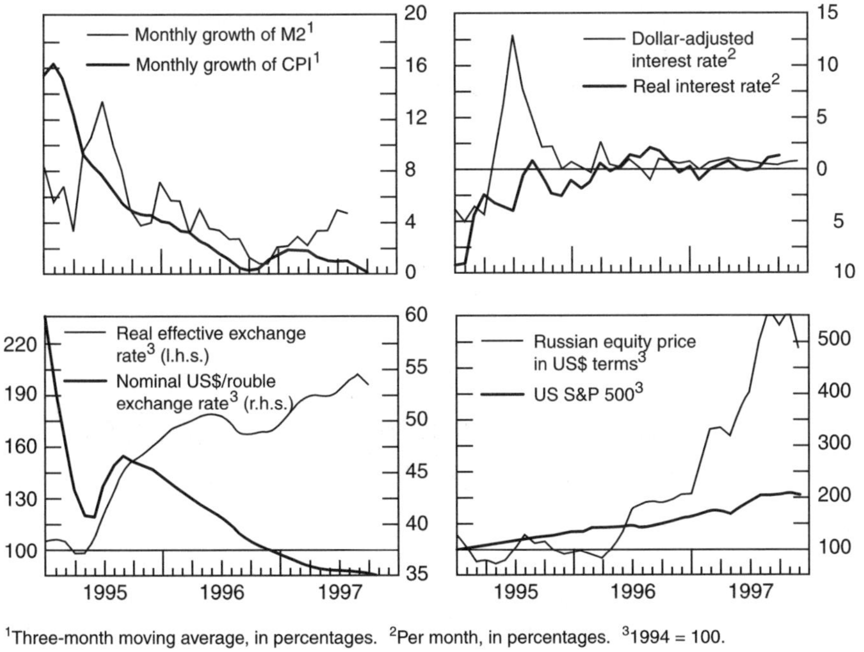

Graph 1. Financial indicators in Russia

The essential lack of any longer-term markets in securities (the introduction in June 1995 of federal loan bonds with a maturity of at least 1 year lengthened the average maturity of all government paper outstanding to about 4.5 months by the end of 1996[19]) and credits not only impedes banks' efforts to diversify their asset portfolios, but also obviously puts some strain on the Treasury as it attempts to turn over the short-term instruments. The system's immanent short-term nature is above all not conducive to longer-term investment or saving. While the holding of short-term securities in dollar terms was very profitable during the second half of 1995 and early 1996, returns more recently remained at 1% or below on a monthly basis. Real rates have also moved in a much narrower range since the introduction of the exchange rate corridor in July 1995. The surge in stock market prices since the

[19] See "Russian Economic Trends", 1 (1997), p. 21. The market in government securities is much more complex than can be explained in this short paper. There are GKOs (short-term government bonds), OFZs (federal bonds with one to 3- year maturities, with interest adjusted quarterly according to yields on GKOs) and MINFIN bonds (dollar-denominated medium- to long-term bonds originally issued to compensate enterprises for hard-currency deposits seized by the Vnesheconombank). GKOs are the dominant instrument and are here called Treasury bills – a more familiar term.

spring of 1996 partly reflects the fact that dollar and real returns on the short-term money market were much more subdued[20] (Graph 1). The relatively high real returns on short-term paper have in the past not been conducive to lending by banks.

In addition, the role of the government in absorbing credit remains pervasive. While in most countries in transition the share of credit available to the economy allocated to the government is steadily moving downwards, this share increased in Russia from 45% in 1993 to 60% in 1996. The absorption of so much credit by the government continues to impede output growth and investment.

11.5 The interest rate channel – beginning to emerge

While there is no transmission of short-term interest rates along the maturity profile to the longer-term end because of the lack of longer-term instruments, it is nevertheless relevant to ask whether the CBR influences other short-term money market rates and, if so, how. While reducing inflation is seen as the CBR's core responsibility,[21] the operational target of monetary policy has been the expansion of net domestic assets under the auspices of the IMF. This narrow target was set in particular to enable any net credit to the government (including the issue of Treasury bills) to be closely monitored and controlled and a tight rein to be kept on credit to commercial banks and thus the growth of the money supply with the aim of holding inflationary pressure in check.

The setting of interest rates in the credit allocation mechanism is free from government interference on the deposit as well as on the lending side. Deposit and lending rates are to be set according to the principle of market forces. These rates are not government regulated nor does the market appear to be subject to collusive behaviour. The concentration of assets in the five largest banks amounts to around 30% of total banking assets and does

[20] Similarly, "Russian Economic Trends", 1 (1997), p. 157. Other factors generally mentioned are a general undervaluation of stocks (low P/E ratios), a portfolio shift in commercial banks' securities portfolios, little incentive for banks to move towards "real" credit allocation, and foreign investments.

[21] The CBR law amended in April 1995 explicitly reaffirms the independence of the central bank, yet it also calls for coordination and consultation with the ministry of finance, for which purpose a joint committee between the two institutions was created.

not give rise to any particular concern.[22] However, the historical dominance of the savings bank Sberbank as the recipient of almost all household deposits persists, but indications are that other banks are now competing effectively with Sberbank.[23]

While providing liquidity support to commercial banks is within the remit of the CBR, the central bank's mechanisms for making short-term credits (or short-term deposit facilities) available are less clear. The CBR has recently introduced instruments to give liquidity support to solvent banks, e.g. through a lombard credit window and repurchase transactions with 'eligible' banks. The lombard rate is held close to the yield on government securities and thus does not serve as a penalty rate as in some other countries.[24] The refinancing rate on overnight credits remains the most important interest rate by the CBR. While this rate is under the control of the CBR, it is usually set by leaning on market rates, that is, it is oriented towards the upper limit of the GKO yield. Under normal circumstances the refinancing rate thus sets a ceiling on the short-term interbank rates. Since late 1996 the refinancing rate has been equal to the interest rate on the longest-term refinancing instrument – the 30-day lombard rate. Access to credit at the CBR is limited to some banks and it appears difficult for banks to assess on what basis rates are charged or when penalty procedures might apply.[25] Rules of conduct for deposit operations at the CBR are also being established.[26] As rules for the use of the CBR facilities may be subject to more changes in the near future, commercial banks may hesitate to avail themselves of these facilities.

It is not obvious what the current transitional uncertainties over the mechanisms at the policy rate level might mean for interest rate formation at the short end of the maturity profile. It appears that the state of uncertain expectations at the short-term policy rate level makes for a very fragile starting point for interest rate formation. Any transmission of the CBR

[22] Comparable ratios in the USA, Germany, Japan and the UK are 14%, 17%, 27% and 57% respectively. In Asia and Latin America, concentration ratios are substantially higher than in Russia.

[23] Three-quarters of all rouble deposits are with Sberbank. Only deposits at Sberbank are subject to the government's deposit insurance. It is difficult to assess whether this leads to an unfair competitive advantage in attracting deposits.

[24] Lombard credits were established in 1996. They are short-term liquidity credits provided three times a month for a 2-week period. (See Khandruev et al. (1996).)

[25] The overdraft rate is set by the CBR as a penalty rate.

[26] The Bank of Russia's annual report (1995) reflects this (p. 52): 'A preliminary procedure for conducting deposit operations was worked out. The Bank of Russia and five commercial banks signed 12 agreements on attracting funds to deposit… .'

short-term interest rate policy to the interbank market will, in addition, have to work through a segmented banking structure. In the wake of the August 1995 interbank liquidity/confidence crises, commercial banks instituted a core market consisting essentially of the larger and more solvent banks while the other banks are basically charged a higher risk premium on their borrowing in this market. The August episode has also led to some retrenchment in this market as outstanding correspondent accounts, which are used to finance inter-regional payments, declined by half from 1994 to 1995. It is less clear whether and when any excess demand for funds or any excess liquidity in the interbank market swaps over into facilities at the CBR. At this point in time, an indicative 'benchmark' money market rate under the more direct influence of the CBR does not appear to exist, especially under a regime where the real positive return on Treasury bills during recent holding periods has still been pervasive as these instruments are evolving into the cornerstone of the CBR's open market operations (repos included). The interest rate on overnight interbank credits and listings of GKO issues with maturities due in 1 to 7 days are the indicators that are most sensitive to market fluctuations.

The impact of any change in interest rates appears also to be undermined by weak credit demand by borrowers. Financing by non-payment is still very prevalent among Russian enterprises; this applies to payments in respect of taxes and employee salaries and to other enterprises (inter-enterprise arrears). There is also a very large developing market for short-term promissory notes (veksels) issued, *inter alia*, by companies. These veksels have a broad circulation and are actively traded. Although this market is very opaque, one could maintain that it is a significant source of external funding for enterprises.[27]

Another factor undermining measurable demand for credit is the rapid emergence of financial-industrial groups. The growth of these groups has been due above all to loans for share transactions as large banks were put in aposition to acquire blocks of shares in major oil, transport and precious-metal industries.[28] As these groups grow, demand for external funds probably weakens – at least initially.

Reserve requirements have been one of the main monetary policy instruments. Bank deposits held with the CBR are not excessive, accounting for 5% of banks' total assets at year-end 1995. Reserve requirements are an active tool for influencing liquidity in the economy. In order to offset the inflationary impact of the transfer of Rb 5 trillion from the central bank

[27] For a more detailed discussion, see OECD (1997).

[28] See Sondhof (1997): "Die Krise der russischen Industrie", Osteuropa-Wirtschaft, 1/1997.

to government accounts in the wake of the presidential elections in June 1996, reserve requirements were raised. In October, the CBR then cut the reserve requirements on rouble-denominated deposits while doubling those on hard-currency accounts to 5%. This shift in the composition of reserve assets was aimed partly at strengthening the rouble as hard currency accounts are converted into rouble accounts. Reserve requirements for the rouble now range from 10% to 16%, high by industrialised country standards but not unusual in emerging markets, providing some downward leeway (although implying a heavy financial burden on domestic banks).[29] In October 1997, minimum reserve requirements on hard-currency reserves were raised in response to uncertainty in the currency market.[30]

11.6 The foreign component – a cautious opening

Effective discrimination in the treatment of domestic and foreign investors with respect to Treasury securities insulate the domestic interest rate-setting mechanism from influences from abroad. The returns on short-term rouble-denominated state paper are capped for foreign investors, and the government has also placed limits on foreign participation in the market. Interest rates came down in 1996. The plans for 1997 to bring more foreigners into the GKO market and lower interest rates further saw a setback in October 1997 as interest rates moved up.

Non-residents were allowed to enter the Russian Treasury-bill market for the first time in February 1996.[31] By April 1997, foreigners had invested US$11 billion in GKOs and OFZs through savings accounts, which amounted to about 25% of the market. Non-residents have to convert their earnings into foreign currency by opening special rouble savings accounts with authorised banks. The effective yield on paper was capped at 19% initially and consecutively lowered to 12% by January 1997. There were also monthly ceilings on foreign participation in the market. The large demand by foreigners and *pari passu* that by domestic savers for rouble

[29] Throughout 1994 and 1995, excess reserves were greater than reserve requirements. This relationship reversed in 1996, but excess reserves remained large (close to 1% of GDP).

[30] One of the major problems for the CBR is the management of the large number of government accounts on the liability side of its balance sheet.

[31] It appears that the initial monthly ceilings on foreign participation were of indicative character only, as investment was not strictly limited. Initially foreigners were granted access to auctions and later to the secondary markets. This resulted in strong capital inflows.

assets were what caused the rapid fall in nominal interest rates and also propelled the real rates in a downward direction.

While current account transactions have been liberalised, capital controls persist. The current account has been positive for some time owing to large trade surpluses (around US$20 billion over the last few years). The recent favourable sovereign credit ratings paved the way for Russia's first eurobond issue in late 1996. The withholding of a tranche payment of the US$10 billion IMF loan based on poor performance in tax revenue collection in 1996 points to continued major weaknesses in the fiscal domain.[32] By contrast, the booming stock market in 1996 and early 1997 may bear testimony to the confidence placed in the longer-term performance of the economy.

11.7 Conclusion

The changes occurring in the current financial landscape in Russia are rapid. The CBR has established itself as a determined and powerful force in this process. Monetary policy currently relies on a fairly strong and direct empirical link between M2 and prices. Owing to rapid developments in financial markets and institutions and potential further changes in the regulatory framework, other links in the transmission mechanism of monetary policy remain weak and subject to further scrutiny. The standard monetary policy transmission channels (interest, credit and the exchange rate) are in the process of being established. The current endemic weaknesses in the financial situation and the emerging role of the transmission mechanisms are being recognised by the CBR. The standard instruments available to the CBR – similar to those used by most other central banks in developed countries – should enable the monetary authority to consolidate progress in the further pursuit of its goals. The main threat to the gains achieved thus far by the CBR is from the fiscal side.

[32] Bank for International Settlements, Annual Report, June 1997.

Appendix A: Money growth and inflation – how close is the link in Russia?

A1 Previous studies and the policy background

Empirical studies on the relationship between the money supply and prices in Russia include those by Koen and Marrese (K & M) (1995), Hoggarth (1995) and Korhonen (1996). Whereas the first two of the studies mentioned do not go beyond December 1994 and contain only prices and lagged money terms, Korhonen's ends in December 1995 and also comprises a real variable (industrial production) and an interest rate. Although methodologies differ somewhat, K & M and Korhonen conclude that prices lag money by about 3 months. Hoggarth deduces that M2 had been a useful guide for future inflation, but that the link has weakened recently. All three studies incorporate several lagged-money and price terms in their final specification and employ percentage changes in monthly data.

In conducting their empirical tests, the researchers had to clear at least the following three hurdles: (1) when to begin the empirical test period, (2) how to define money, and (3) how to treat breaks in series due to policy shifts.

(1) As prices were liberalised in early 1992, the studies by K & M and Korhonen take January 1992 as their starting point. Hoggarth's begins in May 1992 as the monetary overhang may have been large during the first few months of that year. Brodsky (1997) also considers the first 4 months of the same year as a special period, i.e. the beginning of economic reform in Russia. As inflation was still rampant in early 1992, there may be good grounds for excluding that period from empirical tests. In order to make allowance for the question of overhang, in this paper empirical tests include as well as exclude the first four months of 1992.

(2) The definition of money may have to address at least two issues: dollarisation and interenterprise arrears. The standard definition of the money supply in Russia is M2, encompassing cash in circulation and roubles in current and deposit accounts. Dollars held in bank accounts or as cash by the public arc not included in M2. Brodsky (1997), for example, estimates the degree of dollarisation in 1996 at about 38% (dollarisation is defined in his study as dollars held in bank accounts plus dollar cash held by the public, DH, divided by (M2 plus DH). Theory suggests that it is essentially transaction balances which should be included in the definition of money. As dollars in Russia are essentially not held for transaction purposes but for hedging against inflation and/or rouble depreciation, the question of dollarisation

in the definition of money is ignored in the empirical part of this paper.[33] In addition, of course, it would have been practically impossible to estimate a monthly series for dollars held in the Russian economy (as required in the empirical part).

One might consider including interenterprise arrears in the definition of money as they are short-term 'near-money' transaction facilities. Inter-enterprise arrears, defined as enterprises' receivables overdue, in fact stood at a substantial 113% of the money supply (M2) at the end of 1996. However, these arrears are not under any kind of control by the monetary authorities and their statistical base is weak. Nevertheless, K & M add an estimate of interenterprise arrears to M2, concluding that their empirical results are hardly affected. Admittedly, arrears should be carefully monitored as they potentially undermine the effectiveness of monetary policy actions; they are not included in this paper.[34]

(3) How do other studies segment the recent monetary history of Russia, i.e. account for potential breaks/shocks? Gaidar (1997), for example, argues that the economic and political situation in Russia was sharply changing and splits the post-socialist period into four unique subperiods starting in November 1991. He, *inter alia*, claims that one break occurred in January 1995. Without differentiating between periods, Gaidar maintains that: 'By now the relationship between the growth rate of the money stock and inflation rates in postsocialist economies has become a clear statistically proven fact.'

Brodsky (1997) splits the period since 1992 into even shorter subperiods (seven) based on differences observed by him between monthly changes in inflation and the monthly rate of change in the rouble/dollar exchange rate. His major breaks are related to the permissiveness of government finances: the aggressively expansionist credit policy of the CBR in 1992, at the beginning of liberalisation, was motivated by the expectation of a Russian economic miracle and commercial banks received huge amounts of credits from the central bank. While there was some measure of financial stabilisation as budget financing was reigned in to some extent and the growth rate of M2 declined during 1993, the return to new-issue financing of the

[33] Calvo and Vegh (1992) define dollarisation as the extensive use of foreign currency as both a medium of exchange and store of value. In the case of Russia, dollarisation was the main defence against inflation at least during the 1992–94 period (Brodsky (1997), indicating more a store-of-value function. De-dollarisation may have been occurring in 1996–1997.

[34] At the end of 1996, the ratio of M2 to GDP was about 15%. This monetisation indicator is seen by many as too low; yet perhaps a different definition of money may be called for.

budget in 1994 derailed the first attempt at financial stabilisation.[35] However, the return to a tight monetary policy and the recognition that financial permissiveness vis-à-vis central government had dreadful consequences led to a complete rejection of direct credits to finance the budget and the introduction of strict limits on loans to the government in early 1995. While Brodsky also marks the introduction of the rouble corridor in July 1995 as an important stepping stone, both studies, Gaidar's and Brodsky's, recognise the beginning of 1995 as a significant turning point.

A2 The theoretical background and the empirical testing of the hypothesis

While the recent monetary history of Russia may be a stumbling block in the empirical part of this paper, the following takes 1992 as a starting point.

(1) The theoretical starting point is the quantity theory of money. In equilibrium (*):

$$p_t^* = m_t + k.$$

or in first difference form:

$$\Delta p_t^* = \Delta m_t + \Delta k_t. \tag{1}$$

The fractional adjustment in prices may be represented as:

$$\mathrm{D}p = \mathrm{I}\left(p_{t-1}^* - p_{t-1}\right), \tag{2a}$$

$$\mathrm{D}^2 p_t = \mathrm{I}\left(p_{t-1}^* - p_{t-1}\right). \tag{2b}$$

Substituting (1) into (2b) yields:

$$\Delta^2 p_t = \lambda(\Delta m_{t-1} + \Delta k_{t-1} - \Delta p_{t-1}) \tag{3}$$

leading to the final equation:

$$\Delta^2 p_t = \lambda\Delta(m - p)_{t-1} - \theta\Delta k_{t-1}. \tag{4}$$

The variables are defined as follows (all in log terms): p represents consumer prices and m is the money supply, M2.

(2) The time series characteristics of the variables are captured in Graph A1, which plots the levels and the first differences of the variables included in the empirical part of this paper.

---

[35] For a more detailed account of the failure of the policies pursued in 1994 leading to a new bout of inflation, see Gaidar (1997), p. 15.

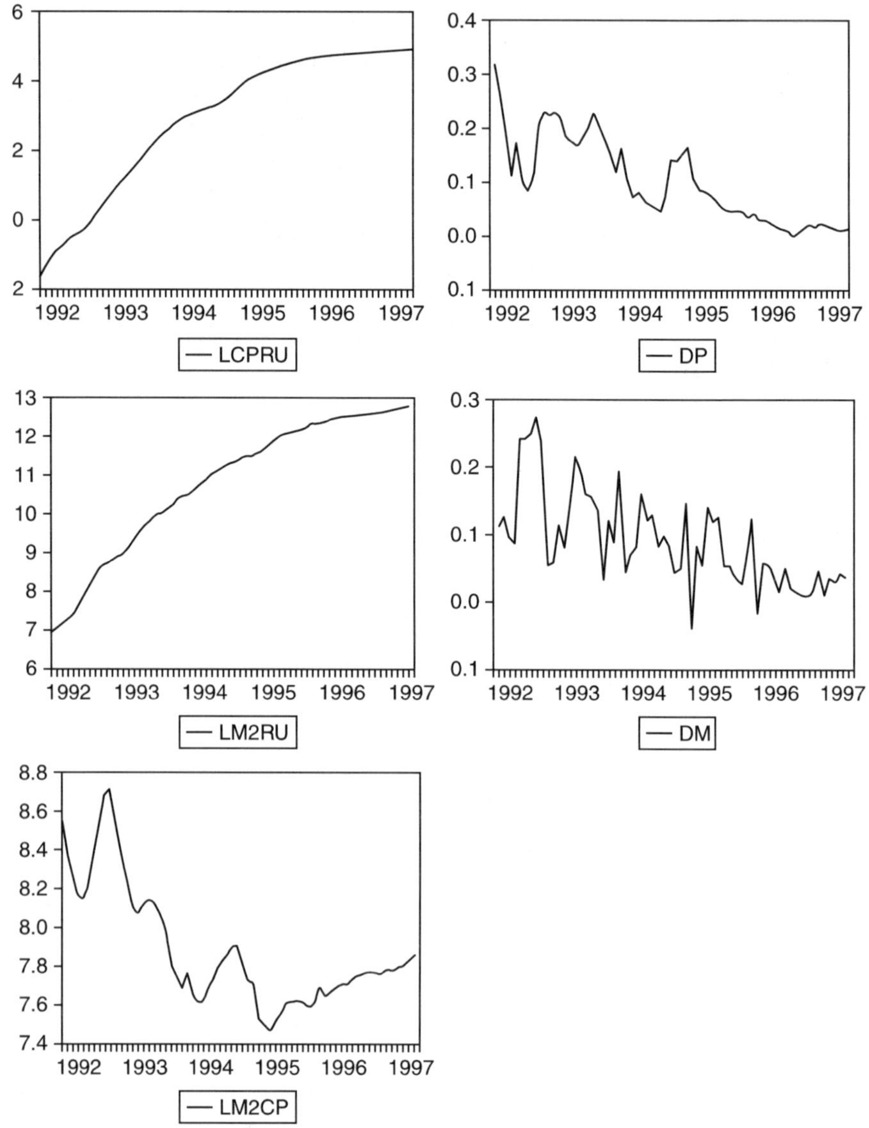

Note: All variables are in log terms. Top panel: Consumer prices (CP) in level and first difference (D). Middle panel: Money supply (M2) in level and first difference (D). Bottom panel: Difference in the level of M2 minus CP.

Graph A1. Inflation and money supply

Even after first differences are considered, it appears doubtful that the inflation and money supply processes are stationary. Should they be represented as in Equation (4)?

The results of the *unit root tests* (tests for stationarity) on a set of variables indicate that p and m may in fact be differenced twice in order to represent stationary processes while $(m-p)$ has to be differenced once. We would have expected similar results from Graph A1. In order to test the null hypothesis that each variable is stationary/non-stationary, Dickey Fuller (DF) and the augmented Dickey Fuller (ADF) tests were run for the entire period. The results displayed in Table A1 are fairly insensitive to the lags chosen. The table shows only a representative six lags for the ADF and lists results with a trend (t) and without a trend (nt).

To reject the null hypothesis of non-stationarity, we require the test statistics to be significantly negative. The evidence indicates that we cannot reject the null hypothesis of a unit root in the levels of p, m, $p-m$, e (the bilateral rouble/dollar exchange rate) and rer (the real effective exchange rate), i.e. all potential variables of interest. What also seems to emerge

Table A1. Unit root tests, 1992:1–1997:6

Variables	DF(t)	ADF(t)	DF(nt)	ADF(nt)
Levels				
p	–0.68	–1.55	–11.40	–3.83
m	–0.68	–2.67	–7.17	–4.98
$m-p$	–1.45	–0.74	–2.41	–1.49
e	–0.09	–2.51	–2.06	–4.92
rer	–3.97	–1.07	–4.30	–1.53
1st difference				
p	–3.66	–3.37	–2.71	–0.52
m	–6.21	–5.05	–3.93	–1.64
$m-p$	4.71	–3.99	–4.73	–3.13
e	–4.68	–4.38	–4.35	–2.14
Rer	–4.50	–3.38	–4.53	–3.10
2nd difference				
p	–7.19	–5.07	–7.24	–5.09
m	–11.93	–6.41	–12.03	–6.36
e	–10.16	–5.00	–10.16	–5.20
rer	–8.56	–5.86	–8.51	–6.02
Critical values: 5%	**–3.48**	**–3.49**	**–2.91**	**–2.91**

Note: All variables are in log terms. The number of lags for the ADF is six (6), t and nt refer to trend and no trend respectively. For m: 1992:1–1997:5.

from the result is that p and m have to be differenced twice and $(m - p)$ differenced once in order to be stationary.[36]

The variable $(m - p)$, also depicted in Graph A1, is of particular interest. The holding of real money balances declined rapidly until about the beginning of 1995, only to then reverse its trend.[37]

Having pointed out the potential econometric weaknesses (as the unit root tests mentioned above present fairly weak evidence) of the theoretical regression Equation (4), the *initial specification* of the regression equation, analogous to Equation (4), is as follows:

$$\Delta^2 p_t = \alpha + \beta\Delta(m - p)_{t-1} + \gamma\Delta^2 p_{t-1} + \delta\Delta^2 m_{t-1} + \mu_t. \tag{5}$$

It should be noted that this regression specification includes the usual intercept (α), an error term (μ) and lagged terms of p and m. The testing of this regression equation led to the simple parsimonious result by sequentially dropping statistically insignificant variables:

$$\Delta^2 p_t = -0.002 + 0.19\Delta(m - p)_{t-1} + \varepsilon_t \tag{6}$$

$$(0.04)\ (4.57).$$

The coefficient 0.19 is very large and indicates that money feeds rapidly into prices.

While this result encompasses the initial period of price liberalisation, the question of the *monetary overhang* at the beginning of the period is dealt with by dropping the first four monthly observations in 1992. The ensuing result is practically identical to that obtained for the whole as the β coefficient in Equation (6) moves down slightly from 0.19 to 0.18. This simple result is somewhat of a surprise as one might have expected a much more complex specification due to the rapid major changes which had occurred in the Russian economy. Some emphasis is thus placed on ensuring that the results are 'solid' in the following section.[38]

---

[36] Based on the DF tests, the conclusion that money and prices are I(2) is weak; the subsequent results, however, tend to confirm this conclusion.

[37] Chow's breakpoint test was applied to the hypothesis that there was a shift in real money holdings in February 1995 and that it proved to be significant (F-statistic: 8.25; probability: 0.006). This would confirm some policy shift (see Section 1 of this appendix).

[38] As the step-wise further liberalisation of administered prices occurred mainly at the beginning of each year, the regression equation was also tested with the inclusion of a dummy variable (1 = January of each year; 0 = the other months). This dummy variable was highly significant. As the basic Equation (5) was hardly changed owing to the inclusion of this variable, it is dropped here in order to render the message more clear-cut.

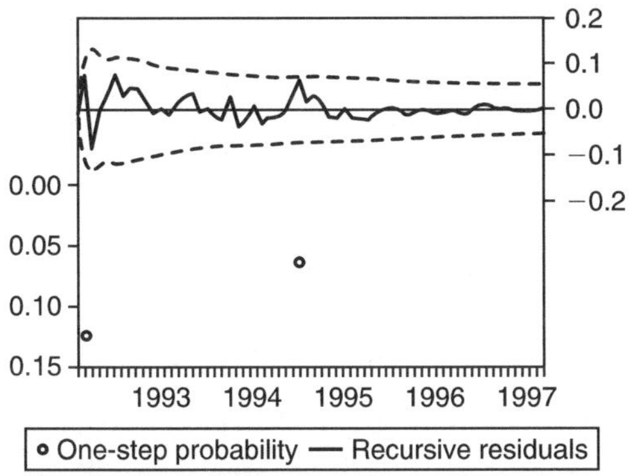

Graph A2. Test for structural changes

A3 Diagnostic tests on the regression results

The regression result was, therefore, subjected to a battery of tests.

(1) As there are potentially many breaks in the time series owing to the rapidly changing economic environment, the stability of the equation was tested using 'recursive residuals'. This procedure is essentially a one-step forward forecast error procedure as the equation is re-estimated for each new observation. The resulting Graph A2 shows that only two observations fall outside the two standard error bands attesting to the structural stability.

(2) The CUSUM test looks at the cumulative sum of the residuals while the CUSUM of squares test assesses the cumulative variance around the regression. Both tests are shown here in graphical form indicating that it was the initial period of the regression in which the cumulative sum of the residuals and then the cumulative variance around the regression moved up rapidly. While the CUSUM test remains within the critical 5% lines, the CUSUM of squares also returns to the 5% boundaries. In particular, the

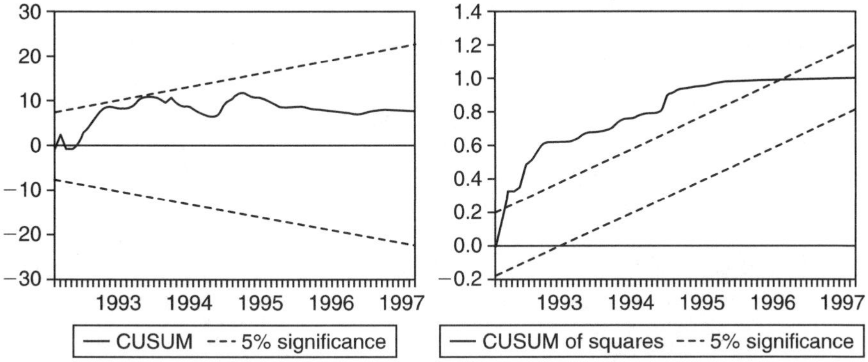

Graph A3. Test for cumulative changes in residuals and variance

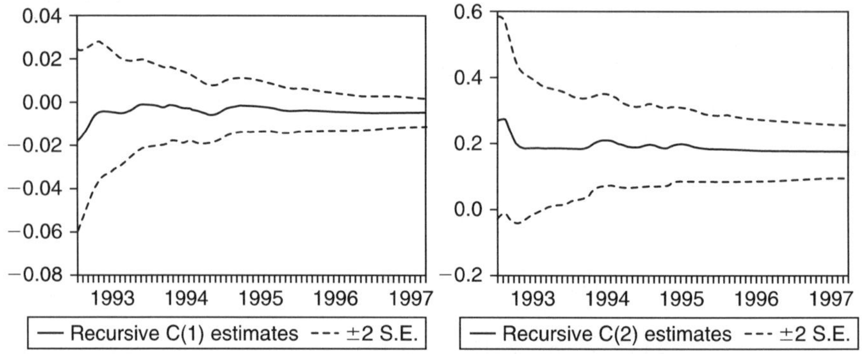

Graph A4. Recursive coefficient estimates

CUSUM of squares test indicates that the variance around the regression was quite strong at the beginning of the observation period.

(3) In order to test for the stability of the coefficients, the basic equation was rewritten in the following form:

$$\Delta p_t = \alpha + \beta(\Delta m_{t-1}) + (1 - \beta)(\Delta p_{t-1}) + \varepsilon_t.$$

That the coefficients are stable is borne out by the following graph. While the coefficients are well within the two standard deviations, the recursive coefficient estimates also do not jump up or down, except at the beginning of the period for the reasons elaborated above.

(4) The residuals of Equation (5) were subjected to the following tests: the Jarque-Bera statistic was 10.53 with a probability of 0.0052. This means that while there are some outliers among the residuals, the hypothesis of the residuals being normally distributed cannot be rejected. In fact, the correlogram of the residuals shows that none of them falls outside a 5% confidence interval.

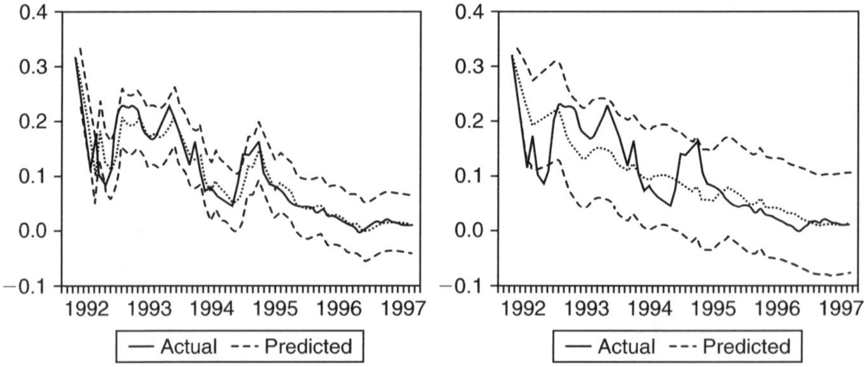

Graph A5. Prediction of inflation – in sample

The ARCH (autoregressive conditional heteroskedasticity) test is motivated by the observation that in many cases the size of the residuals appears to be related to their recent size. The ARCH test was run with four residuals resulting in an F-statistic of 4.2 (with a probability of 0.0048). In addition, with White's Heteroskedasticity Test the F-statistic proved to be 1.58 (with a probability of 0.2136). None of these tests undermines the results obtained in Equation (6).

(5) Another way to ascertain that the obtained regression results are in fact reasonable is to see how the regressions perform against predictions. Graph A5 confirms that the predictions within the sample are somewhat bumpy up to and including the first 2 months of 1995 but that they fall into the range of ±2 standard deviations (except at the very beginning of the period). In general terms, these predictions confirm that the underlying model is quite solid, and has been so in particular since spring 1995.

A natural extension of the model represented above would include real variables. Korhonen's (1996) choice of incorporating industrial production as a proxy for real activity seems logical.[39] The empirical results of the cross-country study by De Broeck et al. (1997) on central and eastern Europe, including Russia, aimed at explaining the behaviour of real money stocks also support the notion that the level of real activity should be included.

[39] It appears that personal consumption or retail sales are less likely to be good proxies. This preliminary judgement is based on graphical inspection of the logs of these variables.

References

Bank for International Settlements, 66th Annual Report, June 1996.

Bank for International Settlements, 67th Annual Report, June 1997.

Bank of Russia, Annual Report, 1995.

Bank of Russia, Bulletin of Banking Statistics, several issues.

Brodsky, B. (1997): "Dollarisation and monetary policy in Russia", Review of economics in transition 6, Bank of Finland.

Calvo, Guillermo A. and Carlos A. Vegh (1992): "Currency substitution in developing countries: an introduction", IMF Working Paper, WP/92/40.

Caprio, Gerard and Patrick Honohan (1993): "Excess Liquidity and Monetary Overhangs", World Development, Vol. 21, No. 4.

Copelman, M. (1996): "Financial innovation and the speed of adjustment of money demand: Evidence from Bolivia, Israel and Venezuela", International Finance Discussion Papers, Board of Governors of the Federal Reserve System, October, No. 567.

De Broeck, Mark, Kornelia Krajnyak and Henri Lorie (1997): "Explaining and Forecasting the Velocity of Money in Transition Economies, with Special Reference to the Baltics, Russia and other Countries of the Former Soviet Union", IMF Working Paper, WP/1997/108 (September).

Gaidar, Yegor (1997): "Applied Economics in Action: The International Monetary Fund", AEA Papers and Proceedings, May.

Hakkio, C.S. and M. Rush (1991): "Cointegration: how short is the long run?", Journal of International Money and Finance, 10, pp. 571–581.

Hoggarth, G. (1995): "Monetary Policy in Russia", in Russia's financial markets and the banking sector, ed. J. Rautava, Bank of Finland Studies, December.

Kennedy, P. (1995): "A guide to econometrics", 3rd ed., Blackwell.

Khandruev, A., Vladimir N. Smenkovskij and Alla M. Chumachenko (1996): "The Modern Bank of Russia", Central Banking, Fall 1996 (7/2).

Koen, V. and M. Marrese (1995): "Stabilisation and structural change in Russia, 1992-1994", Occasional Paper 127, IMF, September.

Korhonen, I. (1996): "An error correction model for Russian inflation", Review of economies in transition 4, Bank of Finland.

Mishkin, Frederic S. (1995): "Symposium on the Monetary Transmission Mechanism", Journal of Economic Perspectives, Vol. 9, No. 4 (Fall).

OECD (1997): "1997–1998 Economic Review – Russian Federation", September.

"Russian Economic Trends", Russian European Centre for Economic Policy, several issues.

Sondhof, Harald (1997): "Die Krise der russischen Industrie", Osteuropa-Wirtschaft, 1/1997.

Zamalloa, Lorena (1997): "Monetary Operations, Money Markets and Public Sector Debt", in Central Bank Reform in the Transition Economies, eds. V. Sundararajan et al., IMF.

12 Exchange rates and monetary policy in central Europe – a survey of some issues

12.1 Introduction

The widening of the exchange rate band in the Czech Republic at the end of February 1996 is the latest major change in the exchange rate policies of central European countries. This paper attempts to provide some discussion input concerning the recently introduced changes in the domain of exchange rate policy in three central European countries (the Czech Republic, Poland and Hungary), with particular reference to how they relate to the conduct of monetary policy. The paper casts a fairly wide net stretching from the actual exchange rate policies pursued via the exchange rate markets to questions involved in the current policy setting.

While large nominal and real depreciations of the currencies in central Europe at the beginning of the transition were the order of the day and may essentially be classified as successful, more recent developments have brought a shift to crawling pegs (Poland and Hungary) or exchange rate bands (the Czech Republic and the Russian Federation).[1] While as recently as 1994 some authors recommended exchange rate bands as a policy alternative for these countries,[2] these bands were, by the spring of 1996, actually introduced by the three countries reviewed here in more detail.[3] These

---

[1] The Russian Federation (or simply Russia) and the Slovak Republic are often included as further reference countries in this paper.

[2] See, for instance, Helpman et al. (1994).

[3] A look at all the countries in eastern Europe reveals that the choice of the exchange rate regime following initial devaluation and associated bouts of high inflation has varied considerably among countries, ranging from currency boards in Estonia and Lithuania through fixed but adjustable pegs in Poland and Hungary to managed floating in Slovenia. This seems to indicate that the choice probably depends less on the progress made on the road to transition than on the broader framework of domestic policies and whether such policies are apt to retain their credibility. Arguments in favour of or against the choice

exchange rate policy measures are quite visible and the underlying framework for monetary policies has been subject to rapid changes and appears now to be comparable to systems existing in industrialised economies. However, market imperfections and financial fragility render the conduct of monetary policy quite delicate. These factors seem to complicate the process of gaining credibility in the foreign exchange markets (policy credibility), and it is not obvious that the normative questions raised by these changes have found satisfactory answers in the literature. One particular aspect of this paper relates to credibility in such a policy context. What is not explored is the next step in the transmission mechanism of monetary policy, i.e. the linkages from exchange rates, interest rates and prices to total spending or vice versa.

The first section of this paper looks at the measures taken by these countries in some detail and relates them to their actual experiences. Section 2 attempts to provide some conceptual backdrop. The third section raises the thorny issue of how to gain credibility.[4] The relationship between the exchange rate and prices is explored in Sect. 4, while a final section brings us back to the real world, before the paper ends with the conclusion.

12.2 Exchange rate regimes

This first section summarises the institutional backdrop of the current exchange rate regime in the three countries under review, keeping in mind in particular the question of the intended aim of the measures, i.e. what macroeconomic impact was foreseen or hoped for and what impact these measures have had on the conduct of monetary policy.

12.2.1 Institutional backdrop

Exchange rate policy is not necessarily the domain of the central bank. In many countries, the choice of the exchange rate regime may for instance lie with the Ministry of Finance or it may be the joint responsibility of the

of a particular regime are not reviewed in this paper: the focus is on 'credibility' once a choice has been made.

4 This stylised differentiation between short and long term is a standard feature of many studies, e.g. Clark et al. (1994, p. 1): 'The time horizon is important…Those factors that have the most influence on exchange rates over the short term are not necessarily the same ones that will exercise the most influence over the long term…Alternative methods of assessing the consistency of exchange rates with economic fundamentals often employ different time horizons and therefore implicitly select different sets of economic fundamentals.'

Ministry of Finance and the central bank. In fact, in most Western countries the choice of the exchange rate regime rests with the government, although the central bank may, to varying degrees, have a role in the decision-making process, while the implementation of the chosen system is normally left to the central bank. In the eastern European countries considered here, the hand of the central bank[5] seems quite strong: in the Czech Republic, the central bank 'proclaims' the exchange rate for the Czech currency vis-à-vis foreign currencies (Article 35 lit.a) and sets monetary policy (Article 2 lit.a).[6]

In Hungary, the National Bank Act (Sect. 13(2)) states: 'The order of fixing and/or influencing the exchange rate is determined by the government in agreement with the NBH.' However, in practice an agreement between the government and the NBH provided more flexibility to the NBH until the crawling peg was introduced in March 1995. Up until then, the NBH had the right to let the exchange rate fluctuate with regard to the basket of foreign currencies within a ±5% range centred on the level established by the government. Any correction of fluctuations beyond this range was for the government to decide upon.[7]

In Poland, decisions on exchange rate policy are much more involved as several parties contribute to this process. Under Article 39 of the Bank Law, the principles for establishing the exchange rate of the zloty against foreign currencies are determined by the Council of Ministers upon a proposal from the president of the NBP in consultation with the Minister of Finance and the Minister of Foreign Economic Relations. While the NBP certainly holds strong cards, the final decision rests with the Council of Ministers.[8]

Even though the institutional set-up is somewhat different between the three countries, the monetary authorities appear to have latitude in the conduct of policy, with the policy framework being set by the government, to whom the monetary authorities are subsequently accountable.

One factor that could strengthen the hand of the central bank and be positive in building credibility in the financial markets is the legal independence of the central bank and whether such independence has indeed

5 See Stanley Fischer (1994, p. 4).

6 Similarly, the National Bank of Slovakia 'establishes' the exchange rate in relation to foreign currencies (28 lit.a) and 'defines' monetary policy (2 lit.a).

7 It may be useful to keep this institutional arrangement for Hungary in mind, especially as many small devaluations occurred while the larger ones seemed to be much more driven by 'political' forces.

8 While the legal framework may indicate that the role of the NBP may be the weakest in terms of determining the exchange rate policy, the political reality may be different. For more detail on the foregoing, see Hochreiter (1995).

provided benefits. These considerations were of paramount importance when the new central bank laws were formulated in these countries. Relating measures of legal central bank independence in particular to inflation has not yet resulted in very firm conclusions for larger groups of countries, while there appears to be an established inverse relationship between these two variables in industrialised countries.[9]

The question of the credibility of monetary policy has experienced a strong renaissance in several industrial countries, in particular owing to the shift to inflation targeting, and has also been fuelled by the ERM debate. This renaissance has demonstrated that central banks should be independent. Independence, however, has to be firmly anchored in order to provide a solid foundation on which to establish credibility. This implies a clear 'legal' statement of the objective of the central bank and consistent policies to implement this mandate. However, confidence would be difficult to earn if central banks were not also made accountable in unambiguous terms to the broader political/social framework.[10]

While the legal 'independence' of a monetary authority by itself may not positively result in a credibility bonus, such 'independence', in conjunction with 'adequate' accountability, appears to be a necessary but not sufficient ingredient of credibility. Whereas the principle of legal independence appears solidly entrenched in the countries under review, the

[9] While many authors attribute a certain credibility bonus to the 'legal' independence of the central bank (e.g. Fischer, 1994), caveats prevail. Fischer concludes, for labour markets, that 'legal' independence does not automatically lead to a credibility bonus in those markets but that 'independent' central banks have to prove their toughness repeatedly. He regresses the sacrifice ratio in recessions since 1962 against a measure of central bank independence and concludes (p. 49): 'The overall relationship is positive and statistically significant. This implies that more independent central banks on average pay a higher output price per percentage point of inflation to reduce the inflation rate. A similar though weaker positive relationship holds between the output loss in recessions and central bank independence. This result is consistent with the Phillips curve being flatter in low inflation than in high inflation economies. But it is nonetheless puzzling, because the more independent central bank should be more credible…' Eduard Hochreiter of the Austrian National Bank pointed out that the reason for the turnover of governors may play a crucial role in this context. This argument may be particularly relevant for Austria.

[10] On a more philosophical note: an analogy may be drawn to the question of 'freedom for what', i.e. of using the freedom wisely. White and Smets (1996, p. 4) also state quite categorically: 'Central bank 'independence', which allows the institution itself to set the mandate and exercise powers without accountability, may have superficial attractions but is unlikely to be a long-lasting feature of a democratic society.'

process of accountability as a *sine qua non* appears to have attracted less attention. The latter arguments hint at a potential weakness: the decision-making process and its accountability in the domain of exchange rate policy may need to be made more transparent to the markets. There is, on the other hand, no evidence that the current legal set-up has harmed credibility in these countries, while for industrialised countries there is some evidence that legal independence has resulted in better performance, at least on the inflation score.[11]

12.2.2 Current exchange rate regime

A fixed exchange rate band or a crawling-peg exchange rate in the countries reviewed here requires a certain degree of commitment from the monetary authorities. Such a commitment to certain rules is, in principle, one way to create a framework for establishing confidence in the policy actions of the authorities.

Russia's band was introduced at a much later time (June 1995) than that of the three countries reviewed here – a time which was still characterised by rapid inflation and fast nominal depreciations and may thus be considered analogous to the early stabilisation period in the three countries (1991–92) – the recent changes in exchange rate policy in these central European countries occurred after some macroeconomic stability had been achieved.

The Czech Republic introduced its exchange rate band in February 1996. The exchange rate was set at CZK 28 to the US dollar at the end of 1990. Since then, the koruna/dollar exchange rate has fluctuated within the narrow margins of CZK 26.4 and 29.4 to the US dollar. The central parity rate has been stable since the foundation of the Czech Republic.[12] The introduction of a wider exchange rate band ranging from ±2.5% to ±7.5% at the end of February 1996 did not change the central parity either.

The Hungarian policy of a crawling peg was officially introduced in March 1995. Before, the Hungarian forint had been fixed against a currency basket and allowed to move within a ±2.25 fluctuation band. However, the forint was adjusted at infrequent intervals.

---

[11] Hochreiter (1995b, p. 5) similarly acknowledges the link between credibility and legal independence: '…it is urgent for the central bank to build reputation and earn credibility as quickly as possible. To achieve this the institutional design is relevant. Thus, legal independence is important.'

[12] The exchange rate of the Czech koruna is set at CZK 1 = USD 0.012305 and DEM 0.036121. The currency basket thus consists of approx. 65% Deutsche Mark and 35% US dollars.

Table 1. Exchange rate systems

Country	Responsibility for exchange rate policy	Exchange rate system	When introduced	Currency basket	Comments
Czech Republic	CNB	Fixed exchange rate system	Late 1990	CZK1 = USD 0.012305 DEM 0.037121	1
Poland	Council of Ministers (see text for more detail)	Crawling-peg devaluation of 1% monthly against a currency basket	January 1996	USD 45% DEM 35% GBP 10% FRF 5% CHF 5%	2
Hungary	Government and NBH	Crawling-peg devaluation of 1.2% monthly against a currency basket (for first 6 months of 1996)	March 1996	USD 30% ECU 70%	3
Russia	CBR	Exchange rate band	June 1995	USD	4

[1]The level of the central rate can be modified within a range of ±7.5%.
[2]Transactions on the domestic foreign exchange interbank market are allowed to deviate within a band of ±7% around the central rate.
[3]The NBH sets the reference exchange rate (middle rate) at noon each day.
[4]A daily sliding band vis-à-vis the US dollar was introduced in June 1996.

Table 2. Eastern Europe and IMF arrangements

Country	Acceptance of Art. VIII, Sections 2, 3 & 4	Exchange rate	IMF arrangements
Czech Republic	1 October 1995	Pegged to basket	
Poland	1 June 1995	Managed floating	
Hungary	1 January 1996	Managed floating	Standby arrangement
Slovakia	1 October 1995	Pegged to basket	
Russia	1 June 1996	Managed floating	Extended arrangement

Source: IMF/IFS (May 1996).

Poland had already introduced the crawling peg policy in October 1991 to replace the fixed exchange rate adopted at the beginning of the reform process. The monthly devaluation of the Polish crawling peg was reduced over time from a level of 1.8% to 1% monthly by January 1996. At an annual rate, the implied devaluation fell from 23.9% to 12.7%.[13]

The IMF characterises the exchange rate arrangements for Hungary, Poland and the Russian Federation as 'managed floating', while the currency of the Czech Republic is 'pegged to a basket'. Although the regime choice problem is of major concern for any country, the 'optimality' of this choice is not addressed in this paper. However, from a historical perspective it may be useful to keep two stylised facts in mind: no exchange rate regime has proven to be permanent, and countries have tended to switch back and forth between exchange rate regimes. Given that the underlying economic structures of the world change over time, the nature of the 'optimal' exchange rate regime can be expected to vary accordingly.[14]

12.2.3 Individual country experience

While central banks most of the time do not bear sole responsibility for the exchange rate system, it is their duty to manage it. In fact, none of the central banks in eastern Europe has left the exchange rate to float as it is

[13] For more detail, see BIS, 'Handbook on Central Banks of Central and Eastern Europe' (1996), and BIS, 66th Annual Report (1996).

[14] The issue of the choice of the exchange rate regime for these countries is taken up in Hochreiter (1995b), while the underlying theoretical issues are discussed in, for example, Flood et al. (1989).

considered to be too important a variable. Do the results of the exchange rate policies in these countries follow a familiar pattern or have there been surprises? Part of the answer may be found in the hopes and expectations voiced by policy makers when the current exchange rate systems were introduced. What follows looks at this experience country by country.

12.2.3.1 Czech Republic

When the Czech Republic introduced its wider exchange rate band at the end of February 1996, two main reasons for doing so were given by the governor of the central bank: one was to create some uncertainty for speculators and the second was competitiveness. A wide band would allow the central bank to make some adjustment if necessary in the future. At the same time, less importance was attached to monetary aggregates: while in the preceding years a target range for M2 had been set and overshot time and again, the central bank in its official publications abstained from indicating a range for the growth of this monetary aggregate in 1996.[15]

The introduction of the exchange rate band was preceded by a long period of nominal exchange rate stability. The exchange rate served as a nominal anchor for monetary policy and price expectation formation. As domestic interest rates remained stubbornly above foreign, in particular German, rates, large amounts of capital flowed into the Czech Republic with the exchange rate risk being very small; the money supply has kept expanding at annual rates above 20% in recent years, as the CNB has not sterilised large amounts of inflows, which amounted to nearly 20% of GDP in 1995.[16] Up until the recent change in policy, the Czech National Bank also regarded the development of the money supply as one of its intermediate targets alongside the exchange rate. Yet, the continuous above-target growth of M2 occurred hand in hand with intervention efforts by the central bank. As sterilisation became more costly to the central bank owing to CNB bills issued to mop up some excess liquidity at interest rates which were not coming down, the question arose as to when such policy would be discontinued.[17]

---

[15] The financial press (Reuter, 16 April 1996) reported that a CNB official saw M2 growth of 14 to 17% as 'desirable' for 1996. The CNB has not officially published any target range for M2. Three reasons spring to mind: (i) a nominal exchange rate goal and nominal money growth are theoretically inconsistent; (ii) the demand for money has been particularly unstable in the Czech Republic (OECD, 1996); or (iii) the overshooting of the money supply range published by the CNB has undermined the credibility of this target.

[16] For more details on the question of sterilised and non-sterilised intervention, see Section 5.4.

[17] See OECD Economic Surveys, Czech Republic, 1996.

The introduction of the exchange rate band was to help in this regard by inducing less short-term capital inflows, relieving the pressure of further monetary expansion. While the band may temporarily increase uncertainty in the forex market, the underlying fundamentals have not changed, and if the band is credible, in the sense that the probability of a realignment is quite small, then one may ask what this band can accomplish or has accomplished. The Czech case seems to prove a point which is also applicable to other countries: when the forex market at the end of February was suddenly faced with a wider band around the central parity rate, rapid outflows occurred (US$600 million within 3 days). As the CNB guided the exchange rate back to the central parity rate after it had weakened somewhat during the first few days following the introduction of the band, and it became clear to the market that the central parity rate was not to be changed – at least in the near future – business as usual and inflows resumed.

The argument that the introduction of the band should strengthen the CNB's anti-inflation policy, keeping Czech products competitive, is the second one used by the governor.

The implicit assumption in the measure taken by the CNB is that the current exchange rate level is some kind of equilibrium level. If one were to define an equilibrium exchange rate as one where the current account can be financed without undue pressure on interest rates, one could argue that in spite of the current account deficit of 3% of GDP in 1995 and a projected current account deficit of around 6% in 1996, the current nominal central parity rate could be maintained. As prices are increasing by around 9% annually (perhaps by ca. 8% by the end of 1996) and as this price rise is quite a bit higher than those in trading partner countries, a loss of competitiveness is implied. Even if we accept the notion that the implied real equilibrium exchange rate of the current situation is somewhat below the true level of the real equilibrium effective exchange rate,[18] the situation will not be sustainable forever.

Stabilisation on the basis of a fixed exchange rate will sooner or later call for a parity adjustment if it is not possible to stop inflation completely.[19] A delayed adjustment would result in an overvaluation, the expectation of a devaluation and the need to keep real interest rates high to ward off a potential speculative attack. In the end, an exchange rate crisis

[18] For a more detailed discussion, see Sect. 4 on exchange rates and prices.

[19] This argument is the standard one in which a fixed exchange rate entails inflationary pressures which ultimately explode in a sudden balance-of-payments crisis, leading to a currency depreciation; see Dornbusch (1990) and Obstfeld (1996). The latter author explores a new set of models which is essentially based on the government's continuous comparison of the net benefits of changing the exchange rate with those of defending it.

could lead to a collapse of the exchange rate arrangement. So one of the main questions at this point in time appears to be: for how long is the current exchange rate arrangement credible, if at all?

12.2.3.2 Poland

Poland was suffering from rapidly accelerating inflation, bordering on hyperinflation, at the end of 1989. After an initial peg to the US dollar and a substantial devaluation of the zloty, the current system of a crawling-peg devaluation of the zloty against a basket of currencies was introduced in October 1991. Initially, monthly devaluations were set at 1.8% (23.9% annualised) and were subsequently lowered in small steps to stand at 1.0% (12.7% annualised) at the beginning of 1996. The downward crawl was complemented by an occasional step devaluation, the last one occurring in August 1993. In December 1995, the value of the zloty's central rate was raised for the first time by 6.4%.

While actual price performance as measured in terms of consumer prices outpaced zloty devaluation by wide margins when the crawl was first introduced, domestic price devaluation has been more in line with actual zloty depreciations since about the end of 1994.

Decisions on discretionary devaluations were taken on the basis of prevailing circumstances, notably as regards the balance of payments and the level of forex reserves. This policy preserved Polish competitiveness, contributing to an 85% rise in the dollar values of merchandise exports to the industrial world between 1992 and 1995. On the other hand, such discretionary interventions raise the question of whether the stabilisation effort pursued by the 'stable' crawling-peg policy was not being undermined. Owing to the solid macroeconomic performance already evident in 1994, the authorities had to begin intervening to resist upward pressure on the exchange rate and reserves started to rise. Further heavy capital inflows in the early months of 1995 led to a widening of the effective exchange rate band in May. Despite a subsequent appreciation of the zloty, capital inflows continued. Accordingly, the latest exchange rate measure was to raise the central parity 6.5% in December 1995, and to reduce the downward crawl from 1.2% to 1% per month from January 1996.[20]

The current exchange rate arrangement has generally served Poland well, as it has contributed to slowing inflation and to providing a measure of assurance that competitiveness is not being undermined. On the other hand, discrete adjustments of the zloty, mainly out of concern for competitiveness, have probably not helped to further confidence in the currency.

[20] See Bank for International Settlements, 66th Annual Report, 1996, p. 49.

The implications of the fixed exchange rate regime for interest rates are probably not very favourable either, as the authorities have been unwilling to let interest rates adjust in step with changes in the balance of payments. With capital mobility increasing, the issue is whether the current exchange rate regime should remain an appropriate anchor or whether more exchange rate flexibility should be allowed.

12.2.3.3 Hungary

In March 1995, the NBH instituted a pre-announced crawling peg with a monthly rate of devaluation of 1.9% from April to June and of 1.3% for the remainder of the year. Starting in January 1996, the monthly devaluation rate was reduced to 1.2%. Up to March 1995, the nominal value of the forint had been fixed but adjusted at discrete intervals.

Up to March 1995, the authorities had pursued a policy aimed at maintaining a constant real exchange rate by compensating for inflation only *ex post* through discrete changes in the nominal exchange rate. The latter policy was to exert downward pressure on prices but ran into problems on two fronts: once it became clear that the current account was moving rapidly into deficit as from around the middle of 1993, pressure mounted on the exchange rate, which had to support two conflicting goals – restraining inflation and supporting the current account.[21] By late spring 1994, it became clear that the current account was to be given priority and that the authorities were willing to relax their commitment to reducing inflation temporarily. In spite of heavy purchases of forints in the order of US$1.5 billion in the summer of 1994, the outcome of this gradual shift in policy was a large nominal devaluation of 8% in August 1994 followed by another large devaluation of 9% in March 1995.

A second reason for the shift in policy was the unsettling effect of the discrete nominal exchange rate changes in the markets. The currency realignment episodes were invariably preceded by anticipatory behaviour in the foreign exchange markets as banks tried to bid up the value of foreign currencies and changes in leads and lags in payments and settlements in foreign trade introduced further cost elements.[22]

---

[21] Riecke (1995) aptly describes the Hungarian policy dilemma, concluding that 'external and internal equilibrium could only be restored through cutting domestic demand' (p. 4).

[22] Such inefficient movements in the exchange rates are aptly reflected by the seesaw movements in the *ex post* dollar rates of return on forint holdings (for more detail, see OECD, 1995a, p. 62).

Table 3. Poland: exchange rate developments

Date	Exchange rate policy	Action	Comments
Before 1990	Multiple exchange rates, adjustable peg to a basket of currencies	Frequent and substantial devaluations	
1 January 1990	Fixed exchanged rate system	Unification of official and black market rates Devaluation (31.6%)	Exchange rate: PLZ 9,500 per USD
17 May 1991	Fixed exchange rate system	Devaluation (16.8% against the dollar, 14.4% against the basket). Shift from a dollar peg to a basket peg	Exchange rate: PLZ 11,100 per USD. Basket includes: US dollar (45%), Deutsche Mark (35%), pound sterling (10%), French franc (5%) and Swiss franc (5%)
19 October 1991	Pre-announced crawling peg	Rate of crawl announced: 1.8% per month (PLZ 9 per day)	
25 February 1992	Pre-announced crawling peg	Devaluation (10.7% against the basket). Rate of crawl: 1.8% per month (PLZ 11 per day)	Exchange rate: PLZ 13,360 per USD
10 July 1992	Pre-announced crawling peg	Rate of crawl: 1.8% per month (PLZ 12 per day)	Basket unchanged Technical adjustment made

Table 3. Continued

Date	Exchange rate policy	Action	Comments
27 August 1993	Pre-announced crawling peg	Devaluation (7.4% against the basket) Rate of crawl reduced: 1.6% per month (PLZ 15 per day)	Exchange rate: PLZ 23,113 per USD.
13 September 1994	Pre-announced crawling peg	Rate of crawl reduced: 1.5% per month	
30 November 1994	Pre-announced crawling peg	Rate of crawl reduced: 1.4% per month	
1 January 1995	Redenomination	One new zloty equal to 10,000 old zlotys	
15 February 1995	Pre-announced crawling peg	Rate of crawl reduced: 1.2% per month	
6 March 1995	Pre-announced crawling peg	Margin in interbank market widened to ±2% around official rate	
16 May 1995	Float within crawling band	Rate permitted to fluctuate ±7% around the central rate, which continues to crawl at 1.2% per month	
21 December 1995		The value of the zloty's central rate is raised by 6.4%	
8 January 1996	Pre-announced crawling peg	Rate of crawl reduced: 1.0% per month	

Table 4. Hungary: exchange rate developments

Date	Exchange rate policy	Action	Comments
Before 21 March 1989	Multiple exchange rate	Substantial devaluation	
21 March 1989	Pegging against a basket according to currency composition of foreign trade	Devaluation (5%)	Major change in policy
14 April 1989		Devaluation (6%)	
18 July 1989		Revaluation (–0.5%)	
25 July 1989		Revaluation (–0.1%)	
29h July 1989		Revaluation (–0.1%)	
1 August 1989		Revaluation (–0.07%)	
8 August 1989		Revaluation (–0.53%)	
15 August 1989		Revaluation (–0.2%)	
15 December 1989		Devaluation (10%)	
31 January 1990		Devaluation (1%)	
6t February 1990		Devaluation (2%)	
20 February 1990		Devaluation (2%)	
7 January 1991		Devaluation (15%)	
8 November 1991		Devaluation (5.8%)	
9 December 1991	Pegging against a basket: 50% ECU, 50% USD	New basket	Major change in policy

Table 4. Continued

Date	Exchange rate policy	Action	Comments
16 March 1992		Devaluation (1.9%)	
23 June 1992		Devaluation (1.6%)	
9 November 1992		Devaluation (1.9%)	
12 February 1993		Devaluation (1.9%)	
26 March 1993		Devaluation (2.9%)	
7 June 1993		Devaluation (1.9%)	
9 July 1993		Devaluation (3%)	
2 August 1993	Pegging against a basket: 50% ECU, 50% USD	Change in basket	
29 Sept 1993		Devaluation (4.5%)	
3 January 1994		Devaluation (1%)	
16 February 1994		Devaluation (2.6%)	
13 May 1994		Devaluation (1%)	
16 May 1994	Pegging against a basket: 70% ECU, 30% USD	Change in basket	
10 June 1994		Devaluation (1.2%)	
5 August 1994		Devaluation (8%)	
11 October 1994		Devaluation (1.1%)	

Table 4. Continued

Date	Exchange rate policy	Action	Comments
29 November 1994		Devaluation (1%)	
3 January 1995		Devaluation (1.4%)	
14 February 1995		Devaluation (2%)	
3 March 1995		Devaluation (9%)	
16 March 1995	Crawling peg introduced	Devaluation (1.9% monthly)	Major change in policy announced 12 March 1995
1 July 1995		Devaluation (1.3% monthly)	Announced 12 March 1995
1 January 1996		Devaluation (1.2% monthly)	Announced 30 August 1995
1 July 1996		Devaluation (maximum 1.2% monthly)	Announced 30 August 1995

While the final goal of monetary policy in Hungary during the past few years has in principle remained unchanged, i.e. the reduction of inflation,[23] the new crawling-peg policy makes the movements in the exchange rate predictable and places a floor under price developments. The exchange rate risk itself becomes calculable, and foreign trade should benefit from such a constellation.

12.2.4 The size of the forex market

In implementing their exchange rate policy, central banks rely on an efficient forex market. While efficiency may be an elusive concept, certain indicators may provide some insight as to whether this market is sufficiently developed. The size of the market is one such indicator.[24]

[23] Hungarian legislation stipulates that the primary and most important task of the central bank is to protect the purchasing power of the domestic currency.

[24] The concentration of players or the large assets of a few players (even though there are quite a number of players) may also be relevant as too few players may, for example, exhibit collusive behaviour.

Table 5. Foreign exchange market turnover[1] (in US$ million per day)

Country	Total FX turn-over	Spot transactions			Outright forwards and FX - swaps		
		With other dealers	With financial institu-tions abroad	All other	With other dealers	Swaps with financial institu-tions - abroad	All other
Czech Republic	1,065	352	441	116	50	72	34
Poland	515	340	150	0	25	0	0
Hungary	694	n.a.	n.a.	n.a.	n.a.	n.a.	n.a.
Russia	190	171	9	0	10	0	0
Total as a %	100	49	34	6	5	4	2
Emerging economies[2]	18,854	7,486	2,999	3,422	1,764	2,086	1,097
Total as a %	100	40	16	18	9	11	6
Global result of Central Bank Survey[3]	1,866,760	640,430	51,657	104,256	797,184	65,776	160,812
As a %	100	34	3	6	43	4	9

[1]The results refer to April 1995; data on a 'gross-gross' basis, i.e. not adjusted for local and cross-border interdealer double-counting.
[2]Brazil, China, Colombia, India, Korea, Malaysia and Thailand.
[3]Includes 26 countries; figures do not add up to total because of incomplete reporting.

The BIS's 1995 'Central Bank Survey of Foreign Exchange and Derivatives Market Activity' (BIS Central Bank Survey) collates data on foreign exchange turnover, an indicator of the size of the forex market, provided by central banks and monetary authorities in 26 countries with regard to their local markets. Table 5 sets out some of the data providing a measure of market activity and can also give a rough indication of market liquidity. In that sense, the data may be useful even if they may not be strictly comparable with the BIS's latest Central Bank Survey data.[25]

While the forex markets in all these countries are young and deepening fast, they are understandably still quite small and exhibit characteristics not uncommon to emerging market economies. The largest forex turnover in the group reviewed in this paper is recorded by the Czech Republic, where it is more than 50% higher than in Hungary. But even the Czech Republic's reported total forex turnover (US$1.1 billion per day) is still quite a bit lower than the smallest figure for the group of 26 countries reporting for the BIS Central Bank Survey (US$2.7 billion per day, in Portugal). The turnover in the three central European markets is growing rapidly. For example, by June 1996, the Hungarian foreign exchange market turnover had reached approx. US$1.2 billion per working day, nearly doubling its size since April 1995.

Spot transactions in the countries under review here have a much greater weight than outright forwards and foreign exchange swaps – a feature not uncommon to fairly new and shallower markets. The latter aspect can also be gleaned from the BIS Central Bank Survey: the market segment accounted for by spot transactions in some of the relatively smaller reporting economies, like Austria, Ireland, Bahrain and Greece, is around 60% of the forex market, with the average for the other countries close to 40%. While a benchmark of around 40% is of course a somewhat arbitrary figure, such an average is nevertheless indicative of the situation in industrial countries. Data collated on an individual country basis for a group of emerging economies indicate that, unlike in industrialised countries, spot transactions have a much greater weight (75% of turnover) than outright forwards and foreign exchange rate swaps. In the countries under study here, this percentage is even higher, amounting to around 90%, indicating that the depth of the forex market, in particular the swap segment, is likely to grow in future.

Business with financial institutions abroad is also much more extensive in this group of central European countries than in a selected group of emerging economies (27%) or in the 26 countries included in the BIS Central Bank Survey (only 7%). This appears to indicate a relatively low liquidity in the domestic market, while dealer-dominated domestic business reflects a relatively high liquidity in the forex markets of the industrial countries.

[25] Bank for International Settlements (1996), Central Bank Survey of Foreign Exchange and Derivatives Market Activity. This is the third triennial survey.

The introduction of Czech koruna convertibility imparted considerable momentum to the development of the interbank foreign exchange market. The fast growth of direct trades among commercial banks has allowed the CNB to gradually relax this market's regulation. In fact, despite a larger volume of foreign exchange purchases by the CNB in 1995 than in 1994, its share of the market dropped. In the Czech Republic, banks and brokers, both domestic and foreign, are the biggest participants in the interbank foreign exchange market. Activities of non-bank financial institutions and enterprises, with some exceptions, have not been decisive for the market.[26]

The forward market in Poland is quite young. It was underdeveloped essentially because of the surrender requirement for foreign export receipts, which was dropped in December 1995, giving some impetus to the expansion of this market. While the spot and forward markets are growing rapidly in Hungary, swap markets are lagging behind.[27]

The forex markets in the countries under review are small, and some segments, like swaps with financial institutions (present only in the Czech Republic), are still missing. In comparison with industrial countries, and to a lesser extent also with regard to larger emerging market economies, the forex markets are still relatively weak. This weakness is reflected in the dominant role played by spot transactions compared with outright forwards and foreign exchange swaps. Low liquidity in domestic forex markets may also be considered a soft spot in their development.[28] Domestic banks are the important players in the forex markets. In all countries, however, the monetary authorities still exercise a lot of discretion in the forex markets and are the main players, albeit with a view to gradually reducing their role in the price-setting mechanism.

12.2.5 Summary

Not surprisingly, the reasons for the recent changes in exchange rate policies appear to be somewhat similar. The exchange rate is viewed as the nominal anchor for inflationary expectations. Poland and, more recently,

---

[26] For more details, see Czech National Bank, Annual Report, 1995 (VI.3, The Interbank Foreign Exchange Market of the CNB).

[27] While nearly 60% of the market is forint trade vis-à-vis other currencies (more than half of which vis-à-vis the US dollar), trade in foreign currencies is dominated by the USD/DEM segment.

[28] The currency breakdown of the forex data indicates that the domestic currency is bought and sold above all vis-à-vis US dollars, except in the Czech Republic, where the Deutsche Mark is slightly more important (53%). Turnover of non-domestic currencies is dominated by USD/DEM forex dealing (80% of the market).

Hungary have been using the exchange rate framework of the crawling peg to bring down inflation. The Czech Republic is looking at its current exchange rate policy more in terms of stabilising inflationary expectations, realising that other factors are dominating the inflationary processes in the country.[29] While aspects concerning competitiveness obviously enter into consideration, all countries also seem to be voicing some concern about rapid capital inflows. However, surprisingly little is being said about the impact of these exchange rate policies on the conduct of monetary policy, in particular interest rate policy. The underlying forex markets still seem to be exhibiting signs of serious weaknesses in terms of depth and liquidity. Central banks are aiming to reduce their involvement in the forex market but at this point may still be classed as the dominant players. Central bank independence in the broader context explained above and the move toward current account convertibility[30] are probably conditions *sine qua non* for further developing the credibility of the central bank's policies.[31]

12.3 Selected issues in current exchange rate regimes

While the appropriateness of the current exchange rate regime remains an issue in all three economies, the above demonstrates that the current choice of regime was essentially the result of economic/political forces prevailing at the time, confirming the historically stylised fact that these regimes have not proved to be permanent and that countries have tended to switch back and forth between different ones. With central bank independence established to some extent and the forex markets in all these countries thin and subject to potential government 'interference', one should ask what light

[29] Another way of looking at this is by differentiating between the endogenous and exogenous crawling peg. In the former case the nominal exchange rate is periodically adjusted to the actual inflation rate, while in the latter the exchange rate is adjusted in steps related to the projected rate of inflation.

[30] Similarly, Hochreiter (1995, p. 9): 'An acceptance of Article VIII would, in our opinion, also be conducive to further raise the credibility of monetary policy and the reputation of the central bank.' And later (p. 10): '...the introduction of (partial) convertibility in countries under consideration has raised the credibility of the reform process.'

[31] It may also be mentioned here that all three countries have signed EU Association Agreements and have applied for EU membership. This led the Austrian National Bank (1996) to conclude that 'harmonizing exchange rate policies with those prevailing in the EU and especially with the future European Monetary Union (EMU) will certainly become a crucial issue in the near future'.

the theoretical and empirical literature may shed on the narrower issue of exchange rate bands.

Such literature on exchange rate bands (captured by the target zone literature) has grown rapidly in the last few years, stimulated by a simple exchange rate behaviour model developed by Krugman (1987 and 1991). His model assumes that the principle of setting limits on the range of exchange rate variations is established. Also, the model does not provide any insight into whether or not such an exchange rate policy might be optimal or preferable in certain circumstances. However, Krugman, in explicitly ignoring the latter two arguments, contends that exchange rate modelling in such an environment should be different from that in an environment of free-floating currencies.

One key result obtained by him is that an exchange rate which is restricted to the band exhibits mean reversion, i.e. the exchange rate has the tendency to revert to its mean central rate.[32] The practical upshot is that the introduction of the band has a stabilising effect on expectations.[33]

Krugman himself raises the question of 'imperfect credibility', admitting that he has assumed throughout that the commitment to defend the target zone is completely credible. However, in the real world, the probability that the band will be defended at all costs or under all circumstances cannot be 1.

Empirical tests have invariably been unable to confirm this simple Krugman model and have consequently led to a range of related research by adding some real-world complexity, i.e. such factors as devaluation risk and intramarginal interventions (and learning processes). For example, Bertola and Caballero (1992) conclude from their study of the exchange rate mechanism (ERM) that the realignment probability, particularly in the early period of the ERM when realignments were more frequent, increases as the exchange rate moves closer to the upper part of the band, clearly negating the mean-reversion hypothesis. The upshot for the behaviour of

---

[32] This holds true in the world of Krugman even in the absence of any 'intramarginal' interventions. The model also posits symmetrical expectations with regard to depreciation and appreciation.

[33] The Krugman model and the subsequent literature assume a 'neo-classical' view: in an open economy, either the money supply or the nominal exchange rate can serve as a nominal anchor. Such an anchor is usually viewed as a necessary condition for macroeconomic stability since, at least in the long run, all nominal variables will converge to the preset rate of growth of either the money supply or the exchange rate. Assuming appropriate fiscal and microeconomic policies, the price stability brought about by a nominal anchor should ensure that the economy will achieve long-run economic growth. (See Calvo et al., 1994.)

the interest rate differential is quite striking: while a Krugman-type model would posit a narrowing of the differential between domestic and foreign interest rates as the exchange rate moves within proximity of the upper bound, the interest differential may be increasing in the Bertola/Caballero world. In fact, the history of the ERM shows that interest rate differentials have grown before realignments. Svensson (1994) concurs with the latter analysis and, by including time-varying realignment expectations in his analysis, concludes similarly that there is no simple deterministic relation between the interest rate differential and exchange rates.[34]

The policy conclusion that appears to emerge from the above is unfortunately less comforting than one might have thought. It is not necessarily the case that the introduction of an exchange rate band provides more 'interest rate flexibility'. In fact, such flexibility may be much more constrained owing to the introduction of the band. It is not clear whether, for example, observed interest rate differentials should increase or decrease as the exchange rate moves towards the upper boundary of the band. There is no simple relationship between the movements in the interest rate differential and the exchange rate as exchange rate expectations are not symmetrical around central parity and as there will always be a residual probability of a realignment of the band.[35] The ultimate answers are to be found in the empirical domain.[36]

From a central bank's point of view, the band is a fairly complex structure. While bands may force the hands of the monetary authorities when the exchange rate reaches its upper or lower limit (intervention and/or adjustment of the central parity), exchange rate changes in the band may also not collate fully with the behaviour of interest rate differentials owing to the uncertain development of market expectations. While the exchange rate band is often seen as providing the authorities with some room for manoeuvre in setting their domestic short-term interest rates, this point is not undisputed. In particular, it is not clear whether any leeway could or should be used in setting short-term interest rates, and if so, how much. The literature demonstrates that claiming more room for manoeuvre in setting interest rates when establishing an exchange rate band is not necessarily valid.[37]

---

[34] I have somewhat simplified the argument (see Svensson, 1992, p. 132).

[35] Similarly, Lysebo and Mundaca (1992).

[36] Other regularities are not included here, but several studies have found that interest rate variability increases on the days before the central parity is adjusted (see, for example, Svensson, 1994).

[37] The experience gained in Chile, Israel and Mexico may be relevant to the countries under review. The aforementioned countries also relied on exchange rate discipline in order to terminate the rapid inflation period, then experienced real exchange rate appreciation and, in order to relax the fixity of exchange rates,

12.4 Exchange rate policy and confidence – a contradiction in terms?

12.4.1 Credibility and exchange rate policy

In spite of some of the problems referred to in the preceding section, all central European countries have introduced bands of ±6 to 7%. Why has such a consensus emerged? The available theoretical literature does not provide us with a guidepost as to the 'optimal' band width. However, the experience with band widths in the European context may have helped: on some counts, the ±2.25% around a central parity in the exchange rate mechanism of the EMS may have proved too narrow, while the ±6% for some currencies may have proved to be a 'feasible' range.[38]

Is there anything in the literature that would tell us when it might be opportune to introduce the band?

The country in which the arguments have to some extent been made explicit is the Czech Republic. Apparently, the authorities had already decided to introduce the band sometime (about 3 months) before its scheduled inception but were looking at market developments, in particular the behaviour of short-term capital inflows, in order to decide on the timing of the introduction. The CNB argues as follows: 'At the same time [last quarter of 1995], the anticipated widening of the crown's fluctuation band strengthened the short-term capital inflow, as it was connected to speculations on the nominal appreciation of the crown promoted by improved economic expectations and an inflation drop in the second half of the year. This complicated the widening of the crown's fluctuation band. To impose it at that time would have led to further intensification of the capital inflow and to either a more substantial one-time nominal appreciation of the

introduced exchange rate bands a few years after the inception of exchange-rate-based disinflation. Also, the nature of the bands seems somewhat similar as they typically feature a crawling-peg parity, a unilateral commitment by the countries' authorities to intervene to support the bands and a much greater width than in Europe before the crisis. On the other hand, there are other countries introducing exchange rate bands. Venezuela is a case in point: after the removal of exchange rate controls in April 1996, the heavily depreciated bolivar was placed into an exchange rate band in May 1996.

[38] Comparisons with the ERM are complicated by at least two important differences: (i) the eastern European countries have taken unilateral decisions, while the ERM is essentially a bilateral parity grid in which a common decision-making process determines any changes; (ii) membership of the ERM provides access to the system's credit facilities, while in eastern Europe each country has to rely on its own reserves to 'defend' its currency (Bofinger, 1990).

crown or an increase in CNB expenditure on sterilisation. Therefore the CNB policy remained unchanged. At year-end, these expectations faded as a result of data on a higher balance of trade deficit, and the inflow of speculative capital stopped.'[39] The band was subsequently widened by the end of February 1996.

As the countries under review here may be considered small open economies and on the assumption of free capital mobility,[40] the frequently chosen starting point for the analysis of the exchange rate is a country with fixed exchange rates. Disregarding any foreign exchange premium, the domestic interest rate equals the foreign interest rate plus the expected rate of exchange rate depreciation/ appreciation until maturity of the interest rate instrument. The domestic central bank has no choice but to let the domestic interest rate rise or fall with the foreign interest rate. If it tries to lower interest rates, investors will shift their capital to a foreign currency, capital outflows will result and the central bank may be inclined to raise interest rates in order to avoid a loss of reserves. If the central bank tries to raise domestic interest rates, this will have the opposite effect: investors will shift their investments to the domestic currency, and foreign exchange reserves will increase liquidity in the economy and force the domestic interest rates down. The domestic interest rate acts as the sole shock absorber in such a simplified world. If one introduces a non-zero band to such a world, the expected rate of currency change relative to some central parity need no longer be zero, thus providing the central bank theoretically with some room for manoeuvre in interest rate policy.[41] However, it is not immediately obvious whether such room should be used and/or whether we actually experience more desirable interest rate behaviour (e.g. measured potentially by interest rate smoothing) and at what cost (at worst, the loss of a fixed anchor).[42]

[39] Czech National Bank, Annual Report, 1995.

[40] Please note that this point is not undisputed (Koch, 1997). While current account transactions are liberalised, capital account transactions have become increasingly so. For example, in the Czech Republic, the following transactions are still subject to regulation: the establishment of accounts abroad by residents, the outright purchase of securities by residents, provision of financial credits to non-residents and real estate purchases by non-residents (Czech Republic, Annual Report (1995), p. 36). (See also Sect. 5.)

[41] For a more technical analysis, see Svensson (1994).

[42] The role of capital flows merits special attention in this connection. While, for example, an increased margin between domestic and foreign interest rates may induce capital inflows, it is difficult to assess the potential magnitude of these flows on the margin. Such flows may potentially play havoc with domestic financial markets. In a simplistic way, the EMS experience is the following: domestic interest rate variability increased before realignments, and with heightened expectations of a realignment and sluggish upward movement in domestic interest rates, large amounts of capital left the country which was under pressure to

While research on exchange rate bands has focused on the resolve of the central authorities introducing and potentially defending the band mechanism and on that of the market in testing the credibility of the band when upper or lower intervention margins are reached, empirical testing of what credibility within the band means and implies has essentially been carried out on a country-by-country basis.[43]

The only available empirical paper in this domain for central European countries concerns the Hungarian experience. The paper, by Darvas (1995), finds that the forward exchange rate exceeded the upper edge of the projected target zones of the forint (simple test proposed by Svensson) after the last forint depreciation in March 1995, implying that covered interest parity does not hold for the present Hungarian foreign exchange market as the interest rate differential is much higher than the expected depreciation and devaluation of the forint would require. Also attesting to the strength was the spot rate of the forint, which hovered at the lower end of the band. According to Darvas, the main factor negating covered interest parity was market imperfections. These were loosely classed as follows: (i) exclusion of foreigners from the domestic forex markets, (ii) lack of mobility for capital inside and outside the country owing to poorly informed domestic investors and to regulations governing capital transactions with non-residents, and (iii) distortions in the financial system which undermine interest rate formation. He concludes that these wedges in the financial system thus make the results of any testing of the credibility of exchange rate bands quite doubtful.

The choice of Hungarian and German 3-month Treasury bills as used by Darvas in his empirical test may violate the principle of instrument homogeneity. Covered interest parity may be violated as the assets considered by him were not comparable in terms of issuer and credit risk. Studies therefore generally employ data on eurocurrency interest rates as these are fairly risk-homogeneous except for their currency of denomination and as they lend themselves best to an assessment of whether a forward rate falling outside the exchange rate band may be indicative of an expected crisis of confidence in the central parity. In Hungary, in addition, custom-tailored Treasury bills and bonds sold outside the regular auctions by the NBH render these markets opaque, and this lack of openness also places an effective lid on foreign participation in this market. The results for Hungary seem to indicate that empirical testing of the confidence in exchange

devalue. After the realignment, short-term capital inflows occurred, reversing the previous outflows, so that the net result around three months after the realignment was about zero.

43 For the Swedish case, see Svensson (1994); for the Norwegian case, see Lysebo and Mundaca (1992).

rate bands may be premature essentially owing to market imperfections and the lack of homogeneous interest rate instruments.

12.4.2 Building credibility

In a wide range of studies, policy credibility is essentially defined as the expectation that an announced policy will in fact be carried out. Although it may be true that apparently 'tough and consistent' behaviour over a longer time horizon may reinforce credibility at one point in time, such a policy over a given period may lower rather than raise the credibility of a non-devaluation pledge subsequently.

The following story captures the credibility conundrum quite well.[44] One afternoon, a colleague announces to you that he is serious about losing weight and plans to skip dinner. He adds that he has not eaten for two days. Does this information make it more or less credible that he really will skip dinner? It appears that with each meal he skips, the 'tough policy' of skipping the next meal becomes more credible, as each observation of playing tough raises the probability we assign to his being a fanatical dieter. However, once we realise that his skipping one meal makes him even hungrier at the next mealtime (i.e. that policy has persistent effects), we are led to the opposite conclusion, namely that it becomes less likely he will stick to his diet the more meals he has skipped.

The foregoing would be borne out by Dornbusch's (1990) view that the probability of no realignment of the central rate can never be zero in a situation in which domestic inflation is higher than inflation abroad, i.e. credibility and thus mean reversion are never definitely established because under some circumstances governments will choose to devalue.[45] The Drazen-Masson paper (1994) seems to indicate that credibility as measured by non-realignment does not necessarily monotonically decrease with the length of time that there has been no devaluation. In fact, a tough policy may actually harm rather than enhance credibility as such a policy constrains the room for manoeuvre in the future. While a policy maker may be able to ignore the very high cost of unemployment for some time in order to keep inflation down, as was the case in the early years of the EMS, mounting unemployment in the absence of realignment was eventually seen by the markets as undermining credibility and the events of the September 1992 EMS crisis were the eventual result.

---

[44] Based on Drazen and Masson (1994).

[45] The counter-argument is as follows: while underlying fundamentals may get out of line with the nominal exchange rate and if it is desirable to keep the existing nominal exchange rate, adjustments may have to be made in other areas of the economy, such as domestic prices and wages (see Clark et al. 1994, p. 2).

Even if credibility is simply seen as a function of the changing link over time between the actual economic situation and the policy maker, it is quite clear that even the most fervent commitments to non-realignment or non-adjustment of the fixed exchange rate will remain credible only if the underlying economic situation remains benign.[46] In that sense, it is probably misleading to say that credibility may be earned. The mere passage of time is certainly a very precarious indicator when one realises that the underlying economic structure[47] or 'unanticipated' shocks may require a change in the exchange rate or exchange rate policy.

In fact, a benign macroeconomic policy environment could on some counts be regarded more the exception than the rule. Indeed, some argue that one of the prominent regularities in the financial and real sectors of the economy is that they undergo periodic turbulence and tranquility with the relative volatility of real and financial shocks, often exhibiting dramatic shocks.[48] If we are living in a world of incomplete and uncertain information *ex ante* about macroeconomic structure and our knowledge of the potential nature of disturbances is incomplete while agents are nevertheless acting in such an environment, this may have implications for the potential credibility of the decision maker, i.e. the monetary authorities.

One strand of literature copes with this problem by proposing an exit strategy or escape clause. For instance, Obstfeld (1991) studies the merits of policy rules with escape clauses, analysing, as an example, fixed exchange rate systems that allow member countries the freedom to realign in periods of stress. He concludes that while well-designed rules with such clauses can improve society's welfare in principle, limited credibility makes it difficult for governments to implement them. The main shortcoming of studies of this type is that the concept of 'stress' or, in more general terms, the conditions governing the use of discretion are ill-defined and hence their application in the real world would undermine 'credibility'. The upshot of this kind of exercise is that one is, in a sense, back at square one: the typical methodology for evaluating any rules and for deriving optimal parameter values for the decision maker is the assumption that market participants expect the authorities to adhere to the rules indefinitely. This means that there is no room for discretion and the problem of

---

[46] The Drazen-Masson paper (1994) starts with the government's objective of minimising an expected discounted loss function (of unemployment and inflation) and is based on a two-period open-economy model. It concludes (p. 738): '… even a tough policy maker who plans *ex ante* to keep the fixed parity (and makes public statements to that effect) will devalue in adverse circumstances.'

[47] In the simple world of Krugman (1991), the monetary aggregate and velocity are, for example, the underlying macrovariables.

[48] See Flood et al. (1989).

credibility remains unresolved. Of course, there is simplicity and relatively easy accountability in this 'permanent rule hypothesis'. Providing an escape clause *ab initio* may thus not be an optimal policy.

A broader approach to the credibility conundrum in the literature seems to indicate that the best 'real world' response of the monetary authorities to the question of enhancing credibility lies in an 'optimal' design of monetary policy. Such an approach attempts to ensure that mechanisms are established for overcoming problems concerning the credibility of monetary policy once it is recognised that discretionary central bank responses to seldom-experienced events might play a valuable stabilisation role.[49]

This broad approach recognises *ab initio* that 100% credibility can never be earned by the central bank in its monetary, or exchange rate, policy. This approach, therefore, confines itself to recognising the following factors as inherently confidence enhancing.

The institutional set-up and the policy maker may make the 'rules of the game' more credible. One topic in this regard is the legal or *de facto* independence of the monetary authorities' central bank (Sect. 1). Another is the identification of the decision maker's economic loss function, which ought to coincide with that of society at large.

Hungary may be a case in point. Independence in the conduct of monetary policy was introduced in earnest only in 1990 in Hungary, first through a public statement from the prime minister, József Antall, that he and his government would not directly influence the decisions to be made at the NBH. While Act LX on the NBH, adopted by Parliament at the end of 1991, marks the start of 'autonomous' monetary policy decisions, it is ultimately the goals of monetary policy that set the stage for their implementation.[50] Monetary policy formulation is an ongoing process and its evolution can to some extent be gleaned from the regular and annual reports of the NBH. It is the president of the NBH who presents the principles of monetary policy for the year ahead to Parliament. These reports reveal that monetary goals and objectives have not yet been formulated consistently over time. The main reasons for the changes in monetary policy formulation appear to be twofold. As the transition process has moved forward, priorities have changed. Monetary policy is part and parcel of the fabric of overall policy, and as the financial problems raised by transition have changed, monetary policy has had to adjust. The second reason may be classed as political. Changes at the helm of the NBH have in the past been due to changes in the political set-up

[49] Flood and Isard (1989), in fact, claim that they are welfare-enhancing.

[50] Act LX of 1991 bestowed a large degree of independence upon the NBH (Article 45) and stipulates that the fundamental task of the bank is to ensure the domestic and external purchasing power of the national currency (Article 4).

of the country. As the president of the NBH essentially sets the tone of monetary policy and it is his ideas which are essentially implemented, non-continuous changes in presidential appointees have led to changes in monetary policy. This does appear to be the case, as presidents of the NBH have had different ideas about monetary policy.[51]

While shifts in underlying economic parameters are continuously time dependent, monetary policy measures and their intent should be made clear to the market from the outset, as should be the case with any subsequent measure. The monetary authorities should constantly ensure that markets understand any policy measures taken. In addition, it would probably increase 'confidence' if the upside and downside risks of such an 'open' policy were stated in unambiguous terms.

A different situation may arise when single and important unpredictable events occur, i.e. events which cannot be captured by probability distributions and which should be classed under 'uncertainty' for the policy maker. In such cases, discretionary action should be allowed which should not undermine confidence in the basic policy strategy of the monetary authorities. This can probably be achieved in part by recognising the existence of such events and by subsequently also making the decision maker accountable to the existing political structure via some rigorous defence mechanism. Such processes, to be credible to the market, should not be opaque but defined in advance, and an active information campaign would ensure that potential information deficiencies would not undermine that credibility.

Although the above-mentioned credibility-enhancing measures do not appear very sophisticated, they seem to provide a solid base to build upon.

12.5 Exchange rates and prices

While price developments are apt to undermine confidence in a policy of more or less fixed exchange rates as pursued in the Czech Republic, they are less likely to lead to any 'confidence' problems in the case of Poland or Hungary, where prices are directly included in the policy framework.[52] On the other hand, the implicit inclusion of inflation which follows from

---

[51] The most recent example is the replacement of Mr Bod with Mr Suranyi. Mr Bod's policy formulation at the beginning of 1995 was changed quite dramatically when Mr Suranyi was appointed in March 1995.

[52] While the 'optimal' choice of the peg remains an unresolved issue, Hochreiter (1995b, p. 5) argues that a single currency peg may be the one with the most potential for gaining credibility: 'In this respect a single currency peg constitutes the simplest rule. It is transparent, easily understood by policy makers and the public and therefore preferred.'

a crawling peg policy may risk cementing the continuation of price inflation or even increase the risk of an acceleration.[53] The latter danger seems to be less pronounced in Poland and Hungary as the monthly devaluation due to the crawling peg has been continuously lowered. However, central banks are obliged to, and do indeed, observe actual and estimated price developments. Exchange rate bands are looked upon by some as helping to restore external price competitiveness after a period of real appreciation, i.e. imposing price discipline or even a reduction in inflation or inflationary expectations. Is a wider band, then, likely to allow competitiveness considerations in the medium run?[54]

One of the key questions in this context is how, if at all, the exchange rate changes feed into domestic prices. Table 6 provides a rough indication. While other factors also play a role in determining domestic price developments or may even be more important than exchange rate changes,[55] it appears that depreciation tends to have a sizeable and immediate impact on domestic prices. The acceleration in the rate of depreciation of the Hungarian forint from mid-1994 led to a sharp jump in the rate of price inflation, although an import surcharge also contributed to this. Conversely, a slower rate of depreciation of the Polish zloty led to a sharp drop in the rate of inflation.[56] Taking peak and trough values for the Czech koruna central rate during the most recent period, one discerns swings in the exchange rate. However, in contrast to the case in the other two countries, the direction of the impact on prices is not unambiguous or at least small. The development of prices in the Czech Republic is thus dominated by other factors. In small open economies, the effect on prices should be almost immediate as traders know clearly in advance the intended nominal behaviour of the domestic exchange rate.

---

[53] See Hochreiter (1996).

[54] See, for example, the statement issued by Governor Tosovsky on Reuter, 9 April 1996.

[55] The problem of price inertia (or downward rigidities) is currently a serious policy concern in all eastern European countries. In the Czech Republic, for example, currently about 10% of prices are still regulated (rents and some energy prices). The envisaged deregulation process is expected to contribute two percentage points to inflation during the next 2 to 3 years. Some rigidities in the factory and labour markets (bottlenecks) also account for the relatively weak inflation outlook (OECD, 1995). Similarly in Poland, relative price adjustment, combined with indexation and inertia, has been part and parcel of Polish inflation (IMF, 1995).

[56] The 66th Annual Report of the BIS (1996) juxtaposes to some extent the experience in the developing world with that in the industrialised world, essentially arguing that in the latter group of countries the exchange rate/price link appears to be much less close or immediate than in many countries in the former group (see p. 39).

Table 6. Exchange rates and inflation

Country	Depreciation[1]	Wholesale prices[2]	Consumer prices[2]	Imports as a % of total expenditure
Czech Republic				
January 1994–July 1995	6.8	6.6	8.2	
July 1995–March 1996	–5.4	5.5	10.9	29.0
Difference	–12.2	–1.1	2.7	
Poland				
January 1993–January 1995	24.5	25.5	31.8	
January 1995–January 1996	4.3	13.8	20.4	26.0
Difference	–20.2	–11.7	–11.4	
Hungary				
July 1993–July 1994	12.2	13.6	19.5	
July 1994–July 1995	34.0	30.2	29.2	19.0
Difference	+21.8	+16.6	+9.7	

[1]Change in local currency per unit of foreign currency. For currency basket, see Table 1 (except for Poland: 45% USD and 55% ECU).
[2]Lagged by one month.

A corollary to the foregoing discussion is the movement of the real effective exchange rate[57] as one indicator of the competitive position of

[57] The calculation of the real effective exchange rate is based on trade-weighted indices vis-à-vis 21 industrial countries. The underlying relative price movement is based on consumer prices. For the difference with regard to the use of producer prices, consult Dittus (1993). In general terms, in all eastern European countries, at certain times the real appreciation has been stronger when measured in consumer as opposed to producer prices. The two most important factors explaining this difference are the phasing out of consumer subsidies and an increased demand for services, combined with an initially small services sector. While there are clearly numerical differences between real effective exchange

a country. Taking the beginning of 1989 as the starting point, the period of the initial large nominal depreciations clearly coincides with the large drop in the real effective exchange rate, implying substantial gains in competitiveness.[58] Notably, the drop in Hungary's real effective exchange rate in the initial stages was rather modest in comparison with the Czech and Polish experience. This may have been one of the main reasons why Hungarian exchange rate policy was continuously plagued by unpredictable and at times substantial nominal devaluations in the subsequent years. However, although this paper does not cover the situation in these countries at the beginning of liberalisation, one major factor that accounted for this difference may have been the level of foreign debt at that time. Whereas the debt/export ratio of the Czech Republic was at a low 40% in 1990 and Poland was at that time already looking back at a history of debt relief/rescheduling agreements, Hungary's debt level stood at US$21.3 billion, its debt/export ratio was 190% and reserves covered only 1 month of imports. Understandably, the Hungarians were more cautious with the initial depreciation of the forint. A second reason was the inherited price structure, as prices were less distorted than in other eastern European countries and peak inflation was the lowest for all countries in the region.[59]

While Poland's initial depreciation was the largest, the subsequent real appreciation was also greater than in the other two countries. More recent developments, in 1995–1996, have indicated the tendency of the real effective exchange rate to depreciate in Hungary. Poland's real effective exchange rate is moving up, implying some loss of competitiveness, while the real appreciation of the Czech koruna seems to be continuing unabated. Graph 1 neatly juxtaposes the different exchange rate policies pursued, on the one hand, by the Czech Republic (stable nominal rate) and, on the other, by Poland and Hungary (relatively stable real effective exchange rate).

---

rate indices based on consumer and industrial prices, they do not seem to undermine the main conclusions drawn in the text.

In order to assess the difference in the behaviour of consumer and producer prices over time, simple correlation coefficients of the quarterly percentage changes in these two time series were in the range of 0.90 for all three countries.

58 Halpern and Wyplosz (1995) suggest four main factors accounting for the initially large undervaluation: (i) the existence of monetary overhang; (ii) pent-up demand for foreign assets; (iii) the lack of credibility on the part of the new authorities; and (iv) total uncertainty about the appropriate equilibrium exchange rate and, therefore, the tendency for risk-averse authorities to err on the side of undervaluation rather than overvaluation.

59 Similarly, Krzak (1995).

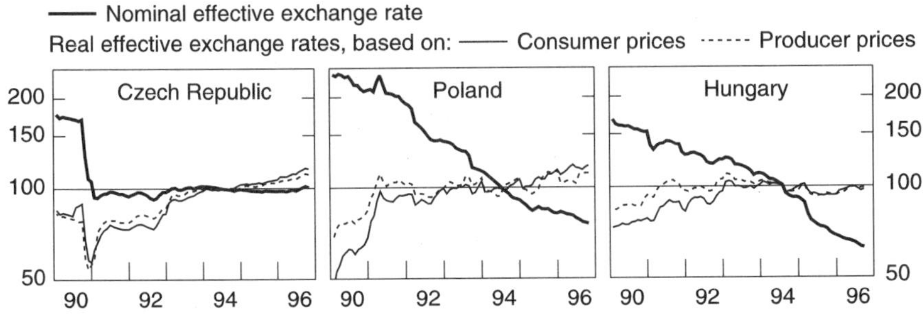

Source: BIS.

Graph 1. Nominal and real effective exchange rates (indices, 1994 = 100 [semi-logarithmic scale])

Interestingly, all three countries' real effective exchange rates were slightly higher by the spring of 1996 than at the beginning of 1989. This does not, however, imply *prima facie* anything directly about their equilibrium level.

Although the concept of an 'equilibrium' real exchange rate may be disputed and it might be difficult to estimate equilibrium rates properly, such considerations are important for the continuous evaluation of a country's competitiveness and may also have a bearing on price performance *per se*. Recent evidence (Calvo et al., 1994) seems to indicate, *inter alia*, that an undervalued real exchange rate is associated with higher inflation. Evidence gleaned through empirical studies on the 'right' real exchange rates seems to indicate that by the end of 1994 the Hungarian forint might have had a slightly overvalued real exchange rate and the Czech koruna seemed to be undervalued by a much larger margin than the Polish zloty (Dittus, 1994). The following discussion explores whether these findings need updating.

One traditional indicator of the scope for further real appreciation is the gap between the dollar value of GNP measured at purchasing power parity (PPP) exchange rates and the actual dollar value of GNP measured at current exchange rates.[60] The rough estimates for 1995 indicate that the room for further real appreciation is greatest in Slovakia and Russia; the ratio is the highest for Hungary.

A look at developments over the last few years confirms that the gap between the actual and the PPP exchange rate has been narrowing rapidly. Most notably in the Czech Republic and similarly in Slovakia, the narrowing has

---

[60] PPP is defined as the number of units of a country's currency required to buy the same amount of goods and services in the domestic market as one dollar would buy in the USA (World Bank Atlas, 1996, p. 33).

Table 7. Real effective exchange rates (% change)

Country	1989–96[1]	Initial depreciation 1989[2]	Subsequent developments	
			up to year-end 94	1995–1996
Czech Republic				
Consumer prices	9.8	–42.7	80.6	6.1
Wholesale prices	6.5	–43.0	78.3	4.9
Poland				
Consumer prices	32.6	–50.0	147.6	7.0
Wholesale prices	7.1	–36.4	73.5	–2.9
Hungary				
Consumer prices	27.4	–10.1	44.8	–1.9
Wholesale prices	0.0	–10.8	14.7	–2.2
Memorandum item:				
Russia				
Consumer prices	–30.5	–98.8	3,423.7	66.0
Wholesale prices	181.6	–98.7	10,664.1	99.4

[1]January 1989 to March 1996.
[2]For the Czech Republic (at that time Czechoslovakia), up to year-end 1990; for Poland and Hungary, up to year-end 1989; for Russia, up to year-end 1991.

been in the order of 50% within the 1993–1995 time span. Such developments imply some loss of competitiveness, but they also hint at fast increases in real incomes.

The discrepancy between PPP and actual exchange rates should, however, be interpreted cautiously, as many studies have pointed out that it may be considered more the rule than the exception and as a large number of empirical studies have also confirmed that the ratio of purchasing power parity to the exchange rate is positively related to real per capita GDP. This higher income bias in the PPP literature has a long tradition in the history of economic thought, developed in some depth by Harrod (1939) and recently applied to OECD countries and confirmed in a study by Turner and Van't dack (1993).[61] The main tenet of this real income bias

[61] The Turner and Van't dack study (1993) provides a range of further references. The World Bank (1993, p.7) states similarly: '…data show that PPC rates (i.e. rates which equalise prices in place-to-place comparisons) are generally lower

Table 8. Equilibrium exchange rates

	1994[1]			1995		Ratio: current USD GNP/PPP-based GNP		
	GNP/ capita (PPP-based)	Population (thousands)	GNP (USD bn)	GNP (USD bn)	GNP[2] (PPP-based USD bn)	1993[3]	1994	1995
Czech Republic	7,910	10,295	33.1	45.6	85.3	35.4	40.6	53.0
Poland	5,380	38,341	94.6	120.7	226.9	45.3	45.9	53.0
Hungary	6,310	10,161	39.0	43.8	66.9	53.2	60.9	65.0
Russia	5,260	148,366	392.5	363.7	770.2	44.8	50.3	47.0
Slovakia	6,660	5,333	11.9	17.4	39.2	29.5	33.5	44.0

[1] World Bank Atlas, 1996.
[2] 1994 PPP-based GNP multiplied by the country's growth rate and the percentage change in US consumer prices (in US dollar terms, 2.8%).
[3] No data available before 1993.

relates to the fact that the actual exchange rate reflects the importance of non-tradable goods, which tend to be more expensive in higher-income countries.

Tables 9 and 10 explore the potential real income bias introduced into the PPP calculation. The methodology adopted here is similar that found in the paper by Turner and Van't dack, the main differences being an extended country coverage (80 countries)[62] and more recent data (1994 instead of 1990); however, the desirable tradable/non-tradable distinction cannot be introduced here owing to a lack of relevant data. The data used, therefore, cover the entire range of final goods and services which make up GDP as a whole, including many items such as construction and government services which are not traded.

---

than market exchange rates for most countries except for the most developed ones… .'

[62] This includes all countries for which the World Bank Atlas (1996) provides PPP data for 1994, except for the economies of the former Soviet Union, as their data are preliminary and potentially subject to large changes, and 36 countries for which the 1994 PPP estimates were based on regression results.

Table 9. Regression analysis of the ratio of the PPP to the actual exchange rate in 1994

Countries[1]	Coefficient of GDP per head[2]	F-statistic	R^2
OECD (25)	0.59 (7.0)	49.4	0.68
Other countries (55)	0.26 (4.6)	21.2	0.29
All countries (80)	0.47 (12.2)	148.1	0.66

[1]OECD countries in 1994. Other countries include all countries from the World Bank Atlas except countries from the former Soviet Union and countries for which the PPP data for 1994 were based on estimates from regressions.
[2]The regressions were estimated in the form:

$$\log \text{PPP/ER} = a + b \log \text{YPC},$$

where: PPP is the purchasing power parity exchange rate for GDP;
ER is the average spot exchange rate;
YPC is per capita income in US dollars valued at PPP.
t-statistics are shown in parentheses.

The results indicate, on the one hand, that shifting the regression from 1990 to 1994 yields similar results. In fact, the strong positive relationship has not changed: on average, a 1% increase in real per capita GDP relative to other OECD countries raises the PPP/ER ratio by 0.59%. In the Turner and Van't dack study, this ratio was 0.55%. While the cross-country results for a large group of lower-level real-per-capita-income countries are weaker, the more global approach covering 80 countries yields results similar to those of the OECD as the coefficient of GDP per head is somewhat lower, but still close to 50%. For the three countries under review, this last regression result involving a broad range of countries was used as a benchmark, not only because by 1994 none of these countries had yet joined the OECD, but primarily as these countries' real PPP income levels were also still relatively low.

Table 10. Actual exchange rate as a percentage of the PPP exchange rate 'predicted' by real per capita income in 1994[1]

	Actual	Predicted	Actual/predicted
Czech Republic	41	59	69
Poland	46	49	94
Hungary	61	53	115
Slovakia	33	55	60

[1]For details, see Table 9.

Differences between the actual and the predicted PPP/exchange rate ratio, determined using the GDP equation for 80 countries, are shown in Table 10. The results for the three individual countries indicate that relative to other countries' real per capita PPP income, the results for the Czech Republic were quite a bit below the regression line, implying that the PPP/exchange rate ratio is about 40% lower than what relative real per capita income in the Czech Republic would lead one to expect. A small upward revision of the nominal exchange rate relative to the PPP exchange rate also emerges for Poland, while the estimate for the Hungarian ratio is above the regression line, suggesting a small downward adjustment of the ratio. The results of the adjustment due to the real income bias for the three countries indicate that perhaps the differences in the levels of competitiveness ought not to be exaggerated.

Further indirect evidence on this point may be gleaned from a look at the nominal wages earned by workers in US dollar terms. On that score, it appears that wages in manufacturing are substantially below wages in other Western competitor countries. Table 11 confirms this impression as hourly labour costs in the manufacturing sector are only as high as 10% of German labour costs.[63] However, the development of this indicator also corroborates the empirical finding on the level of the real effective exchange rate: wages are somewhat higher in Hungary than in the Czech Republic and Poland.[64]

More recently, the real effective exchange rates seem to collate well with the earlier findings on the level of the exchange rate, as they appear to be moving in the right direction: the Hungarian forint has tended to depreciate, while the Czech koruna, in particular, continues to appreciate substantially in real terms.

The tentative conclusions drawn above have to be accompanied by several caveats. The real effective exchange rate is only one indicator of a country's competitiveness. Examining competitiveness alone, independent of structural and cyclical developments in output and demand, changes in policy and financial market conditions, generally provides only a partial account of developments in external trade.[65] One approach to overcoming

[63] Table 11 also shows relatively high non-wage labour costs for Hungary. The implications of such costs for the labour market are explored to some extent in the 66th BIS Annual Report, p. 23.

[64] Unit labour costs would be the preferred indicator as productivity is not considered in dollar wage costs.

[65] The underlying proposition is the standard argument: a country with a real appreciation should suffer export losses and experience current account deficits, so that later the real appreciation is reversed. However, this proposition is not undisputed owing to facts (e.g. Japan has experienced larger current ac-

Table 11. Total labour costs in manufacturing

Country	Total hourly labour costs in 1994[1]			Social security contributions and payroll taxes as a percentage of total taxes (1993)
	Indices based on data in a common currency	Of which		
		Wages	Non-wage labour costs	
Germany	100	55	45	39
Czech Republic	7	60	40	35
Poland	8	55	45	25[2]
Hungary	10	50	50	39
Bulgaria	4	57	43	25[2]
Slovakia	6	59	41	–
Romania	3	63	37	29[2]
Russian Federation	2	59	41	36[2]
Austria	80	50	50	40
Finland	73	54	46	26
France	66	52	48	47
Italy	62	50	50	37

[1] 1993 for eastern European countries.
[2] 1994.

this drawback is to provide a broader macroeconomic framework which essentially attempts to estimate the equilibrium real effective exchange rate as a value that is consistent with internal and external balance over the medium term.[66] An analysis of export market shares may also indicate whether

count surpluses in conjunction with real appreciation) and to theory (the portfolio balance approach notes that a country with increasing net foreign assets, given accumulating current account surpluses, should experience a real appreciation).

[66] It is beyond this paper's scope to show such a framework. For example, the macroeconomic balance approach provides a framework for calculating equilibrium exchange rate positions at internal and external equilibrium. It defines the equilibrium real exchange rate as the value that is consistent with internal and external equilibrium over the medium term. Internal balance is normally

or not a country is losing competitiveness. The related indicators may provide different or supporting evidence. Market-based indicators may usefully complement the aforementioned indicators by focusing on anticipated movements in exchange rates and their fundamental determinants,[67] while studies of individual segments of the economy, beyond the traditional look at the tradable/non-tradable differentiation, may further complement the competitiveness picture.

At this point in time, it seems futile to attempt to assess internal or external balance for these countries, i.e. to try to find a base period in which the internal and the external balance of these countries were in equilibrium.[68] If internal balance is defined as a situation in which real output is at its potential level and inflation is at a low and non-accelerating rate, none of these countries exhibits internal balance. All three countries are for the first time emerging from a transition recession (the Czech Republic and Hungary since mid-1993 and Poland since somewhat earlier), and only since then have they been experiencing positive growth rates.

We also know very little about potential output or output gaps on the capital side. As far as inflation rates are concerned, the three countries are also yet to reach values comparable to those of other industrialised countries; the values are not low, and inflation was even accelerating in Hungary in 1995 compared with 1994. It does not appear possible to assess easily what the 'internal balance' might be and therefore provide a macroframework in which to determine the 'right' level for the real effective exchange rate.

Another more fundamental point is raised by Hochreiter, who argues (1995b) that a real exchange rate which is appreciating from a low point after the initial devaluation is not *a priori* a cause for concern but may well reflect 'good' economic policy. In fact, he points out that if the eastern European countries are to catch up with the West, they must raise productivity to enable them to pay higher real wages. He therefore concludes,

---

defined as achievement of the underlying potential output, while external balance is defined as attainment of an equilibrium position in the current and capital accounts (see Clark et al., 1994).

[67] These indicators may include forward exchange rates, interest rate differentials, forward interest rates, yield curves and option-based estimates of future exchange rate volatility.

[68] One pragmatic approach to computing equilibrium exchange rates is to assume that PPP holds over a longer time horizon. While this paper draws on the World Bank's method of calculating PPP (1996) in this regard, a time horizon of 5 to 6 years since price liberalisation appears to be too short to allow such an approach. Also, the price distortions during this period, due essentially to structural factors existing at the beginning of liberalisation, drive a sizeable wedge between domestic and external price developments (even in tradable goods).

Table 12. Internal and external balance

	1992	1993	1994	1995	1996[1]
	Real GDP				
Czech Republic	–6.4	–0.9	2.6	4.8	4.8
Poland	2.6	3.8	5.2	7.0	6.3
Hungary	–3.0	–0.8	2.9	1.5	1.0
	Consumer prices (annual averages)				
Czech Republic	11.1	20.9	10.0	9.1	8.9
Poland	43.0	35.3	32.2	27.8	20.0
Hungary	23.0	22.5	18.8	28.2	23.0
	Unemployment rates (end of year)				
Czech Republic	2.6	3.5	3.2	2.9	3.3
Poland	13.6	16.4	16.0	14.9	13.5
Hungary	12.7	12.6	10.9	10.9	10.6
	External current account balance (% of GDP)				
Czech Republic	–1.7	0.4	–0.1	–4.0	–6.9
Poland[2, 3]	–0.3	–2.7	–1.0	–1.9	–6.0
Hungary[2]	0.9	–9.0	–9.4	–5.7	–3.5

[1]Estimates.
[2]Only transactions in convertible currencies.
[3]Excluding unclassified cross-border exports (1996: about 5% of GDP).

contrary to standard reasoning, that the (equilibrium) real exchange rates should typically appreciate. Such considerations are welcome as they may point to a correct assessment of the underlying causes of, for example, an appreciating real effective exchange rate. If the appreciation were to be interpreted as a monetary phenomenon, i.e. a sign of excess demand, serious concerns may arise;[69] by contrast, if the appreciation is mainly related to changes in terms of trade between traded and non-traded goods due to

[69] Upward pressure on non-traded goods prices could be interpreted as a sign of excess demand if it stemmed from less benign origins like large budget deficits or rapid credit growth. None of this had come to light by the middle of 1996: the Czech Republic runs a small budget surplus, while Poland as well as Hungary run small deficits. Credit growth appears depressed in Hungary, and at a reasonable level in the Czech Republic (real growth around 0%), while credit growth is quite fast in Poland (more than 10% real growth in 1995), calling for a more cautious assessment of the real appreciation in the latter country.

'real' developments, such appreciation should be tolerated and may even be welcome.

The evidence presented above seems to indicate that the current level of the real effective exchange rates does not appear to be seriously out of line with the underlying fundamentals. The direct PPP evidence appears to show that the Czech Republic and perhaps also Poland have some room for real appreciation; Hungary seems to have used more or most of its initial room for manoeuvre, perhaps partly because the initial depreciation was not as strong as in the other two countries. The continued real appreciation of the koruna and the fact that the 'real income bias' has probably led us to overestimate the gap between the nominal and the PPP-based exchange rate are indicative of less room for manoeuvre in the Czech Republic than thought hitherto.

Evidence concerning the level of nominal wages in all three countries, however, seems to indicate quite a bit of room for further price increases without competitiveness being seriously undermined, with further developments in labour productivity set to play a crucial role. Although recent movements in the real effective exchange rate appear to be in line with the underlying levels, it should be borne in mind that any further real appreciation may be warranted on the grounds of developments in the real sector of the economy.

Strong productivity growth reduces the loss of competitiveness due to higher inflation. As productivity is estimated to increase by about 4% in the Czech Republic in 1996, this fact can contribute to a longer viability of the current band around the current central parity.

12.6 Monetary policy in the real world

12.6.1 Money supply and exchange rates

Choosing the exchange rate as an intermediate target for monetary policy implies that the money supply is, to some extent at least, endogenous.[70] Money balances are in that sense accommodating, i.e. they are determined in conformity with agiven exchange rate. If the central bank is to keep the ex-

[70] Targeting of any kind of monetary aggregate has been consistently rejected by the academic literature. For example, Bofinger (1990) notes that none of the parameters for a policy of monetary targeting with flexible exchange rates vis-à-vis foreign currencies is given: there is no stable trend path of potential output, as it is highly variable, and consensus and conditions determining minimum inflation rates, which are compatible with price stability, are not in sight. The situation today in the Czech Republic (OECD, 1996) is similar.

change rate within a pre-announced band, it may have to intervene. If the monetary authorities choose to sterilise capital inflows,[71] which tend to push the exchange rate up, by absorbing them into their reserves, there is no impact on the monetary base and the authorities may have bought time in order to assess whether such flows are of a temporary or of a permanent nature. However, buying time through sterilised intervention may become costly and may thus be difficult to maintain over longer periods. The monetisation of capital inflows through unsterilised intervention is not without pitfalls either: this sequence of events may lead to too fast a growth of the monetary base with the perhaps usual and predictable impact on inflation and/or it may lead to an undesirable real appreciation of the exchange rate with unpalatable consequences for trade performance. The interest rate may play a useful role in such a scenario, e.g. adjusting the domestic rates may slow down capital inflows. Such use of the interest rate usually assumes that the central bank has some leverage in modifying such short-term interest rates. Do interest rates react reasonably well in the context of credit supply and demand?

12.6.2 Interest rates and financial fragility

The interest rate may have to be used to keep the exchange rate within its band. Such a situation has presented itself in many individual countries. While it is, for example, possible to raise the short-term nominal interest rate to high levels and ensure that the exchange rate does not 'fall through the roof', such a situation proves invariably unsustainable, as subsequent high real interest rates not only result in large domestic financial disturbances but will also constantly stifle real investment, with potentially very negative effects for growth prospects. While pre-announced rates of devaluation may provide a first limit for differentials between the domestic and foreign interest rates, the additional factors to be considered in relating the exchange rate to the difference between domestic and foreign interest rates are the potential movement of the exchange rate within the band and the abandonment of the central parity within the band.

While the argument above may imply a still large degree of variability in interest rates, it is generally put forward that the exchange rate band should enforce interest rate smoothing: as the exchange is allowed to move within the band, any 'shocks' to the interest rate may be smoothed by moving the exchange rate in the opposite direction within the band.

The relevance of the two contradictory propositions above depends partly on whether or not the room for manoeuvre within the band should

[71] The following assumes that, in fact, large and 'hot' capital inflows occurred in these countries. For related evidence, see, for example, Koch (1997).

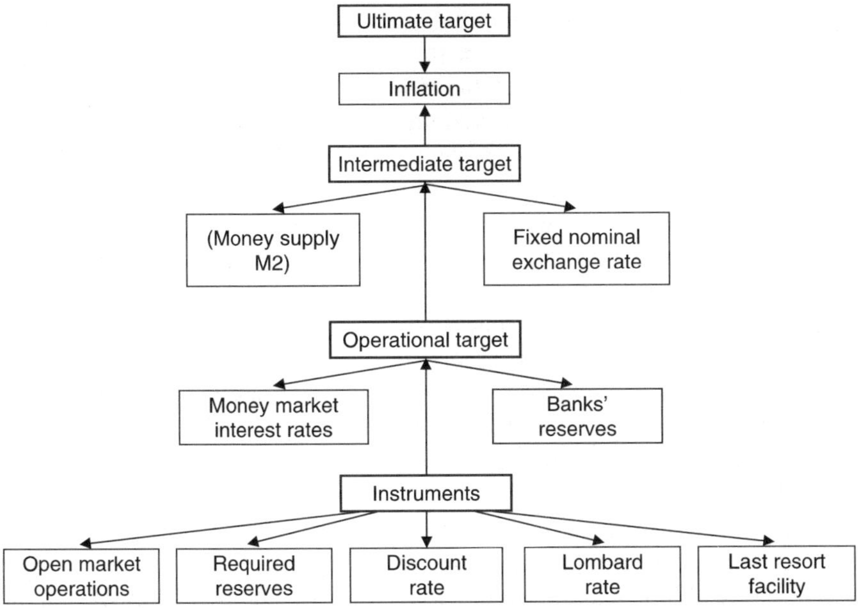

Graph 2. Monetary policy targets and instruments of the CNB

be used and how extensive this room actually is. Part of the answer is based on the immediacy and directness of this link. Interest rate arbitrage in the financial markets is fairly direct and immediate, as the investor will consider the interest differential between the domestic and foreign currency as well as the potential for change in the foreign exchange rate over the time horizon of the investment. One may, however, dispute the applicability of interest rate arbitrage as, for example, capital movements are not completely free, i.e. imperfections exist in the international capital flow (especially portfolio flow) mechanism as well as in the domestic money market mechanism (interest rate formation may be distorted).

One indicator of such imperfections would be that domestic interest rates were higher vis-à-vis foreign interest rates than would follow from the pre-announced rate of devaluation.

Another more fundamental query concerns the reason why interest rate smoothing may be desirable from a policy point of view. In a recent study, Goodhart (1996) finds interest rate smoothing for a group of large industrial countries and argues that the manicured changes in selected industrial countries' short-term policy rates are too small and too late to have the desired impact on policy. He points out that whenever inflation begins to deviate from its desired path, the authorities prefer to make relatively small changes instead of adjusting interest rates by a large enough jump, but the rationale for such smoothing is not spelt out.

While institutions (Sect. 1.1) and instruments in the interest rate domain were obviously lacking at the beginning of transition, by 1996 monetary authorities had put in place a monetary framework which is not substantially different from that of some western European countries. In a nutshell, monetary authorities use their monopoly control of a high-powered monetary base to influence a short-term money market rate. Besides their control of the (finer) instrument of setting a money market rate, the authorities also maintain a more formal, more visible discount or refinancing rate, which is varied less frequently, but in larger steps with more of an announcement effect.[72] While reserve requirements are still high, nominal short-term interest rate instruments quite similar to those of other, industrialised economies had been developed. The monetary authorities have now abandoned direct credit allocation to the private sector, and credits to the government have been seriously constrained.[73] In all three countries, the money markets had matured to such a point that open market operations had become a standard daily feature. While changes in the depth, breadth and resiliency of individual market segments are continuous, it appeared that a significant amount of interbank business was taking place with the result that relatively unbiased short-term interest rates were emerging.

A good case in point may be the Hungarian money market interest rates. The NBH posts repo (overnight) and reverse repo (weekly) rates, providing a sort of interest rate tunnel for other market interest rates. At the beginning of 1993, this tunnel ranged from 5% for the reverse repo rate to 20% for the overnight repo rate. Over time, this tunnel narrowed, and by the end of 1995 its upper value was 31% and its lower value 27%. While the overnight interbank rates generally followed this tunnel, the fairly large daily swings of 15% during 1993 and at the beginning of 1994 abated and had calmed down even more by year-end 1995. The daily monthly Treasury bill rates are also more consistently inside the tunnel. The effect of these developments is that the spread between the individual instruments on the money market has narrowed, probably indicating more efficiency.

This is not to rule out the possibility of sluggishness in the adjustment of the interest rate in particular markets. Sluggishness may be understood to refer to anything that slows down the impact of market forces in the adjustment process. The slowing down of market force processes may still be at

[72] See the section on interest rates in Goodhart (1996).

[73] For example, by early 1992 the most important tool of monetary policy was the quantitative regulation of the overall and individual access of banks to credit refinancing from the NBH (Estrin et al., 1992).

work in economies which have only recently introduced measures to liberalise their interest rate policy.

While the tools of monetary policy were apparently less developed in the countries under review than in western European economies, the move from direct to indirect monetary instruments appears to have been more or less completed by 1996. In general, it appears that the rudimentary ingredients for successful monetary policy implementation are present in all three countries: a two-tier banking system that clearly separates money from reserve money and vests sole responsibility for policy implementation in the monetary authority, as well as sufficient technical and institutional capabilities for managing the system. The monetary policy framework currently in place appears similar to that of western economies (see attached stylised graph for the CNB).

Monetary policy may remain 'weak' in some respects, reflecting the more recent historical development and structure of the emerging domestic money markets, as 'inherited' problems are not yet fully resolved. These elements may lead not only to distorted markets but also to a weak and/or unpredictable monetary transmission mechanism. A good case in point may be client interest rates. While credit criteria should dominate, other factors may play an overriding role, thus negating the more direct link with the money market rates. The demand for credit on on the part part of big enterprises facing liquidity problems may be driven by pure survival criteria, given that they are willing to pay/accept any kind of interest charged to them. Attempting to place ahard budget constraint on these enterprises may endanger the existence of the banks themselves. On the other hand, one may find small new companies which use credit in agamble to make huge profits. If they go under having used bank loans, it is the banks that get stung. These financial idiosyncrasies weaken the standard link in the transformation process from shorter-term liabilities to longer-term assets on the banks' books. However, some evidence has also recently emerged that in the Czech Republic the link between the interbank market rates and the interest rates on newly extended credits is quite close, i.e. more immediate in terms of time.[74]Whereas distortions in the interest rate formation process are one aspect, the legacy of the past financial system may also place aparticular burden on monetary policy owing to other weaknesses as financial transition as an ongoing process is beset with further problems. The more prominent ones are inadequate payment and settlement systems[75] and non-performing loans. Both these factors may be indirectly feeding into interest rate formation as

[74] Czech National Bank, Annual Report, 1995, pp. 49–50.

[75] This point is not developed further here. Long settlement lags in the domestic banking market were at one time particularly noticeable in Poland.

Table 13. Monetary policy framework

	Czech Republic	Poland	Hungary
Key interest rate	Short-term repo rate	Rediscount rate	Base rate
Reserve requirement			
Calculation basis	Average	Average	Average
Liabilities	Domestic and foreign	Domestic (17% on demand and 9% on time deposits) and foreign (2%)	Domestic (15.5%) and foreign (24%)
Refinancing			
Discount policy	Negligible	Seasonal	Negligible
Lombard policy	Marginal	Some	Not used
Open market	Substantial	Extensive	Some
Repos	Mostly	Substantial	Mostly
Swaps	Not used	Not used	Parallel with repo
Auction credits	Not used	Not used	Not used
Direct credits	Not used	Not used	Some
Overdraft credits	Not used	Not used	Small
Special refinancing	Redistribution credits	Not used for short-term refinancing	Project credits
Banker for government	Yes	Yes	Yes
Agent for	Government securities	Government securities	Government securities
Credit to government (legal ceiling)	5% of government revenue	2% of government revenue	3% of government revenue

Source: Handbook on Central Banks in Central and Eastern Europe, BIS (1996).

they increase the operating risks and costs for banks. Non-performing loans may influence the process of interest rate formation directly and are one of the factors accounting for the high interest rate margins required by banks. High reserve requirements may also enter into the banks' interest rate policy

Table 14. Structural financial indicators (end-1995)

	Czech Republic	Poland	Hungary	*Memo item: Russia*
Domestic				
M2/GDP (as a %)	86.0	36.0	43.0	40.0
Stock market capitalization (in USD bn)	18.3[1]	8.0[1]	4.2[1]	15.0
Size of Treasury bill market (in USD bn)	1.5	10.0		30.0[2]
External				
International reserves (in USD bn)	13.8	15.0	12.0	14.4
Liabilities to BIS reporting banks (in USD bn)	7.5	7.9	8.0	49.4

[1]June 1996. [2]June 1996; all government securities.

and should be assessed with regard to the burdens already borne by these banks (e.g. non-performing loans). These financial legacies ought to be kept in mind when interpreting the behaviour of the 'usual' indicators of the stance of monetary policy (e.g. interest rate spreads, nominal and real short-term interest rates, structural factors such as M2/GDP, and nominal and real credit to the private sector).

The implication of low ratios appears to be that the current stock of money is probably insufficient in some countries to accommodate real transactions. This type of ratio frequently goes hand in hand with the use in the domestic economy of a surrogate currency such as the US dollar or the Deutsche Mark.

Financial fragility may also be due to other weak or missing elements in the financial structure, such as bankruptcy regulation. In Western economies, bankruptcy laws play a permanent but minor role. In central Europe, companies often still suffer from systemic insolvency. In such a situation, bankruptcy laws probably have only a limited part to play, as it is questionable whether the threat of insolvency is the right tool to instil financial discipline.

Even though the Czech Republic (1991), Hungary (1992) and Poland have introduced bankruptcy laws, enforcement of bankruptcy proceedings coupled with the potential restructuring of companies has been difficult because of the unemployment consequences. In the Czech Republic, which enacted bankruptcy law in 1991, subsequent measures effectively prevented this law from being applied until about the middle of 1993, and by the end of 1993 only some 300 bankruptcy proceedings had been completed. This low level of enforcement is in stark contrast to the situation in Hungary and Poland, where the number of insolvencies is up to ten times greater, partly accounting for the much higher level of unemployment in these two countries. The Czech government has regarded bankruptcy as a post-privatisation issue, while in Hungary the original bankruptcy law refers to a '90-day trigger', whereby bankruptcy proceedings are initiated automatically if debts have not been settled within 90 days. In Poland, banks are the driving force behind the 'bankruptcy' system and have started 6,000 bankruptcy proceedings. Polish law treats state-owned enterprises differently from private enterprises, as the courts are becoming involved in restructuring the enterprises rather than liquidating them.[76]

As financial restructuring is being placed on a sounder footing, the ongoing process in the area of bankruptcy is an additional aspect of inherited financial fragility which makes it even more difficult to achieve confidence in the underlying.

This paper has treated financial fragility only summarily. Even though differences exist between individual country experiences, it nevertheless appears in general that the interest rate formation process is still subject to many imponderables (which are difficult to assess systematically). High interest margins continue to be a strong case in point.

12.6.3 Capital flows

It is not immediately obvious how a foreign investor would react to a widening of the exchange rate band. Perhaps investor behaviour is driven more by general considerations of country risk and the outlook for economic/political stability as well as risk assessment for individual instruments, rendering the introduction of the exchange rate band essentially irrelevant for longer-term considerations. Actual restrictions and barriers in the domain of capital flows may also play an important role. Table 15 provides some background information, drawing attention to the fact that most of the impediments are now on the outflow side.[77] At any rate, the process of capital account liberalisation took on a new dimension in 1995 (Sect. 1), and this has in general terms provided more room for more diversified capital inflows from non-residents. Participation in the growing domain

---

[76] See Finance East Europe, Vol. 5, No. 23, 1st December 1995.

[77] Sokolowska (1995) provides the legal background to the abolishment of foreign exchange restrictions in Poland.

Table 15. Capital account restrictions

	Czech Republic	Poland	Hungary
Non-residents in country			
Loans/borrowing			
Foreign currency			
Domestic currency			
Securities			
Bonds			
Equity	Participation not limited		
Direct investment		New businesses need to register locally and need permits in several areas	Foreign participation exceeding 10% of equity requires government approval
Repatriation of capital	None		
Transfer of profits	None		
Purchase of real estate	None	Permission required (except in the case of inheritance)	Not allowed
Residents abroad			
Loans/borrowing	Approval by the CNB	Limits are set for the private and public sectors by the government	Financial institutions report to the NBH; other institutions subject to approval by the NBH

Table 15. Continued

	Czech Republic	Poland	Hungary
Securities Bonds Equity		All categories of capital transfer, including gifts, require a foreign exchange permit	Hungarians may acquire bonds and shares in OECD countries via exchange rate offices (since 1st July 1996)
Direct investment	Approval by CNB and Ministry of Finance	Acquiring an interest in a foreign enterprise requires a foreign exchange permit	Approval needed
Purchase of real estate	Not allowed, except by approval of Ministry of Finance		

of financial assets has been more noticeable as the share of portfolio flows in total capital flows has become significant. This has probably increased the potential vulnerability to sudden withdrawals of funds. Speculative attacks on the currency are thus more easily administered by non-residents (and residents) in this more liberalised environment. In this sense, increased liberalisation of capital flows might have a detrimental effect on the credibility of the policies pursued by the monetary authorities.

12.6.4 Intervention

One way of mitigating the impact of capital flows is intervention by the central banks, which is a feature of the foreign exchange markets in all central European countries. Episodes abound, and in that sense intervention is a daily routine for the central banks. For example, in March 1996 the NBP sold domestic currency to the market in order to slow down the upward drift of the zloty; and after the widening of the band for the Czech koruna at the end of February 1996, the CNB bought domestic currency for a few days in order to stabilise it. These interventions were intra-marginal. Hungarian interventions have been marginal. The first intramarginal intervention occurred on 29 August 1995.[78] Whereas in January and February 1995 the NBH sold foreign exchange, the months following the introduction of the March 1995 policy package saw the central bank purchasing substantial amounts of it. However, little is known about the actual strategies pursued by individual central banks, their exact timing or the currency involved. The evidence concerning the 'effectiveness' of such intervention, which essentially looks at the short-term results, cannot therefore be assessed with any appreciable confidence.[79] The aforementioned episodes seem to indicate, however, that the 'success' rate may be reasonably high, probably owing in part to the fact that central banks still play quite a dominant role in the forex markets.[80]

Interventions led to an increase in foreign exchange reserves (assuming the case of capital inflows, i.e. non-residents wishing to hold more assets in zlotys, korunas and forints). Since all three countries recorded large increases in reserves in 1995 (Table 16), banks may also experience a concomitant broadening of liquidity (unsterilised intervention) as their balances at the central bank expand, which would, other things being equal, imply an easing of monetary conditions. Whereas the scale of sterilisation in different countries is difficult to compare as it is reflected in various items on central bank balance sheets, one indicator is the rise in monetary authorities' gross foreign assets in relation to the increase in the monetary base.

The rise in foreign exchange reserves at the CNB seems to have generally led to a commensurate growth of the monetary base throughout the period under review, implying that sterilisation seems to have played only a minor role. This also implies that the CNB in principle pursued a loose monetary policy as commercial banks had ample liquidity. Most recently, however, the CNB decided to raise the reserve requirement from 8.5% to 11.5% (August 1996), implying a certain reining-in of liquidity.

---

78 See Darvas (1995, p. 23).

79 According to views widely held in the 1970s, exchange market intervention – insofar as its effects on the monetary base (or interest rates) were sterilised – would not provide the authorities with an effective policy instrument in addition to the monetary base (or interest rates). More recently, it has come to be recognised that even if the hypothesis of uncovered interest rate parity were valid, sterilised intervention could be effective if it signalled new information about the intentions of policy makers to adjust interest rates or other policy instruments, as necessary, in order to achieve their exchange rate objectives (for more details, see Isard, 1995).

80 Admittedly, this is quite a weak conclusion as episodes of 'unsuccessful' intervention would probably not be reported.

Table 16. Changes in foreign exchange reserves and monetary base

Period	Czech Republic			Poland			Hungary		
	Forex reserves	Monetary base	Ratio	Forex reserves	Monetary base	Ratio	Forex reserves	Monetary base	Ratio
	In billions of US dollars								
1988–92	–	–		2.0	0.6	3.33	3.2	5.1	0.63
1993	2.8	2.4	1.17	0.0	–1.9	0.00	2.3	–0.5	–4.60
1994	2.4	2.5	0.96	1.7	0.5	3.40	0.0	0.5	0.00
1995–96[1]	6.9	6.5	1.06	8.9	3.5	2.54	5.2	–0.4	–13.00

[1]Czech Republic, March 1996; Poland and Hungary, end-1995.

Table 17. Import coverage ratio[1]

		Czech Republic	Poland	Hungary
1993	Q1	25.2	103.0	144.8
	Q2	49.4	80.6	148.8
	Q3	71.0	78.5	175.2
	Q4	72.6	87.5	131.5
1994	Q1	114.9	109.0	249.4
	Q2	103.8	108.4	182.0
	Q3	109.8	114.9	182.2
	Q4	110.2	101.2	158.8
1995	Q1	134.9	114.2	161.7
	Q2	139.6	152.8	155.5
	Q3	174.6	165.0	175.1
	Q4	179.3	178.1	195.9
1996	Q1	182.8	211.6	240.4
	Q2	155.7	207.3	193.6

[1]Official reserves as a percentage of goods and non-factor services imports.

Poland and, since 1995, also Hungary have, in contrast to the Czech Republic, partly sterilised inflows. While Poland experienced an expansion of the monetary base by US$3 billion in 1995, Hungary's monetary base even contracted that year, attesting to the tight monetary policy being pursued. Hungary has in the past used high reserve requirements to automatically sterilise some inflows (Table 13).[81]

The main channel for absorbing banks' increased liquidity due to capital inflows appears to have been the domestic banks themselves, as the central banks in general sold domestic securities to them.[82] Attempts were also made to sell securities to other investors. These attempts may have mitigated the effect that sterilisation may have had on upward pressure on interest rates.

However, the upshot of the pressure on the nominal exchange rate is visible in the rapid accumulation of reserves over the last 2 years. While the monetary authorities may be able to calculate approximately the cost of the accumulated reserves by looking at the interest differential between low-interest-bearing foreign reserves and high-interest domestic securities, it is even more taxing to judge optimal reserve accumulation as this assumes an assessment of the probability of having to defend the currency and an evaluation of the potential amounts involved at the margin. One rough indicator in this connection is the import coverage ratio, which provides an initial impression of whether or not reserves are adequate. On this score, all three countries appeared to have accumulated a reasonable level of reserves by the middle of 1996. These foreign exchange reserves might bolster confidence in current exchange rate policies as the countries seem to have sufficient 'ammunition' to 'defend' their currency.[83]

12.7 Conclusion

The approach of this paper is more to raise issues and not necessarily to provide answers. While exchange rate policy is the driving force behind monetary policy in the Czech Republic, Poland and Hungary, monetary authorities

[81] In 1996, Hungary discontinued the option of meeting part of the reserve requirements by using government securities (April) and widened the reserve base in the calculation of the required reserve ratio (February). The compulsory reserve ratio was decreased gradually from 14.8% in February to 12% by June. (See BIS, Handbook on Central Banks in Central and Eastern Europe, 1996).

[82] However, if securities sold to the commercial banks are of the type which also qualifies for subsequent sale to the central bank, sterilisation may not be fully effective.

[83] Some weakening of this ratio had appeared in all the countries by the middle of 1996.

naturally always also attempt to monitor interest rate developments very closely, not losing sight of their main task of keeping price developments in check. The credibility of the monetary authority in this process is very important as it underpins their resolve to follow sound policies. Although the role of the central bank as guarantor of price stability has been established in principle in legal terms in all three countries, governments play the decisive part in setting exchange rate policy (except in the Czech Republic, where the central bank may also set policy). Building credibility in such an environment has many facets. This paper argues that 'institutional' credibility may probably be enhanced by several further measures being taken, and that the credibility of the policy maker may be strengthened by ensuring longer-term continuity in that sphere, i.e. not changing the governor (chairperson) of the central bank just for political expediency. Policy credibility can probably only be tested empirically if the underlying markets are functioning efficiently. However, stumbling blocks in the foreign exchange and money markets as well as obstacles to the free flow of domestic and external capital and, in general terms, financial fragility, partly due to the problems of the past, render policy credibility an elusive goal in these countries.

The domestic foreign exchange markets appear less liquid than in other countries, the money markets still seem to be subject to many imponderables, and restrictions on the external flow of capital, albeit eased considerably in 1995, are still prevalent since domestic financial fragility continues to impact seriously on the play of the supply of and demand for credit as the free flow of domestic funds remains a goal to be pursued. Preliminary work at the NBH demonstrates these impediments for the exchange rate market, and it is not at all clear whether the introduction of exchange rate bands has any impact on the credibility of the monetary authorities, nor is it evident whether this policy increases or decreases the scope for interest rate flexibility. However, the move toward general current account liberalisation should in the longer run be one that is conducive to building confidence.

In general, the probability of government involvement in all markets may still be higher in these countries than in most other, industrialised countries, making it more difficult to establish the credibility of the monetary authorities on that score, too. Gaining credibility implies being able to achieve objectives which are explained to the market in clear terms and are subject to a governmental auditing process. Policy makers should also clearly state the upside and downside risks involved in these policies. This is particularly relevant for the countries under review, as some of these risks have different repercussions in these economies than in developed countries. Confidence in policy is probably not helped by asserting that there will not be any change whatsoever, for example in exchange rate policy. Obviously, underlying macroeconomic performance (e.g. domestic prices rising faster than foreign prices) may make change unavoidable. Although it may not be optimal to publish an exit strategy from the existing exchange rate policy, any change to the policy should probably not be allowed to come as a total surprise to the markets, so that any potential modification can be perceived and understood as a continuation of policy. This includes current policy moves and also future intentions. Any potential change in policy should be made clear from the beginning, avoiding the problem of any loss of confidence in future policy action.[84] The mere passage of time, however, is not propitious for building confidence in policy, especially where the markets are beginning to 'smell a rat'. Holding onto policy may then even have detrimental effects, as policy changes prove to be either too late or too little.

Although exchange rate policy had an impact on price developments in the short run, study of the adequate level of the real effective exchange rate revealed that none of the countries had a seriously overvalued exchange rate, but the likelihood of any serious undervaluation leading to further price increases must also be invalidated. Under certain circumstances, it may even be desirable to tolerate some further appreciation of the real effective exchange rate if it can be linked to higher real incomes. Particularly noteworthy in this regard is the continued rapid real appreciation of the koruna, although it must be realised that the gap between the actual exchange rate and the PPP exchange rate may be overestimated. The actual performance of the three economies may not immediately raise the question of the credibility of the current exchange rate system as the present high level of capital inflows and a satisfactory level of reserves may provide some breathing space in the near term. In fact, the latter aspects appear to be the positive indicators in the current scenario. However, the large capital inflows continue to expose the problem of too loose a monetary policy or potentially too high interest rates.

[84] Similarly, White and Smets (1996, p. 14): '...such episodes clearly indicate that market perceptions of the future intentions of the authorities are as important as, and perhaps even more important than, their current policy setting. It is for this reason that constant reiteration of the medium-term goal of price stability is useful as a means of conditioning market expectations.'

References

Austrian National Bank – Oesterreichische National Bank (1996): 'Focus on transition', Exchange rate policy in transition – developments and challenges in central and eastern Europe, I/1996.

Bank for International Settlements (1996): 'Handbook of Central Banks of Central and Eastern Europe'.

Bank for International Settlements (1996): 'Central Bank Survey of Foreign Exchange and Derivatives Market Activity, 1995', May.

Bank for International Settlements (1996): '66th Annual Report', June.

Bertola, Giuseppe and Ricardo J. Caballero (1992): 'Target zones and realignments', American Economic Review, May.

Bofinger, Peter (1990): 'The role of monetary policy in the process of economic reform in eastern Europe', CEPR, Discussion Paper Series, No. 457.

Calvo, Guillermo A., Carmen M. Reinhart and Carlos A. Vegh (1994): 'Targeting the real exchange rate: theory and evidence', IMF, Research Department, WP/94/22, February.

Clark, Peter, Leonardo Bartolini, Tamim Bayoumi and Steven Symansky (1994): 'Exchange rates and economic fundamentals – a framework for analysis', IMF, Occasional Paper 115.

Cukierman, Alex, Steven B. Webb and Bilin Neyapti (1992): 'Measuring the independence of central banks and its effect on policy outcomes', World Bank Economic Review, September.

Czech National Bank, Annual Report and Monthly Bulletin (several issues).

Darvas, Zsolt (1995): 'Exchange rate premia on the Hungarian foreign exchange market', paper presented at the XXI Century Foundation/CEPR Conference on Convertibility and Exchange Rate Policy, Sofia, September.

Dittus, Peter (1993): 'Consumer prices outpacing producer prices: a problem?', Bank Review, 4/1993.

Dittus, Peter (1994): 'Capital flows and monetary policy in central Europe', internal BIS draft.

Drazen, Allan and Paul R. Masson (1994): 'Credibility of policies versus credibility of policy makers', The Quarterly Journal of Economics, August.

Estrin, Saul, Paul Hare and Marta Suranyi (1992): 'Banking in transition: Development and current problems in Hungary', The Centre for Economic Performance, The London School of Economics, Discussion Paper No. 68, March.

Fischer, Stanley (1994): 'Modern Central Banking', prepared for the tercentenary of the Bank of England, Central Bank Symposium, June.

Flood, Robert P. and Peter Isard (1989): 'Monetary policy strategies', IMF Staff Papers, September.

Flood, Robert P., Jagdeep S. Bhandari and Jocelyn P. Horne (1989): 'Evolution of exchange rate regimes', IMF Staff Papers, December.

Goodhart, Charles (1996): 'Why do the monetary authorities smooth interest rates?', LSE Financial Markets Group, Special Paper No. 81.

Halpern, Laszlo and Charles Wyplosz (1995): 'Equilibrium exchange rate in transition', CEPR, Discussion Paper.

Helpman, Elhanan, Leonardo Leiderman and Gil Bufman (1994): 'New exchange rate bands', Economic Policy, October.

Hochreiter, Eduard (1995): 'Central Banking in Economies in Transition', in Establishing Monetary Stability in Emerging Market Economies, eds. Thomas Willett et al., The Political Economy of Interdependence.

Hochreiter, Eduard (1996): 'The case for hard currency strategies for emerging market economies' in Exchange rate policies for emerging market economies, eds. Thomas Willett et al., Westview Press.

IMF (1995): 'Republic of Poland, Staff Report for the 1995 Article IV Consultation', December.

Koch, Elmar (1997): 'Capital flows in eastern Europe: Some lessons from the emerging markets in Latin America and Asia', in conference papers on Banking, International Capital Flows and Growth in Europe, Potsdam, October 1995, Springer Verlag (forthcoming).

Krugman, Paul R. (1991): 'Target zones and exchange rate dynamics', Quarterly Journal of Economics, August.

Krzak, Maciej (1995): 'The experience of east European countries with different exchange-rate regimes', The Vienna Institute for Comparative Economic Studies, Research Report No. 217, April.

Lysebo, Tore A. and B. Gabriela Mundaca (1992): 'Does the credibility of the exchange rate depend on the width of the target zone?', Arbeidsnotat, Norges Bank, August.

Obstfeld, Maurice (1996): 'Models of currency crisis with self-fulfilling features', Discussion Paper Series, No. 1315, CEPR.

OECD (1995): Purchasing Power Parities and Real Expenditures – 1993.

OECD (1995): Economic Surveys, Hungary.

OECD (1996): Economic Surveys, Czech Republic.

Riecke, Werner (1995): 'Final goals, intermediate targets and the use of instruments of monetary policy within a changing exchange rate regime', Oesterreichische Nationalbank and The Vienna Institute for Comparative Economic Studies, Central and Eastern Europe Conference.

Sokolowska, Barbara (1995): 'Foreign exchange policy', in Poland's Foreign Trade Policy 1994–1995, Foreign Trade Institute, Warsaw.

Svensson, Lars E.O. (1991): 'The simple test of target zone credibility', IMF Staff Papers, September.

Svensson, Lars E.O. (1994): 'Why exchange rate bands?', Journal of Monetary Economics 33, pp. 157–199, North-Holland.

Turner, Philip and Jozef Van't dack (1993): 'Measuring international price and cost competitiveness', BIS Economic Papers, No. 39, Monetary and Economic Department, November 1993.

White, William R. and Frank Smets (1996): 'From inflation reduction targets to price stability: Experience and prospects', Bank for International Settlements, lecture prepared for Norges Bank and Sveriges Riksbank, May/June.

World Bank (1993): 'Purchasing Power of Currencies', International Economics Department, Washington.
World Bank (1996): World Bank Atlas, Washington.
Wu, Yangru (1996): 'Are real exchange rates nonstationary? Evidence from a panel-data test', Journal of Money, Credit and Banking, Vol. 28, No. 1, February.
Wyplosz, Charles (1995): 'Links between monetary policy and the exchange rate', paper presented at the BIS, November.

13 Financial intermediation: efficiency, fragility and polices for reform

This paper seeks to provide a brief overview of financial intermediation. The first section considers the importance of efficient intermediation and briefly examines some of the academic literature on the relationship between efficient intermediation and growth. A second section outlines the main causes of financial fragility – both macroeconomic and microeconomic. A final section considers what needs to be done. Particular emphasis will be put on the *Core Principles for Effective Banking Supervision* recently issued by the Basle Committee. This, it will be argued, is a policy document that could have far-reaching effects.

13.1 Financial intermediation

The *mobilisation of savings and intermediation* to investors is the core function of financial intermediation. What are the *basic ingredients* required to *implement* these functions? A first basic requirement is the existence of financial *institutions*, be these government or privately owned, operating under clear rules, subject to internal and external auditing processes and disciplined by the market. *Diverse markets* are also essential. This might include the foreign exchange markets, the interbank and money markets, capital markets including equity and the market for derivatives in order to be able to hedge against various risks. Of course there are many specialised markets (e.g. for different types of insurance, for different kinds of consumer credits and mortgages).

Participants in each market vary. They may range from domestic players (government, finance ministry/central bank, banks, non-bank financial intermediaries, enterprises, households) to foreign players (foreign banks, investment companies, individuals). It is often important to distinguish between the different players not only because the role they play in economic activity differs but because their actions are often conditioned by different incentives. Basic *principles of the market economy* imply that the rule of law prevails and contracts are enforceable. A large shadow economy

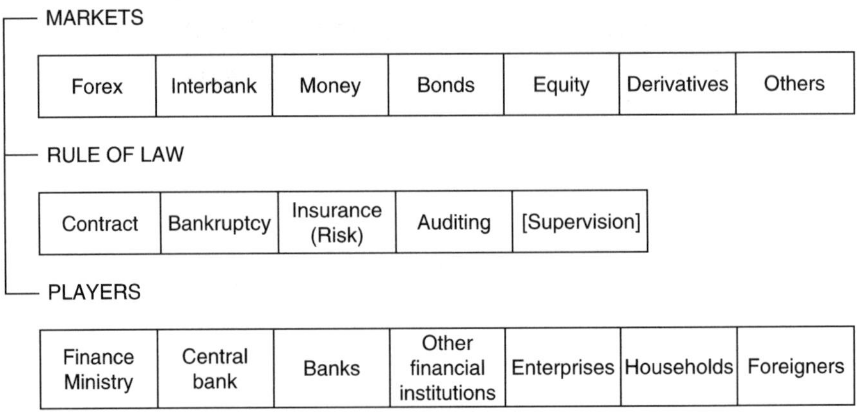

Chart 1. A stylised financial framework

may be indicative that the principles of the market economy are not working. The rules of the game should not only be clear for institutions but also for each individual market. Fair competition among the various participants is key. Bankruptcy laws, deposit insurance laws and supervisory laws may be needed to reinforce the market principles.

These distinctions are commonplace enough. In reality, of course, there is a constant pressure for change. Moreover, interactions between the various elements adds a complex layer of analysis. While it may be possible to adequately capture the structure of a financial system and perhaps also its changes, it may be much more delicate to assess *what* informational/incentive structure *drives the financial system.*[1]

Hence some recent academic work has sought to explain what drives the financial system. Some of this literature takes a closer look at the behaviour of individual agents in the market place: are they acting under a reasonable incentive system (or adverse incentives) and are these incentive systems compatible with each other? This revival of the more detailed look at the various agents in the market and how they arrive at their decisions has to some extent led to a re-examination of accepted macroeconomic

[1] Similarly, Bisignano (1995), who discusses four elements of financial structure, instruments, institutions, markets and flows. He points out that a theme common to all four elements is *homogenisation*: that there is greater substitutability and incrementally less differentiability within each one of these four units of financial structure, domestically and increasingly internationally. His focus is on the *function* of these elements along 'C.I.A.' (*contracts, information and agency*) lines.

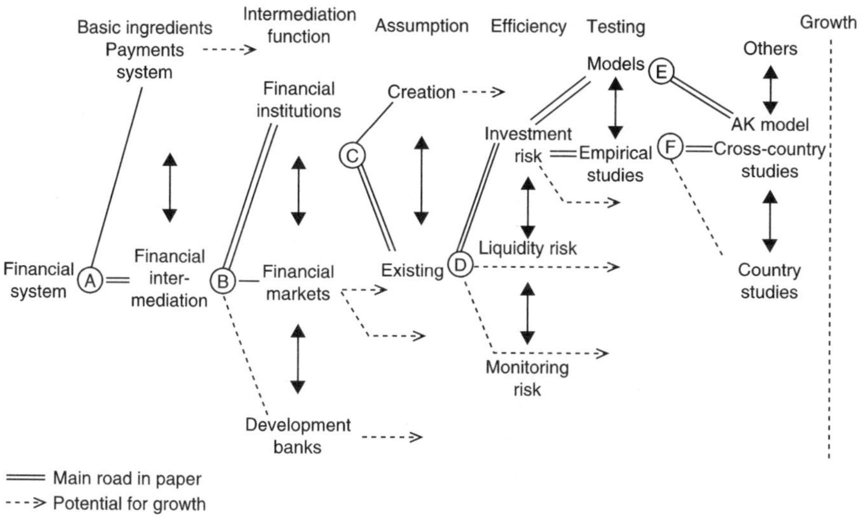

Chart 2. Financial system: a road map

assumptions.[2] (To be explained verbally by reference to Chart 2). Chart 2 attempts to show another stylised road map of how the financial system might influence growth. Please bear in mind that again there is no time sequence involved in this road map. For example, the creation/existing split could occur right at the beginning. Nor does the road map capture all the possible feedback/interaction effects, the major one being the one back from growth onto the financial system. The stylised map, however, aims to indicate major nodes (from A to E) in order to place the major thrust of the first section of this paper into perspective (indicated by the double lines in the chart) and it again indicates the complexity of the financial system. While individual elements should all be sound, soundness unfortunately also applies to all the potential links/interactions within the financial system.

---

[2] Mishkin (1990), for example, explains adverse selection: borrowers have an informational advantage over lenders because borrowers know more about the investment projects they want to undertake than lenders. As the lender cannot distinguish between the borrowers of good quality and bad quality, he will only make loans at an interest rate that reflects the average quality of good and bad borrowers. 'The result is that high-quality borrowers will be paying a higher interest rate than they should because low-quality borrowers pay a lower interest rate than they should. One result of this *lemon problem* is that some high-quality borrowers may drop out of the market and so profitable investment projects that should be undertaken will not be.' (p. 3).

One issue that has preoccupied researchers has been the complex relation between financial intermediation and growth.

While probably a large part of the economic profession would generally agree that efficient financial intermediation favours economic growth and development,[3] our understanding of what drives growth, and more importantly for this paper the role of the financial system in this process, is still very limited.[4] In a recent conference on growth sponsored by the Federal Reserve Bank of Boston, reference to the role of finance in growth was virtually absent.[5] That conference examined the determinants of growth in terms of neoclassical models and the new growth theories based more on innovative processes and spillovers. While the classical determinants of growth are widely agreed to be capital, labour and technology, the interaction between these three elements is not clearly understood. In particular, the role of the financial system in the interaction between these factors has not been greatly illuminated by systemic empirical research. While model builders understand the complexity of the financial system, the thrust of more recent models has relied in essence on the (traditional) savings/investment link. The article by Pagano (1993) is used here as an illustrative example of how the intermediation function can be explicitly included within a growth framework (endogenous growth model):

$$y = Ak, \tag{1}$$

$$\gamma = sA - \delta, \tag{2}$$

$$\gamma = s\mu A - \delta, \tag{3}$$

where y is per capita output, k is per capita capital and A is the level of technology (Equation 1).[6] With this production function, steady-state growth γ in a closed economy equals Equation 2, where s is the savings ratio and δ is the rate of depreciation. An increase in the savings/investment ratio raises the rate of economic growth. Pagano specifies that a fraction $1 - \mu$ of savings is lost in the intermediation process and arrives at Equation 3, which shows that financial development could affect growth by influencing A, s or μ. Growth can thus be influenced by A, the marginal productivity of capital, by s, the private saving rate, and μ, the

---

3 Sepp (1995).

4 For a recent review of broad trends in the literature on growth in the USA, see Jorgenson (1996).

5 Fuhrer and Little (1996).

6 While these so-called AK models are widespread, they are not undisputed, especially the assumption that the growth rate is proportional to the investment rate (Jorgenson, 1996).

proportion of saving funnelled into investment. The empirical testing (see below) is then subsequently based on such or similar work. If, for example, the marginal productivity of capital is to be higher in the private than in the public sector, then it is generally more efficient to provide credits to the private sector than to the public sector. Higher private savings rates have for some time been considered crucial in fostering growth.[7]

These developments in coping with integrating ideas/theories from the macro- and microfinancial structure is overlaid by continuous and deep changes in the structure of financial intermediation. These include changes in bank relations, the growth of non-bank financial intermediaries, the major growth in international investment and trading, the growth in merger and takeover activity in both the financial and non-financial sector and the innovations in new financial instruments.[8] The change in the financial landscape over the last few years in industrialised economies has been profound.

It is hardly surprising that empirical testing of the link between financial systems/intermediation and economic growth has therefore invariably been plagued by at least three major issues. The *complexity* of existing domestic financial systems, the *continuous changes* taking place in the financial system as borders between markets and players and the concepts of the 'rules of law' are blurred and overlap, and *changing 'concepts' of growth.*

What is the evidence of the positive relationship between growth and financial intermediation? More recent studies include those by King and Levine (1993) and Johnston and Pazarbasioglu (1995).[9] These studies attempt to follow the endogenous growth model approach by using regression analysis. At this very general level, where growth as dependent variable is mostly defined as real growth per capita, it is not surprising that the financial variables that are identified as having an impact are very few and that their role is only considered in the longer run. Fry (1995) explicitly levels this criticism as all the financial development models using endogenous growth ignore the dynamic process of financial liberalisation or stabilisation.

What are the relevant variables in these models? Table 1 summarises three typical cross-country studies. The variables included are indicative without being exhaustive.[10] One major problem in identifying the role of

---

[7] For an application of this conceptual framework to assessing the effect of financial reform on each one of the factors influencing growth, see Andersen and White (1996, their Sect. 2).

[8] Bisignano (1995).

[9] On the numerous new contributions on finance and economic development, see Fry (1995, Chap. 4).

[10] The paper ignores that the interrelationship between financial development and growth may give rise to threshold effects, that is, as there is a cost involved in

Table 1. Linkages between financial markets and growth: the financial variables in cross-country regressions

World Bank (1989)	King and Levine (1993)	Johnston and Pazarbasioglu (1995)
M3/GDP	Liquid liabilities1/GDP (DEPTH)	M2/GDP
	Banks' domestic assets/(banks' plus central bank's) domestic assets	
	Credit to private enterprises/total credit2	
	Credit to private enterprises/GDP	Claims on private sector/GDP
		Reserve money/GDP
Real interest rate		Real interest rate
		Lending minus deposit rate

[1]Currency held outside the banking system plus demand and interest-bearing liabilities of banks and non-bank financial intermediaries.
[2]Credit issued to central and local governments plus credit issued to public and private enterprises.

developing financial systems, the current real income level may not be high enough to shoulder such costs. The basic tenet of the *literature on thresholds* is that economies can only choose to develop a particular type of financial intermediation system when they have passed a certain threshold in terms of per capita income as it is only then that they can reap the benefits of the financial system's positive effect on growth. While regressions show that certain levels of income are important in developing the financial system, these levels are usually treated as exogenous. How do you get the system off the ground? In principle, an underdevelopment trap is possible where low income makes the development of a financial system impossible, which in turn blocks the allocation of resources to investment and weakens growth. The positive scenario (i.e. all the scenarios discussed above) supports the financial development/growth nexus. While most studies on underdevelopment/poverty traps highlight thresholds for the accumulation of human capital, i.e. a certain level of education as a precondition for growth, financial underdevelopment can be a very severe constraint on growth once this precondition is met (Berthelemy and Varoudakis, 1996b).

financial variables in the longer run are basic systemic changes that occur in the financial landscape in individual countries and/or actual banking crises. Johnston and Pazarbasioglu (1995) therefore adopt an individual-country approach arguing that the role of financial variables in the growth process is quite different depending on whether the financial system is essentially liberalised or not. They identify the major time perivods (5 years) of liberalisation as reflected in the elimination of credit ceiling and/or credit controls and the monetary direct government financing. Their approach thus keeps the individual country specificity and at the same time permits a cross-country analysis. Their study included 40 countries, of which 13 were industrialised economies, and appears to be particularly relevant to the countries in transition.

The variables shown in Table 1 were identified as being important for growth in addition to the traditional growth variables found in these kinds of analyses (significant in a statistical sense).[11] Two of the relevant variables had already been studied by the World Bank (1989) – *financial depth* and the real interest rate – and the findings at that time appear to have influenced our thinking and are of policy relevance today. The indicator of financial depth was demonstrated to correlate positively with per capita income. Greater financial depth was seen to contribute to growth by improving the productivity of investment, i.e. productivity was seen to be significantly higher in the faster-growing countries, which also have deeper financial systems. The indicator captures the volume of financial services provided. There is of course a two-way causation – higher income leads to deeper financial markets. However, several studies included the *initial* level of financial depth in their regressions in determining growth, and this variable was found to be significant.

A similar argument probably holds true for the *real interest rate*, which is supposed to hover in the positive range (this rate is to reflect the cost of capital). The World Bank (1989) had grouped countries according to their real interest rate into positive, moderately negative (0 to –5%) and strongly negative. The first group had lower inflation rates, deeper financial sectors, higher investment rates and significantly more productive investments than the others. 'More importantly, the growth rates of the countries with positive real interest rates were considerably higher on average than those of the others.'[12]

[11] Other explanatory variables include, *inter alia*, government expenditure/GDP, GDP deflator, % change in CPI, exports plus imports/GDP, foreign direct investment/GDP and primary school enrolment rate. For a summary of traditional growth determinants see Bank for International Settlements, Annual Report 1993, pp. 62–65.

[12] For more detail, World Bank (1989), Chap. 2.

Most economists would probably still agree with the preceding paradigm. While it may be possible that countries with faster growth may tolerate somewhat higher real interest rates, the World Bank has emphasised the detrimental effect of very negative real interest rates (scarce capital resources were wasted in these countries). However, very high real interest rates may also have seriously damaging effects on the economy, in particular if they remain very high for a long period of time.

A third factor that has shown persistent relevance in cross-country studies is the *private sector/public sector split.* A banking system that simply collects savings to allocate them to the public sector is not likely to channel resources effectively towards productive investment. While this factor is particularly relevant in developing economies, its recognition has also had profound influences on the conduct of public finances as most countries have moved away from direct financing of the government toward a system whereby the government is competing effectively for resources in 'competitive' markets.

Indicators such as the *reserve money/GDP* ratio are found in a variety of studies. This ratio essentially is intended to capture a tax on financial intermediaries and is therefore an indicator of the more general phenomenon of financial repression.[13] Fry (1995) shows that the similar indicator of reserves to deposits was three times higher in developing countries than in industrial countries and he has put forth a figure of 2.8% of GDP for the inflation tax alone in a single year in developing countries.

The *spread* between the *lending and deposit rate* usually enters the regression equation as an efficiency indicator of (usually) banking intermediation. The a *priori* assumption is that lower intermediation costs imply more efficient banking, that is competition seems to work in this sector (Pagano's factor μ). While some studies confirm this inverse link from financial intermediation margins to real GDP per capita, lower margins may in fact weaken the banking system as profits are being eroded, rendering banks more vulnerable.[14] Increased vulnerability may lead to a fall in the volume of loans accorded to the private sector with a detrimental impact on growth.

In general terms our a *priori* assumptions about certain indicators hold in the context of cross-country regressions. Certain variables promote economic growth: a reasonable level of financial depth, a positive real interest rate, sufficient room for manouevre for private sector initiatives, a low level of financial repression and reasonable interest rate margins. Excesses

[13] Next to low-yield required reserves, financial repression may also be due to ceilings on lending or deposit interest rates or the inflation tax on monetary assets.

[14] Similarly, Berthelemy and Varoudakis (1996a).

in any of these variables often undermine the efficient allocation of resources and retard growth: very low financial depth, very low negative interest rates, a pervasive government stronghold on the financial system,[15] excessive financial repression and high interest rate margins.

13.2 Financial fragility

Macroeconomic factors have been at least a contributing factor in all of the banking crises; in many, they provided the trigger for the crisis.[16] The severity of the recession in the Nordic countries, for example, is seen as one of the major contributing factors in the banking crisis.[17] High inflation tends to introduce distortions in relative prices and efforts to bring it under control. Yet risks persist even in countries where inflation stays low. Overvalued exchange rates have been a significant element in several crises. Macroeconomic instability (measured, e.g., by standard deviations of annual percentage changes in GDP and inflation) often goes hand in hand with even larger fluctuations in banking business (as measured by standard deviations of bank deposits/GDP and bank credit to private sector/GDP ratios). An unstable macroeconomic environment inevitably makes it harder for banks to assess credit risks. On the other hand, macroeconomic stability and financial system soundness appear to be mutually reinforcing.[18] In particular, macroeconomic stability helps to ensure a sound banking system.

But an adverse macroeconomic climate has not been the only cause of poor performance. Other contributing factors have included a more *difficult environment*, an *uneven institutional fabric, bad banking practices, weak prudential oversight mechanisms* and, finally, the inevitable problems encountered in the *transition to a more liberal system.*

An important aspect of increased vulnerability has been attributable to certain *developments* which are more *outside the control of individual*

---

[15] On this particular aspect, see Honohan (1997).

[16] See the extensive study by Caprio and Klingebiel (1996).

[17] Sigurdsson (1994).

[18] In their recent consultative paper (Basel Committee on Banking Supervision, 1997), banking supervisors accord an even more prominent role to sound and sustainable macroeconomic policies: 'Providing sound and sustainable macroeconomic policies is not within the competence of banking supervisors. Supervisors, however, will need to react if they perceive that existing policies are undermining the safety and soundness of the banking system. In the absence of sound macro-economic policies, banking supervisors are faced with a virtually impossible task. Therefore, sound macro-economic policies must be the foundation of a stable financial system.' (p. 12).

Table 2. Factors contributing to the crisis

United States 1984–1991	• Deficient bank management • Inadequate supervision and poor regulation • Macro volatility, regional recessions
Estonia 1992–1994	• Implementation of currency board brought growing bad debt problem of some banks to surface which could no longer earn large profits from foreign exchange trading or by lending central bank credits at high spreads • Deficient bank management and inappropriate lending policies • Frozen deposits in Russia • Collapse of Social Bank caused by bad loans and fraud
Finland 1991–1993	• Deregulation of financial system without adequate strengthening of regulatory and supervisory framework • Boom-and-bust cycle • Collapse in Soviet trade, deterioration of ToT • Rise in real interest rates adversely affected repayment capacity of banks' borrowers • Depreciation of markka also adversely affected repayment capacity of private sector indebted in foreign exchange • Excessive risk-taking in lending, poor decisions, lack of internal controls
Hungary 1990s	• Inheritance of largely non-performing portfolio from former monobanks • impact of recession of real sector on economy; demise of CMEA • Lack of banking expertise and poor lending policies • Moral hazard due to repetitive bank bailouts
Latvia 1994–	• Deficient bank management • Inadequate supervision and regulation • Fraud
Poland 1992–1994	• Severe economic shocks that Polish enterprises suffered in 1990 and 1991 (e.g. demise of CMEA trade) • Poor lending decisions and lack of banking expertise

Table 2. Continued

Spain 1977–1985	• Combination of '73/'74 oil shock and inappropriate policy responses to shock • Rapid liberalisation of banking sector without adequate strengthening of regulatory and accounting framework as well as bank supervision • Deficient bank management and concentration of loans to related parties
Turkey 1982–1985	• 1979/80 Turkey slid into a recession brought on by tight monetary policy; reduced sharply corporate sector's ability to service its debt, which in turn adversely affected banks • Liberalisation of banking system without adequate strengthening of regulatory and accounting framework and bank supervision • Lending to related parties

Reproduced from Caprio and Klingebiel (1996), Table 2.

banks, and they have generally contributed to banks' reduced profitability and greater downward pressure on profit margins, especially in traditional intermediation activities. Credit ratings of banks have generally weakened, and widespread failures are a sign of this increased vulnerability.[19]

The increased vulnerability can be traced to some regime change,[20] induced by policy or external conditions. The main features of structural change are well known: a quantum leap in the variety and complexity of new instruments; a blurring of functional distinctions between different types of institutions, with combinations of business lines ranging from traditional commercial and investment banking to insurance and, in some cases, even non-financial activities;[21] the internationalisation and globalisation of finance; the institutionalisation of savings; an unprecedented surge in trading and hence in payment and settlement flows; and a marked heightening of competitive pressure (i.e. from non-bank financial intermediaries). These changes have implied that a rising proportion of banks' revenue has come from non-interest sources.

[19] Honohan (1997).

[20] Not all changes in the structure of financial intermediation may have led to 'increased vulnerability'. Other changes strengthened the intermediation process.

[21] Borio and Filosa (1994).

A major source of difficulty has been the *uneven institutional fabric* inherited from years of government control and protection. Two elements of this unsatisfactory structure have been of particular consequence: inefficient banks and an inadequate legal framework.

At the start of many liberalisation programmes, banks – protected by controls and regulation – were often very inefficient. In many countries, moreover, state-owned banks had traditionally played an important, and sometimes dominant, role in the banking system. With loan policies subject to government direction or other forms of political pressure, banks did not always evaluate credit risks properly. They could also afford to be overstaffed or to maintain excessive branch networks. A banking system will become more efficient only if liberalisation is accompanied by measures to enable the more competitive banks to absorb and reform the weaker banks or to allow new entrants to drive out the incompetent banks. But the takeover mechanism was frequently obstructed by various restrictions that have remained in force even after liberalisation.

Secondly, the legal framework was still ill-attuned to the needs of a market-oriented financial system. Banks depend on an effective legal framework. The promptness of legal procedures necessary for banks to be able to get control of the collateral they hold has an obvious bearing on its value, particularly in a crisis: long delays and unpredictable adjudication of claims in the event of bankruptcy are also essential.

A third source of difficult has been *poor banking practices*. The inadequate diversification of bank assets has been a central failing. Specialist banks have been overly dependent on the particular sector or region served. Another weakness has been concentration on loans for real estate.

In a number of developing countries, lending to *connected* enterprises (e.g. industrial companies which have a major stake in the bank) has often compromised objective risk assessment and increased the temptation of fraud. Rules in different countries on maximum exposure to a single borrower vary significantly in their restrictiveness. Some supervisory authorities impose a limit of 10% of capital or net worth, but others permit up to 30%. Moreover, the intent of these regulations is sometimes undermined by increased exposure through subsidiaries, by offshore or off-balance-sheet operations or by counting each of several companies within a group as a single borrower.

Another dangerous practice is excessive *maturity and currency mismatches* between assets and liabilities. Where bank finance is practically the only source of investment finance, even for long-term projects, as it is in many developing countries, banks whose funds are drawn from short-term deposits face potentially serious maturity mismatches. When interest rates are liberalised, banks lose the protection of the controlled structure

Table 3. Resolution costs of banking crises

	% of GDP		% of GDP
Spain (1977–85)	17	Venezuela	18
Finland (1991–93)	8	Bulgaria	14
Sweden (1991)	6	Mexico	12–15
Norway (1987–89)	4	Hungary	10
United States (1984–91)	3	Argentina	>25
Japan (1993–)	3½	Chile	>25
		Côte d'Ivoire	>25

Source: Lindgren et al. (1996).

that typically kept short-term rates below long-term rates. Attempts by banks to avoid this interest rate risk by charging their long-term borrowers variable interest rates (linked to short-term rates) may rebound on them as a credit risk if their customers face servicing difficulties when short-term rates rise sharply. Similar conditions apply to foreign-currency lending to domestic borrowers. Such lending typically surges in the early stages of reform programmes as borrowers seek to avoid the higher domestic currency interest rates that usually accompany liberalisation.

A fourth important cause of difficulties has been the failure to strengthen the system of *prudential oversight* sufficiently to cope with the increased risk that is almost inevitably associated with liberalisation. Very often, the responsible authorities lack the resources to adequately monitor banks or the powers to enforce the rules. In some cases, supervisory guidelines remained lax or were easy to evade: when supervision was not on a consolidated basis, for instance, banks could transfer problems offshore or to other members of their conglomerate group.

Officially enforced rules and regulations can, of course, be only part of any oversight mechanism; disclosure and market-based control mechanisms also have an essential role to play because any regulation inevitably prompts attempts to avoid or to evade. This is all the more true when the structure of financial markets is changing rapidly and may at times outgrow specific regulatory provisions.

13.3 Banking crises

The literature on banking crises clearly shows the costs of resolving crises have been very high. Firstly, the direct costs incurred (*ex post*, i.e. after the crisis is considered to be resolved)[22] have been enormous. Secondly, and perhaps as important, banking crises have been expensive in terms of the GDP foregone as they have almost always induced a marked slowdown in growth.[23]

The incidence of banking crises has been much greater in developing and transition economies than in the industrial world. While the individual country crises are not alike in any group of countries, one can probably broadly differentiate between two types: the *macroeconomic* type in the industrialised world (leading to boom-and-bust cycles) and the *microeconomic* variety with pervasive government involvement in the banking system, which has been more common in developing and transition economies.[24] Some indication of the scale of the problem is given by comparing the scale of non-performing loans (Table 4). While peak values for non-performing loans in industrial countries were around 10% of total loans in single years, these values were above 20% for an extended period of time in eastern European countries.

Crises in the developing countries are often based simply on poor management, recklessness and fraud ('looting') and a government-permeated banking system,[25]factors which are less prevalent in economies that have been more market-oriented for longer. The upshot of this basic differentiation is that a somewhat modified set of indicators reflecting actual or potential weakness is relevant for different kinds of countries.[26] Why do these crises occur? Some broad considerations may help our understanding. While all the factors listed above may have played a role, their importance in individual episodes varies. Often it is not possible to distinguish between cause and effect, and the individual factors are inextricable intertwined. The lack of a single overriding cause points to the conclusion that no single remedy is likely to apply to all crises. However, what is important here is that weaknesses in any of these factors may have a detrimental effect on growth.

---

[22] Caprio and Klingebiel (1996).

[23] For a summary of these indirect costs, see Goldstein and Turner (1996).

[24] This differentiation is based on Honohan (1997).

[25] For more detail, see Honohan (1997). Countries included in the government-permeated group are Cameroon, Egypt, Hungary, Pakistan, Philippines and Poland.

[26] Honohan (1997) uses in the end seven fairly straightforward indicators in the empirical part of the paper: share of reserves to deposits, government share of lending, central bank refinancing of bank lending, government deficit, loan-to-deposit ratio, foreign borrowing/deposit ratio and the growth rate of real bank credit.

Table 4. Non-performing loans (as a percentage of total loans)

	1990	1994	1995	1996
Asia[1]	7.6	6.2	5.1	4.0
India	–	23.6	19.5	17.3
Latin America[2]	6.2	8.4	7.8	6.0
Eastern Europe				
Czech Republic	19[3]	38	36	36
Hungary	11[3]	21	15	13
Poland	30[3]	28	22	14
Industrial countries				
United States	3.3	1.9	1.3	1.1
Japan[4]	–	3.3	3.3	3.4
Italy	5.2	8.1	9.3	10.1
Finland	8.0[3]	4.6	3.9	2.7
Norway	9.1[3]	5.4	4.1	3.2
Sweden	11.0[3]	6.3	4.4	3.0

[1]Hong Kong, Korea, Indonesia, Malaysia, Taiwan and Thailand.
[2]Argentina, Brazil, Chile, Colombia, Mexico, Peru and Venezuela.
[3]For Eastern Europe and the Nordic countries (peak year of the banking crisis): 1992.
[4]Fiscal years.

13.4 Strengthening financial intermediation

It is clear that policy to improve and strengthen the financial intermediation process requires both macroeconomic and microeconomic measures.

There are a couple of points to be made about macroeconomic policies. First, it is essential to adopt policies that *preserve monetary discipline*. When faced with insolvent banks, many governments have in the past yielded to the temptation of relaxing monetary policy so much as to generate high inflation, negative real interest rates and devaluation. By eroding the real value of banks' bad loans, this tactic can appear to pay short-run dividends. But such policies typically provoke capital flight, shrinking the domestic deposit base of sound as well as unsound banks. Moreover, the memory of expropriation through inflation endures long after lax macroeconomic policies have been reversed.

The second warning about macroeconomic policy is that governments need to be wary of allowing *misaligned exchange rates* to persist for too long.

In many Latin American countries, tight monetary policies and/or fixed exchange rates led to significant reductions in inflation in the 1990s, but at the price of real exchange rate appreciation and widening current account deficits. Several eastern European countries now face a similar dilemma.

Microeconomic policies are also important. As the scope of such policies is very broad, this paper will conclude by focusing on one important aspect – the *quality of bank supervision*.

To help supervisors and banks worldwide to ensure that adequate steps are taken to strengthen financial systems, the Basel Committee on Banking Supervision has been widening the scope of its activities, both in terms of the range of issues addressed and in terms of involving a wider range of countries. During the last 6 months or so, the Basel Committee has been working on a set of Core Principles for effective banking supervision. These principles were published as a discussion document last month and are meant to form the basis for the further evolution of supervisory practices in the coming years.

The preparation of these Core Principles represents a significant departure from the Basel Committee's practice in at least three ways. Firstly, they cover all banks, not just internationally active banks. This is obviously very important for the transition economies. Secondly, they are comprehensive and not targeted to specific industrialised country concerns. Thirdly and most importantly, there has been broad participation of many non-G10 countries in the preparation of the principles. In addition to the G10 country supervisors that are permanent members of the Basel Committee, some 15 supervisory authorities have been closely involved. The discussion process is now being extended more widely with a view to finalisation in September at the IMF/World Bank meeting. These Core Principles are of great importance, and it is difficult to exaggerate the effect they could eventually have in strengthening the international financial system, although one cannot expect dramatic results in the short term. These principles seek to set out some broad features of a robust supervisory regime. They do not attempt to lay down specific guidelines for individual banks or supervisors. For example, they suggest that a satisfactory supervisory system must have clear procedures for provisioning against bad loans, and these must be in line with best international practice. But they do not attempt to lay down precise rules about how banks should provision for bad loans.

There are 25 Basel Core Principles that need to be in place for a supervisory system to be effective. The Principles relate to:

- Preconditions for effective banking supervision – Principle 1,
- Licensing and structure – Principles 2 to 5,
- Prudential regulations and requirements – Principles 6 to 15,

- Methods of ongoing banking supervision – Principles 16 to 20,
- Information requirements – Principle 21,
- Formal powers of supervisors – Principle 22, and
- Cross-border banking – Principles 23 to 25.

In addition to the Principles themselves, the document contains explanations of the various methods supervisors can use to implement them. They are meant to apply to the supervision of all banks within their jurisdictions. The Principles are minimum requirements and in many cases may need to be supplemented by other measures designed to address particular conditions and risks in the financial systems of individual countries.

It is noteworthy that the very first recommendation relates to the need for *independent* supervisors vested with the necessary powers. In the past, the effectiveness of supervisors has been undermined either because they have been subject to undue political influence or because they have lacked the resources needed to carry out effective supervision. In many cases, they have lacked the legal authority to enforce their judgements (say, by revoking a firm's licence). So it is very important that supervisors have the legal powers to take and enforce decisions. To do this, they must be adequately protected against litigation.

The second group of principles deals with the *licensing* and structure of banks. Supervisors must be able to control effectively the criteria and standards for the establishment of banks and have the ability to reject applications that do not meet the required standards – so-called 'fit-and-proper' tests. This applies equally to requests by existing banks to change ownership structures or to acquire other institutions.

The third group of recommendations deals with the *nature of the prudential requirements* supervisors should impose – this is of course close to the Basel Committee's traditional focus. The first guideline deals with the need to hold adequate capital, the Basel ratios. The other guidelines, however, cover the equally important matter of checking banks' internal operational procedures. Credit assessment, monitoring loan quality, controlling connected lending and the measuring of risks and so on are at least as important as capital adequacy. Supervisors will need to be able to independently assess procedures for granting credits and for the valuation of assets. Internal information and control systems must be adequate to monitor the risks run. Supervisors need to be able to detect any lending to connected enterprises or individuals. They must have the capacity to check that market risks are adequately measured and that adequate procedures are in place to deal with such risks. Finally, supervisors must ensure that banks have adequate safeguards against operational risks by, for example, ensuring the strict separation of risk-taking and risk-monitoring activities.

The fourth set of recommendations relates to the *methods of conducting supervision*. They emphasise four key aspects. First, supervisors need to develop a good 'feel' for the banks they supervise, and this will require some form of both on-site and off-site supervision. It will also require regular contact with bank management and a thorough understanding of the institution's operations. Secondly, supervisors must have a means of collecting, reviewing and analysing detailed statistical information from banks. Thirdly, supervisors must have a means of independently auditing the supervisory information they receive – perhaps by doing this themselves or perhaps by using external auditors. A final but essential element of effective supervision is the ability to supervise each banking organisation's operations on a consolidated basis worldwide.

13.5 Concluding remarks

This paper touched upon some broad aspects of financial intermediation. The following conclusions may be drawn:

- Our theoretical and empirical understanding of the relationship between financial intermediation and growth is still being developed.
- Financial fragility is a complex concept which we try to avoid by providing solid macro and micro policies and a supervisory framework.
- A large part of the efforts by the central banking community is aimed at building a sound framework for financial intermediation. The Core Principles of the Basel Committee on Banking Supervision is an important initiative in this process.

Bibliography

Akerlof, George A. (1970): 'The market for 'lemons': quality uncertainty and the market mechanism', *Quarterly Journal of Economics*, pp. 488–500.

Andersen, Palle and William R. White (1996): 'The macroeconomic effects of financial sector reforms: an overview of industrial countries', OECD conference on 'Interactions between structural reform, macroeconomic policies and economic performance', Paris, January.

Bank for International Settlements (1993): Annual Report.

Bank for International Settlements (1996): Annual Report.

Bank for International Settlements (1996): 'Changing financial systems in small open economies', Monetary and Economic Department, *Policy Paper* No. 1, December.

Barro, Robert J. (1991): 'Economic growth in a cross-section of countries', *Quarterly Journal of Economics*, May, issue 2.

Basel Committee on Banking Supervision (1997): 'Core Principles for Effective Banking Supervision', Consultative Paper, Basel, April.

Berthélemy, Jean-Claude and Aristomene Varoudakis (1996a): 'Models of financial development and economic growth', eds. Hermes and Lensirik, *Routledge Studies in Development Economics*, London and New York.

Berthélemy, Jean-Claude and Aristomene Varoudakis (1996b): 'Financial development policy and economic growth', eds. Hermes and Lensirik, *Routledge Studies in Development Economics*, London and New York.

Bisignano, Joseph (1995): 'Paradigm for understanding changes in financial structure: instruments, institutions, markets and flows', paper prepared for the conference 'Structural change and turbulence in international financial markets', International Center for Monetary and Banking Studies, Geneva, 9–10 November (first draft).

Borio, Claudio E.V., N. Kennedy and S.D. Prowse (1994a): 'Exploring aggregate asset price fluctuations across countries: measurement, determinants and monetary policy implications', *BIS Economic Paper* No. 40, April.

Borio, Claudio E.V. and Renato Filosa (1994b): 'The changing borders of banking: trends and implications', *BIS Economic Paper* No. 43, December.

Caprio, Gerard and Daniela Klingebiel (1996): 'Bank insolvencies, cross-country experience', The World Bank, *Policy Research Working Paper*, 1620, July.

Claessens, Stijn (1996): 'Banking Reform in Transition Countries', The World Bank, Policy Research Working Paper, 1642, August.

Fry, Maxwell J. (1995): 'Money, interest and banking in economic development', Johns Hopkins University Press, Baltimore and London.

Fuhrer, Jeffrey and Jane Sneddon Little (1996): 'Technology and growth: an overview', 'Technology and Growth', Federal Reserve Bank of Boston, Conference Proceedings, June.

Gertler, Mark (1988): 'Financial structure and aggregate economic activity: an overview', *Journal of Money, Credit and Banking*, August, Part 2.

Goldstein, Morris (1996): 'Presumptive indicators/early warning signals of vulnerability to financial crisis in emerging-market economies', Institute for International Economics, January.

Goldstein, Morris and Philip Turner (1996): 'Banking crises in emerging economies: origins and policy options', *BIS Economic Paper* No. 46, October.

Goodhart, Charles and Dirk Schoenmaker (1993): 'Institutional separation between supervisory and monetary agencies', Financial Markets Group, London School of Economics, February.

Haggard, Stephan, C.H. Lee and S. Maxfield (1993): 'The politics of finance in developing countries', Cornell University Press, Ithaca and London.

Honohan, Patrick (1997): 'Banking system failures in developing and transition countries: diagnosis and prediction', *BIS Working Paper* No. 39, January.

IMF (1996): *World Economic Outlook*, May and October.

Johnston, Barry R. and Ceyla Pazarbasioglu (1995): 'Linkages between financial variables, financial sector reform and economic growth and efficiency', IMF, WP/95/103.

Jorgensen, Dale W. (1996): 'Technology in growth theory', in Technology and Growth Conference Proceedings, Conference Series No. 40, Federal Reserve Bank of Boston, June.

Karvalits, Ferenc (1997): 'The Hungarian Banking System: 10 years of two-tier banking', Paper prepared for the Euro-Forum Seminar, March (draft).

Kindleberger, Charles P. and Jean-Pierre Laffargue (1992): 'Financial crises', Cambridge University Press.

King, Robert G. and Ross Levine (1993): 'Finance, entrepreneurship, and growth', *Journal of Monetary Economics* No. 32, pp. 513–542.

Lindgren, Carl-Johan, Gillian Garcia and Mathew I. Saal (1996): 'Bank soundness and macroeconomic policy', IMF.

McClam, Warren D. (1982): 'Financial fragility and instability: monetary authorities as borrowers and lenders of last resort', in *Financial Crises*, eds. Charles P. Kindleberger and Jean-Pierre Laffargue, Cambridge University Press.

Mishkin, Frederic S. (1990): 'Asymmetric information and financial crises: a historical perspective', National Bureau of Economic Research, Working Paper No. 3400.

Mishkin, Frederic S. (1995): 'Symposium on the monetary transmission mechanism', *Journal of Economic Perspectives*, Vol. 9, No. 4, Fall.

Mondschean, Thomas S. and Timothy P. Opiela (1997): 'Banking reform in a transition economy: The case of Poland', *Economic Perspectives*, Federal Reserve Bank of Chicago, March/April.

Pagano, Marco (1993): 'Financial markets and growth', *European Economic Review* No. 37, April.

Sachs, Jeffrey, Aaron Torvell and Andrés Velasco (1996): 'Financial crises in emerging markets: the lessons from 1995', *Brookings Paper on Economic Activity* I.

Schwartz, Anna J. (1986): 'Real and pseudo-financial crises', in *Financial Crises and the World Banking System*, eds. F. Capri and G.E. Wood, Macmillan.

Sepp, Urmas (1995): 'Financial intermediation in Estonia', *Review of Economies in Transition*, Bank of Finland, Unit for Eastern European Economies, 2.

Sigurdsson, Jón (1994): 'The Nordic model in crises', *Economic and Financial Review*, Summer/Autumn.

Solow, Robert M. (1982): 'In the lender of last resort', in *Financial Crises*, eds. Charles P. Kindleberger and Jean-Pierre Laffargue, Cambridge University Press.

Sundararajan, V. and Tomás J.T. Baliño (1991): 'Banking crises: cases and issues', IMF.

Vihrälä, Vesa (1996): 'Theoretical aspects of the Finnish credit cycle', *Bank of Finland Discussion Papers*, August.

White, William R. (1996): 'Pitfalls and policy options particular to the financial systems in emerging markets', paper presented at the 12th Pacific Basin Central Bank Conference, Singapore, November.

World Bank (1989): *World Development Report* 1989 (Financial Systems and Development).

14 The monetary policy transmission mechanism in China

The Chinese financial system is undergoing a transformation. Although 5-year plans continue to be published, they are increasingly being overtaken by events. While planning for the real economy is tending to take the back seat, centrally controlled credit allocation still plays a major role, at least officially.

14.1 The changing financial sector

The bulk of the state-allocated credits to individual sectors of the economy continue to be granted by the 'policy banks' dedicated to the implementation of economic policy objectives and by the state-owned commercial banks.[1] Interest rates have not been liberalised, but certain 'free-market' aspects seem to have a bearing on rate setting. In the recent past, moreover, the central bank, the People's Bank of China, has given consideration to far-reaching financial system changes that could serve to lay the foundation for a freer play of market forces in this area. This would be all the more welcome in that consumer prices have already been liberalised, and prices on the factor markets are also moving in this direction.[2]

The aim is to alter the official 'credit policy' framework in certain respects: the structure of credit is to be adjusted by targeting lending more specifically to the most important sectors of the economy; the interest rate management system is to be reformed by authorising certain instruments that are not directly under state control; and the rural credit cooperatives

---

[1] There are three 'policy banks' (State Development Bank of China, Export-Import Bank of China und Agricultural Development Bank of China) and four state-owned commercial banks (Industrial and Commercial Bank of China, Agricultural Bank of China, Bank of China and People's Construction Bank of China).

[2] Allocating state-controlled resources at below-market prices leads to highly inefficient reallocation ('rent seeking').

are to be gradually transformed into 'genuine' commercial banks.[3] These changes are to be implemented on a step-by-step basis.

These 'limited' changes in the financial sphere are taking place against the backdrop of other major projects: financial services to state-owned enterprises – which are themselves being reformed – are to be improved, and the reform of the exchange rate regime is to be speeded up. In November 1996, current account convertibility of the renminbi was officially implemented. In 1995 the development of a provisional legal framework marked a major breakthrough in financial legislation.

Currently, credit allocation plays the biggest role in the monetary policy transmission mechanism. In what follows, we examine this mechanism more closely and also discuss some more recent measures taken by the Chinese central bank to strengthen the market in this area. The current exchange rate regime would seem to be in line with the declared aim of monetary policy, namely to maintain price stability and thereby foster economic growth.

14.2 The credit policy perspective

The financial landscape is dominated by the four state-owned commercial banks, which hold 72% of total financial assets (Table 1). The State Development Bank of China, the Export-Import Bank of China and the Agricultural Development Bank of China continue to finance major state projects in their respective areas of specialisation. By contrast, the credits allocated to other commercial banks appear to have very little weight. The prevailing credit restrictions, however, are circumvented by the large regional banks and cooperatives, which the government (deliberately) controls less tightly. While credit growth by the state-owned banks has been over 20% per year in the 1990s, implying a sizeable real credit expansion, it is likely to have been higher still at some regional banks.

An expansion of credit due to relaxation of credit restrictions or circumvention of credit ceilings is generally not matched by a corresponding rise in savings, so that banks are obliged to create money, with potentially inflationary consequences. Since the non-state sector has recently been showing the most dynamic growth (Table 2), the government does not necessarily see any reason to put an immediate stop to 'irregularities'.

[3] People's Bank of China, *Annual Report* 1995, p. 4.

Table 1. The Chinese banking system[1]

	Number	Assets at end-1995 (Yuan 100 billion)
Deposit money banks		
State commercial banks	4	45.9
Other commercial banks[2]	11	4.3
Rural credit cooperatives	50,000	6.8
Urban credit cooperatives	4,900	3.1
Finance companies	65	0.5
Specific depository banks	348	3.3

[1] Not including two policy banks (State Development Bank of China and Export-Import Bank of China), six nationwide commercial banks that conduct investment business with each other, and all foreign financial institutions.
[2] Regional banks (e.g. Guangdong Development Bank, Shenzhen Merchants Bank, Fujian Industrial Bank, Beijing Urban Cooperation Bank).

Table 2. Financial indicators

	1991–93	1994	1995	1996
	Percentage changes			
Credit from state banks	20.4	18.4	24.6	–
M2	34.0	32.1	31.9	25.0[1]
Retail prices	7.1	21.7	14.8	6.1
Wage growth	18.6	35.3	21.7	–
Exchange rate (yuan/US$)	5.6	8.6	8.4	8.3
Memo items:				
GDP	12.3	11.8	10.2	9.7
Industrial output	19.4	21.4	16.0	15.0[1]
Of which:				
State-owned enterprises[2]	*10.1*	*6.5*	*8.6*	*7.0*[1]
Collective enterprises[2]	*30.3*	*29.4*	*20.2*	*25.0*[1]
Other enterprises[2]	*54.0*	*42.2*	*27.2*	*17.0*[1]

[1] Estimated.
[2] Share of industrial output: 31%, 43% and 26% respectively (1995).

For efficient credit allocation, interest rates would be a suitable instrument, but they have tended to play a rather passive role in this process to date. The government has hesitated to raise interest rates to curb surging investment or to combat inflation. The repercussions of such a policy, which leads not only to inefficient resource allocation but also to wide fluctuations in real interest rates, are unlikely to be conducive to a more stable investment behaviour on the part of the dynamic non-state production sector.

14.3 Difficulties in recovering loans

In setting interest rates, however, the margin between lending and deposit rates is maintained (Table 3), and in principle this should enable the banks to earn healthy profits. There is no incentive to change anything since a credit risk assessment is superfluous. The banks are not exposed to any interest rate risk, as deposits earn lower interest than loans across the entire yield curve (in particular at the short end, where the deposit rate is 3 to 5% but the rate payable on loans for working capital is over 10%).

Lending also seems to be quite rigorously segregated along the maturity spectrum: for example, loans for working capital cannot be converted into loans for fixed investment. This does not make loan recovery easier, particularly where the borrowers are state-owned enterprises. However, poor-quality loan portfolios, which evidently affect most financial institutions, can be viewed in quite a different light given that all banks are nationalised (there is only one single private investment bank in China), and the omnipresent hand of the state goes some way beyond the problem of lending to borrowers who are themselves involved in the business of the bank concerned ('connected lending').

In its latest annual report (1995), the Chinese central bank makes explicit mention of the structural weakness (in the financial sector) that is partly reflected in the poor quality of financial institutions' loan portfolios.[4] In view of the fact that the banking sector is still highly compartmentalised, that directed lending still predominates and that state-owned enterprises are not obliged to aim for profits (since credit is allocated on the

---

4 Corporate indebtedness and the problem of the 'chain of indebtedness' can be broken down as follows: 1. internal liabilities (chiefly to staff pension funds); 2. liabilities to other enterprises; 3. liabilities to banks. An attempt to break this chain in the early 1990s failed because new lending from the central bank was used mainly to settle internal liabilities (amortisation of pension fund liabilities). In 1996, 45% of the 68,000 state-owned industrial enterprises in China recorded losses estimated at over US$8 billion, with non-performing loans being put at some 20% of total banking system credit.

Table 3. Return on banks' on-balance-sheet assets and liabilities (1995) in per cent

Maturity	Treasuries	Building loans	Savings deposits
3 years	14	13½	12
5 years	16	15	14

basis of non-economic criteria), the rather closed financial sector would not seem to be internationally competitive at present.[5]

14.4 Moving away from planning and towards a free market

One might imagine that a market-oriented economic policy conducted via interest rates and the exchange rate would be best suited to allocate scarce resources most productively, but with the system described above China has nonetheless achieved truly impressive rates of growth. Over the last 5 years, real GDP, underpinned by persistently high rates of investment above 40%, has been remarkably stable at around 12% annually.[6] During this period, annual inflation averaged around 13%. 1996 was called the year of the 'soft landing', as robust economic growth coincided with action to bring down the high rate of inflation to below 7%. Below, we examine the general macroeconomic situation and the ambivalent attitude of Chinese economic policy in reconciling these seemingly contradictory influences.

In the 1970s and 1980s, China's economy underwent a series of 'boom and bust' cycles, i.e. periods of heady growth followed by steep downturns. For example, in 1981 real gross business fixed investment declined by 13%, only to rise again by 28% the following year. Such cycles frequently began with efforts by the state to accelerate reforms, which – via an expansionary credit policy – directly triggered a strong increase in investment. This led in turn to an upswing and the attendant danger of a pickup in inflation,[7] followed by a downturn due to a tighter policy with more stringent administrative restrictions.

---

[5] Liberalising interest rates is currently one of the most important monetary policy issues for the People's Bank of China.

[6] China's foreign trade was equally buoyant, with exports growing between 1978 and 1995 from US$10 billion a year (0.8% of global exports) to 14 times as much, at almost US$150 billion (3.4% of global exports).

[7] This is a simplified account; it was only in 1985 that a major step was taken towards price liberalisation.

With such restrictions ending the cycle, the reform process came to a halt or in some cases was even reversed. Demands for speedier reforms were then obviously interpreted by economic agents as a signal to strengthen investment, so that investment spending surged once more. Excess demand during the last growth cycle pushed annual inflation to almost 20% in 1988.

14.5 No signs of overheating in the current cycle

The current cycle, which started in 1991, seems on the other hand to be following a slightly different path. Inflation peaked at 22% in 1994 and has since declined, while economic activity has remained buoyant throughout the period. Figures for 1996 underscore this success, that is, it seems as though any potential overheating is being successfully countered without jeopardising growth.

One explanation for this is that the supply of credit has remained stable (Table 2), with surplus demand being met through unofficial channels. Firms have realised that the government has been tolerating a more flexible attitude to credit ceilings.[8] The danger of overheating has this time been addressed not through strict restrictions by the authorities, but by the government keeping a steady hand, that is growth of the money supply M2 has been gently brought back down to around 25% in 1996. The weight attached to the money supply underscores the state's willingness to provide the economy with an adequate 'mantle of liquidity' so as to give private initiative room to develop.

Credit ceilings are evidently bound to become gradually less binding, as the state sector is rapidly shrinking and interest rates are beginning to move to the forefront of monetary policy instruments. The central bank has lent major support to this development by developing reference short-term interest rates for the emerging interbank market.

14.6 The exchange rate policy perspective

This success on the domestic front has increasingly borne fruit on the external side as well, as massive capital inflows (chiefly in the form of direct investment) and rapid growth in official reserves have been accompanied by a stable exchange rate of the yuan against the US dollar

---

8 According to the Chinese central bank's 1995 annual report (p. 10), 'the central bank should gradually improve the mode by which credit ceilings are managed and expand the use of indirect instruments'.

since the unification of the exchange rate regime in early 1994 (with the fixed exchange rate being superseded by a managed float).[9] The contemporaneous depreciation of the currency by 45% stimulated exports and boosted growth, albeit at the cost of a temporary rise in domestic prices. The recent decline in inflation increases the likelihood that the current level of around 8.5 yuan to the US dollar will be maintained in the near term, a rate likely to foster further growth going forward.

9 At that time the quota system for retention of foreign exchange was abolished and the procedure for approving the use of foreign exchange was relaxed (firms needing foreign exchange can now acquire it against renminbi directly from the foreign exchange banks set up for the purpose upon presentation of a valid permit).

15 Capital flows in eastern Europe: some lessons from the emerging markets in Latin America and Asia

15.1 Introduction

Given the scale of the transformation of the economies in eastern Europe, it is perhaps not surprising that the revival of capital flows into that region has occurred somewhat later than that of flows into Asia and Latin America. Although events are still unfolding at the time of writing, it may be useful to take a look at emerging capital flow trends in central Europe[1] in the light of the experiences in Latin America and Asia. Section 1 briefly reviews recent developments in global capital flows. Section 2 looks at the size of the capital flows for the three regions under review. Section 3 juxtaposes in a highly stylised way some factors which influence the capital flow experiences in Latin America, Asia and central Europe. A more detailed analysis of the composition and nature of the capital flows in the three groups of countries is contained in Sect. 4. Three important policy-related issues are then addressed in Sect. 5: the effect of inflows on monetary policy (including the issue of sterilisation); whether inflows reflect excessive domestic consumption rather than investment (including the relationship with fiscal policy); and, finally, how far foreign direct investment has been export-oriented. Some conclusions follow in Sect. 6.

15.1.1 The integration of world financial markets

The last decade has seen an explosion in the volume of capital movements.[2] The main general contributory factors to this development have been the

---

[1] This paper defines eastern Europe as comprising Bulgaria, the Czech Republic, Hungary, Poland, Romania, the Slovak Republic and Slovenia; central Europe encompasses only the Czech Republic (or the former Czechoslovakia), Hungary and Poland. These definitions have been chosen for presentation purposes only.

[2] One possible measure of this is cross-border transactions in bonds and equities (gross purchases and sales). See Bank for International Settlements (1992), p. 193.

removal of exchange controls in all major industrial countries and, in many emerging market economies, domestic financial liberalisation and rapid advances in financial technology. These general developments have been helped and accelerated by financial market developments themselves, the evolution of derivative instruments to facilitate new forms of hedging and position taking, the boom in securitisation through an increase in the share of financial liabilities and assets that are readily tradable, and greater institutionalisation of investment activity, as restrictions on financial institutions' investment abroad have been eased.[3] A distinguishing feature of recent trends is the increased significance of portfolio capital movements – as opposed to bank or official lending, which predominated in the 1970s and 1980s. Unlike bank or official lending, such flows are not closely linked to particular end-users or particular investments.

There has been a sharp rise in the proportion of financial assets held by non-residents. Such holdings are, in general, very sensitive to shifts of sentiment in international financial markets. Unrealistic exchange rates or inadequate economic policies have become more subject to the sanction of capital markets. A large amount of funds can now easily be moved into individual countries – and out again just as easily. This increased volatility of capital flows, and their potential reversibility, has become a key concern of policy makers everywhere.

15.2 Capital inflows to central Europe

Capital flows into central Europe did not rise strongly until 1993. During the 2-year period 1993–1994, the inflow of capital to the eastern European countries amounted to US$26 billion.[4] Of this total, more than one-third accrued to Hungary and roughly the same amount to Poland and the Czech Republic together.[5] This represented about 8.5% of total inflows to the three regions shown.[6]

[3] For a more detailed analysis of these individual factors, see Crockett (1994) and Bank for International Settlements (1993), pp. 147–148.

[4] Calvo et al. (1994, pp. 2 et seq.) also review the period leading up to the watershed years 1990–1991. They show that for the period 1987–91 capital outflows for the region as a whole (Bulgaria, Czechoslovakia, Hungary, Poland and Romania) amounted to US$24 billion, financed by a reduction in reserves.

[5] This implies that capital inflows have been unevenly distributed in the region and justifies to some extent the focus in this paper on the three central European countries: the Czech Republic, Hungary and Poland.

[6] Capital flows into these groups of countries account for about 20% of global flows, with the countries in central Europe receiving nearly 2% of 'world' capital inflows during this period.

Inflows to central Europe reached about 7% of GDP in 1993 and stayed high, at nearly 5% of GDP, in 1994. This is well above the rates seen in Asia in recent years and close to the peak values of almost 5% reached in Latin America in 1992 and 1993.[7] Asia has seen a steady growth of capital inflows, which have hovered around 3% of GDP during the last 2 years. In terms of exports, however, the average capital inflow of around 14% for the central European countries over the period 1990–1994 is closer to the Asian experience.

Yet what has happened to these inflows in general terms? Have they been absorbed by the official foreign exchange reserves? All three country groups saw their reserve position strengthen during the period 1990–1994 (Table 1).

The Latin American countries absorbed only about one-third of their inflows (a US$65 billion increase in reserves, with a US$182 billion capital inflow) and the proportion going into the reserves fell during the early 1990s. The rate of absorption was much higher for Asia. In the central European countries, around one-half was taken into the reserves. The change in central European official reserves grew from small amounts in

Table 1. Capital flows and reserves

	1975–1982 annual average	1983–1990 annual average	1990	1991	1992	1993	1994	Cumulative 1990–1994
	In billions of US dollars							
	Net capital flows (inflows = +)							
Eastern Europe[1]	–	–	2.2	5.4	3.2	13.7	11.9	36.3
Czech Republic	–	–	–0.2	–0.3	0.2	2.6	2.1	4.4
Hungary	–	–	–0.8	2.4	0.4	6.0	3.3	11.4
Poland	–	–	1.7	0.5	0.9	2.1	2.7	7.9
Latin America[2]	20.4	4.6	10.9	29.2	52.8	57.6	31.1	181.7
Asia[3]	8.3	7.6	8.3	30.1	43.1	44.1	49.2	174.8

[7] Inflows into Mexico decreased by about US$20.5 billion from 1993 to 1994, while the decrease for all other Latin American countries was US$3.5 billion.

Table 1. Continued

	1975–1982 annual average	1983–1990 annual average	1990	1991	1992	1993	1994	Cumulative 1990–1994
	Net change in reserves (increase = +)							
Eastern Europe[1]	–	–	–0.1	3.7	2.0	5.5	7.6	18.7
Czech Republic	–	–	–0.5	0.8	–0.1	3.0	2.4	5.5
Hungary	–	–	–0.6	2.7	0.8	2.6	–0.6	4.8
Poland	–	–	2.4	–0.8	0.6	–0.2	1.7	3.7
Latin America[2]	0.9	1.3	12.4	16.4	24.4	19.7	–7.6[4]	65.3
Asia[3]	3.4	16.4	19.8	34.6	45.9	33.1	45.8	179.3
Memorandum items: total developing countries								
Net capital inflows	*22.4*	*37.5*	*36.1*	*156.4*	*145.3*	*151.2*	*129.8*	*618.7*
Net increase in reserves	*9.4*	*15.4*	*32.6*	*70.5*	*68.9*	*66.0*	*52.8*	*291.1*

[1]Bulgaria, the Czech Republic, Hungary, Poland, Romania, the Slovak Republic and Slovenia.
[2]Argentina, Brazil, Chile, Colombia, Mexico and Venezuela.
[3]China, India, Indonesia, Korea, Malaysia, Singapore, Taiwan and Thailand.
[4]The drop in Mexico's reserves was US$17.7 billion.
Source: National sources.

1990 to a cumulative US$14 billion by 1994.[8] By the end of 1994, the cumulative change in reserves was broadly similar in the three countries

[8] The definition of official reserves varies: for the Czech Republic, they comprise convertible foreign exchange and SDRs; for Hungary, non-gold reserves in convertible currencies (excluding SDRs and IMF reserve position); for Poland, gold, convertible foreign exchange and IMF reserve position (excluding SDR holdings).

concerned.[9] However, individual country experience varied widely. The Czech Republic channelled all inflows into reserves. Indeed, inflows have grown more rapidly than in the other two countries since the separation from the Slovak Republic in January 1993. Poland took nearly half of its inflows into reserves. The increase was smallest in Hungary, where reserves actually fell in 1994.

15.3 Stylised macroeconomic features influencing capital flow experiences in Latin America, Asia and central Europe

Some comparisons of broad macroeconomic indicators for Asia, Latin America and central Europe are shown in Table 3. Sound macroeconomic performance will underpin consistent and substantial capital flows. One major component of good macroeconomic performance is the recipient country's domestic growth.

At 8%, GDP growth in Asia was more than two and a half times as high as in Latin America during 1990–1994. Moreover, gross national savings and investment ratios (of around 34% each) were much higher in Asia than in Latin America (19 and 21% respectively). The high export ratios and strong export growth in Asia also suggest a better capacity to service any future external liabilities arising from capital inflows.

The divergence in inflation performance – very marked in the 1980s, when inflation was far higher in Latin America than in Asia – has persisted but is now somewhat smaller. The fairly good inflation performance in Asia also helped to keep real effective exchange rate appreciation in check or low, while in Latin America anti-inflation policies using exchange-rate-based nominal anchors contributed to a sizeable real appreciation.[10] GDP growth and saving/investment ratios in central Europe have all been closer to those of Latin America than those of Asia. Thus, both Latin America and central Europe share the low investment/low growth characteristics.

Domestic savings are the major source of future investments. Saving rates in central Europe were high before transition, largely because limited consumption opportunities led to forced saving.[11] The low saving rates seen

---

[9] The developments in 1995 confirm those in 1993–1994. Official reserve accumulation accelerated in the Czech Republic (US$9.8 billion at the end of July) and Poland (US$11.0 billion at the end of July), while Hungarian reserves stagnated (US$7.5 billion at the end of June).

[10] See Bank for International Settlements (1994), p. 154.

[11] IMF (1995, pp. 68–69): 'There is little doubt that aggregate savings in these countries are much lower than they were before transition'.

Table 2. Capital flows

	1990	1991	1992	1993	1994	Average 1990–94
	As a percentage of GDP					
Central Europe[1]	0.5	2.0	1.0	6.9	4.7	3.2
Czech Republic	–0.7	–1.3	0.8	8.3	5.8	2.9
Hungary	–2.5	7.3	1.2	15.7	8.0	6.2
Poland	2.7	0.7	1.1	2.5	2.9	2.0
Latin America[2]	1.2	3.0	4.9	4.8	2.3	3.2
Asia[2]	0.8	2.6	3.3	3.0	3.1	2.7
	As a percentage of exports					
Central Europe[1]	2.2	8.6	4.6	30.1	19.2	13.8
Czech Republic	–2.5	–4.0	2.6	19.7	14.5	8.2
Hungary	–8.3	23.0	4.1	67.9	30.6	22.6
Poland	56.7	4.1	6.3	15.5	25.2	11.6
Latin America[2]	10.5	28.7	49.4	51.2	24.0	32.8
Asia[2]	2.7	8.5	11.0	10.1	9.0	8.3

[1]The Czech Republic, Hungary and Poland.
[2]See Table 1 for a list of countries.
Source: National sources.

more recently may owe something to high and variable inflation rates in the past, as well as to weak financial intermediation.[12] These low saving rates have gone hand in hand with low investment rates, which stood at around 20%, close to the levels seen in Latin America during the last few years. In fact, since 1989, capital investment in almost all countries in central and eastern Europe has fallen by more than GDP, only to rise somewhat in 1994 in the countries most advanced in the transition process. The lack of

[12] Weak' intermediation refers to a whole gamut of problems, ranging from, *inter alia*, inadequate financial instruments to large gaps between lending and borrowing rates. Admittedly, by increasing uncertainty about the future, high and variable inflation may promote precautionary saving. On the other hand, by heightening the uncertainty about the effective rate of return on saving, variable inflation may directly discourage saving. This latter effect may have prevailed in central European countries with extremely high and variable inflation rates.

Table 3. Selected macroeconomic indicators

	Central Europe[1]			Latin America	Asia
	1990–1992	1993	1994	1990–1994	1990–1994
GDP growth (in %)	–5.8	1.9	4.0	2.8	7.8
Gross national savings (as % of GDP)	29.8	24.5	21.9	18.8	33.6
Gross domestic investment (as % of GDP)	23.3	19.5	15.6	20.6	34.0
Government consumption (as % of GDP)	19.3	20.0	17.3	11.6	9.4
Budget deficits (as % of GDP)	–2.8	–2.6	–2.7	–0.0	–2.1
Total exports[2] (as % of GDP)	25.3	27.5	28.7	11.3	28.6
External debt/export[2] ratio	251.0	228.0	184.0	272.0	147.0
Monthly inflation (in %)	4.4	2.5	2.0	11.4	0.8
Monthly inflation variance	2.3[3]	1.4[3]	0.7	57.4	0.2
REER[4] appreciation (cumulative, in %)	24.1	5.8	0	15.7	–4.6

[1]The Czech Republic, Hungary and Poland (weighted by the 1990 purchasing power parity (PPP) valuation of country GDPs).
[2]Export earnings (goods, services and income).
[3]Excluding the initial months of price liberalisation.
[4]For Latin America and Asia, in terms of consumer prices; for central Europe, consumer prices and wholesale prices are given equal weight.
Source: National sources.

Table 4. Central Europe: inflation and real effective exchange rates

	Consumer price inflation (in %)				Real effective exchange rate appreciation (cumulative, in %)			
	Monthly rate		Monthly variance		CP	WP	CP	WP
	1991–1994	1994	1991–1994	1994	1991–1994[1]		1994–1995[2]	
Czech Republic	2.5	0.8	0.2	0.3	11.8	5.0	6.0	1.2
Hungary	3.0	1.8	1.8	0.4	22.5	–0.1	–5.4	–9.1
Poland	6.5	2.5	4.1	0.9	18.1	3.2	2.6	–8.3

Note: CP consumer prices; *WP* wholesale prices (industrial producer prices).
[1]For Hungary and Poland, starting in March 1991; for the Czech Republic, starting in February 1993.
[2]To June 1995.
Source: National sources.

investment funds,[13] reflecting low levels of saving, is probably themost serious constraint on growth in central Europe in the medium-term perspective.[14] Finally, government consumption is proportionately higher in central Europe than in either Latin America or Asia.

Central European economies appear to be more open and more reliant on foreign trade than Latin America and nearly match the high export/GDP ratio of Asia. Debt/export ratios for central Europe fall between those in Latin America and those in Asia. Another important similarity is that both Latin America and central Europe recorded substantial real effective exchange rate appreciation during the period up to 1993.

In 1994–1995, however, the real effective exchange rate for central Europe as a hole depreciated. Hungary's real effective exchange rate depreciated substantially during 1994–1995, while the real effective exchange rate of the Czech koruna appreciated somewhat, reflecting to some extent

[13] The investment ratios look much more dismal when all central and eastern European countries are included. For example, the saving ratio for Russia was reckoned to be close to 10% in 1994 (UN, 1995).

[14] The UN (1995, May, p. 89) agrees, arguing that 'the lack of investment funds, reflecting low savings levels, modest levels of foreign investment and official assistance, high interest rates and inefficient financial intermediation, is probably one of the most binding constraints on growth in transition economies in the medium-term perspective'.

the pressure on that currency. The evidence for Poland is less clear (Table 4). While the real effective exchange rate based on consumer prices shows a small appreciation, the indicator based on wholesale prices exhibits a fairly substantial depreciation. The large discrepancies in the real effective exchange rates based on consumer and wholesale prices are remarkable and are attributable to a relatively faster rise in service prices, as the backlog of demand was particularly large in this area and this sector continues to grow faster than others.

The evolution of the real effective exchange rate over time, however, does not indicate whether or not the real exchange rate of a country is under- or overvalued. In this context, it was a well-established strategy at the beginning of the transformation process to devalue by a large margin in order to provide the tradable goods sector of the economy with the necessary room for manoeuvre. Since then, the real effective exchange rates in all three countries have been appreciating, eroding this room for manoeuvre. By 1994, it appeared that the Czech koruna was, indeed, still substantially undervalued in relation to its estimated 'correct' real exchange rate level. Evidence for the other two countries appears to be less firm, indicating that perhaps the Hungarian forint may be slightly overvalued, while the Polish zloty may be slightly undervalued.

The implications for capital flows appear to be that they are more likely to be sustainable in the case of the Czech Republic.

Returning to Asia and Latin America, another factual difference between these two regions concerns the volatility of the return on financial assets. Asia may look back on a history of fairly stable implied returns of the order of 8 to 10% during the 1980s and 1990s, more or less in line with growth performance during most of this period. Latin American countries, in contrast, experienced depressed returns in the 1980s, followed by extremely high returns during the 1991–1993 period and a sharp drop in 1994. Of course, this volatility reflects to some extent the risks involved in these flows. The experience has, to say the least, been less positive for the stock exchanges in central Europe. The large see-saw movements on the Warsaw Stock Exchange bear ample witness to this.[15]

---

[15] The volatility of the emerging stock markets does not necessarily deter foreign capital from flowing into these markets. One argument follows the familiar portfolio line that the low correlation of these markets with financial markets in industrial countries provides significant scope for diversification (IMF, 1994, p. 70). In addition, the macroeconomic literature tends at times to ignore the potential for gain in falling stock markets.

Table 5. Central Europe: selected macroeconomic indicators

	GDP growth			Budget balance[1]			Exports[1]		
	1990–1992	1993	1994	1990–1992	1993	1994	1990–1992	1993	1994
Czech Republic	–6.9	–0.9	2.6	–0.8	0.1	1.0	31.0	47.5	47.0
Hungary	–5.8	–0.8	2.0	–3.9	–5.6	–7.5	35.2	30.6	28.3
Poland	–5.4	3.8	5.1	–2.8	–2.8	–2.7	20.0	18.6	21.5

[1]In percentages of GDP.
Source: National sources.

As far as fiscal balances are concerned, the average for the central European countries hides important differences. While the Czech Republic had a central government budget surplus amounting to 1% of GDP in 1994, the Hungarianbudget deficit has been deteriorating during the last few years, to stand at 7.5% of GDP in 1994 (Table 5).

While the fiscal deterioration in Hungary owes something to the initial drop in output and the associated rise in unemployment at the beginning of transition, the government also experienced difficulties in decisively reducing its role in resource allocation and streamlining social programs. Whereas subsidies were lowered during this period, transfers increased. The government's interest payments were also a drag, as they increased from 2.3% of GDP in 1989 to 6.8% in 1994. Austerity measures were introduced in March 1995 and included a sharp 9% forint devaluation, an 8% import surcharge and cuts in welfare spending (in particular by placing a cap on the rise in public sector wages). However, the final judgement on whether they had a salutary impact on budget balances is still outstanding, owing to parliamentary opposition to some of these measures.[16]

15.4 Composition of capital flows

Past experience may not be a good basis for predicting future events, in particular in the area of capital flows. In any case, if any lessons are to be

[16] The IMF (1995) considers these measures to be 'important steps' and adds (p. 55): 'Further measures will nevertheless be needed, including a broadening of the income tax base, a reduction of the burden of the pension system, and an acceleration of privatisation'.

Table 6. Composition and nature of capital flows

	Central Europe	Asia	Latin America
Sterilisation	Approx. 1/2 sterilised (but large country differences)	Approx. 2/3 sterilised; little difficulty in sterilisation	Approx. 1/3 sterilised; difficulty in sterilisation
Direct investment (FDI)/portfolio mix	Small portfolio flows	2/3 FDI flows	2/3 portfolio flows
Investment/ consumption	FDI inflows have tended to increase consumption (initially)	FDI inflows have tended to increase investment	FDI inflows have tended to increase consumption
Nature of FDI flows	Privatisation; some greenfield operations, but only in Hungary	More in the form of greenfield operations and joint ventures	Major privati sation and debt/equity swaps
Return on financial investment	Very volatile equity markets; returns dependent on holding period	Higher in past on average and less volatile	Lower in past on average and more volatile

drawn from the capital flow history in Asia and Latin America, a closer look must be taken at the individual components of capital flows and how they might differ between these country groups (Table 6).[17]

[17] There is a long history of looking at and interpreting individual capital flow items from the balance of payments. Recently, Claessens et al. (1993) pointed out that there is sufficient substitution between and interaction among the various flows to make an analysis of the time series of one flow possibly misleading. They also find little evidence that the composition of flows is of use in forecasting the overall levels of flows, suggesting that the overall capital account is independent of the type of flow. The upshot of these results is that the distinction between 'hot' and 'cool' flows based on balance-of-payments labels is questioned and that 'the preoccupation with analysing the time-series properties of short-term (portfolio) flows is overdone. The root cause of volatility is more likely changes in institutional structure than an inherent property of a certain

Table 7. Foreign direct investment (FDI) and portfolio investment (P)

	1990	1991	1992	1993	1994	Cumulative 1990–1994
	FDI as a percentage of FDI plus P					
Central Europe	–	–	–	57	48	66
Latin America	25	30	23	17	57[1]	28
Asia	85	81	79	65	72	73

[1]Due to a sharp drop of P from US$68 billion in 1993 to US$17 billion in 1994.
Source: National sources.

For a recipient country, it may be most important whether inflows are of a debt-creating or non-debt-creating nature.[18] Furthermore, it is important to know whether or not any inflows are easily reversible, in particular, if they can bewithdrawn at short notice. It would, for example, be quite useful to have a maturity profile for all debt-creating flows.[19] One aspect of the statistical nature of some of these inflows has been that the differentiation between short-term and long-term instruments, which was a standard feature of balance-of-payments presentation in many major industrialised countries in the 1980s, has fallen more and more into discredit. At that time it was realised that, for example, a 3-month eurocredit can be as long-term as a 5-year bond issue, while a Treasury bond with a 30-year maturity can easily be more liquid than a time deposit at a commercial bank.[20]One standard classification has been the distinction between foreign direct investment (FDI) and portfolio investment (P). FDI flows[21] are thought to be

type of flow, and adverse effects of sudden, large movements in a particular type of flow are likely a result of distortions in the domestic economy'.

18 Neither official flows nor banking flows are considered in the following discussion. Moreover, the whole question of arrears, financing by non-payment, is left out.

19 The World Bank's 'World Debt Tables' provide some insight.

20 Claessens et al. (1993) warn against evaluating capital flows according to their label (for example, the instrument traded or the transactor recorded in the balance-of-payments statistics).

21 FDI data in eastern Europe are based on balance-of-payments concepts and currently do not capture any retained earnings. However, this latter component of FDI will become more important with the passage of time. Inotai and Marer (1993) classify profit repatriation on past direct investment as still 'insignificant' in the case of Hungary. Another methodological question concerns direct investment outflows: several eastern European countries publish only net direct

determined more by long-term fundamental economic considerations and are not easily reversible, whereas portfolio flows are more oriented towards shorter-term rates of return and, thus, are potentially more volatile, that is they are more easily reversible.

In fact, one of the hallmarks of the difference between capital flows has been the dominance of direct investment flows to Asia, while the reverse has been true for Latin America, rendering Latin American countries in general more vulnerable than Asia to swings in foreign investor sentiment.[22]

Whereas about two-thirds of the flows to Asia have been FDI flows (and only one-third portfolio flows), the reverse is true for Latin America. This difference is probably due in part to the better long-term prospects in Asia, as explained above, and more prudent financial policies. It also appears that, in a number of Asian countries, controls on both inward portfolio investment and domestic financial markets have been kept tighter, while there has been less tight control of portfolio inflows into Latin America. The prospects for short-term gains from portfolio investment looked relatively more promising in Latin America during the 1991-1993 period, as it re-emerged from the 1980s depression, than in Asia, in which foreign investment was already occurring. Another factor was high nominal interest rates, combined with the policy of adjusting the exchange rate only partially for inflation: this meant that domestic interest rates, when converted into dollars, were extremely high.

About 65% of the cumulative capital inflows to central Europe during 1990–1994 were in the form of direct investment.[23] The remaining 35% covers flows of quite diverse characteristics. About three-quarters of non-direct investment flows were accounted for by *Hungary* during 1993 and 1994. These flows were mainly attributable to the large borrowing programme of the National Bank of Hungary, which took the form of international bond

investment data. As direct investment abroad by these countries has, until now, been very small, net direct investment has, therefore, at times been equated with FDI inflows. For example, the volume of Czech direct investment abroad has not yet been particularly noteworthy. Its value in 1994 amounted to US$21 million (Czech National Bank, 1995, p. 30).

[22] See Turner (1995), p. 18.

[23] Cumulative FDI flows for all central and eastern European countries during 1990–1994 amounted to about 2.5% of global FDI flows. About one-third of these flows was invested in Hungary, while another third went to Poland, the Czech Republic and Russia together. Hungary emerges as the largest recipient when these flows are scaled against GDP or per capita.

Table 8. Central Europe: net bond issues

	1992	1993	1994	1995, H1	*Memorandum item: debt/export earnings in 1994*
	In billions of US dollars				%
Central Europe	0.8	4.3	2.7	1.0	
Czech and Slovak Republics	0.0	0.6	0.3	0.1	*60.0*
Hungary	0.8	3.7	2.4	0.6	*250.0*
Poland	0.0	0.0	0.0	0.3	*210.0*

Source: National sources.

issues (Table 8).[24] This programme reflected increasing budgetary and external deficits. The fiscal deficit widened to 6–7% of GDP in 1992 and 1993 and 7.5% in 1994, while the debt/export ratio (at 250%) was the highest in central Europe.

A large proportion of what is recorded as short-term capital inflows to *Poland* apparently reflects unrecorded export earnings: the foreign exchange inflows are deposited at exchange offices located near border posts. This interpretation is also supported by the large discrepancy between customs and balance-of-payments data. Foreign participation in the Warsaw Stock Exchange is still quite limited. Some of the flows to the *Czech Republic* are in the form of government bonds but the bulk of the inflows is attributable to the private sector.[25]

If these features are borne in mind, it appears, indeed, that only about 10% of the capital inflows into central Europe (some flows to the Czech Republic and small amounts of equity inflows) during the 1990–1994 period may be considered as easily reversible 'hot' flows. For this reason, it is instructive to examine the Czech experience in more detail, as it raises a number of important issues of domestic monetary policy management.

[24] The Hungarian balance-of-payments statistics do not include a category for 'portfolio' flows. The classification in Table 6 follows the IMF/IFS taxonomy. (The IMF identifies these flows as 'nie' = not included elsewhere.) Less than one-quarter appears to be in the form of flows into the equity markets.

[25] The portfolio flows into the Czech Republic include the central bank bond issues of 1993 and the city of Prague eurobond issues (US$250 million) of 1994.

15.5 Some key policy issues

15.5.1 Inflows and monetary policy: a case study of the Czech Republic

The capital inflows episode has been particularly important and has probably raised the most concerns in the Czech Republic. A closer look at that country's capital account confirms the significance of portfolio flows during 1993–1995, which coincided with fairly consistent FDI inflows. However, other long-term capital, which usually accounts for one-quarter of inflows, was essentially in the form of corporate borrowing and appears to have contributed to strong inflows in 1995. Moreover, 1995 seems to have yielded a new development: short-term capital flows – which are apparently due in the main to enterprise and bank borrowing abroad – predominated in the first quarter.

The capital flow experience of the Czech Republic since mid-1993 appears to display the typical symptoms associated with rapid capital inflows: strong reserve growth, providing a cushion against adverse capital movements; a further real appreciation of the koruna, albeit very modest in scale, as the 1991–1992 period had seen a much faster real appreciation; higher-than-projected money growth, which could put at risk the move towards a low-inflation path; and a significant pick-up in imports, leading to a weakening current account position.

How has the Czech National Bank (CNB) reacted? In general, countries are not prepared to adopt alaissez-faire stance and simply allow, for example, the nominal exchange rate to drift upwards as aresult of large capital inflows. The response to capital inflows will depend on the monetary policy/exchange rate policy framework in place when such flows occur. In the Czech Republic, anominal anchor, the exchange rate, was chosen to provide

Table 9. Czech Republic: capital accounts

	1992	1993	1994	1995 Q1
	In millions of US dollars			
Foreign direct investment	980	520	840	110
Portfolio investment	–25	1,060	820	85
Other long-term capital	320	530	500	505
Short-term capital	–1,280	535	–50	1,170
Total	**0**	**2,650**	**2,110**	**1,870**

Source: National sources.

Table 10. Czech Republic: financial and external indicators

	1991	1992	1993	1994	1995
Koruna/$ exchange rate	29.5	28.3	29.2	28.8	26.0(7)
Consumer price inflation (in %)	56.7	11.1	20.9	10.0	9.7(7)
Official reserves (US$ billion)	0.8	0.8	3.8	6.1	9.8(7)
Broad money (change in %)	26.7	23.0	20.2	22.1	17.1(6)
Real broad money (change in %)	–19.1	10.7	–0.6	11.0	6.4(6)
Imports (in US$) (change in %)	–	46.5	24.0	14.5	28.0(5)
Current balance (US$ billion)	1.1	–0.3	0.4	0.3	–0.7[1]
Banks					
Loan/deposit ratio	–	1.002	0.983	0.977	1.003[1]
Margin between lending and borrowing (in %)	–	6.34	7.06	6.05	5.81[1]
Term structure:					
– deposits					
up to 1 year	–	71.9	72.1	72.0	70.8[1]
1–4 years	–	20.5	21.0	22.6	23.6[1]
over 4 years	–	7.6	6.9	5.4	5.6[1]
– loans					
up to 1 year	–	38.3	41.2	40.7	40.0[1]
1–4 years	–	27.3	28.8	30.1	30.5[1]
over 4 years	–	34.4	30.0	29.2	29.5[1]
– new loans					
up to 1 year	–	–	73.2	73.1	77.7[1]
1–4 years	–	–	18.7	16.9	15.0[1]
over 4 years	–	–	8.1	10.0	7.3[1]

[1]First quarter.
Source: National sources.

aframework for the development of stable expectations.[26] When confronted with such flows, countries invariably tend to err on the side of caution, that is the initial reaction is to sterilise these flows – if it is not certain whether they are permanent or temporary in nature – in order to minimise their impact on the anchor. This essentially reflects the policy stance of the CNB.

[26] The Czech koruna is currently pegged to a currency basket consisting of US dollars (35%) and Deutsche Mark (65%). The daily rate may deviate by 0.5% from the value calculated by the CNB.

Open market operations involving CNB bills, T-bills and National Property Fund (NPF) bills were used to sterilise excess liquidity, with most of them winding up in bank portfolios. The transfer to the CNB of some NPF deposits held by commercial banks and the decline in government indebtedness to the CNB, both in 1994, can also be included among the further sterilisation measures.[27] Furthermore, the short-term capital inflows were partially eliminated, as instalments had to be paid for exceeding the marginal credit in the clearing account with the Slovak Republic.[28] In addition to using open market operations and administrative measures, the CNB also mopped up some liquidity by raising reserve requirements in August 1994 and June 1995. The Czech Republic partially liberalised capital outflows in October 1995 – the first country in central Europe to do so – and this may also be interpreted as a typical response to soften the impact on the exchange rate of rapid capital inflows.

These policy measures raise a number of questions for the CNB. When should it seek to limit mounting reserves, for example, by allowing a nominal appreciation? Should the CNB continue its policy of sterilised intervention, or should some non-sterilised intervention be allowed, permitting the money supply to expand at a faster rate?

Allowing a nominal appreciation of the currency could serve to reduce short-term inflows, but perhaps at the risk of causing overvaluation in real terms. Much depends on the prospects for real productivity growth: if productivity rises strongly, then anti-inflation policy would be better served by taking the associated real wage increase in nominal appreciation rather than in higher nominal wages.

Opinions in the literature seem to be divided on the desirable rate of monetary expansion. While Calvo et al. (1995) attribute enterprise borrowing abroad to a 'genuine shortage of credit' in the economy, leading to the policy recommendation of monetary loosening and perhaps non-sterilisation of some of the inflows, the IMF in its report on the Czech Republic (1995) considers the inflows simply as substitution of foreign credit for domestic credit and the role of banks in this process as crucial and does not interpret this as an increase in money demand, thereby implying that continued sterilisation may perhaps be called for.

The substitution of foreign credit for domestic credit has supposedly occurred because there is a maturity mismatch between credit demanded and credit supplied: demand for bank credit by enterprises is concentrated at the longer end of the maturity spectrum. Long-term domestic bank lending (over 4 years) as a share of total lending dropped by more than

[27] See CNB (1995b), p. 19.
[28] See CNB (1995b), p. 12.

4 percentage points in 1993, but appears subsequently to have stabilised at around 30%. In addition, more than 75% of new loans are currently short-term, lending further support to the argument that banks are keen to reduce the risk in the maturity mismatch originating from short-term deposits and long-term lending. Banks' unwillingness to transform maturities may also owe something to the fact that in the past they were being overburdened with long-term credit which was both low-yielding and non-performing. The latter argument also explains to some extent the still-high margins between banks' borrowing and lending, which have not yet moved substantially below 6% but which, nevertheless, have come down from a level of 7% at the end of 1992 to stand at 5.8% in March 1995.[29] Taken by themselves, high domestic interest margins may be a factor encouraging borrowing from abroad, especially in cases where the domestic 'real' interest rate for borrowed funds is high.[30] Another explanatory factor appears to be the relative movement between the domestic and the 'foreign' interest rate on bank credits.[31] If we were to proxy[32] the latter rate by the German bank credit rate, this would show that domestic borrowers may have substituted foreign for domestic credits as the rate on domestic credits came down by 1% from late 1992 to March 1995, while the German rate came down substantially faster, namely by 2.5% during this period.

Examination of the data does not confirm a general credit crunch as neither the nominal nor the real interest rates have moved up, but have in fact moved down. The banks' behaviour reflects a degree of understandable adjustment in their maturity transformation role, but there seems to be little indication of their squeezing out long-term borrowers. As the loan/deposit ratio has remained more or less unchanged, there is no general indication that banks have been reluctant to extend credit.[33] It appears that the prime mover may have been simply the relatively lower borrowing costs abroad in the context of a stable or even slightly appreciating currency. A subsidiary factor, however, might be that the reluctance of local banks to grant anything but short-term loans may have led some enterprises to borrow from banks abroad.

---

[29] It is also argued that these high margins continue to reflect inefficiencies in the intermediation process itself.

[30] With inflation running at around 10% since the beginning of 1994 and the nominal interest rate on loans at about 13%, and moving recently towards 12.5%, the implied 'real' interest rate does not seem to be excessive.

[31] Calvo et al. (1995) arrive at a different conclusion, as they compare the relative development in the CNB and T-bill markets.

[32] Obviously this is a very crude proxy as foreign interest costs are difficult to pinpoint since they vary according to lender, loan maturity, currency denomination and the risk assessment of the borrower.

[33] On this point, see Calvo et al. (1995).

15.5.2 Saving, investment and deficits

Table 3 shows that investment, which tends to be much more import-intensive than the other demand components, has accounted for a far larger and more buoyant share of GDP in Asia than in Latin America.

Heavy imports of capital goods in Asia have not only increased the productive potential but probably also attenuated upward pressure on the exchange rate.[34] The central European countries, however, have experienced a falling investment/GDP ratio. The larger current account deficits in these countries thus mainly reflected increases in (private) consumption rather than investment.[35]

Table 11. Gross Fixed Investment (GFI) and Foreign Direct Investment (FDI)

	1990	1991	1992	1993	1994
	In percentages				
Central Europe					
FDI/GFI	1.3	7.3	10.2	9.9	6.8
Czech Republic					
GFI/GDP	26.3	23.1	28.5	26.6	26.7
GFI growth	–2.1	–17.7	9.0	–7.7	4.4
Hungary					
GFI/GDP	19.2	20.7	19.7	18.7	19.7
GFI growth	–7.0	–10.4	–2.7	1.7	11.5
Poland					
GFI/GDP	21.0	19.5	16.8	16.0	15.5
GFI growth	–10.6	–4.4	2.3	3.0	7.0
Latin America					
FDI/GFI	3.4	5.7	5.5	5.6	8.4
Asia					
FDI/GFI	4.5	4.7	6.4	7.2	7.9

Source: National sources.

[34] See Welfens (1994).
[35] See Calvo et al. (1995).

Table 12. Central Europe: consumption in the private and public sectors

	1990	1991	1992	1993	1994
	As a percentage of GDP				
Total consumption	68	83	85	87	83
Household consumption	50	63	65	67	66
Czech Republic	50	45	52	56	58
Hungary	62	70	73	74	74
Poland	46	69	67	69	67
Public consumption	18	20	20	14	12
Czech Republic	20	19	23	23	22
Hungary	11	11	12	14	12
Poland	19	23	22	20	17

Source: National sources.

As in Latin America, there was abacklog of unsatisfied demand for private consumer goods in central Europe after the initial liberalisation in 1990–1991, and the share of consumption in GDP moved up rapidly. Household consumption dominated this process. By 1992–1993, the share of total consumption in GDP had reached over 85% in Poland and Hungary and more than 75% in the Czech Republic. Preliminary data for 1994 – at least for the three countries in this sample – suggest that there has not been much change since then, except for some marginal reversal in Poland.

One possible interpretation is that the current capital inflows are financing a permanently higher level of consumption and that, by 1994, a certain equilibrium level had been reached, that is the initial buying spree had run its course. Yet there has not been any rebound in savings, and consumption levels, while not increasing, have remained rather high – at least by the standards of countries with major development potential.

At times, parallels are drawn with the experience in Latin America and Asia in this regard. Capital inflows have been employed more wisely in Asia, as they have been used to support high rates of investment. For Latin America, on the other hand, the evidence indicates that the increase in inflows coincided to some extent with falling average investment and rising consumption.[36] In central Europe, the consumption boom clearly occurred before the more substantial flows to this region and is thus to be associated more with the general liberalisation tendencies of that period,

[36] See Turner (1995, pp. 14 ff.).

namely trade liberalisation and concomitant import growth. Yet it could be argued that capital inflows allowed the high rates of consumption attained during the boom to be prolonged.

It appears, therefore, that the behaviour of the central European countries is tending towards 'Latin American behaviour' that is, greater consumption. However, there has been marked diversity across countries. Hungary, for example, seems to be 'overconsuming', as its consumption share reached 86% of GDP by 1994, compared with 73% in 1990.[37]

15.5.3 Direct investment: export-oriented?

Direct investment is often regarded as a form of investment which leaves the recipient country less exposed to swings in foreign investor sentiment. It allows the recipient country to share the risks of investment with the investor: the 'servicing' of direct investment liabilities depends on the generation of profits and does not create a fixed burden in the same way as bank or bond debt. From an external point of view, this self-stabilising feature of direct investment is reinforced when direct investment is export-oriented.

Figure 1 reproduces a graph originally designed to show that direct investment has been much more export-intensive in Asia (i.e. the regression line shown in the figure is flatter) than in Latin America. Observations for the three central European countries have been superimposed on this figure.

The difference in export orientation suggested by this graph is supported by surveys conducted in Latin America and Asia on the behaviour of foreign companies in these areas, which show that relatively more is exported by foreign companies in Asia than by those in Latin America.[38] On this score, Hungary clearly shows the least export-oriented performance of the three central European countries, and of all countries contained in the graph, its high FDI inflows contrast with the lowest export growth. The Polish experience is close to the Asian regression line; data for Poland are comparable to those for Korea, India and Taiwan. In fact, export performance may have

[37] Clearly this argument simplifies the process as, for example, a lot will depend on the 'efficiency' of investment. Turner (1995) proxies efficiency by looking at the reciprocal of ICOR (incremental capital output ratio of gross investment to GDP divided by the average rate of real growth for the period), which is twice as high in Asia as in Latin America for the 1984–1993 period.

[38] Bank for International Settlements (1995, p. 68): 'While US firms in Asia export more than one-half of their output, those in Latin America export only about one-quarter of their production. (...) Chinese statistics (...) suggest that the exports of foreign-funded enterprises (...) have accounted for an average of about 60% of the increase in China's exports during the 1990s, with this percentage rising in the last few years.'

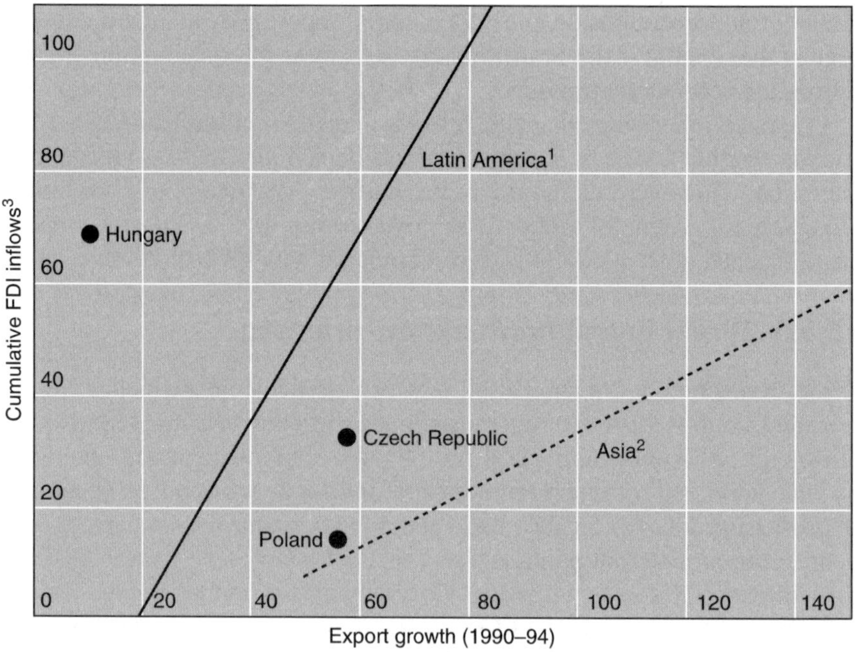

[1]Argentina, Brazil, Chile, Colombia, Ecuador, Mexico, Peru and Venezuela. [2]China, Hong Kong, India, Indonesia, Korea, Malaysia, Philippines, Singapore, Taiwan and Thailand. [3]For central Europe, 1990–94; otherwise, 1989–92.

Fig. 1. Foreign direct investment and exports (as percentages of 1989 exports)

been even stronger if exports have been under-recorded, as suggested earlier. The Czech Republic's performance ranks between that of Colombia and Chile (Latin American countries), on the one hand, and of the Philippines and Indonesia (Asian countries), on the other.[39]

Perhaps more importantly, the nature of FDI has differed between Latin America and Asia: in Latin America it has mainly taken the form of debt/equity swaps and privatisation, which do not necessarily generate additional capital formation. In Asia, by contrast, FDI has mostly been in the form of acquisitions or the setting-up of new enterprises. Data on central Europe seem to indicate that greenfield investments have had a relatively insignificant share of FDI inflows in Poland and the Czech Republic, whereas they may have amounted to as much as one-third in Hungary.[40]

[39] The Czech National Bank notes that even though inflows were 'directed towards large enterprises and joint ventures their share of exports has not as yet been substantial' (Czech National Bank (1995), p. 28).

[40] Inotai (1995) states that 'greenfield investments have been spreading in most of the central European countries; if you look at Hungary, more than one-third of

While this dichotomy is relevant, it may, however, be worth bearing in mind that the second-round effects of these investments may be poorly captured by the statistical classification, for the purchase of a run-down factory by a non-resident (privatisation) may lead to further substantial investments.

15.6 Conclusion

Central Europe has experienced a dramatic capital account turnaround since the beginning of transition, as capital outflows have given way to large capital inflows, which, during 1993 and 1994, were greater when scaled by GDP than those experienced in Latin America and Asia. The capital flow experience of the three regions displays certain similarities, but also important differences. Central Europe has attracted about 2% of world capital inflows since transition started. International capital has flowed unevenly into eastern Europe, being attracted to those countries most advanced in the transition process, that is the central European economies. This phenomenon, namely that only a certain number of countries in a particular region attract capital inflows, is also not unknown in Latin America and Asia.[41]

The integration of 'world' capital markets will in future also encompass the emerging markets in central (and eventually also eastern) Europe, as portfolio inflows – which have so far been fairly small – will continue to increase and are potentially a more volatile element of capital flows. How far these capital inflows (and also outflows) should be permitted ought to be the subject of a serious policy discussion in the countries concerned. A stable macroeconomic environment is probably one condition for maintaining sustainable capital inflows.

In Asia the build-up of credibility due to solid financial institutions and markets and good macroeconomic performance has rendered the countries of the region less vulnerable to any harmful capital flow shocks than Latin American countries. In fact, the Asian economies appear to have had much less difficulty in sterilising capital inflows than those in Latin America.

---

total investment has been greenfield, which is about 3 billion dollars'. It should be noted that Inotai's data for Hungary refer to the CSO data, which differ from the BOP data of the National Bank of Hungary (HNB). The HNB statistics cover only cash payments by foreigners, while the CSO data also cover payment in kind (e.g. machinery). This methodological difference means that by the end of 1994 the FDI stock was about US$8.5 billion (CSO) or US$7.5 billion (BOP).

[41] See Fernandez-Arias and Montiel (1995).

While FDI inflows to eastern Europe have occurred since the beginning of transition, portfolio inflows are a more recent phenomenon (1993–1995). Only the countries most advanced in the transformation process have been able to attract such flows, and they have also been the first ones to register small amounts of FDI outflows (the Czech Republic, Hungary and Poland). The fairly successful transition experienced by the Czech Republic, and in particular its stable nominal exchange rate, have recently led to short-term capital inflows, and the case study has demonstrated that the way in which these inflows have been handled by the CNB corresponds in many respects to the standard policy response of neutralising the effects with a mix of policy measures, which is no different from policy responses in other 'industrialised' developing economies. In Poland, despite the boom and bust periods of the Warsaw Stock Exchange, there has recently been a resumption – albeit limited – of foreign participation in this market, against the background of a relatively favorable macroeconomic outlook, the resolution of the external debt problem and a fairly positive risk assessment of Poland's recent borrowings on capital markets. The composition of capital flows may thus shift more to portfolio investment during the coming years.

The capital flows into eastern European countries since 1990 have not left these countries vulnerable to any sudden withdrawals, as they have been predominantly in the form of FDI. In the cases of Poland and the Czech Republic, these flows have been fairly export-intensive, with positive effects on the current account balance in the longer run. By contrast, inflows to Hungary do not appear to have been export-intensive. The nature (privatisation) and fairly modest size of these flows have not, however, had a noticeable impact on depressed fixed investment activity. Nor does privatisation necessarily generate any additional investment.

The consumption/investment counterpart of the inflows does give grounds for concern. Consumption picked up rapidly at the beginning of transition. Although this phenomenon can be interpreted as anormal reaction to the forced saving during the 'pre-transition' period, high levels of consumption have persisted. In Hungary, current consumption levels are now extremely high. A particularly worrying aspect of this is Hungary's high budget deficit (around 7½% of GDP in 1994), while the final judgment on the austerity measures introduced in March 1995 is still outstanding.

Investment ratios appear to be too low to sustain rapid growth. They are similar to those found in Latin America but substantially below ratios in Asia. It appears that domestic savings are the essential ingredient any substantial and sustained increase in investment.

Although this paper has attempted to present certain common elements in the capital flow experiences of the transition economies, it has become clear that individual country experiences differ markedly. Nevertheless, there are lessons to be learnt from the experiences of Latin America and Asia, and these two regions provide convenient benchmarks with which to begin the analysis of capital flows to central Europe.

References

Bank for International Settlements (1993), 63rd Annual Report, 1992–1993.

Bank for International Settlements (1994), 64th Annual Report, 1993–1994.

Bank for International Settlements (1995), 65th Annual Report, 1994–1995.

Calvo, G. A., Sahay, R. and Vegh, C. A. (1995), 'Capital flows in central and eastern Europe: Evidence and policy options', IMF Working Paper No. 57, May.

Christensen, B. V. (1994), 'The Russian Federation in Transition: External Developments', IMF Occasional Paper No. III.

Claessens, S. and Gooptu, S. (eds.) (1993), 'Portfolio investment in developing countries', World Bank Discussion Paper No. 228.

Claessens, S., Dooley, M. P. and Warner, A. (1993), 'Portfolio capital flows, hot or cool', in Claessens, S. and Gooptu, S. (eds.).

Corbo, V. and Hernandez, L. (1993), 'Macroeconomic adjustment to capital inflows: Rationale and some recent experience', in Claessens, S. and Gooptu, S. (eds.).

Corbo, V. and Hernandez, L. (1994), 'Macroeconomic adjustment to capital inflows: Latin America Style vs. East Asian Style', World Bank Policy Research Working Paper No. 1377, November.

Crockett, A. (1994), 'Monetary policy implications of increased capital flows, in changing capital markets: implications for monetary policy', Federal Reserve Bank of Kansas City, August 1993.

Czech National Bank (1995a), *Annual Report, 1994.*

Czech National Bank (1995b), *Report on the monetary development in the Czech Republic*, first quarter.

Dittus, P. (1994), 'Capital flows and monetary policy in central Europe', Mimeo, Bank for International Settlements.

Fernandez-Arias, E. and Montiel, P. J. (1995), 'The surge in capital inflows to developing countries', World Bank Policy Research Working Paper No. 1473, June.

Gulati, S. (1988), 'Capital flight: causes, consequences and cures', *Journal of International Affairs*, Vol. 42, No.1, 165–185.

IMF (1995), *World Economic Outlook*, May.

IMF (1994), *World Economic Outlook*, October.

IMF (1995), *Czech Republic, Economic Reviews*, April.

Inotai, A. and Marer, P. (1993), 'Foreign investment in Hungary', Joint Hungarian Blue Ribbon Commission, December.

Inotai, A. (1995), 'Five years of reform in countries in transition: assessment and prospects', Round-table discussion, UN Economic Commission for Europe, June.

Podkaminer, L. (1995), 'Accelerated growth in central and eastern Europe, slower decline in Russia and Ukraine', Research Report, The Vienna Institute for Comparative Economic Studies, July.

Reisen, H. (1993), 'South-east Asia and the impossible trinity', *International Economic Insights*, May/June, 21–23.

Turner, P. (1995), 'Capital flows in Latin America: A new phase', BIS Economic Papers, Bank for International Settlements, May.

UN (1995), *Economic Survey of Europe in 1994–1995*, Economic Commission for Europe, March (prepublication version; final version, May 1995).

Welfens, P. J. J. (1994), 'Foreign Direct Investment and Privatization', in Schipke and Taylor (eds.), *The Economics of Transformation*, Springer Verlag.

Williamson, J. (1993), 'Issues posed by portfolio investment in developing countries', in Claessens, S. and Gooptu, S. (eds.).

World Bank (1995), *Global Economic Prospects and the Developing Countries*, April.

Annex

A1 The Bank for International Settlements (BIS)

The BIS was established in 1930. It is the world's oldest international financial institution and remains the principal centre for international central bank cooperation. The BIS was established in the context of the Young Plan (1930), which dealt with the issue of the reparation payments imposed on Germany by the Treaty of Versailles following the First World War. The BIS was also created to act as a trustee for the Dawes and Young Loans (international loans issued to finance reparations) and to promote central bank cooperation in general. Since 1930 the Bank has developed its own research in financial and monetary economics and makes an important contribution to the collection, compilation and dissemination of economic and financial statistics.

In the monetary policy field, cooperation at the BIS in the immediate aftermath of the Second World War and until the early 1970s focused on implementing and defending the Bretton Woods system. In the 1970s and 1980s, the focus was on managing cross-border capital flows following the oil crises and the international debt crisis. The 1970s crisis also brought the issue of regulatory supervision of internationally active banks to the fore, resulting in the 1988 Basel Capital Accord and its 'Basel II' revision of 2001-2007. More recently, the issue of financial stability in the wake of economic integration and globalisation, as highlighted by the 1997 Asian crisis, has received a lot of attention.

The BIS has also always performed 'traditional' banking functions for the central bank community (e.g. gold and foreign exchange transactions), as well as trustee and agency functions. The BIS has also provided finance in the context of IMF-led stabilisation programmes (e.g. for Mexico and Brazil).

A2 The Group of Ten (G10)[1]

The G10 is made up of 11 industrialised countries (Belgium, Canada, France, Germany, Italy, Japan, the Netherlands, Sweden, Switzerland, the United Kingdom and the United States) which consult and co-operate on economic, monetary and financial matters.

The ministers of finance and central bank governors of the Group of Ten meet once a year in connection with the annual meetings of the International Monetary Fund and the World Bank. The deputies of the Group of Ten met as needed, but usually between two and four times a year. *Ad hoc* committees and working parties of the Group of Ten were set up as needed. The meetings of the deputies have been discontinued since 2006.

In recent years, work by the Group of Ten has included reports on collective action clauses, insolvency arrangements and contract enforceability, turbulence in asset markets, and the implications for financial markets and economic policies of ageing and pension system reform. These reports and the communiqués of the ministers and governors of the Group of Ten are available from the website of the BIS, IMF and OECD.

[1] For the historical link between the BIS and the G10, consult Toniolo, Gianni (with the assistance of Piet Clement) (2005) *Central Bank Cooperation at the Bank for International Settlements, 1930-1973*, (Chap. 11.8) Cambridge University Press.

Author

Elmar B. Koch

is a German lawyer and holds MBA and PhD (in finance) degrees from the USA. He was in the Secretariat of Central Banking Studies at the Bank for International Settlements (BIS). Earlier assignments at the BIS included the Secretariat of the G10 Ministers and Governors (2002–2006), Secretariat of the Central Bank Governance Forum (2003–2006), mediator between Governments of the former Yugoslavia (2001–2002), Senior Economist for "Special Meetings" (2000–2001) and Senior Economist for "All Governors and Emerging Market Economies" (1995–2000). Before 1995 he held positions as Deputy Head of Statistics and Documentation, in the Eurocurrency Standing Committee and the Secretariat of Data Bank Services.

He has published in economics, finance and law in the USA, Europe and Asia. He was associate professor of finance in the USA and lectured in particular in Europe at the Joint Vienna Institute, the Financial Stability Institute, the University of Basel and central banks worldwide. He is on the editorial board of the Journal of International Economics and Economic Policy (IEEP) and referees for other journals. His experience covers macroeconomics (monetary and financial policy), the international financial architecture and such areas as monetary policy instruments/transmission mechanism, pension funds, 'collective action clauses', IMF finances, sovereign debt, e-finance, bank restructuring, corporate finance, central bank law and insolvency law, governance, real effective exchange rates and statistical methodologies.

Printing: Krips bv, Meppel
Binding: Stürtz, Würzburg